Forging Freedom in

W. E. B. DU BOIS'S

Twilight Years

Forging Freedom in W. E. B. DU BOIS'S Twilight Years

No Deed but Memory

Edited by Phillip Luke Sinitiere

University Press of Mississippi / Jackson

Margaret Walker Alexander Series
in African American Studies

The University Press of Mississippi is the scholarly publishing agency of the Mississippi Institutions of Higher Learning: Alcorn State University, Delta State University, Jackson State University, Mississippi State University, Mississippi University for Women, Mississippi Valley State University, University of Mississippi, and University of Southern Mississippi.

www.upress.state.ms.us

The University Press of Mississippi is a member of the Association of University Presses.

Manufactured in the United States of America

First printing 2023
∞

Library of Congress Control Number 2023008547
Hardback ISBN 978-1-4968-4616-7
Trade paperback ISBN 978-1-4968-4617-4
Epub single ISBN 978-1-4968-4618-1
Epub institutional ISBN 978-1-4968-4619-8
PDF single ISBN 978-1-4968-4620-4
PDF institutional ISBN 978-1-4968-4621-1

British Library Cataloging-in-Publication Data available

To Arthur McFarlane II and Jeff Peck

CONTENTS

ACKNOWLEDGMENTS

While this particular book has one editor, the collective labor of many people brought it into the world. This project germinated from a panel on Du Bois's late career I organized for the 2011 Organization of American Historians annual meeting in Houston. (This is the second book on Du Bois that materialized from that panel. The first, *Citizen of the World: The Late Career and Legacy of W. E. B. Du Bois*, appeared in 2019.) Conversations with the panel participants, Lauren Louise Anderson, Jodi Melamed, and Eric Porter, helped to craft the ideas and perspectives behind what became *Forging Freedom in W. E. B. Du Bois's Twilight Years: No Deed but Memory*. The thoughtful observations and insightful audience questions, including a productive post-panel discussion with Shawn Leigh Alexander, improved this book. As this project took shape over many years, Robert Sloan, formerly of Indiana University Press, and Duke University Press's Gisela Fosado, offered feedback that helped to clarify its ideas and arguments. I'm also very grateful to anonymous readers from University Press of Mississippi whose suggestions strengthened this book.

At the University Press of Mississippi, the following individuals all had a hand in bringing this book to fruition over the long period of its development: Craig Gill, Lisa McMurtray, Vijay Shah, Emily Snyder Bandy, Katie Turner, Joey Brown, and Jackson Watson. I'm also very thankful for copyeditor Robert Norrell's superb skills. It was truly a pleasure to work with you all. I am honored that this book is part of the Margaret Walker Alexander Series in African American Studies.

I'd also like to offer a particular note of thanks to the late Rob Cox, formerly head of Special Collections at the University of Massachusetts Amherst. I will not soon forget his energetic support of my work and his hospitality during my research trips to work in the W. E. B. Du Bois Papers. I also offer heartfelt gratitude to other members of what I affectionally call my Amherst family: Aaron Rubinstein, Blake Spitz, Caroline J. White, and Danielle Kovacs, along with Whitney Battle-Baptiste, director of the W. E. B. Du Bois Center at UMass, and assistant director Adam Holmes. Research fellowships funded by the Andrew W. Mellon Foundation helped to make this book possible. In Nashville, I thank DeLisa Harris, Robert Spinelli, Brandon Owens, and Brynna Farris at Fisk University's Special

Collections. I'm also grateful to the Johns Hopkins University Press for permission to include previously published material. I offer special applause to this book's cross-disciplinary cohort of contributors for their enlightening scholarship and for their forbearance as the volume materialized over the course of many years. I'm honored to collaborate with such brilliant scholars.

Finally, to mark the urgency of forging freedom in the contemporary era and to honor Du Bois's devotion to Black liberation, I humbly dedicate this book to two of Du Bois's descendants: his great-grandsons Arthur McFarlane II and Jeff Peck.

Forging Freedom in W. E. B. DU BOIS'S Twilight Years

INTRODUCTION

Du Bois Has Left Us, but He Has Not Died

—Phillip Luke Sinitiere

It was 1968, a signal year in African American history and the Black freedom struggle. Perhaps most famously, in April James Earl Ray murdered Martin Luther King in Memphis as the civil rights icon traveled to lend his support to striking sanitation workers in search of economic democracy. The Black Power movement was in full force, despite the presence of the US government's notorious COINTELPRO program. While the Black Panther Party laid Bobby Hutton to rest in Oakland the same month King died, the Black fists of Olympians John Carlos and Tommie Smith (along with the silent solidarity of Peter Norman) rose in global protest that October in Mexico City. In part spurred by the Olympic Project for Human Rights, Carlos and Smith's Black Power salute symbolized the insurgent strivings of many. In a final example, student protests and marches erupted at places such as Howard and Columbia, where activists called for the enactment of educational and curricular democracy in the form of Black Studies programs.

The year 1968 is also significant for understanding W. E. B. Du Bois's late career and legacy. In his hometown of Great Barrington, Massachusetts, the convergence of Cold War anti-Black anticommunism shaped how residents sparred over commemorating his life. In New York City, Martin Luther King praised the late scholar in a moving oration at Carnegie Hall. On the west coast, Pacifica Radio aired a 120-minute program that covered Du Bois's life as a scholar and activist. Finally, the Marxist scholar Herbert Aptheker edited and published Du Bois's posthumous and final memoir *The Autobiography of W. E. B. Du Bois: A Soliloquy on Viewing My Life from the Last Decade of Its First Century.*

In the aesthetically alluring Berkshires of western Massachusetts where Du Bois hailed from, the politically radical orientation of the late civil rights leader divided the town in the late 1960s over efforts to commemorate his legacy. For many residents, Du Bois's choice to join the Communist Party in 1961 was the unforgivable sin. Op-eds and letters to the editor in local Great Barrington newspapers reflected typical Cold War ideological combat. Opposition expressed in racially coded language manifested fears and anxieties swirling about militant civil rights. Despite stiff resistance, some of it likely instigated through the Boston office of the FBI, in 1969 a multiracial memorial committee succeeded in hosting an event to honor Du Bois. The contest over Du Bois's legacy would continue to divide friends and foes alike. Many refused to remember the towering African American intellectual apart from his support of communism and socialism.[1]

To honor what would have been Du Bois's one hundredth birthday, in February 1968 *Freedomways* magazine sponsored a commemorative ceremony at Carnegie Hall. At the event—only three months before his assassination—Martin Luther King delivered a speech titled "Honoring Dr. Du Bois." King's powerful presentation appreciatively reviewed Du Bois's long and distinguished career by connecting his decades-long civil rights activism to an extensive publication record of books on both American and African history. He called Du Bois an "intellectual giant," bringing attention to his role as a tireless educator. "He would have wanted his life to teach us something about our tasks of emancipation," King said in opening remarks. His speech called for a revitalized analysis, assessment, and recognition of the late scholar's work. "History cannot ignore W. E. B. Du Bois," thundered the civil rights leader and minister. King also insisted on a robust reckoning with Du Bois's leftist politics. He stated, "Some people would like to ignore the fact that he was a Communist in his later years. . . . It is time to cease muting the fact that Dr. Du Bois was a genius and chose to be a Communist. Our irrational obsessive anticommunism has led into too many quagmires." Cognizant of how politicized Du Bois's legacy had become by 1968, King's coupling of racial and economic justice emboldened his solidarity with a noted radical. "Dr. Du Bois has left us," King said, "but he has not died."[2]

Keeping the spirit of Du Bois alive, three months after King's speech the Pacifica Radio station in Berkeley, KPFA, aired a two-hour program called "The Life of Du Bois." Produced by Gene Dealessi, it placed Du Bois in the larger context of African American history. "The Life of Du Bois" quoted excerpts from his books and writings and played audio clips from various interviews and two late-career speeches. Listeners heard an extraordinarily timely message as Du Bois assailed America's complicity in colonialism and its perpetuation of the global color line. "Today the United States is fighting world progress; progress which must be towards socialism and against colonialism and war," Du Bois commandingly stated on the Pacifica broadcast.[3]

Finally, historian Herbert Aptheker published Du Bois's autobiography in 1968, five years after Du Bois's death and a few years after excerpts of the *Autobiography* appeared in China, Germany, and Russia. Du Bois took the manuscript with him to Ghana in 1961 and left it in the care of his second wife Shirley Graham Du Bois, who delivered it to Aptheker in 1966 after she fled Ghana for Egypt in the midst of political unrest.[4] The Du Bois–Aptheker friendship dated to the 1940s, when Du Bois invited the radical historian to oversee and edit his archives. Aptheker's extraordinary efforts produced over forty volumes of his comrade's intellectual labor, including the posthumously published *Autobiography*. In 1997, he recalled, "Du Bois has filled my life—first as a teacher, then as a guide, inspiration and father. . . . In his office I was literally at his feet. I loved him. His wife, Shirley Graham, told my wife, Fay, that he thought of me as his son. Happily I devoted much of my life to him and his work in scores of volumes. I had the opportunity and honor of bringing forth his writings." The honor about which Aptheker wrote also required a responsibility for his teacher's legacy. "Let those who remain," he observed, "emulate Du Bois' courage and persistence and help realize his dream of a decent, equitable and peaceful world."[5]

Whereas Aptheker praised *Autobiography*, early scholarly reviews criticized Du Bois's radical politics, reflecting a distinct Cold War context vexed about communism. Writing in the *Journal of Southern History*, Hugh Davis Graham lamented that it fell "pitifully short" of Du Bois's scholarly standards and dismissed the late scholar's "mindless apology for Stalinism." Despite assailing the "preachy little postlude," Graham asserted that Du Bois "can be forgiven for pulling the rank of age and lecturing us for having lost the Vision of the Fathers." Nevertheless, he admitted that at least two-thirds of the book "represents thoughtful recollection of a high order."[6] In the *American Historical Review*, Louis Filler's assessment more resolutely praised the book even as he found Du Bois's leftist politics "controversial" and insisted on interpretive pluralism that forcefully countered communism as the singular perspective of the age.[7] W. M. Brewer showered countless superlatives upon the *Autobiography*, and used multiple exclamation points and italicized phrases for emphasis in his *Journal of Negro History* review. For Brewer, Du Bois's status as a leader was "peerless and incomparable," and the late scholar's writings "literally poured acid in the veins of bigots, racists, and exploiters of cheap labor and natural resources, sources of great wealth through the ages and now." About Du Bois's decision to join the US Communist Party (CPUSA), Brewer stated, "He was merely pleading with America to save its soul by practicing its principles of Christianity and democracy!" On the book's literary merits, Brewer promised that readers "will be fascinated and rewarded by the subtle thought and craftsmanship in writing."[8] In *Political Science Quarterly*, St. Clair Drake addressed Du Bois's final decade, and attempted to universalize his doctrine of double consciousness. Persecuted for his political convictions, Drake described Du Bois's "escalating alienation from the land of his birth" that made him "bitter and indignant." As a result, Drake observed that in Du Bois's writings he "heaps scorn and contempt upon what he conceived of, after he passed the age of eighty, as a corrupt, money-mad culture with a 'war-mongering,' arrogant, governmental elite in control of the society." Reflecting a sensitivity to the racial psychology Du Bois revealed in the *Autobiography*, Drake wrote that "the intellectual and personal crises faced by all black intellectuals, however, are highlighted in Du Bois's *apologia pro vita sua*. I suspect there is no American black man who has not, at some time, had fantasies about shaking the dust of racist America from his feet. . . . Du Bois acted out in one long lifetime moods that most Negroes feel sometimes."[9]

The preceding episodes from 1968 illustrate how both scholars and citizens attempted to make meaning out of Du Bois's work and legacy, and how they responded to matters of the political and intellectual developments of his late career between the 1930s and 1960s. The seemingly intractable disputes over his memory and his legacy that surfaced in the wake of his passing all centered on how both individuals and institutions understood freedom, conflicts that continue into the present day.[10] It is such contestations about freedom with which *Forging Freedom in W. E. B. Du Bois's Twilight Years: No Deed but Memory* is most especially concerned.

The postlude of Du Bois's *Autobiography* inspired this volume's short title. It narrates his perspective on the state of midcentury American democracy. Given his own late career persecution at the hands of the US government, and at particular moments the alienation he felt and experienced, Du Bois had many reasons for pessimism. Yet an enduring conviction that democracy remained an active idea and political possibility—however dim it might have been in Du Bois's mind in the early 1960s—prompted how his thoughts on the past, present, and future converged in several creative expressions on the *Autobiography*'s closing pages. "For this is a beautiful world; this is a wonderful America, which the founding fathers dreamed until their sons drowned it in the blood of slavery and devoured it in greed. Our children must rebuild it," he stated in the book's final paragraph. "Let then the Dreams of the Dead rebuke the Blind who think that what is will be forever and teach them that what was worth living for must live again and that which merited death must stay dead," Du Bois wrote. "Teach us, Forever Dead, there is no Dream but Deed, there is no Deed but Memory."[11] Based on the conviction that indeed the "Forever Dead" have something to teach those of us still living, and that "no Deed but Memory" is the particular lot of scholars interested in analyzing Du Bois's latter years, the short title of this volume comes directly from the *Autobiography*'s final line.

As a verb, forging speaks of a refining process. After a piece of metal passes through the heat of fire, a metallurgist forms and shapes the object into something stronger and more durable. The book's title, *Forging Freedom*, also resonates with the *Autobiography* given its narration of freedom's unfolding in Du Bois's life, especially from the 1930s through the 1960s. Those were not easy years for Du Bois from the standpoint of his personal and political life, especially the anticommunist heat he experienced during the McCarthy period. Those experiences metaphorically brought him through a refining process resulting in even deeper conviction about freedom's horizon of possibility. As a result, Du Bois's attempts to puzzle out a conception of freedom during his late career took many forms: books, essays, newspaper articles, creative writings, speeches, and lectures. Interpreting and expositing such expressions of liberation is this volume's task.

In its broadest conceptualization, Du Bois's definitions of freedom emphasized independence of thought and the autonomy to simply exist as a human being in the world—in all of one's emotional, intellectual, psychological, and relational specificities—so long as it did not actualize exploitation of or discrimination against others. In other words, for Du Bois freedom was living life through one's individual subjectivity in light of humanity's universal and collective existence, experience, and interdependence.[12] Several of Du Bois's publications illustrate the expressive range of his articulations of freedom.

For example, his 1944 essay "My Evolving Program for Negro Freedom" explained how his definition of freedom changed over the span of his career while it specified his late-career conceptualization. "Finally and in summation, what is it that in sixty years of purposive endeavor, I have wanted for my people? Just what do I mean by 'Freedom'?" he proposed. Using italics for emphasis, Du Bois continued: "Proceeding from the vague and general plans of youth, through the more particular program of active middle life, and on to the general and at the same time more specific plans of the days of reflexion. I can see, with overlappings and contradictions, these things: By 'Freedom' for Negroes, I meant and still mean, *full economic, political and social equality with American citizens, in thought, expression and action, with no discrimination based on race or color*."[13]

On the role of creative endeavor as one barometer of freedom's embodiment, a 1946 *Chicago Defender* column on concerts he attended over the years at Carnegie Hall put it this way: "As I look back upon our path in this land I can see nothing that has guided us more consistently toward freedom and accomplishment than our literature and music, our sculpture and painting, our drama. Our political efforts despite our triumphs have failed us; our economic emancipation has hardly more than begun; our physical revolt died a-borning. But our art forms have not only made America, they are an integral part of the 20th century."[14]

A particularly powerful conclusion to his 1947 text *The World and Africa* titled "The Message" announces a creative clarity about Du Bois's conceptual register of freedom and helps to frame how the essays in this volume grapple with the idea. "Reader of dead words who would live deeds," he began his interpretive summary, "this is the flowering of my logic." He wrote:

> I dream of a world of infinitive and valuable variety; not in the laws of gravity or atomic weights, but in human variety in height and weight, color and skin, hair

> and nose and lip. But more especially and far above and beyond this, is a realm of true freedom: in thought and dream, fantasy and imagination; in gift, aptitude, and genius—all possible manner of difference, topped with freedom of soul to do and be, and freedom of thought to give to a world and build into it, all wealth of inborn individuality. Each effort to stop this freedom of being is a blow at democracy—that real democracy which is reservoir and opportunity. . . . There can be no perfect democracy curtailed by color, race, or poverty. But with all we accomplish all, even Peace.[15]

Fast approaching seventy years of age, the post–World War II moment in which Du Bois penned these freedom words possessed sharp meaning—anticolonial resistance abroad, demands for Black freedom in the US, and a surging anti-Black anticommunism ringing from Washington, DC, and echoing across the nation, among other developments. Beyond merely performing an expression of freedom's individuality, or touting diversity for diversity's sake, he indicated that bound and correlated are individual freedom (i.e., "freedom of soul," "freedom of thought") and collective emancipation (i.e., "with all we accomplish all"). This is an alternative formulation of Du Bois's mantra of all for one, one for all, which is a way of life, an orientation with which to exist in the world. But there also was in *The World and Africa* a certain simple yet robust summary of his life's intellectual and political work: the world and Africa, and this idea's connections to and entanglements with global history. The concept of the world and Africa, then, as Du Bois wrote about it in the late 1940s, was a verbalization of Black internationalism. It also keyed his pan-Africanism, while it demanded that Black Americans exceed the limits of provincialism for a global perspective since Black freedom abroad related directly to freedom at home.[16]

Any number of quotes and phrases from Du Bois's late-career writings capture his notion of freedom; in reality, his notions of freedom were more than simply conceptions about political possibility, or miscellanies of liberty. At a basic but profound level, the act of assembling thoughts on a page, or formulating ideas in speaking realized the very freedom for which he strove across his lifetime.

His twilight years, as this volume defines it, commenced in 1934, the year he exited the NAACP, and continued to his death in 1963. However, topics such as historical memory and issues of legacy and heritage, questions this book probes, are also germane to analyzing Du Bois's twilight years. To grasp the historical significance and cultural meaning of such vital subjects, *Forging Freedom* covers selected chapters of Du Bois's final three decades. Building on a growing number of studies that assess his life from the 1930s to the 1960s, *Forging Freedom* renders W. E. B. Du Bois's closing years during the Cold War not as a story of advancing alienation into rigid socialist doctrine or communist ideology, but as the life of an energetic intellectual who, in a world that often tried to subvert justice and equality in the name of political and economic power, evaluated the present in light of the past in purposeful, passionate commitment to freedom of thought, expression, and being for Black people and other people of color in the US and across the globe. Du Bois's commitment to freedom's flourishing animated the civil rights movement's war against white supremacy. In sum, *Forging Freedom* demonstrates that the durability of Du Bois's intellectual achievements remain relevant for the twenty-first century.[17]

This volume's genesis began with a panel on Du Bois's late career I assembled for the 2011 Organization of American Historians annual meeting. For this book, I invited contributors to consider freedom in its most capacious sense, but also dialectically, as a way to excavate the intellectual, cultural, social, and political significance of Du Bois's closing decades particularly in relation to American society. While his global horizons are not absent in *Forging Freedom*—a subject addressed more fully in my 2019 book *Citizen of the World: The Late Career and Legacy of W. E. B. Du Bois*—the US context is front and center. No volume is able to cover the full scope of Du Bois's twilight years. The selective shape of topics that *Forging Freedom* explores cohere thematically around the subjects of politics and protest, identity and culture, and literature and legacy.

Part I: Politics and Protest, explores a wide variety of oppositional strategies Du Bois directed towards the wide expanse of inequality in US society. Analyzing W. E. B. Du Bois's books *Black Reconstruction*, *Dusk of Dawn*, and the *Black Flame* Trilogy, Lisa J. McLeod explains how he employed rigorous academic research and philosophy, the crafting of historical narrative, and the deployment of creative expression through protest literature to mount sophisticated assaults on whiteness's perpetuation of innocence, especially as liberal individualism gained more political traction towards the end of his life. Du Bois's later work examined the psychological and social structures that normalize white entitlement, and he offered portraits of "well-meaning white people" that exposed the often-shameful opacity of white Americans to the harm white supremacy causes. This chapter traces Du Bois's evolving belief that reasoned argument with such an obtuse population is not effective in the struggle against white supremacy; it also demonstrates that he nevertheless worked to investigate that obtuseness with an antiracist eye toward its eradication.

Similarly, Carlton Dwayne Floyd and Thomas Ehrlich Reifer center W. E. B. Du Bois's *Black Reconstruction* as a text of literature and history through which to understand domestic and global circulations of capital in slavery's afterlife. Since that afterlife continues into the contemporary historical moment of ongoing class and racial conflict, Floyd and Reifer contend that *Black Reconstruction* remains a compelling text of political theory and possibility for its attention to the present through the past. Du Bois's unparalleled analysis of the centrality of white supremacy in the defeat of Black Reconstruction and in the changing social foundations of US global power allows *Black Reconstruction* to speak to our present moment as few other works. Du Bois's powerful analysis and creative literary and historical mix of politics, poetry and prose illuminates its implications for scholars and activists seeking to transform the US and the global system today.

Moving more from political theory into the realm of protest, in a chapter on political protest, Werner Lange narrates the depth of Du Bois's radical peace activism in the face of anticommunist repression. It was the state's chokehold on freedom, not freedom itself, which grew exponentially during the last years of Du Bois's heroic life as the elderly and seemingly indefatigable peacemaker unrelentingly took on the interlocked forces of war, ignorance, racism, and colonialism. The twin barriers to freedom's more complete realm, however, proved to be increasingly intransigent and bolstered by the rapid rise of America's military-industrial complex. However, as Du Bois's peace praxis demonstrates, the Cold War's fortified barriers to peace were not entirely insurmountable. Du Bois spoke militant truth to militaristic power at the dawn of the Nuclear Age, and his voice in the wilderness, then almost totally muted, continues to resound with renewed vigor throughout the world.

Complementing Lange's connections between Du Bois's democratic expressions and the politics of peace, Reiland Rabaka probes the intellectual expanse of Du Bois's unique Marxist formulations through his anticapitalist writings that analytically combined a critique of imperialism, white supremacy, racial capitalism, and white theorists of Marxism. This led Du Bois at the outset of his critique of capitalism to simultaneously critique capitalism *and* the white critics of capitalism. Du Bois's "socialism," according to Rabaka, may have never been as scientific, dogmatic, or orthodox Marxist as many intellectual historians have claimed, or would like to claim. His thought often exhibited internal tensions, sometimes appearing race-centered, and at other times seeming overly concerned with class, labor, and economic justice issues. For Du Bois, it was not simply capitalism and class struggle that impeded the democratization of socialism, but racism, sexism, and colonialism as well. Du Bois's discourse on democratic socialism offered a distinct Black radical frame of reference, distinguished by its antiracist sociopolitical ethics.

Cumulatively, the chapters in Part I explain in substantial detail across Du Bois's late-career intellectual production how he not only solidified his commitment to Marxism but clarified the material manifestations of political and economic democracy in Black American life, and how such expressions of freedom existed within the broader US body politic.

In Part II: Identity and Culture, Andre E. Johnson's exploration of Du Bois's 1956 *The Nation* column "Why I Won't Vote" uses the lens of rhetoric studies to show how and why Du Bois's "pessimistic prophecy" recalibrated a rationale for political participation that exceeded casting ballots. Johnson argues that Du

Bois's rhetorical trajectory from advocating voting to his decision to abstain from voting in the 1956 US presidential election coincided with his shift from a mission-oriented prophet to a pessimistic one. He explains how for Du Bois pessimism was not cynicism; rather, the lament tradition within this pessimistic prophecy gave Du Bois purpose to keep speaking, writing, and visioning a better day for democracy. Johnson shows how despite such shifts, Du Bois continued to harbor democratic hope.

Murali Balaji reveals how Lala Lajpat Rai, an Indian nationalist leader and one of the leading voices of Arya Samaj, a reform movement in Hinduism that called for a return to living life according to the Vedas, shaped and inspired Du Bois's thinking about Afro-Asian solidarity. For Du Bois, Rai's faith—and his willingness to sacrifice himself for a cause greater than himself—profoundly stirred a newfound political awakening. Balaji shows how the Hindu concept of *dharma*, or righteous action, which Rai and Gandhi claimed as underpinning their approaches to resisting British imperialism, influenced Du Bois merging his ideals of anticolonialism and socialism. Through a close reading of Du Bois's correspondence with Indian intellectuals and works like his novel *Dark Princess*, Balaji maps out how the dharma of socialism through Hindu conceptions of selflessness, sacrifice, and communalism inspired his attempts to foster Afro-Asian solidarity.

The final two chapters of Part II look explicitly at Du Bois's complex relationship to religion. Christopher Cameron locates Du Bois's critique of religion and skepticism about divinity in the longer history of Black freethought to posit a connection between his late career turn to Marxism and irreligion. This essay broadens the scholarly understanding of Du Bois and religion within the context of the African American humanist movement by connecting his religious skepticism and political radicalism. In embracing humanism, Du Bois became part of a growing movement of Black artists, intellectuals, and political activists who denied the existence of God, an afterlife, and other central teachings of American Christianity. By rejecting the supernatural, embracing human potential, and working to transform their world through science and reason, African American humanists such as Du Bois laid the foundations for one of the most significant streams of twentieth century Black thought and culture. Meanwhile, Phillip Luke Sinitiere examines the intellectual history of W. E. B. Du Bois's dialectical analysis of American Christianity during his last three decades. This chapter reveals how Du Bois understood the interrelationship of religion and culture in the United States from the 1930s to the early 1960s. It explores the creative ways that his Black radicalism fostered an idiosyncratic, nuanced assessment of religion's political and social significance. It also documents Du Bois's abiding attention to how the ruling class wielded a spiritualized anticommunism that used religion to silence dissent and subvert freedom. Finally, Sinitiere's study catalogs the reception of

Du Bois's materialist explorations of religion amongst religious professionals and ordinary people while disclosing ways that Du Bois, through thoughtful considerations of religion and culture, conceptualized and practiced freedom at a critical stage of his late-career life.

The volume's final section of essays, Part III: Literature and Legacy clusters analysis of what Du Bois meant politically, socially, and intellectually to peers and comrades at the end of his life and beyond. Section III thus translates the history of Du Bois's late career and legacy into an intellectual urgency of action in the contemporary political moment.

Charisse Burden-Stelly underscores the importance of political networks, what she calls the "mutual comradeship" between Du Bois and radical Black women that produced social and intellectual solidarity in the midst of anti-Black political repression during the Cold War. This chapter shows how Du Bois's move toward the US Communist Party reflected the connections he made after World War II between communism, freedom for racialized and oppressed people at home and abroad, and international peace. This chapter defines mutual comradeship as an affective practice of collaborative freedom, reciprocal care, and collective learning constituted by the enduring commitment to, advocacy for, and protection of those engaged in radical political struggle on behalf of the racialized, colonized, and oppressed. Mutual comradeship offers collective economic and moral support for radical organizations, institutions, and periodicals as well as the lateral and intergenerational practice of legacy maintenance and preserving Black radical thought in historical memory.

In a complementary way, Robert Greene II illuminates the relationship between the intellectual politics of Martin Luther King and W. E. B. Du Bois. Greene tracks how the convergence of King and Du Bois in 1968—when King delivered his famous "Honoring Dr. Du Bois" speech at Carnegie Hall in February of that year to honor what would have been Du Bois's hundredth birthday—entangled their respective legacies within the Black radical tradition. This chapter examines the rhetorical and ideological relationship between the two men. Inexorably bonded due to their shared passions for advancing the cause of equal rights, it shows how the links between Du Bois and King go even deeper. Both men were giants in American society's long-running debates about racism, and by the later years of their lives both were largely ostracized by an America gripped with fear about communism and the rise of nonaligned African and Asian nations.

Jodi Melamed's chapter, a revision with Tyler Monson of her 2006 *African American Review* essay on Du Bois's posthumously published *Autobiography*, places Du Bois's critique of capitalism alongside of the nascent democratic liberalism of the Cold War era. The authors explain how in revisiting the essay in the Trump era it was the criminalization of Du Bois for his witness for communism—and thus, according to the protocol of his witness in the *Autobiography*, for his critical consciousness of racial capitalism—that stands out. Melamed and Monson ask how Du Bois's anticapitalist legacy orients the radical possibility of a "hermeneutic of disloyalty" in the era of Black Lives Matter and Donald Trump's authoritarian administration. They also consider how the story Du Bois tells in the *Autobiography*, of coming into a critical consciousness about the role of race in capitalism, can inform contemporary struggles to actualize antiracial capitalist thinking and politics.

Finally, Camesha Scruggs's chapter uses public history to analyze the politics of memory and the politics of place at Du Bois's Boyhood Homesite in Great Barrington, Massachusetts. Scruggs documents a history of the site from a place of commemoration in the 1960s and '70s, to one of archaeological excavation in the 1980s to the early 2000s, to one of public historical memory in the early twenty-first century. Throughout this chapter, in autobiographical mode she intertwines her practicum experiences as a tour guide at the W. E. B. Du Bois Boyhood Homesite with scholarship regarding Du Bois, memory, and preservation. The chapter argues that Du Bois spearheaded his own preservation project while showing how the memorial imprints about the homesite from scholars and community members both expand the geography of freedom in addition to being active participants in preservation.

Rather than produce a comprehensive narration of Du Bois's closing decades, the essays in *Forging Freedom* collectively analyze particular aspects of his intellectual and cultural production from the 1930s to the early 1960s while also accounting for the historical meaning of his late career and legacy in politics and culture. The chapters in this book emphasize the vitality and the complexity of Du Bois's twilight years while aiming to produce innovative details about how he forged American freedom in his late-career life. This volume spotlights Du Bois's unwavering devotion to freedom in both theory and practice. It maintains that the importance of revisiting his long and distinguished career at the dawn of the twenty-first century is a fitting pathway to liberation for those committed to no deed but memory.

NOTES

1. Amy Bass, *Those About Him Remained Silent: The Fight Over W. E. B. Du Bois* (Minneapolis: University of Minnesota Press, 2009).

2. Martin Luther King, "Honoring Dr. Du Bois," in W. E. B. Du Bois, *W. E. B. Du Bois Speaks: Speeches and Addresses, 1890–1919*, ed. Philip S. Foner (New York: Pathfinder, 1970), 12–20.

3. "The Life of W. E. B. Du Bois," produced by Gene Dealessi, KPFA (May 19, 1968), Pacifica Radio Archives, Archive Number BB1719.03B, North Hollywood, California.

4. Herbert Aptheker, *The Literary Legacy of W. E. B. Du Bois* (White Plains, New York: Kraus International Publications, 1989), 331–34; Hamilton Beck, "Rewritten Autobiography: W. E. B.

Du Bois' *Soliloquy on Viewing My Life* in the German Democratic Republic," *Lebende Sprachen* 64, no. 1 (2019): 47–77.

5. Herbert Aptheker, "Personal Recollections: Woodson, Wesley, Robeson and Du Bois," *Black Scholar* 27, no. 2 (Summer 1997): 42–45.

6. Hugh Davis Graham, review of *Autobiography* in *Journal of Southern History* 34, no. 4 (November 1968): 640–41.

7. Louis Filler, review of *Autobiography* in *American Historical Review* 74, no. 1 (October 1968): 315–16.

8. W. M Brewer, review of *Autobiography* in *Journal of Negro History* 54, no. 1 (January 1969): 72–75.

9. St. Clair Drake, review of *Autobiography* in *Political Science Quarterly* 86, no. 2 (June 1971): 292–94.

10. On recent developments with respect to Du Bois's legacy both among scholars and in Great Barrington set in the wider context of his memory in history, see Phillip Luke Sinitiere, Edward Carson, and Gerald Horne, "'If we neglect to mark this history, it may be distorted or forgotten': Socialism and Democracy in W. E. B. Du Bois's Life, Thought, and Legacy," *Socialism and Democracy* 32, no. 3 (2018): 1–13.

11. W. E. B. Du Bois, *The Autobiography of W. E. B. Du Bois: A Soliloquy on Viewing My Life from the Last Decade of Its First Century* (New York: Oxford University Press, 2007 [1968]), 275.

12. Nahum Dimitri Chandler, *"Beyond This Narrow Now": Or, Delimitations of W. E. B. Du Bois* (Durham: Duke University Press, 2022).

13. W. E. B. Du Bois, "My Evolving Program for Negro Freedom," in David Levering Lewis, ed., *W. E. B. Du Bois: A Reader* (New York: Henry Holt, 1995), 613–14.

14. W. E. B. Du Bois, "The Winds of Time," *Chicago Defender*, February 23, 1946, in Herbert Aptheker, ed., *Newspaper Columns by W. E. B. Du Bois, Volume 2: 1945–1961* (White Plains, NY: Kraus-Thomson, 1986), 676–77.

15. W. E. B. Du Bois, *The World and Africa* (New York: Oxford University Press, 2007 [1947]), 165.

16. Mahmood Mamdani, "Introduction," in W. E. B. Du Bois, *The World and Africa*, xxv–xxx; Eric Porter, *The Problem of the Future World: W. E. B. Du Bois and the Race Concept at Midcentury* (Durham: Duke University Press, 2010), 103–44.

17. For a fuller account of the history of Du Bois studies, particularly work that covers his latter years, see Phillip Luke Sinitiere, "'A Legacy of Scholarship and Struggle': W. E. B. Du Bois's Life after Death," in *Citizen of the World: The Late Career and Legacy of W. E. B. Du Bois*, ed., Phillip Luke Sinitiere (Evanston, IL: Northwestern University Press, 2019), 227–66.

PART I

Politics and Protest

CHAPTER 1

The Rational and the Irrational: W. E. B. Du Bois's Excavation of Whiteness, 1935–1960

—Lisa J. McLeod

But what on earth is whiteness, that one should so desire it?
—W. E. B. Du Bois[1]

The Dream persists by warring with the known world.
—Ta-Nehisi Coates[2]

From his earliest works to his final ones, Du Bois illustrates that whiteness and white supremacy were the foundation and ongoing font of racism worldwide.[3] By the 1930s, he had become so convinced of the intransigence of American whiteness that he began promoting a strategic form of economic and educational self-segregation for African Americans. Reflected in his later work is Du Bois's increasing conviction that white Americans were not prepared even to contemplate a racially just society. It is, I think, a conclusion he reached only reluctantly, and after long experience with white Americans. It is therefore not surprising that Du Bois did not offer to white America a step-by-step program for dismantling white supremacy, given how few would read, let alone honestly engage it.

The problem of freedom is not unconnected to this problem. Black freedom depends on the end of whiteness—or at the very least, the end of white supremacy. If Du Bois was pessimistic about the willingness of whites in the mid-twentieth century to confront and demolish the destructive aspects of whiteness, he nevertheless bequeathed to us an analysis of white supremacy that could allow white Americans to develop our own program for transforming white racial identity. Du Bois's later work not only examines the psychological and social structures that normalize white entitlement, but he also offers portraits of "well-meaning white people" that expose the often-shameful opacity of white Americans to the harm they cause. He presents implicit and explicit diagnoses of the complex tangle of perceptual and cognitive practices that allow white people to brutalize Black Americans (as well as people of color around the world) while maintaining a mantle of innocence. The freedom of white people to think and act unencumbered by these mistaken perceptions, and the freedom of people of color from a social, political, economic, and cultural world drenched in white misperceptions, depends on remediating whiteness. In this chapter, I will trace Du Bois's evolving belief that reasoned argument with such an obtuse population is not effective in the struggle against white supremacy; I will also demonstrate that he nevertheless worked to investigate that obtuseness with an eye toward its eradication.

1. *Black Reconstruction* (1935): The Wages of White Supremacy

> I used to say to our audiences: "It is difficult to get a man to understand something, when his salary depends upon his not understanding it!"
> —Upton Sinclair[4]

Du Bois's epic sociohistorical work, *Black Reconstruction in America*,[5] is the first major work of American history to emphasize Black agency in the eras just prior to, during, and immediately after the Civil War. Du Bois had been working on the several "revisionist" arguments of *Black Reconstruction* since at least 1909;[6] the ongoing mischaracterization of this period among professional historians amounted to race libel, and Du Bois's 1934 departure from the NAACP and return to Atlanta University offered him the chance to finally publish the work. Famously, Du Bois wished to correct the prevailing image of Reconstruction as, at best, a failure of government caused by avaricious Northerners manipulating ignorant, formerly enslaved African Americans. He also helped to answer a crucial question about the relative paucity of political leverage among the American laboring class. Thanks to David Roediger, Du Bois's claim that white labor's failure to join forces with Black labor was due in great part to the "public and psychological wage"[7] of white racial identity has become familiar. However, it is important to emphasize that for both Roediger and Du Bois, the white working class's attachment to racial supremacy "undermined not just working-class unity but the very *vision* of many white workers."[8] Thus, succumbing to the myth of white supremacy supported white workers' material exploitation and involved real damage to their critical faculties.

The dynamic accounting for the construction of white racial identity and its attendant epistemic failings is not only complex but also involves some local variations. Roediger opines that Irish American Catholics in New York, for example, "mutilated the corpses of the free Blacks they lynched in the 1863 Draft

Riot in New York City," an act that cannot be explained by "political [or] psycho-economic calculations" alone. Even more difficult to explain is the fact that the workers kept authorities from retrieving those bodies for days.

> The psychological wages of Irish whiteness were sometimes of the sort based on rational, if horribly constrained, choices. But as frequently they were the products of what Frantz Fanon called "the prelogical thought of the phobic"—the fevered thinking in which the racist nurtures his hatred as he "project[s] his own desires onto the Negro" and behaves "as if the Negro really had them."[9]

Whatever needs Irish Americans satisfied by defining themselves as white and therefore not only in competition with but superior in every way to free Black workers (and later the emancipated), the results were ruinous to both groups.

Crucially, neither the temptations of whiteness nor the material and epistemic toll of being in its thrall were limited to the white working class. As I have elsewhere discussed,[10] Du Bois in *Black Reconstruction* devotes a chapter to Andrew Johnson's sudden "transubstantiation" from an enemy of the plantocracy to its most powerful friend at a *tremendous* cost to the federal treasury. As Du Bois explains, within a month of the war's end Johnson had reversed his stand on Confederate land forfeiture, depriving the Union of millions of dollars in land and (nonhuman) chattel in order to ensure that freed slaves would not receive a penny—let alone forty acres and a mule. Indeed, the white supremacist ideology that survived the Civil War has so enthralled most Americans that the failure of the traitorous South to make reparation for its treason is neither remarked on in popular (white) literature about the Civil War, nor addressed in the classroom.

For Du Bois, the motivation for the Union's choice to "reconcile" with the white South is clear. Johnson and others realized that excluding the "Southern oligarchy" from economic and political participation would mean a majority-Black South, and so, to prevent the unthinkable, set about eviscerating federal support and protection of the "freedmen." As Du Bois explains, Johnson "was a thick-and-thin advocate of universal suffrage in the hands of the laborer and the common man, until he realized that some people actually thought that Negroes were men."[11] Of course, allowing former Confederates to recapture political as well as economic power meant leaving formerly enslaved Black Americans to a veritable hell on earth, but most white liberals, including Johnson, were willing to sacrifice Black Americans in service to "national reconciliation"—an exchange that makes sense only if they conceived of the nation as white.

Johnson's choice of "reconciliation" over "radical" Reconstruction, and the eventual triumph of white "redemptionism," meant that the end of the war brought the end of slavery in name only. Indeed, by 1877 white Southerners were able murderously to "redeem" their treasured way of life in every way that mattered:

free labor and exclusive access to the polls meant that slavery was as good as restored, and the rise of Jim Crow laws meant even less unwanted contact with Black Americans than had been the case before.[12] By 1900, despite the (apparent) ongoing authority of the Fifteenth Amendment, African Americans were excluded from voting, one way or another, in every state in the South.[13]

For Du Bois, then, Andrew Johnson helped bring about the triumph of white supremacy over the potential for racial justice provided by Reconstruction:

> The transubstantiation of Andrew Johnson was complete. He had begun as the champion of the poor laborer. . . . Suddenly thrust into the Presidency, he had retreated from this attitude. He had not only given up extravagant ideas of punishment, but he dropped his demand for dividing up plantations when he realized that Negroes would largely be beneficiaries. *Because he could not conceive of Negroes as men*, he refused to advocate universal democracy, of which, in his young manhood, he had been the fiercest advocate, and made strong alliance with those who would restore slavery under another name.[14]

Black Reconstruction not only documents the retrenchment of white supremacy in the death of Reconstruction, but it also represents a major development in Du Bois's analysis of the problem of whiteness and white supremacy. Unlike the heartfelt appeal of *The Souls of Black Folk* and the wicked, angry lampoonery of "The Souls of White Folk," his work here is neither an appeal to well-meaning white people nor a call to arms. Instead, the Du Bois of *Black Reconstruction* offers empirical observations about similar, puzzling behavior in two rather different classes of white men: the politically powerful, and those with almost no political power. Both groups, he finds, cling to an identity that prevents them from acknowledging readily available evidence of Black humanity. The failure of white Americans to recognize the humanity of their Black fellow citizens is palpably devastating to those Black citizens; the destruction of hopes, life's work, and even lives is the very antithesis of freedom. As Du Bois subtly implies, white freedom is also curtailed by the obsession with white supremacy: whites are hardly free when they are constrained by such warped epistemic and moral faculties.

This reading of *Black Reconstruction* helps answer Keith Byerman's concern that Du Bois treads perilously close to propaganda in this work, despite his avowed commitment to history as "science." The final chapter of *Black Reconstruction* is, as Byerman notes, a kind of bibliographical essay in which Du Bois examines the writing of history in general, and the history of Reconstruction in particular.[15] Yet, Byerman argues, there is a kind of propaganda at work in *Black Reconstruction*: "Blacks come close to canonization. . . . Despite their experience of slavery for generations, blacks have few faults, many virtues, and they consistently return good for evil."[16] Whether this is a fair characterization of the depiction of Black

Americans throughout the book, the focus on Black contributions to the US before, during, and after the Civil War is, for Du Bois, a remediation project. On an uneven playing field, "objective facts" might still be selectively presented in order to combat an existing and biased representation—rarely more needed than in the case of the role of freed Black Americans during Reconstruction.

As has long been recognized, Du Bois's aim in *Black Reconstruction* was primarily to answer the Dunning School's interpretation of Reconstruction as a dismal failure caused by the rampant corruption and ignorance of newly empowered Black Americans after the Civil War. Whether or not these historians were *consciously* working to "defend the white race,"[17] they would have begun with the implicit conviction that whiteness was normal and superior, and in telling the story of post–Civil War America, their concern would have been to articulate the necessity of white reconciliation. They would not have recognized the contributions and even the humanity of Black Americans during Reconstruction as a concern, let alone a priority, in telling this story—and *this* is the context in which Du Bois's work must act. Thus, "objective" or "balanced" depictions of African Americans would have been of little use; producing an *accurate* image of the postwar nation required just the sort of narrative Du Bois offered.

In this light, Du Bois is less a propagandist than a therapist (*à la* Wittgenstein),[18] working to improve the field of history; in any case, Du Bois is offering to establish "the things that actually happened in the world"[19] in order to balance the false representations of the Dunning school. Thus, rather than becoming "a propagandist for a particular view," he is, I would argue, trying to overcome the white inability to recognize Black achievement and thus the possibility of the equal humanity of African Americans. Byerman's concern that Du Bois is instead using history as a "tool for political change," rather than as a science,[20] and that his moral imperative (to improve conditions for Black Americans) reveals Du Bois's self-interest is on its face legitimate. However, as Du Bois was aware, Du Bois's readers were not neutral observers who could or would "objectively" weigh his work against those of previous, white supremacist scholars. Rather, he is writing within a milieu that always already interprets African Americans as subhuman. History as science could only be aspirational in such circumstances, and Du Bois's writing of history can only ever be political so long as he must work to undermine the white supremacist assumptions of historical scholarship.[21]

In sum, Du Bois recognizes the social and psychological complexity of white supremacy in the case of Andrew Johnson but is still more or less compelled to attempt to combat the white supremacist conception of American history by offering clear evidence of its inaccuracy. In doing so, he is struggling against the background assumptions of white supremacist historians like William Archibald Dunning's followers, but also of white Americans more generally. In the following sections, I will explore how Du Bois's work in the decades after *Black*

Reconstruction's publication reflect his growing conviction that white supremacy was too psychologically complex to be dismantled by rational means alone. Du Bois's growing understanding of white thought and behavior tested his faith in the power of human reason, especially the ongoing imperialist ambitions of the US and European powers in the first half of the twentieth century. Du Bois thus began looking to the tangled undergrowth of emotion and the unconscious for explanations regarding the problem of whiteness.

2. *Dusk of Dawn* (1940): "Unconscious and Subconscious Reflexes of Living Things"

In *Dusk of Dawn: An Essay Toward an Autobiography of a Race Concept*, published just five years after *Black Reconstruction* but long after Du Bois had completed his research (if not his revisions) on that work,[22] Du Bois addresses at length the history and uses of race, both in the US and worldwide. For my purposes, part of his project in *Dusk* involves offering insight into the role of whites and whiteness in maintaining the race concept and its ongoing salience. Specifically, he emphasizes the lack of self-awareness in white Americans' racial thinking, in part by tracing the development of global white supremacy as background to the First World War. As I will demonstrate below, Du Bois pays particular attention to the apparently irrational source of whites' desire to maintain white racial identity as a ground of superiority in contrast to their demeaned and degraded illusion of the nature of Black folk.

As Eric Porter explores in *The Problem of the Future World*,[23] Du Bois in *Dusk* commits to the dual nature of racial categories: insupportable by any known science, and nevertheless relevant to the causes and explanations of everyday individual and systemic human interactions. Quoting Kate Baldwin, Porter characterizes Du Bois's conception of race in *Dusk* as "both an impossibility and a fact."[24] Without doubt, understanding the odd ontological structure of racial categories is necessary to the struggle for social, political, and economic justice in the US and globally.[25] The material effects of race must be faced head on, in order to combat "the continued subordination of identifiable groupings of human beings by other identifiable groupings of human beings."[26] Porter urges, convincingly, that Du Bois's analysis in *Dusk of Dawn* still offers useful insights to antiracist scholars and activists. Du Bois lifts up a set of "epistemological-ethical questions regarding the necessity of developing knowledge about race's changing foundations and being attuned to the ways refusals of such knowledge enable its reproduction."[27] Like so many complexes that function below the level of consciousness, aspects of racial ideology thrive in conditions of ignorance, and so does the resulting oppression.[28] The difficulty of convincing American whites that they must seek knowledge about the ongoing construction of race and the fiction of white supremacy is thus a significant obstacle to justice, in which light Du Bois's nuanced work in *Dusk of Dawn* is particularly urgent.

In *Dusk*, Du Bois understands that the material changes that would improve Black lives would be more or less simple, if not easy, to accomplish: improved education and access to political and economic power chief among them. The primary obstacle to such changes, then and now, is white opposition. In passages that presage Fanon, Du Bois contends that combating—even simply understanding—white supremacy would mean "charting . . . a path . . . through a jungle of ideas conditioned on unconscious and subconscious reflexes of living things . . . blind unreason and often irresistible urges of sensitive matter."[29] Ignorance, greed, and hatred do not simply produce and reproduce white supremacy; imbricated within all forms of social and political relations via unconscious associations, impulses, and habitual behaviors, white supremacy consists only in part of mistaken ideas. Furthermore, whiteness acts like a living force—a jungle—and it can be pruned or even killed in one place, only to sprout new growth elsewhere.

In sum, education and "objectively" persuasive demonstration are inadequate tools for dismantling white folks' commitment to maintaining the color line. "[I]gnorance and ill will" alone do not drive white supremacy but also, Du Bois asserts, "certain more powerful motives less open to reason or appeal."[30] This conviction about white irrationality sets him apart from white liberal critics of American racism, such as Gunnar Myrdal, whose 1944 book *American Dilemma* explained white racism as a product of whites' ignorance about Black Americans. "There is no doubt," Myrdal wrote, "that a great majority of white people in America would be prepared to give the Negro a substantially better deal if they knew the facts."[31] Whatever Myrdal may have had in mind, "the facts" about white supremacy and the oppression of African Americans (and others) had been available for over a half century to the white world in general, and to Du Bois's white acquaintances, in particular. It was far from clear that any amount of clarity in terms of facts could have convinced white America to give the Negro a "better deal."

The rapacious undergrowth of white supremacy has, of course, a fairly obvious connection to white material and psychological gain. What Myrdal and his ilk neglected—and Du Bois did not —was the tremendous profitability of institutional and mercantile endeavors that relied on the presumed subhumanity of people of color, as well as those "psychological wages" garnered from white identity. White leaders and historians hailed such entrepreneurship as a triumph of "human" ingenuity—who could have thought that so much labor could be got so cheaply *in a democracy*? The answer, of course, lies in the fact that the economic and political colonialism of the early twentieth century were possible only through a sort of elemental disidentification of whites from people of color. Despite extensive and manifest evidence of their humanity, white leaders initiated policies that immiserated "black slaves and colored serfs." The mental and moral gymnastics through which white people engaged in such projects is central to much of Du Bois's later work and comparable to the work of anticolonial thinkers and activists in the decades that followed.

Du Bois, the one-time champion of European civilization, was reluctant to conclude that white supremacist racism would "not yield to argument" but only—if at all—to slow and gradual efforts at diverse forms of suasion.[32] Du Bois recounts as pivotal in this growing realization the devastating lynching of Sam Hose and its aftermath a full forty years prior to *Dusk*. Hose, a Black grocer with whom Du Bois had been acquainted, was burned, hanged, and dismembered in 1899 in Coweta County, Georgia, southwest of Atlanta. Horrified by the event, Du Bois set off from Atlanta University for downtown Atlanta to convince Joel Chandler Harris, then the editor of the *Atlanta Constitution*, to publish an editorial denouncing lynching as the criminal horror that it was. Well before he had reached the *Constitution*'s offices, Du Bois was stopped cold by the news that Hose's knuckles were on display at a grocery down the street.[33] This celebration of torture and murder made a mockery of Du Bois's errand: how could any editorial, however powerful, reach the hearts and minds of a community so twisted as to make human bones public souvenirs? While Du Bois had surely heard of whites' proclivity toward celebrating such trophies in other instances, it was likely the first so proximate in space and time to his own home.

How to imagine the devastation Du Bois felt when so viscerally confronted with the merciless glee in white hearts and minds in the face of this particular atrocity? Whites *in his own community* remained complacent, at *best*, against the spirit-murdering aftermath of literal butchery.[34] In the words of the late Joel Olson, the "mad rationality of lynching and segregation" shattered Du Bois's faith in science.[35] Nevertheless, Du Bois remained in Atlanta for ten more years, publishing in 1903 what remains his most famous work, *The Souls of Black Folk*—a work that enfolds the presentation of social science data within richly poetic expression of the humanity, the soulfulness, to be found in the Black community.

Indeed, even when he left academia (the first time) in 1910, his faith in white rationality accompanied his agreement to head the National Association for the Advancement of Colored People's (NAACP) Publicity and Research arm. Recalling the event forty years later, Du Bois notes that in this early turn from scholarly work to activism,

> my basic theory [in starting *The Crisis*] had been that race prejudice was primarily a matter of ignorance on the part of the mass of men, giving the evil and anti-social a chance to work their way; that when the truth was properly presented, the monstrous wrong of race hate must melt and melt quickly before it. *All human action to me in those days was conscious and rational. There was no twilight zone.*[36]

In retrospect, Du Bois believed that the jarring reality of whites' anti-Black violence gutted *his* ability to act as a rational scientist.[37] It would be long years of experience and study, weaving in and out of the scholarly world, before he developed a vocabulary that effectively described the epistemic and moral disaster of whiteness. In *Dusk*'s fifth chapter, written some forty years after the Hose murder, Du Bois offered the metaphor meant to illustrate "the full psychological meaning of caste segregation."[38] Du Bois describes a cave in which Black folk are trapped and from time to time observed by passing whites. In contrast to Plato's notion, those *outside* Du Bois's cave cannot and do not want to recognize the truth of those entombed therein, and in fact cannot hear them at all.[39] "It gradually penetrates the minds of the prisoners that the people passing do not hear; that some thick sheet of invisible but horribly tangible plate glass is between them and the world."[40] As this reality dawns on those trapped inside the cave, behind this plate glass, they increase their efforts, desperate to be heard.

> They get excited; they talk louder; they gesticulate. Some of the passing world stop in curiosity; these gesticulations seems so pointless; they laugh and pass on. They still either do not hear at all, or hear but dimly, and even what they hear, they do not understand. Then the people within may become hysterical. They may scream and hurl themselves against the barriers. . . . *They may even, here and there, break through in blood and disfigurement, and find themselves faced by a horrified, implacable, and quite overwhelming mob of people frightened for their own very existence.*[41]

The importance of this metaphor, for present purposes, is its depiction of the *fear* whites feel in the face of increasingly frantic efforts by Black Americans to be heard. The imagery of "disfigured and bloody" African Americans is all-too-relevant as I write this in the summer of 2016.[42] Also distressingly accurate is the image of white Americans, unable or unwilling to hear the messages about pain and exclusion shouted out by Black Americans.[43] Importantly, Du Bois describes these white witnesses as fearful *for their "very existence"* at the sight of this broken glass and blood.

I contend that Du Bois's insight here reveals that white identity is built on a brutally murderous lie of innocence. When I, as a white American, face evidence that—far from innocent or even "normal"—my people are capable of every wrong they have accused others of doing, and *then some*, my very existence *as the person I believed myself to be* is placed in doubt. To return to Du Bois's metaphor, my confidence in my very humanity might well be shaken by the suspicion that I am responsible for the injuries of those who break through the glass. As well, because superiority constitutes whiteness's foundations, the thought that white superiority has been maintained by inhuman acts that inherently deny such superiority must be unthinkable. Immediately, I would deny the evidence before me—the injuries to Black bodies, if caused by white folk, must be deserved. Whites' motivation to deny Black suffering (by presuming their subhumanity) while simultaneously asserting our own justification is all too clear. In turn, we will at great pains deny this complex; our identity is put at risk even at the hint of such an explanation.

White folks, then, have a deep-seated motivation to ignore evidence of their own wrongs. In fact, we engage in active efforts to deny such wrongs, and to minimize the suffering of all people of color that can reasonably be linked to whites' behavior. Du Bois here makes use not of the "veil" metaphor of his earlier work, but of "invisible but horribly tangible" plate glass—less obscuring but harder to breach. This metaphor suggests that the lives of Black folks, their humanity, struggle, and *pathos* is not *unavailable* to the white world, but rather that we have built barriers in order plausibly to ignore it. Convincing white folk of the ultimate benefit of putting aside the barrier, or reaching across it, is, unsurprisingly, a difficult task, as it means endangering the supposed foundation of our very existence.

The publication of *Dusk of Dawn* accompanied rapid changes worldwide, with a decade of economic depression behind and decades of war, including Cold War, ahead. The white supremacy driving these economic and political developments resulted in the immiseration of thousands of African, Latin American, and Southeast Asian people. Du Bois writes:

> The progress of the white world must cease to rest upon the poverty and the ignorance of its own proletariat and of the colored world. . . . To attack and better all this calls for more than appeal and argument. . . . [T]he quickest way to bring the reason of the world face to face with this major problem of human progress is to listen to the complaint of those human beings today who are suffering most from white attitudes, from white habits, from conscious and unconscious wrongs which white folks are today inflicting on their victims. The colored world therefore must be seen as existing not simply for itself but as a group whose insistent cry may yet become the warning which awakens the world to its truer self and its wider destiny.[44]

Of course, anyone who could enjoy the advantages of superiority while engaging in work that supports the oppression of others would appear to be a moral monster. Du Bois generously remarks that most white folk are "painfully human,"[45] that is, they are understandably concerned to maintain the privileges to which they have become accustomed. I nevertheless would contend that the fear, uncertainty, and self-loathing always nipping at the heels of even the most unreflective white folk surely impairs any meaningful sense of freedom we might claim; it further creates a moral and epistemic complex as difficult to detect in oneself as it is to ameliorate.[46] In Du Bois's *Black Flame* trilogy, Du Bois's capacity for empathy helps us to see the impact on human freedom of such twisted epistemic patterns on white America.

3. The *Black Flame* Trilogy (1957–1961)

The three novels that make up the *Black Flame* trilogy combine semi-autobiographical narrative, sociological commentary, and historical analysis, offered in the sometimes-disarming mix of poetic and didactic prose that characterize so much of Du Bois's work. As Gerald Horne has written, Du Bois turned his prodigious creative energies to the trilogy after losing many of his beloved political organizations (e.g., the Council on African Affairs) which withered in the anticommunist (and not incidentally anti-Black) glare of the late 1940s.[47] The result sometimes lacks grace—and is often tremendously affecting. Eric Porter notes that critics often perceive Du Bois's later works as reflecting his weakening faculties, not to mention his increasingly ideological bent.[48] Du Bois's trilogy nevertheless transcends most midcentury treatments of race and includes rich and multi-layered depictions of white (and "nearly white") characters, as well as African American protagonists. Du Bois's insight into whiteness and white people, as well as continuing reflection on "the Black experience" in the US, remains exceptional. A detailed analysis of these works is beyond my scope here; the following discussion offers only a preliminary account of the complex conception of whiteness with which Du Bois grappled at the end of his career.

Du Bois's accomplishment in the *Black Flame* trilogy is prodigious: 1,200 typed pages produced over the six years between May 1949 and 1955, *beginning* when Du Bois was eighty-one.[49] According to Brent Edwards, and perhaps unsurprisingly, Du Bois had a difficult time finding a publisher, as the manuscript must have seemed to be a "sprawling, quixotic indulgence in nostalgia by a very old man."[50] The books are unjustly neglected at this point, given Du Bois's particular perspective—and especially given the view of Herbert Aptheker, Du Bois's literary executor—that they were the "most revealing work from Du Bois's pen."[51] These novels do not fit neatly into the genre, ranging within a single chapter from fictional narrative to historical lesson to political *cri de coeur*;[52] they also provide an inimitable perspective on the psychosocial, political, and theoretical moments in a long American century.

Eslanda Robeson recognized Du Bois's primary motivation in writing the trilogy as presenting a clear account of the dismantling of Reconstruction by white plantocracy in collaboration with the white worker.[53] Had the aristocracy united with the recently emancipated Black Americans, they might have been able to create a thriving South—after all, hadn't Black Americans brought "schools and civilization" to a benighted land during Reconstruction? Whites had retaken South Carolina, one Black character points out in *Ordeal*, but as a people had lost everything of true value, having "not a statesman, not a poet, not an artist, not a writer" among them. The analysis put forth by this character, Sanford, the former foreman and steward of the Breckinridge planation, reveals the cost to white people of white supremacy. While attempting to maintain their elevated position, the white aristocracy could not recognize the benefit to their own humanity of recognizing the humanity and talents of African Americans.

Some vignettes occasioned by Du Bois's purpose may strike the reader as overly "on the nose." As Edwards writes, Du Bois presents the tableau of a grand conspiratorial meeting of white supremacist world leaders without comment or qualification[54] and other portraits of wealthy white businessmen, which, however sardonically intended, could support the case that Du Bois was no longer "reasonable" in his view of corporate America. On the other hand, given Du Bois's entirely reasonable critique of neocolonialism as early as *Dusk of Dawn*, caricatures of greedy white supremacists are hardly out of bounds given Du Bois's project in the trilogy. The stylistic eccentricities of the trilogy do not negate the scholarly value of these works, whatever their quality as novels (which is well beyond my expertise). They offer a rare perspective on American social and political life, particularly in small Southern towns, and include shrewd commentary on the experience of individuals served and those subjugated by the racism of American institutions.

Contemporary reviews in relatively friendly periodicals agreed that the original characters around which Du Bois weaved the narrative needed more fleshing out, a flaw more apparent with each passing book.[55] J. Saunders Redding, in the *Afro-American*, feared that the faults of the first book—the inattention to the nuances of fictional world- and character-building—were "compounded" in the second. Redding complains, I think accurately, that each book really contains elements of four different works: a history of the American period covered, a sociology of the South, a political commentary, and only then, a fictional narrative of original characters. Perhaps as a result, the narrative is more melodramatic than subtle, with stark divisions of characters into Black and white, good and bad, respectively. However, he notes, the result—particularly the mythology of Manual Mansart as "the Black Flame," burning long and low for love and justice—is "very interesting."[56] One may or may not read this is a compliment.

While I cannot engage at length with the (admittedly limited) more recent commentary on the *Black Flame* trilogy, I do want to note that its shortcomings as literature are again oft-observed. Lily Wiatrowski Phillips characterizes them as "odd, perhaps flawed, work," and rightly indicates that they are seldom read.[57] Byerman reads the postscript to the first book as "conced[ing]" that "the plot . . . is merely a thread on which are hung his assorted observations about American life," and thus contends that "art here has been brought into the service of social science."[58] Rampersad is more generous toward the trilogy but notes that the prose is often "torpid" and "sluggish"—which does not necessarily distinguish Du Bois from other writers of the period (or "his" period, the Victorian), but can be discouraging. Rampersad further points out that Du Bois's charting of family trees, while careful, is not flawless.[59] Against my own thesis regarding the centrality of whiteness as problem in this trilogy, Rampersad argues that capitalism replaces racism as the nemesis of Du Bois's late life.[60] While I will not take up these critiques in detail here, I hope in the remainder of this chapter to offer a slightly different read on the trilogy.

It should come as no surprise that art takes a back seat to argument in Du Bois's final work of fiction; after all, he had propounded the use of Art as Propaganda (and Beauty as Truth) since 1926 and never, to my knowledge, retracted this commitment.[61] Further, as Byerman and Rampersad both indicate, Du Bois's commitment to the accurate revision of the historical record was in some tension with the creation of Beauty, and he lacked time to craft the revisions necessary to balance these aims.[62] Nevertheless, I contend that the scope of the *Black Flame* and its varied characters—fictional as well as historical—allow readers to see white supremacy taking its toll on generations of both Black and white Americans, sometimes ending in profound tragedy and always spoiling the potential for flourishing. The players, major as well as minor, reveal the many-headed hydra of American "race relations" under white supremacy. Du Bois's own observations and inclinations are distributed amongst various African American characters—male and female—in the trilogy, even if Manual Mansart is the presumptive stand-in for the author.[63] Moreover, Du Bois maps out the narrative in such a way that a white audience may begin to understand the diversity of African American experience in the early twentieth century—a trademark element of his works. Gifted and promising young Black men and women find themselves frustrated in the pursuit of the lives to which they are entitled and are wounded or killed by systemic and interpersonal racism; several white characters thrive materially despite lacking any virtue beyond their fortunate birth.

In tracing the lives of several African American characters, Du Bois in the trilogy offers white readers insight into how our world appears from the perspective of those who are by this very same world denied full humanity. The range of outcomes for talented, even brilliant, Black characters, even the luckiest and most capable of whom fail to achieve a full measure of flourishing, illustrates the continual violence of "the white world." The protagonist, Manual Mansart, rises to the presidency of a Black college, but never has the resources or autonomy (due to the white board of trustees) to realize his vision of African American education. Du Bois gives us deep and prolonged insight into Mansart's frustrations, and glimpses of what might have been. For the white reader, such access to the interiority of African Americans' experiences amounts to moments of "white double-consciousness,"[64] the ability to see whites and their behavior from an African American perspective.

The omniscient viewpoint used in these novels also allows us access to Du Bois's conception of the range of white subjectivities. A white working-class character named Scroggs, shaped by poverty and the shame of witnessing his mother having to steal food from "Negroes," reveals powerful resentment at his own station in life while desperately holding onto the fiction of white supremacy. Scroggs kills a Black man during a lynching spree, then quells his consequent guilt by appealing to divine purpose: "God wanted Black folk restrained—to not live 'like other men,' for [Scroggs] learned that they were 'not really human.' Learned something of it in school, more in the newspapers, and read one or two frightening books."[65] His own experiences dealing with African Americans, perhaps even especially the charity some had extended to the family in Scroggs's childhood, was no match for the lessons in school and church that whites were the true humans and children of God.

Du Bois relates vignettes featuring at least three generations of Scroggses: Sam, Abe, and Joe, who "represented the same type": "desperately afraid of losing their heritage as 'white folk,' of sinking to the level of Negroes. They represented, on the whole, disinherited people, dispossessed of land and property, but frantically clinging to their 'rights.'"[66] For whites of all classes, Black Americans were resources to be tapped or threats to be dealt with, rather than human beings entitled to their own life goals and the means to attain them. As Du Bois suggests in other works, the end of slavery put whites in fear of an end to white supremacy, and instead of questioning the worth of white supremacy, they found new ways to degrade Black Americans. From the working class Scroggses to the multimillionaire Cecil Rhodes, whites in Du Bois's trilogy depend on the degradation of Black people in order to maintain their illusions of self-worth.

Perhaps the most incisive nonwhite character is the singular Jean Du Bignon, who may well be one of the most interesting female characters in midcentury American literature. Du Bignon reflects elements of Du Bois himself, both in her conviction about her identity and her commitment to the work of racial uplift, but also, for my purposes, in her fierce determination to understand whiteness. Du Bignon, a light-skinned, mixed-race African American woman, could, we are told, have passed for white, but is determined instead to remain wedded to "her people." As Du Bois makes clear, the lightness of her complexion makes Du Bignon's acceptance in the "Black world" a dodgy thing. Born and raised in New Orleans, Jean battles with her aristocratic (and white-identified) great-grandmother over what type of life she will lead, and where she will lead it.

> "But," stormed the old woman, "there is many a person here in New Orleans with as much black blood as yours, passing as white. Why shouldn't you?"
>
> "Simply because I do not want to. I am interested in this matter of colored people because they explain the whites."
>
> "But you can work with them here."
>
> "No, I cannot. Here I am neither one nor the other unless I entirely desert the one. I won't do that."[67]

Indeed, she does not; instead, she obtains a PhD in sociology at "Chicago University," determined to travel and study the "races of the world." After some misadventures, she presents herself as a "colored" candidate for the job of secretary to Manuel Mansart, now president of the "colored" State College in Georgia. Even traveling to the College for her interview is challenging, as she is read as white and thus cannot find a cab that will transport her from dignified white society to the Black college. When she finally reaches Mansart's office, Mansart's son, Douglass, objects to her taking the position, when there are "plenty of *colored* girls who need the work."[68] The senior Mansart, impressed with her academic credentials, gives Du Bignon the position, "with the vague promise [that she would teach] a class in Sociology 'as soon as practical.'"[69] Over the years, Du Bignon becomes Mansart's most trusted ally, in spite of the criticisms and doubts of both Black and white folk in the local community. Later, Mansart considers making Du Bignon a dean, because she is trustworthy and able, but "in the South and among Negroes" the fact that she is a woman is "distinctly against her. He dare not attempt such an innovation at this time."[70]

Du Bignon is a fascinating character for any number of reasons, and her perspective on whiteness is particularly acute. Her aforementioned claim that she wanted to live with and come to know "colored people" because "they explain the whites"[71] indicates that white people need explanation; with this suggestion, Du Bois upends the centuries-long tradition of presuming whiteness as the norm that needs no explanation. A glaring example of the opposite standpoint is found in the scientific community's response to Jesse Owens's triumph at the 1936 Olympic Games in Berlin. Hitler was not the only one surprised by Owens's abilities, and thus white American physiologists studied Owens's muscles, bones, and ligaments to determine how he was able to defeat white athletes in track and field events. On Du Bois's apparent view—not only as spoken by Du Bignon but as demonstrated with his work on this trilogy—whites, not African Americans, present as pathological, and ultimately in need of study.

Observing Black lives, for the author as well as the character, reveals whiteness. Through ideology, practices, and policies, white Americans have worked tirelessly to define what is possible for Black Americans. While the metaphor of a photographic negative would be too simplistic, it does point to the phenomenon to which Du Bignon refers: Black experience constitutes a reflection of white pathology around race, because it is the outcome of that pathology.[72] The segregation of education, religion, and public institutions, as well as the instances of violence that destroyed Black individuals and communities were—and are—demanded and sustained by white desires.

Without a single example of white individuals being harmed by contact with African Americans (indeed, there are centuries' worth of evidence that the opposite is true), whites behaved as if they could not work or live or be educated or entertained alongside and on an equal basis with African Americans. The persistence of such racial injustice reflects the pathology of the white psyche in US culture. Through Du Bignon's narrative, as well as those of other Black characters in the trilogy, we are witness to the depth of the white need to control Black Americans—and the brutality that results when whites feel that their control is at risk. In the end, Du Bignon's confidence that she can solve the problem of whiteness through study gradually erodes into hopelessness—perhaps a reflection of Du Bois's own experience of the United States.

From this brief discussion it is clear, I hope, how Du Bois's picture of whiteness developed following his 1940 publication *Dusk of Dawn*. He reveals some sympathy for the befuddled white characters in even the worst villains of the trilogy; rather than evil, desperation and smug self-assurance shape his white characters, but all focus on maintaining their superiority. Du Bois does not excuse such characters from responsibility but uses them to illustrate the fact that white supremacy is "bigger" than all of those held within its grasp, whatever color. Many of these white characters are simply helpless in their own fear, and most are as dreadfully contorted by their place in a white supremacist system as are the Black Americans to whom they feel so superior.

Of course, the *Black Flame* trilogy offers a wealth of Du Boisian insight on any number of topics; I have barely scratched the surface even of his portrayal of whiteness in its pages. For now, I note how and why whiteness counts as a hindrance to accurate perception and clear thinking among white people. Du Bois portrays each white Scroggs as significantly more perplexed by the demands of whiteness than "colored" Jean Du Bignon. For the purposes of this chapter, every Scroggs is also in every important sense lacking freedom; he is unable to act autonomously, or even get out from under the burden of performing whiteness. This performance, of course, includes the active suppression of African Americans, both politically and economically. While Du Bignon and Manuel Mansart understand how whiteness operates, they cannot leverage their understanding of whiteness except to attain minor successes. All three are entangled in the demands of white supremacy and thus cannot live out the sort of freedom of movement or even thought that democracy promises.

Perhaps most tragically, Mansart's children and grandchildren are, one by one, swallowed up in different ways by white supremacy. Their political and economic aspirations—even the musical talent of Mansart's youngest—are warped or even destroyed altogether by the inescapable constraint of living in a white supremacist nation. And despite his chillingly accurate diagnosis of white supremacy as the cause of these many tragedies, great and small, Du Bois does not, in his white characters, offer much hope for the deconstruction of whiteness. Nevertheless, his portrayal of the ways in which white supremacy socializes white individuals into misconceptions and epistemic weaknesses offers to the white reader necessary insight, if not hope. He knows that many white Americans suspect the vulnerability of their status. Ultimately, it must be up to white Americans to understand how to release their tenuous grip on racial supremacy and make their way toward full humanity.

The change in Du Bois's description and analysis of whiteness over time is, as outlined above, connected to his changing strategy to combat the color line. So long as he believed greed and ill will drove white supremacy (and Black suffering), his program of research and education aimed to prove to white America (and Europe) that those of African descent were as varied, and capable of greatness, as any European folk. Over time, he came to see white racial perceptions as built on irrational fears and protected by psychological mechanisms that were fairly opaque to whites themselves. This combination meant obvious failures of perception and cognition were accepted by white people as normal and accurate. Challenges to these faulty epistemic patterns were met with everything from disbelief and disdain to the fear and anger indicative of a sense of existential threat. According to Gerald Horne, Du Bois believed that the Rev. Martin Luther King Jr.'s strategy of appealing with nonviolence to whites' sense of morality was not sufficiently attentive to the fact that whites were "diseased with racism and may be unreachable by [Gandhian] methods."[73]

The basic diagnosis of the problem of whiteness I am attributing to Du Bois has much in common with the conception of "white ignorance" put forth by Charles Mills. Mills's identification of the white moral and epistemic failures that characterize modern political theory (such as social contract theory) has prompted a reexamination of the "problem" of racism in American philosophy.[74] Like Mills, Du Bois offers a picture of whites' motivations to maintain white supremacy; however, Du Bois's account is less explicit. The intuition sketched out in *Black Reconstruction*, that much of white supremacy is not only irrationally motivated but ultimately resistant to reason, is fleshed out in portrayals of white irrationality and fear in his later work, both nonfiction and fiction. In this sense, Du Bois appears to transcend modernity entirely, in his growing conviction that human action owed more to "chance and unreason"[75] than rational self-interest.

In short, white and Black Americans in Du Bois's writings from 1935 to 1960 seem to inhabit two different worlds, with two different habits of perception. Du Bois makes clear that white supremacy was not simply a relic of slavery; in fact, the fervor with which whites retrieved white identity in the Reconstruction era only became more entrenched with time. As numerous public opinion polls and countless census data repeatedly confirm, Du Bois's certitude that white and Black America live in two different spheres with very different perceptions and chances of success was well founded. The ability to change this state of affairs lies squarely in the hands of white Americans, if only they can overcome the psychological and ideological tangle that they have created, much to their detriment.

As Eric Porter notes, those who seek a more just society, both locally and globally, neglect Du Bois at our peril.[76] In my view, Du Bois is an invaluable genealogist of the "problem of the twentieth century," even as it becomes a key problem of the twenty-first, and especially from the perspective that "whiteness"—the behavior, convictions, and beliefs (conscious and unconscious) of white-identified people—is a deadly obstacle to the pursuit of racial justice. Du Bois's deft portrayal of whites' commitment to their own superiority offers a tremendous opportunity for white antiracists to examine themselves and their institutions with an eye toward real change.[77] Knowing how well we do not know ourselves or our motivations, white Americans must be willing to accept that our best intentions are likely to be fraught with undertones of supremacy and shot through with the presumption that we not only know best but *are* best: after all, who *was* the Tolstoy of the Zulus?[78]

Of course, Du Bois's time was not our time; Porter's insight again is useful here: "As I situate Du Bois's thought at midcentury, I explore his insight into longue durée processes that he saw shaping his past, present, and future. . . . we can pay close attention to how he interrogated social and ideological projects that were emergent at this moment but which continue to shape our present. Yet I also recognize the ways that Du Bois and his analysis were bound by history."[79] In particular, Porter notes, the situation in many African nations is not what Du Bois had hoped for, and certainly not what he worked for: rather than independence, many analysts find that "neocolonialism" best describes the "postcolonial" future for which Du Bois toiled. Perhaps his greatest shock and disappointment would be the status of China and Russia. No longer even putative utopias, as Porter points out, they are both (a) capitalist and (b) apparently exploiting the global South. Like Porter, then, I "consider how Du Bois's ideas might be revised as they are brought to bear on a very different present than he imagined."[80] With no example of a just, antiracist nation on the horizon, we must make use of the tools Du Bois left us with in order to make a new way toward racial justice. In doing so, we may find that at last we are free.

NOTES

1. W. E. B. Du Bois, "The Souls of White Folk" in *Darkwater: Voices from within the Veil* (Mineola: Dover, 1999), 18.

2. Ta-Nehisi Coates, *Between the World and Me* (New York: Spiegel and Grau, 2015), 11.

3. See "Jefferson Davis," "The Conservation of Races," in W. E. B. Du Bois, *Writings* (New York: Library of America, 1986); also, "A Vacation Unique," in Shamoon Zamir, *Dark Voices: W. E. B. Du Bois and American Thought, 1888–1903* (Chicago: University of Chicago Press, 1995).

4. Upton Sinclair, *I, Candidate for Governor: And How I Got Licked* (Berkeley: University of California Press, 1994 [1935]), 109.

5. Du Bois, *Black Reconstruction in America: 1860–1880* (New York: The Free Press, 1998).

6. David Levering Lewis, "Introduction," *Black Reconstruction*, viii.

7. *Black Reconstruction*, 700.

8. Roediger, *The Wages of Whiteness: Race and the Making of the American Working Class* (New York: Verso, 1991/1993), 13, citing *Black Reconstruction*, 27–30.

9. Roediger, *The Wages of Whiteness*, 150.

10. "The Transubstantiation of Andrew Johnson: White Epistemic Failure in Du Bois's *Black Reconstruction*," *Phylon* 51, no. 1 (Fall 2014).

11. Du Bois, *Black Reconstruction*, 281.

12. See Eric Foner *Reconstruction: America's Unfinished Revolution* (New York: Harper Perennial, 1989), and Nicholas Lemann, *Redemption: The Last Battle of the Civil War* (New York: Farrar, Strauss, and Giroux, 2007).

13. Glenda Gilmore, *Gender and Jim Crow: Women and the Politics of White Supremacy in North Carolina 1896–1920* (Chapel Hill: University of North Carolina Press, 2006); see also Carol Anderson, *White Rage: The Unspoken Truth of Our Racial Divide* (NY: Bloomsbury, 2016).

14. Du Bois, *Black Reconstruction*, 322, emphasis mine.

15. Keith E. Byerman, *Seizing the Word: History, Art, and Self in the Work of W. E. B. Du Bois* (Athens: University of Georgia Press, 1994), 61.

16. Byerman, *Seizing the Word*, 74.

17. Byerman, *Seizing the Word*, 61.

18. Ludwig Wittgenstein, *Philosophical Investigations*, trans. G. E. M. Anscombe (Oxford: Blackwell, 1953/1986), 133 (p. 51).

19. Du Bois, *Black Reconstruction*, 722, quoted in Byerman, *Seizing the Word*, 61.

20. Byerman, *Seizing the Word*, 79.

21. As Celena Simpson has written, "This historical project . . . forms the base upon which Du Bois's political projects against white racism, both structural and personal, rely." Celena Simpson, "Du Bois's Dubious Feminism: Evaluating through *The Black Flame Trilogy*," *Pluralist* 10, no. 1 (2015): 54.

22. See David Levering Lewis, *W. E. B. Du Bois: The Fight for Equality and the American Century 1919–1963* (New York: Henry Holt, 2000), 363–65.

23. Eric Porter, *The Problem of the Future World: W. E. B. Du Bois and the Race Concept at Midcentury* (Durham: Duke University Press, 2010).

24. Porter, *The Problem of the Future World*, 30, citing Kate Baldwin, *Beyond the Color Line and the Iron Curtain* (Durham: Duke University Press, 2002), 183.

25. Anthony Appiah and others have argued that Du Bois appears never to have surrendered the notion that racial groups had some biological or otherwise physical, ontological foundation. This question is not relevant to my discussion here, but I should point out that I disagree; toward midcentury, Du Bois's occasional poetic flights regarding the deep differences between the races should, I contend, be read *only* as poetic flights, and not as evidence of his intellectual commitments regarding racial metaphysics.

26. Porter, *The Problem of the Future World*, 31.

27. Porter, *The Problem of the Future World*, 34.

28. See, e.g., Charles Mills's germinal work *The Racial Contract* (Ithaca: Cornell University Press, 1999) for the epistemological conditions of the Racial Contract, as well as his more recent piece, "White Ignorance," in *Epistemologies of Ignorance*, eds. Shannon Sullivan and Nancy Tuana (Albany: State University of New York Press, 2010), 11–38.

29. Du Bois, *Dusk of Dawn*, 551; see Porter, *The Problem of the Future World*, epigraph, vii.

30. Du Bois, *Dusk of Dawn* in *Writings*, 557.

31. Myrdal, *American Dilemma*, 48, quoted in Joel Olson, *The Abolition of White Democracy* (Minneapolis: University of Minnesota Press, 2004), xiv.

32. Du Bois, *Dusk of Dawn*, in *Writings*, 558.

33. Du Bois, *Dusk of Dawn*, in *Writings*, 602.

34. Patricia Williams refers to the impact of white supremacy on people of color as "spirit murder"; Patricia Williams, *The Alchemy of Race and Rights* (Cambridge: Harvard University Press, 1991).

35. Joel Olson, "W. E. B. Du Bois and the Race Concept," *Souls* 7, no. 3–4 (2005): 118–28, quoting 118. As David Levering Lewis also notes, "It was the bitterest of revelations to a Calvinist and a Hegelian that scientific truth, repeatedly broadcast, was apparently impotent to ameliorate collective behavior." See Lewis, *W. E. B. Du Bois*.

36. Du Bois, *Dusk of Dawn* in *Writings*, 760, emphasis mine.

37. Du Bois, *Dusk of Dawn* in *Writings*, 603.

38. Du Bois, *Dusk of Dawn* in *Writings*, 649.

39. My thanks to Charles Mills for this connection. "W. E. B. Du Bois: Black Radical Liberal," in *A Political Companion to W. E. B. Du Bois*, ed. Nick Bromell (Lexington: University Press of Kentucky, 2018), 48.

40. Du Bois, *Dusk of Dawn* in *Writings*, 650.

41. Du Bois, *Dusk of Dawn* in *Writings*, 650, emphasis mine.

42. And remains so six years later, as the anniversary of George Floyd's murder is met within a week by a racially motivated mass shooting in Buffalo, New York.

43. Examples include the cases of Renisha McBride, who was shot and killed by a white homeowner after she came to his door for help following a car accident, and Jonathan Ferrell, who was shot and killed by Charlotte, North Carolina, police officers, called by a homeowner who feared Ferrell was a homebreaker, when in fact he, too, was seeking help after a traffic accident. See, for example Renisha McBride, "Detroit Area Man Gets 17 to 32 Years for Shooting Visitor on Porch," *Los Angeles Times*, September 3, 2014, http://www.latimes.com/nation/nationnow/la-na-nn-porch-killer-sentenced-20140903-story.html; Jonathan Ferrell, "Video Is Released from 2013 North Carolina Police Shooting of Jonathan Ferrell," *New York Times*, August 6, 201, https://www.nytimes.com/2015/08/07/us/dashboard-camera-video-is-released-from-2013-north-carolina-police-shooting.html?_r=0.

44. Du Bois, *Dusk of Dawn* in *Writings*, 679–80.

45. Du Bois, *Dusk of Dawn* in *Writings*, 650.

46. This is not to say that whites suffer the greatest harm of white supremacy; as Thomas C. Holt notes, for Du Bois, Black consciousness developed as a consequence of the extreme alienation Black Americans faced in a white supremacist United States that rejected their very humanity. Thomas C. Holt, "The Political Uses of Alienation: W. E. B. Du Bois on Politics, Race, and Culture, 1903–1940," *American Quarterly* 42, no. 2 (June 1990): 201–23.

47. Gerald Horne, *W. E. B. Du Bois: A Biography* (Santa Barbara: Greenwood Press, 2010), 180.

48. Porter, *The Problem of the Future World*, 3.

49. Brent Hayes Edwards, introduction to *The Ordeal of Mansart* (New York: Oxford University Press, 2007), xxv.

50. Edwards, introduction, xxv.

51. Edwards, introduction, xxv.

52. Keith Byerman says of the trilogy that these writings are "cast in the form of novels": "a blending of history, fiction, social commentary, political criticism, and autobiography." Byerman, *Seizing the Word*, 138.

53. Eslanda Robeson, "The Ordeal of Mansart," *National Guardian* (July 22, 1957), 4.

54. Edwards, introduction, xxix.

55. Meridel Le Sueuer, in her review, wrote that the richness of even minor characters "make one wish that the author had perhaps a little more faith in his magnificent powers of characterization. . . . Under the magnificent structure of the historical building, the fine tendrils and penetrating portraits of a hundred people leave the reader exasperated and hungry for more and to follow and see the growth or destruction of these people under the steam pressure of history." "Ordeal of Mansart—Passion and an Illumination of History," Meridel Le Sueuer, *Daily Worker* (September 29, 1957), 6.

56. J. Saunders Redding, "Latest Work of W. E. B. Du Bois," *Afro-American* (February 16, 1960), 2.

57. Lily Wiatrowsky Phillips, "*The Black Flame* Revisited: Recursion and Return in the Reading of W. E. B. Du Bois's Trilogy," *CR: The New Centennial Review* 15, no. 2 (Fall 2015): 157–70.

58. Byerman, *Seizing the Word*, 138.

59. Arnold Rampersad, *The Art and Imagination of W. E. B. Du Bois* (Cambridge: Harvard University Press, 1976), 268; also 315, n. 2.

60. Rampersad, *The Art and Imagination of W. E. B. Du Bois*, 270.

61. Du Bois, "Criteria of Negro Art," *The Crisis*, October 1926, in *Writings*, 993–1002.

62. Byerman, *Seizing the Word*, 139; Rampersad, *The Art and Imagination of W. E. B. Du Bois*, 269. Rampersad here compared Du Bois's work not unfavorably to Dos Passos's *U.S.A.* trilogy.

63. Henry Louis Gates points out that several characters "stand for aspects of Du Bois's personality and professional life," including at least two fictional academics, Sebastian Doyle and James Burghardt. Henry Louis Gates, "Series Introduction," Du Bois, *The Ordeal of Mansart*, xviii.

64. See Linda Martin Alcoff, *The Future of Whiteness* (Cambridge: Polity, 2015).

65. Du Bois, *The Ordeal of Mansart*, 150.

66. Du Bois, *Mansart Builds a School*, 216.

67. Du Bois, *Mansart Builds a School*, 83.

68. Du Bois, *Mansart Builds a School*, 87.

69. Du Bois, *Mansart Builds a School*, 87.

70. Du Bois, *Mansart Builds a School*, 111.

71. Du Bois, *Mansart Builds a School*, 83.

72. I want to point out that the notion of "pathology" as I use it here should in no way imply that white Americans lack culpability for the ongoing consequences of white supremacy. It is a feature of Du Bois's account of white epistemic and moral failure, as discussed above, that white Americans must work to end white supremacy despite the psychological barriers to such work they have inherited. See my *What the Old Man Knew: Du Bois and the Problem of Whiteness*, chapter 5, work-in-progress on file with the author; see also Olson, "W. E. B. Du Bois and the Race Concept"; John Shuford, "Four Du Boisian Contributions to Critical Race Theory," *Transactions of the Charles S. Peirce Society* 37/3 (Summer 2001): 301–37.

73. Gerald Horne, *Black & Red: W. E. B. Du Bois and the Afro-American Response to the Cold War, 1944–1963* (Albany: State University of New York Press, 1986), 240.

74. Mills, "White Ignorance."

75. Du Bois, *Dusk of Dawn* in *Writings*, 558.

76. Porter, *The Problem of the Future World*, 2.

77. Such change may or may not include the abolition of "whiteness," as some have argued; e.g., Olson, "W. E. B. Du Bois and the Race Concept," 126; it does, I think, require whites to understand whiteness—at least for the time being—as a form of ontological indebtedness, as argued by John Shuford, "Four Du Boisian Contributions to Critical Race Theory," 330.

78. That white Europeans have produced the recognized "greats" of classical literature and music has worried a great many college students committed to racial equality. Saul Bellow is reported to have mused that the Zulus had produced no Tolstoy during an interview, and this specific question bedeviled a young Ta-Nehisi Coates, as he recounts in his memoir, *Between the World and Me* (New York: Spiegel and Grau, 2015), 43; in a 1994 *New York Times* op-ed, Bellow denied that the question had meant to uphold white superiority, http://www.nytimes.com/books/00/04/23/specials/bellow-papuans.html. Coates answers the question in a way that should be obvious: *Tolstoy* is the Tolstoy of the Zulus, and is, in fact, everyone's Tolstoy.

79. Porter, *The Problem of the Future World*, 15.

80. Porter, *The Problem of the Future World*, 16.

CHAPTER 2

Politics, Poetry, and Prose: W. E. B. Du Bois, *Black Reconstruction*, and the Origins of Our Times

—Carlton Dwayne Floyd and Thomas Ehrlich Reifer

> The most magnificent drama in the last thousand years of human history is the transportation of ten million human beings out of the dark beauty of their mother continent into the new-found Dorado of the West. They descended into Hell; and in the third century they arose from the dead, in the finest effort to achieve democracy for the millions of working men the world has ever seen. It was a tragedy that beggared the Greek; it was an upheaval of humanity like the Reformation and the French Revolution. Yet we are blind and led by the blind. We discern in it no part of our labor movement; no part in our industrial triumph; no part in our religious experience.
>
> —W. E. B. Du Bois, *Black Reconstruction*

> The problem of class is . . . the problem of the ruling class—of a capitalist class so immensely wealthy that they are capable of destroying the world as a side effect of their pursuit of private gain.
>
> —Erik Olin Wright[1]

W. E. B. Du Bois's *Black Reconstruction* is one of the most powerful works of historical sociology ever written. More than this, it put forward a historical sociology of slavery and freedom that underscored the crucial role of the realities of slavery and freedom in human culture, which would only be taken up as a crucial subject of scholarly inquiry in the late twentieth century. In this work, as no other, Du Bois deploys a rich understanding of the souls of Black folk and in creating the "Black Radical Tradition," drawing on but going beyond Marx, to analyze the problem of the twentieth century: the color line.[2] Yet as Du Bois realized, the color line was more mysterious than imagined. Du Bois's sojourns in Europe and the Warsaw Ghetto, in the aftermath of the destruction of European Jews in the Holocaust, revealed to him:

> the race problem in which I was interested cut across lines of color and physique and status and was a matter of cultural patterns, perverted teaching and human hate and prejudice, which reached to all sorts of people and caused endless evil to all. . . . So that the ghetto of Warsaw helped me to emerge from a certain social provincialism.[3]

Europe was formative for Du Bois in other ways as well. During his time in Germany, Du Bois knew or studied with many of the greatest classical sociological theorists and historical political economists of his time, including Max Weber and Gustav Schmoller. Despite this, Du Bois's landmark *Black Reconstruction*, is all but ignored.[4] This racialized "epistemology of ignorance" is especially tragic as the problem of the color line Du Bois poignantly underscored increasingly intersects with the question of human survival.[5] Part of the explanation of this ignorance is that Du Bois's *Black Reconstruction* is rarely read.[6]

Du Bois's *Black Reconstruction* reveals a scholar activist, like Oliver Cox or C. L. R. James, who while adumbrating much of the best in historical sociology and world-systems analysis, went far beyond. For Du Bois provided an unparalleled analysis of the centrality of white racism in the defeat of Black Reconstruction and in the changing social foundations of US global power. Here, Du Bois argued that the defeat of Black Reconstruction involved "a tremendous change in the whole intellectual and spiritual development of civilization in the United States because of the predominant political power of the South, built on disenfranchised labor."[7] Du Bois's powerful sociological, narrative, and moral imagination; mastery of African American oral and literary traditions; and wide ranging study of literature, poetry, prose, Latin, Greek and German (he was once a professor of classics) allow *Black Reconstruction* to speak to our present moment as few other works.[8] Herein we explore Du Bois's powerful analysis and mix of politics, poetry, and prose, illuminating its implications for scholars and activists seeking to transform the US and the global system today.

Du Bois, *Black Reconstruction*, and the Origins of World-Systems Analysis

Du Bois's scholarship was profoundly influenced by studying the political economy of the German historical school with Gustav Schmoller in Germany, during which time he also attended the lectures of Max Weber. And it was in London, at the Pan-African Congress, where he met many anticolonial intellectuals, that Du Bois made his famous statement that the problem of the twentieth century was the color line. London was a prime vantage point for seeing the world as a whole during the era of British hegemony. Upon his return from Europe, racism in the US ensured that the only job he could get in the emerging discipline of sociology was in the South, at Atlanta University, and this along with his own activism ensured that Du Bois would split his time between Atlanta and New York City. In New York, Du Bois became a central person in the National Association for the Advancement of Colored People (NAACP), of which he was a key founder and the leading force in its magazine, *The Crisis*. And of course, Atlanta and New York, as London before, were prime vantage points for seeing the fusion of race and class, and wealth and poverty, in the capitalist world-system.

Du Bois was of course part of what Italian socialist Antonio Gramsci called the "subaltern classes."[9] Gramsci is relevant for situating Du Bois's unique contribution. For with the North-South divide in Italy, Gramsci was forced to confront *The Southern Question*, which as Edward Said noted, "under-read and under-analyzed," gives "paramount focus to the territorial, spatial, geographical foundations of social life."[10] For Gramsci, from Sardinia in the South of Italy, the country was a "microcosm of world capitalism inasmuch as it contained in a single country both metropolis and colonies, advanced and backward regions," encapsulating development and underdevelopment on a global scale.[11] Gramsci saw the South as a crucial element of the ruling hegemonic bloc in Italy, which if left unchallenged would ensure a rightward fascist trajectory. Similarly, Du Bois was also forced to confront the Southern question, America's North-South divide and its intimate relationship with white supremacy and racism, in *Black Reconstruction*. Here Du Bois argued for the centrality of slavery and its legacy in the changing social foundations of the US and the global system.

There are profound similarities between Du Bois, especially his emphasis on the crucial role of geoeconomic regions in the capitalist world economy, and the world-systems analysis of Immanuel Wallerstein. In the context of the social movements of the 1960s, Wallerstein created world-systems analysis out of a fecund synthesis of critical currents in social science. Inspired by Marx Fanon, the French *Annales*, and German Historical Schools, with their emphasis on geoeconomic regions and Third World radicalism, Wallerstein brought these all together in startlingly original ways. Here, like the London of Marx's later years, New York City was crucial in Wallerstein's experience and global focus, as was his Jewish background and time in Africa.

Wallerstein's most essential work was his multivolume *The Modern World-System*. But it was left to world-systems scholar Giovanni Arrighi to develop Gramsci's insights about hegemony in ways that deeply resonate with the work of Du Bois.[12]

For Du Bois was perhaps the first to develop the evocative adumbrations of the world-systems perspective in Marx's *Capital*, with its emphasis on the social foundations on which global capitalism rested, noting that the "black workers of America [were] bent at the bottom of a pyramid of growing commerce and industry."[13] Yet in the work of Marx and world-systems, this crucial role of Blacks in the historical development of the modern world-system in general, and US hegemony in particular, foregrounded by Du Bois, often remains in the background.[14]

Black Reconstruction in World-Systems Perspective, and the World-System in Du Boisian Perspective

> In the United States of America, every independent workers' movement was paralyzed as long as slavery disfigured a part of the republic. Labour in a white skin cannot emancipate itself where it is branded in a black skin.
> —Karl Marx, *Capital*

> The unending tragedy of Reconstruction is the utter inability of the American mind to grasp its real significance, its national and world-wide implications.
> —W. E. B. Du Bois, *Black Reconstruction*

The origins of *Black Reconstruction* date back as early as Du Bois's *The Souls of Black Folk.* The deeper origins of Black Reconstruction as historical process go back to white settler colonialism and Black African slavery. In this process, unilateral transfers of capital and labor, forcible and voluntary, that Arrighi saw as fundamental in the production of wealth and poverty on a global scale, and related processes of development and underdevelopment, led the way.[15] In Du Bois's terms, presented in our first epigraph, the slave trade was the "most magnificent drama in the last thousand years of human history." It is significant that Du Bois frames this horror as the "most magnificent drama" over millennia, though later his encounter with Nazi evil in the Holocaust probed the limits of his own understanding of tragedy.

Nevertheless, at this point, in writing *Black Reconstruction* Du Bois relies on literary and theatrical tropes to unearth its framing as encompassing the breadth and depth of those narratives accorded the status of a Greek tragedy, or any other narrative of unmatched significance, in what it displays concerning the depraved depths of humanity, as well as its majestic heights. Here in the kidnapping of and slave trade in Black bodies, in "the transportation of ten million human beings out of the dark beauty of their mother continent into the new-found Dorado of the West," Du Bois refers to three narratives; two of which have received significant attention, that of the colonization of the so-called "Dark Continent," and that of the legendary quest for a "City of Gold," El Dorado, about which many a tale has been told, and that of what Paul Gilroy called the Black Atlantic.[16] That the latter tale is far less favored in relationship to those aforementioned tragedies, is in Du Bois's estimation and ours, deeply unfortunate.

Du Bois continues by citing yet another historic, fabled reference, that of "The Resurrection," of biblical origins, when he notes that these slaves, now in "El Dorado," who found that they had "descended into Hell," rose "in the third century," invoking the act of Christ rising from his grave on the third day, "from the dead, in the finest effort to achieve democracy for the millions of working men the world has ever seen." By drawing on the most revered literature of America and Western Christendom and its themes of slavery, freedom, death, and resurrection, Du Bois illuminates how Black slaves seeking and gaining freedom, however fleetingly, is akin to a beleaguered Christ seeking and gaining some form of life after death, for our salvation. Moreover, Du Bois signifies that this "finest effort to achieve democracy for the millions of working men" mirrors Christ's efforts to provide salvation to the suffering multitudes both then and in the worlds to come. The central point for us in this comparison is that Du Bois frames *Black Reconstruction*, literally and figuratively, or materially and fictively, as one of the greatest stories ever told, to use a much-referenced phrase.

Du Bois was among the first to really underscore the centrality of freedom and slavery in Western culture, themes brilliantly explored subsequently by David Brion Davis and Orlando Patterson, today seen as responsible for fundamentally transforming historical understandings of these questions.[17] In this, they followed trails blazed by Frederick Douglass and W. E. B. Du Bois, as well as the deep wellsprings of African American oral and literary traditions, which remade Christianity. It is no accident that the epigraph of Orlando Patterson's *Slavery and Social Death* is taken from *The Narrative of Frederick Douglass*: "I felt as I never felt before. It was a glorious resurrection from the tomb of slavery, to the heaven of freedom."

Africans in the New World, Du Bois among them, early on understood the importance of freedom, as well as the denial of their freedom on which the freedom of others rested. Orlando Patterson would start off his book *Freedom* by noting, "No one would deny that today freedom stands unchallenged as the supreme value of the Western world," arguing that the very idea of freedom came out of the experience of slavery and what David Brian Davis called *Inhuman Bondage*.[18]

In *Black Reconstruction*, Du Bois underscored this centrality of what Robin Kelley calls *Freedom Dreams* in the philosophy of freedom of the eighteenth century and the abolitionist movement, which

> demanded that ordinary human freedom and recognition . . . which slavery blasphemously denied. This philosophy of freedom was a logical continuation of the

> freedom philosophy of the eighteenth century which insisted that Freedom was not an End but an indispensable means to the beginning of human progress.[19]

Though key aspects of this drama Du Bois references in the story of Black Reconstruction are the ways in which race and class function intertwined within it, the centrality of Black women in ideas of and struggles for freedom would only begin to get its due as a scholarly subject in its own right with the emergence of Black feminist and womanist theory. Nevertheless, Du Bois's work paved the way for such work in emphasizing African slavery, the one part of the global proletariat that was literally in chains, and among whom women carried an especially heavy burden.[20]

> Above all, we must remember the black worker was the ultimate exploited. . . . It was thus the black worker, as founding tone of a new economic system in the nineteenth century and for the modern world, who brought civil war to America. . . . That dark and vast sea of human labor . . . that great majority of mankind, on whose bent and broken backs rest today the founding stones of modern industry—shares a common destiny; it is despised and rejected by race and color; paid a wage below the level of decent living; driven, beaten, prisoned and enslaved in all but name; spawning the world's raw material and luxury—cotton, wool, coffee, tea, cocoa . . . how shall we end the list and where? All these are gathered up at prices lowest of the low, manufactured, transformed and transported at fabulous gain; and the resultant wealth is distributed and displayed and made the basis of world power and universal dominion and armed arrogance in London and Paris, Berlin and Rome, New York and Rio de Janeiro. Here is the modern labor problem . . . the problem of . . . Democracy, of Humanity. Words and futile gestures avail nothing. Out of the exploitation of the dark proletariat comes the Surplus Value filched from human beasts which, in cultured lands, the Machine and harnessed Power veil and conceal. The emancipation is the emancipation of labor and the emancipation of labor is the freeing of that basic majority of workers who are yellow, brown and black.[21]

Moreover, Du Bois understood, as did Sojourner Truth, Harriet Tubman, Frederick Douglass, Karl Marx, and so many others before, that the overriding importance of slavery in the US Civil War necessitated a revolutionary war of abolition. This transformation was exemplified in what Du Bois called a "general strike" of slaves, women and men, as well as Lincoln's Emancipation Proclamation, and the serving of some 180,000 African Americans in the Union armies.[22] The abolition of slavery and African American enfranchisement and electoral participation across the South following these measures were crucially supported by the Union armies, resulting in two thousand African Americans being elected across the South, including to positions in the US Congress and Senate.[23] And yet, the beginning of the Great Depression—1873–1896—saw the intensification of what Du Bois called the "counterrevolution of property" and the "propaganda of history," putting winds in the sails of a white supremacist backlash against the Black freedom struggle.[24]

In large part, these particular tragedies resulted from an inability (and arguably a lack of desire) to link Black labor with white labor, or to understand the need for such linkage. In the face of subterfuge that focused on machines and animals in labor to "veil and conceal" the revelation that what really mattered for any revolutionary labor-empowering arc was that awe-inspiring drama of Black labor. Here, newly arisen from Hell, Blacks offered the ways and means for all labor to imagine their freedom. The descent into hell and the apocalypse gestures towards uncovering, revealing the truth of the world at the end of time, at the crossroads.

And in underscoring Blacks as the foundation stone of modernity, Du Bois sought to reveal, as in Ecclesiastes, that "the stone which the builder refuses becomes the cornerstone."[25] It is no surprise then, that this refrain became one of Bob Marley's songs of freedom and the title of the third volume of Madison Smartt Bell's trilogy on the Haitian Revolution, the only successful slave revolution in world history, albeit one also largely unthinkable within the framework of Western-enlightenment thought, as Michel-Rolph Trouillot argues in *Silencing the Past*.[26]

While Du Bois sought to encourage struggles for freedom that would allow material and spiritual freedom for all, the majority of whites refused. Here then, Du Bois notes, "was a tragedy that beggared the Greek; it was an upheaval of humanity like the Reformation and the French Revolution. Yet we are blind and led by the blind. We discern in it no part of our labor movement; no part in our industrial triumph; no part in our religious experience."[27] As Marx noted and Du Bois demonstrated, slavery truly disfigured the Republic. Here, the defeat of Black Reconstruction solidified this region's reactionary influence as part of the US hegemonic ruling bloc, with decisive implications for the US and the global system, as Du Bois predicted and subsequent analysis confirms.[28]

Du Bois's *Black Reconstruction* thus helps answer the classic question of American exceptionalism, the failure of the US to generate a major long-standing socialist or labor party, and the related right turn of the US polity and global system. The failure of labor in a white skin to recognize their affinities with workers of color split the working class in the US and abroad, fatally undermining possibilities for social democracy and democratic socialism right up to the present.[29] For example, the New Deal, while uplifting first and second-generation immigrants on the white side of the color line, simultaneously depressed that of Blacks, ensuring their continued disenfranchisement and exploitation.[30]

It was only after World War II, when Blacks once again served in the US armed forces in large numbers, that the civil rights movement forced America to once again confront the limits of American freedom. Ironically, it was right before the 1963 March on Washington—one hundred years after Lincoln's Emancipation Proclamation—that Du Bois passed away at age ninety-five. And yet, the March on Washington for Jobs and Freedom brought together central themes of *Black Reconstruction*.[31] And in the book *Where Do We Go from Here: Chaos or Community?* penned by Dr. Martin Luther King Jr. shortly before and published after his assassination, he recognized the fundamental reality underscored by Du Bois, as well:

> Since before the Civil War, the alliance of Southern racism and Northern reaction has been the major obstacle to social advancement. The cohesive political structure of the South working through this alliance enabled a minority of the population to imprint its ideology on the nation's laws. This explains why the United States is still far behind European nations in all forms of social legislation.[32]

King, like Du Bois before him, moved from civil rights to labor and human rights. Towards the end of his life, King spoke out against the Vietnam War and sojourned with the Black garbage workers on strike in Memphis, Tennessee. King also spoke of integration as shared power and radical redistribution, identifying as obstacles what he called the three interrelated evils, "racism," "exploitation," and "militarism," arguing you couldn't really get rid of one without getting rid of the others, again echoing Du Bois. Since King's assassination, though, radical redistribution has primarily been upward from the poor majority to the rich, with the US embracing racism, militarism, and materialism.

From Civil Rights to Corporate Rights: Du Bois's Tales of Two Reconstructions, Nineteenth to Twenty-First Century, and Their Defeat

The weakness of US labor, underscored in the failure of labor unity across lines of race, class, gender, and nation, and the obverse side of this, the strength of the capitalist class during the era of Reconstruction and beyond, curbed the progressive transformation of the US and the global system, as Du Bois argued it would.[33] An important but seldom-discussed aspect of Black Reconstruction's defeat were fears that redistribution of wealth and related social reform in the South wouldn't stop there but would threaten capitalist property relations more generally. Because of these threats, as Richard Franklin Bensel underscores, finance capital played a crucial role in ending Black Reconstruction.[34] Moreover, the incorporation of 180,000 African Americans in the armed forces, the emancipation of the slaves and the military defeat and occupation of the South by the Union armies, created powerful supports of hatred and resentment towards the federal government among whites, especially but not only in the former Confederate states. The abolition of African slavery also created long-lasting fears among whites of government redistribution of wealth and property that continue today.

Thus, as Du Bois understood, the past was prologue, with understanding the past essential for making more egalitarian, multicultural futures.[35] The defeat of Black Reconstruction and the failure of the Congress of Industrial Organization's (CIO) Operation Dixie to democratize the Jim Crow South solidified for a time the Democratic Party as the party of white supremacy throughout the South.[36] As the cause of civil rights was embraced, first by the CIO and later the Democratic Party under the pressure of the Left and civil rights movement, this was to change.[37] Critical here was the "long Southern strategy," where the Republican Party capitalized on the backlash against civil rights and feminism by reaching out to white Southern voters, especially evangelical ones.[38] And as David Bateman, Ira Katznelson, and John Lapinski note in *Southern Nation*, "The white South took up the Republican Party's offer to transform into a radically conservative Southern Party."[39] In fact, as Glenn Feldman states, "the South did not become Republican so much as the Republican Party became *southern*."[40] Of course, as some six million Blacks moved out of the South in the Great Black Migration, Jim Crow moved with them, providing recurrent opportunities for Southern-inspired strategies to remake the political map across the nation as well.[41]

Central in this transformation, as Du Bois underscored, was the recurrent failure of the white working class to decisively ally with the Black freedom struggle so as to remake the social foundations of the US polity. This failure, more than any other factor, paved the way for right-wing white supremacist backlashes, from the defeat of Black Reconstruction in the late nineteenth century to the defeat of the more ambitious goals of the civil rights movement, or what activists called the Second Reconstruction in the 1960s.[42] Both the late nineteenth and twentieth centuries, then, saw a move away from civil rights to corporate rights, with long economic downturns followed by successive Gilded Ages, including the one we are currently in.

By the late seventies, both US political parties abandoned civil rights and the working classes as a whole. And increasingly the Republican Party embraced the Christian Right, rooted in the white evangelical South. This set the stage for Trump's targeting of white working-class voters hit hard by globalization in the Rust Belt, constituencies all but ignored by Hillary Clinton, who threw her lot in with Wall Street instead. The resulting Clinton deficit in voter support was enormous.[43]

Doug McAdam and Karina Kloos summarize the critical lessons, in ways that shows the prescience of Du Bois's predictions about the depths of white racism in the South and its political implications for US politics.

> Quite simply, nothing explains the rightward shift in federal policymaking over the past two decades more than the partisan realignment of the South. . . . Since 1930, the shifting policy fortunes of the two parties owe to a single source: whichever party has been favored by the South—make that the white South—has exercised effective policy control over the federal government.[44]

Decades of the neoliberal assault allowed Trump to emerge as the George Wallace of the twenty-first century, representing the continued Southernization of US politics.[45] The dominance of Southerners in Congress illustrates this clearly.[46] Disarmed by lack of knowledge of the reality and lessons of *Black Reconstruction* and its defeat, and related understandings of intersectionality, there was a near universal failure to grapple with the remaking of the Republicans as a party of the far right, based especially in the white evangelical South, and a Trump victory.[47]

Though the 2016 presidential election surprised most experts, from the vantage point of Du Bois, it was no surprise. Obama was elected president in part as a reaction to the Republican role in bringing on the Wall Street meltdown of 2008 and global financial crises, despite the Democrats being deeply implicated here. Voters were even willing to give Obama a second chance, rebuilding the multiracial coalition four years later. Yet the lack of hope and change to believe in, the loss of manufacturing jobs, especially in the rustbelt and the Midwest, and growing sexism and xenophobia doomed Clinton.[48]

Formerly, non-college-educated white voters, affluent or not, were more evenly distributed between the parties. Not too attuned to politics and often bearing significant racial antipathies towards Blacks, minorities, Muslims and immigrants, the Obama presidency and the rise of Trump solidified their identification of Blacks, minorities, immigrants, and Muslims with the Democratic Party. This played a major role in a racial sorting-out process among the parties, as those with anti-Muslim, anti-immigrant, and racist sentiments increasingly identified with and moved into the Republican Party. The right wing "othering" of President Obama, accused of being a non-US born Muslim, played a major role here, as did the right-wing media more generally.[49]

Today's Republican Party, in the context of the great wave of foreign immigration following the 1965 Immigration and Nationality Act, became ascendant by adopting the virulent anti-immigrant and racist rhetoric of the Know Nothing party and the former Democratic Party when the latter was the party of Southern white supremacy.[50] The South has played a key role in this reincarnation. Notably, Alabama senator Jeff Sessions was the first senator to support Trump, going on to become his first US attorney general. Sessions and his aide Stephen Miller were crucial in torpedoing comprehensive immigration reform and mainstreaming the anti-immigrant racism that became a centerpiece of Trump's presidential campaign. Miller went on to become Trump's number-one adviser on immigration. Here, the South returned to its historic role as the region with the most exclusivist stance on immigration since the passing of the landmark 1924 National Origins Act. This act racially and spatially remapped the nation, drawing the color line around Europe, dramatically restricting immigration, and is a model for the Trump administration today.[51]

There are analogies, too, that can be made with the current white supremacist backlash and the undoing of the first Reconstruction. As seen in *Black Reconstruction*, when progressive coalitions fail to deliver on ambitious programs of social uplift, or otherwise fail to address prolonged economic stagnation in the aftermath of economic downturns and financial crises, right-wing racist and proto-fascist movements reap the political benefits. Of course, these developments in the US are part of a worldwide wave of revolt on the Left and Right across the globe.[52]

Du Bois, *Black Reconstruction*, and the Origins of Our Times

> The plight of the white working class throughout the world today is directly traceable to Negro slavery in America. . . . The resulting color caste founded and retained by capitalism was adopted, forwarded and approved by white labor, and resulted in the subordination of colored labor to white profits the world over. Thus the majority of the world's laborers, by the insistence of white labor, became the basis of a system of industry which ruined democracy and showed its . . . roots in World War and Depression.
> —W. E. B. Du Bois, *Black Reconstruction*

Though Du Bois is rarely seen as relevant for the study of fascism, in fact American racism and the white South arguably pioneered many features that would become integral to the growth of early twentieth- and twenty-first-century fascism.[53] Du Bois sought to drive home the irony of a United States of America that pays homage to the expansive possibilities for freedom while worshipping at the altar of a racism that, in tragicomic fashion, ensures freedom's destruction. As Du Bois argued, in the early nineteenth century,

> America . . . stepped forward . . . and added . . . a vision of democratic self-government. . . . What an idea and what an area for its realization—endless land of richest fertility, natural resources such as Earth seldom exhibited before, a population of infinite variety . . . It was the Supreme Adventure, in the last Great Battle of the West, for that human freedom which would release the spirit from lower lust for mere meat, and set it free to dream and sing.[54]

Given the ways in which environmental destruction is trending, with signs increasingly clear to many of impending and irrevocable decimation of the planet, it is clear that Du Bois's work was prescient in thinking through where white supremacy and capital might lead us. And indeed, this land is clearly such a place for an increasingly select group of the very rich profiting off the ever-growing poor. For Du Bois, this scenario is the direct result of the choice of white labor to choose white capital over an alignment with Black labor. Du Bois alludes to this choice and its impact on freedom dreams when he remarks concerning such that in the midst of all this promise

> some unjust God leaned, laughing, over the rampart in heaven, and dropped a black man in the midst. It transformed the world. It turned democracy back to Roman Imperialism and Fascism; it restored caste and oligarchy; it replaced freedom with slavery and withdrew the name of humanity from the vast majority of human beings. But not without struggle.[55]

Du Bois's "The Propaganda of History," the last chapter of *Black Reconstruction*, provides an instructive lesson in the importance of historical memory, real and fabricated, in social change.[56] After the election of President Obama, few anticipated progress towards racial and gender equality would stop. Yet as Ibram X. Kendi articulated, in words that conjure Du Bois's work, "If Barack Obama came to embody America's history of racial progress, then Donald Trump should come to embody America's history of racist progress. And racist progress has consistently followed racial progress."[57]

At a time when many worry as to whether any nation "dedicated to the proposition that all men are created equal . . . can long endure," it is time to reimagine the present in the context of past struggles for freedom, betrayed, and American dreams deferred. This reimagining is all the more important given the centrality of the theme of freedom in the work of Du Bois. Animated by the light of freedom, *Black Reconstruction* reminds us of it, in our own time, with its powerful parallels to periods where the dawn of freedom seemed to arise, only to be followed by the bitter dusk of slavery reborn.[58] Or as Du Bois put it, "The slave went free; stood a brief moment in the sun; then moved back again towards slavery. . . . Democracy died save in the hearts of black folk."[59]

Throughout history, ordinary people went to extraordinary lengths to keep the dream of freedom alive.[60] What Du Bois showed, though, was how freedom can be reversed. Victories won on military battlefields can be turned back.[61] In these cultural battles for hegemony, *Black Reconstruction* never became part of what Michael Denning called the "Cultural Front," nor did it gain much of a renaissance later, albeit with some notable exceptions.[62] While Obama's election held out a promissory note for a profound cultural shift, it resulted in a white supremacist backlash that mirrored that during the first Black Reconstruction. This backlash was part of a global resurgence of right-wing and fascist movements combining anti-Semitic tropes and racism in increasingly dangerous ways. Du Bois, who came to understand the profound linkages between the color line and racism in all its forms, would not have been surprised.[63]

Following Trump's victory, the 2017 Unite the Right rally of white supremacists in Charlottesville, Virginia, with their chants of "The Jews will not replace us," gave a glimpse of the increasingly destructive racism, antisemitism, and xenophobia, as did the murderous attacks against Jews and synagogues in Pittsburgh, Pennsylvania, in October 2018 (targeted for their work supporting immigrants and refugees) and Poway, California, in April 2019. More generally, the racist anti-Semitic trope of immigrants invading and replacing whites, supposedly masterminded by the Jews who control the world, the so-called great replacement theory, has been used to try and justify a growing list of atrocities, such as the August 2019 massacres in El Paso, Texas, and Dayton, Ohio, and the massacre of African Americans again in Buffalo, New York, in Spring of 2022.[64]

As Du Bois reminded us, African Americans played leading roles in abolitionism and Reconstruction, among the first interracial movements and experiments of interracial democracy in world history.[65] Taking Du Bois's insights into account and placing them in wider frames can help us confront the challenges of reconstructing the US and global system today, on new and enlarged social and ecological foundations, as we move towards an increasingly nonwhite majority. Here, the voices of indigenous peoples and their allies, exemplified in the struggles against the Dakota pipeline, which united over three hundred Indian Tribes across North America and beyond, foreshadow possibilities for truly multicultural futures.[66]

◆ ◆ ◆

> The chief obstacle in this rich realm of the United States . . . to the coming of that kingdom of economic equality . . . is the determination of the white world to keep the black world poor and themselves rich. A clear vision of a world without inordinate individual wealth, of capital without profit and of income based on work alone is the path out, not only for American but for all. . . . Across this path stands the South with flaming sword.
>
> —W. E. B. Du Bois, *Black Reconstruction*

Du Bois's *Black Reconstruction* speaks to the origins of our times, most especially the remaking of the US-dominated global system on increasingly narrow oligarchic, racist, and patriarchal social foundations, in ways that today imperil the survival of the human species and other sentient beings. In 2019, over eleven thousand scientists from some 153 countries sounded the alarm of climate emergency, "The climate crisis is closely linked to the excessive consumption of the wealthy lifestyle."[67] Here the focus of Du Bois dovetails with Arrighi's work on oligarchic wealth, centrally implicated in the global climate crisis, as well as Wright's articulating of the world-destroying capacities of today's oligarchic elites.[68]

Today is the age of truly systemic crisis, as Immanuel Wallerstein argued before his death in 2019. Thus, there has never been a more urgent time for the remaking of the US and global system on newly enlarged, more peaceful and sustainable global foundations. And though the obstacles are great, recent election cycles in the US saw what will hopefully be an even more significant development than the victory of the resurgent xenophobic right, in the rise of politicians such as Bernie Sanders, Elizabeth Warren, Julian Castro, Alexandria Ocasio-Cortez, and many others. Today polls show that the majority of young people, the most diverse and progressive generation in US history, have a more favorable view of socialism than capitalism. And while it's unclear what exactly this means, it appears to indicate values of solidarity, multiculturalism, diversity, and egalitarianism.[69]

Among the most significant and enduring aspects of Du Bois's argument is the capacity of the oppressed to transform the world. The changing demographics of the US as registered in the recent blue wave in Virginia, former center of Confederate power, giving the Democratic Party control over the statehouse; and the election in 2020 of the first African American and Jewish American senators in Georgia, which turned blue—albeit in a state that also hosts the far-right congresswoman Marjorie Taylor Greene—indicate there are opportunities for new multicultural coalitions aiming to understand and change the world for the better.[70] For scholars and activists to seize these opportunities in ways that promote the hopes of Du Bois's *Black Reconstruction*, it is time to return to this powerful work, so as to get ready for the immense effort it will take to create a more just, sustainable, multicultural future.

NOTES

Thanks to Phil Sinitiere, and anonymous reviewers for helpful suggestions.

1. Quoted in Kathleen Q. Seeyle, "Erik Olin Wright, 71, Marxist Sociologist Who Offered Alternatives to Capitalism," *New York Times*, 3 February 2019, A22. Erik Olin Wright, *Understanding Class* (New York: Verso, 2015); Charles Tilly, *Durable Inequality* (Berkeley: University of California Press, 1998); Giovanni Arrighi, Terence K. Hopkins and Immanuel Wallerstein, *Antisystemic Movements* (New York: Verso, 1989); Etienne Balibar and Immanuel Wallerstein, *Race, Nation, Class* (New York: Verso, 1991); Carlton D. Floyd and Thomas E. Reifer, "What Happens to a Dream Deferred? W. E. B. Du Bois and the Radical Black Enlightenment/Endarkenment," *Socialism and Democracy* 32, no. 3 (November 2018): 52–80.

2. Jonathan Schneer, *London: The Imperial Metropolis* (New York: Yale University Press, 1999), 203–28; Cedric J. Robinson, *Black Marxism: The Making of the Black Radical Tradition*, 3rd revised and updated ed. with a new foreword by Robin Kelley and a new preface by

Damien Sojoyner and Tiffany Willoughby-Herard (Chapel Hill: University of North Carolina Press, 2020).

3. As Du Bois noted, "I have seen something of human upheaval in this world . . . but nothing in my wildest imagination was equal to what I saw in Warsaw in 1949. I would have said before seeing it that it was impossible for a civilized nation with deep religious convictions and outstanding religious institutions; with literature and art; to treat fellow human beings as Warsaw had been treated. There had been complete, planned, and utter destruction." W. E. B. Du Bois, "The Negro and the Warsaw Ghetto," *Jewish Life* (April 1952): 14–15.

4. There are, of course, important exceptions, notably the work of Bernard Magubane and Zine Magubane. See, in particular, Zine Magubane, "Overlapping Territories and Intertwined Histories: Historical Sociology's Global Imagination," in *Remaking Modernity: Politics, History, and Sociology*, Julia Adams, Elizabeth M. Clemens and Ann Shola Orloff, eds. (Durham: Duke University Press, 2005), 92–108.

5. Shannon Sullivan and Nancy Tuana, eds., *Race and the Epistemologies of Ignorance* (New York: SUNY Press, 2007); Reiland Rabaka, *Against Epistemic Apartheid* (New York: Lexington Books, 2010); Aldon D. Morris, *The Scholar Denied* (Berkeley: University of California Press, 2015).

6. See Moon-Kie Jung, "The Enslaved, the Worker, and Du Bois's *Black Reconstruction*," *Sociology of Race and Ethnicity* 5, no. 2 (2019): 157–68; Claire Parfait, "Rewriting History: The Publication of W. E. B. Du Bois's *Black Reconstruction in America* (1935)," *Book History* 12 (2009): 266–94; Isaac Martin, "The Comparative Historical Sociology of W. E. B. Du Bois," *Trajectories* 27, no. 3 (Spring 2015): 23–26. As David Roediger notes, "In my own field, that of history, the leading U. S. professional organization recently published a poll which asked members to list the most important historians and books treating the American South. Not a single respondent named W. E. B. Du Bois's *Black Reconstruction*. This omission, the rough equivalent of a group of theologians neglecting the Bible in listing important books bearing on Christian tradition, came as part of a pattern." See *Black On White: Black Writers on What it Means to Be White*, edited with an introduction by David R. Roediger (New York: Schocken Books, 1998), 8. Oliver Cox's legacy as one of the founding fathers of world-systems analysis was recognized by Immanuel Wallerstein and Giovanni Arrighi (the latter in personal conversations with me, Tom), where Arrighi spoke of how influential Cox was for his *The Long Twentieth Century: Money, Power, and the Origins of Our Times* (New York: Verso, 1994, 2010). See also Immanuel Wallerstein, "Oliver C. Cox as World-Systems Analyst," Herbert M. Hunter, ed., *The Sociology of Oliver C. Cox* (Stamford, CT: JAI Press, 2000), 173–84; Christopher A. Mcauley, *The Mind of Oliver Cox* (Notre Dame, IN: University of Notre Dame Press, 2004).

7. W. E. B. Du Bois, *Black Reconstruction: An Essay Toward a History of the Part Which Black Folk Played in the Attempt to Reconstruct Democracy in America* (New York: Oxford University Press, 2007), 517. Subsequent studies have powerfully amplified this basic insight, notably V. O. Key, Jr's., *Southern Politics in State and Nation* (Knoxville: University of Tennessee Press, 1984); Angie Maxwell and Todd G. Shields, eds., *Unlocking V. O. Key Jr.: Southern Politics for the Twenty-First Century* (Fayetteville: University of Arkansas Press, 2011); Rocket Mickey, *Paths Out of Dixie: The Democratization of Authoritarian Enclaves in America's Deep South, 1944–1972* (Princeton: Princeton University Press, 2015).

8. In Summer 2013, the *South Atlantic Quarterly* devoted a special issue to Du Bois's masterwork. More recently, in 2017 *Boston Review* published a coedited volume by Walter Johnson and Robin Kelley, *Race, Capitalism, Justice*, with a sustained focus on *Black Reconstruction* and Cedric Robinson's *Black Marxism*, the latter begun when he was in the Sociology Department with Giovanni Arrighi and Immanuel Wallerstein at SUNY Binghamton, then the global center for world-systems analysis. In an interview in the *New York Times Book Review*, 10-19-17, Chris

Hayes noted that he was "reading a ton of history books about Reconstruction, in fact it's basically all of what I'm reading," and when asked "what's the one book you wish all Americans would read right now?" he replied: "*Black Reconstruction*, by Du Bois." In 2019, Henry Louis Gates also mentioned the importance of *Black Reconstruction* as well as Eric Foner's *Reconstruction*, before the showing of his landmark 2019 PBS series, *Reconstruction*. Chris Hayes, "By the Book," *New York Times Book Review*, 19 March 2017, 8 (and for the extended electronic version, see nytimes.com/books). "By the Book: Henry Louis Gates, Jr.," *New York Times Book Review*, 28 March 2019, https://www.nytimes.com/2019/03/28/books/review/by-the-book-henry-louis-gates-jr.html.

9. Antonio Gramsci, *Subaltern Social Groups: A Critical Edition of Prison Notebook 25*, edited and translated by Joseph Buttigieg and Marcuse E. Green (New York: Columbia University Press, 2021). Buttigieg also translated the now standard English edition of Gramsci's *Prison Notebooks* and was the father of Democratic presidential candidate, secretary of transportation, and former mayor of South Bend, Indiana, Pete Buttigieg.

10. Edward Said, *Culture and Imperialism* (New York: Vintage, 1993), 49. Quoted in Antonio Gramsci, *The Southern Question*, translated and introduced by Pasquale Verdicchio (New York: Bordighera Press, 2015), 2.

11. Eric Hobsbawm, *How to Change the World* (London: Abacus, 2011), 317; Perry Anderson, *The Antinomies of Antonio Gramsci* (New York: Verso, 2017).

12. Giovanni Arrighi, *The Long Twentieth Century* (New York: Verso, 2010).

13. Du Bois, *Black Reconstruction*, 2; Karl Marx, *Capital, Volume 1* (New York: Vintage Books, 1976), 798, 925.

14. See for example, the otherwise brilliant and fundamental analysis of Giovanni Arrighi, "Marxist Century, American Century: The Making and Remaking of the World Labour Movement," *New Left Review* 179 (January/February 1990): 29–64, and his *The Long Twentieth Century*, both of which bear rereading in Du Boisian perspective. For a foregrounding, see Immanuel Wallerstein, "Response: Declining States, Declining Rights?" *International Journal of Labor and Working-Class History* 47 (Spring 1995): 24–27. Among world-systems scholars who put the Black experience and African slavery in the foreground are the brilliant and fundamental works of Dale Tomich, whose works remain essential reading.

15. See Tom Reifer, "The Battle for the Future Has Already Begun: The Reassertion of Race, Space and Place in World-Systems Geographies and Anti-Systemic Cartographies," *World Society Studies*, Christian Suter and Christopher Chase-Dunn, eds., *Structure of the World Political Economy and the Future of Global Conflict and Cooperation* (Berlin: Verlag, World Society Studies, 2014), 129–53.

16. Paul Gilroy, *The Black Atlantic: Modernity and Double Consciousness* (Cambridge: Harvard University Press, 1993).

17. David Brion Davis, *Inhuman Bondage* (New York: Oxford University Press, 2008); Orlando Patterson, *Slavery and Social Death* (Cambridge: Harvard University Press, 2018); Orlando Patterson, *Freedom in the Making of Western Culture* (New York: Basic Books, 1991); David Brion Davis, *The Problem of Slavery in Western Culture* (Ithaca: Cornell University Press, 1966); Eric Foner, *Gateway to Freedom: The Hidden History of the Underground Railroad* (New York: W. W. Norton, 2015); R. J. M. Blackett, *Making Freedom: The Underground Railway and the Politics of Freedom* (Chapel Hill: University of North Carolina Press, 2017); R. J. M. Blackett, *The Captive's Quest for Freedom* (New York: Cambridge University Press, 2018).

18. Davis, *Inhuman Bondage*.

19. Du Bois, *Black Reconstruction*, 16. See also Robin Kelley, *Freedom Dreams: The Black Radical Imagination* (Boston: Beacon Press, 2003).

20. Jennifer L. Morgan, *Laboring Women: Reproduction and Gender in New World Slavery* (Philadelphia: University of Pennsylvania Press, 2004); Saidiya Hartman, "The Belly of the World: A Note on Black Women's Labors," *Souls* 18, no. 1 (January–March 2016), 166–73; Alys Eve Weinbaum, *The Afterlife of Reproductive Slavery* (Durham: Duke University Press, 2019).

21. Du Bois, *Black Reconstruction*, 11. See also Walter Johnson, *River of Dark Dreams: Slavery and Empire in the Cotton Kingdom* (Cambridge: Harvard University Press, 2013); Sven Beckert, *Empire of Cotton: A Global History* (New York: Vintage, 2014); Brian Schoen, *The Fragile Fabric of Union: Cotton, Federal Policies, and the Global Origins of the Civil War* (Baltimore: Johns Hopkins University Press, 2009); Eric Foner, *The Fiery Trial: Abraham Lincoln and American Slavery* (New York: W. W. Norton, 2010).

22. Alys Eve Weinbaum, "The Gender of the General Strike: W. E. B. Du Bois's *Black Reconstruction* and Black Feminism's Philosophy of History," in *Citizen of the World: The Late Career and Legacy of W. E. B. Du Bois*, Phillip Luke Sinitiere, ed. (Evanston, IL: Northwestern University Press, 2019), 133–64; Thavolia Glymph, "Du Bois's *Black Reconstruction* and Slave Women's War for Freedom," *South Atlantic Quarterly* 112, no. 3 (Summer 2013): 489–506; Thavolia Glymph, *The Women's Fight* (Chapel Hill: University of North Carolina Press, 2020); Chandra Manning, *Troubled Refuge: Struggling for Freedom in the Civil War* (New York: Knopf, 2016); Steven Hahn, *A Nation Under Our Feet* (Cambridge, MA: Harvard University Press, 2003); Steven Hahn, *The Political Worlds of Slavery and Freedom* (Cambridge, MA: Harvard University Press, 2009); Stephanie McCurry, *Confederate Reckoning* (Cambridge, MA: Harvard University Press, 2010).

23. Eric Foner, *Freedom's Lawmakers* (Baton Rouge: Louisiana State University Press, 1993); Henry Louis Gates Jr., *Stony the Road* (New York: Penguin, 2019), 1fn1; Eric Foner, *Reconstruction: America's Unfinished Revolution, 1863–1877* (New York: Harper Perennial, 2014); Eric Foner, *The Second Founding: How the Civil War and Reconstruction Remade the Constitution* (New York: W. W. Norton, 2019); Gregory P. Downs, *After Appomattox* (Cambridge: Harvard University Press, 2015).

24. See also Manisha Sinha, *The Counter-Revolution of Slavery* (Chapel Hill: University of North Carolina Press, 2000); Gregory P. Downs, *The Second American Revolution: The Civil War-Era Struggle Over Cuba and the Birth of the American Republic* (Chapel Hill: University of North Carolina Press, 2019).

25. There are interesting resonances here with Christianity and the Bible once again, as well as with the related work of Rene Girard, *Things Hidden Since the Foundation of the World* (Stanford: Stanford University Press, 1987). See also Rene Girard, *Violence and the Sacred* (Baltimore: Johns Hopkins University Press, 1979).

26. Michel-Rolph Trouillot, *Silencing the Past: Power and the Production of History* (Boston: Beacon Press, 2015). For a sympathetic but powerful critique, see Dale Tomich, "Thinking the 'Unthinkable': Victor Schoelcher and Haiti," *Review* 31, no. 3, Fernand Braudel Center, vol. 31, no. 3, 2008, 401–32. The second volume of Madison Smartt Bell's trilogy on the Haitian Revolution is *Master of the Crossroads*, and the third, *The Stone that the Builder Refused*. See also Mark C. Carnes, *Novel History* (New York: Simon and Schuster, 2001), 184–208.

27. Du Bois, *Black Reconstruction*, 595.

28. Desmond S. King and Rogers M. Smith, *Still a House Divided* (Princeton: Princeton University Press, 2011); Sean Farhang and Ira Katznelson, "The Southern Imposition," *Studies in American Political Development* 19 (Spring 2005): 1–30; Ira Katznelson and Quinn Mulroy, "Was the South Pivotal?," *Journal of Politics* 74, no. 2 (March 2012): 604–20; Ira Katznelson, *Fear Itself* (New York: Liveright, 2013); David A. Bateman, Ira Katznelson and John S. Lapinski, *Southern Nation: Congress and White Supremacy after Reconstruction* (Princeton: Princeton

University Press, 2018); Christopher H. Achen and Larry M. Bartels, *Democracy for Realists* (Princeton: Princeton University Press, 2017); Evelyn Nakano Glenn, *Unequal Freedom* (Cambridge: Harvard University Press, 2014); Cybelle Fox, *Three Worlds of Relief* (Princeton: Princeton University Press, 2012); Devra Weber, *Dark Sweat, White Gold* (Berkeley: University of California Press, 1995); Linda Gordon, *Pitied But Not Entitled* (Cambridge: Harvard University Press, 1994); Linda Gordon, "Welfare Reform," *Dissent* (Summer 1994): 323–28; Jill Quadagno, *The Color of Welfare* (New York: Oxford University Press, 1994); Felicia Kornbluh, *The Battle for Welfare Rights* (Philadelphia: University of Pennsylvania Press, 2007); Ira Katznelson, *When Affirmative Action Was White* (New York: W. W. Norton, 2006); Ira Katznelson and Suzanne Mettler, "On Race and Policy," *Perspectives on Politics* 6, no. 3 (September 2008): 519–37.

29. Michael Goldfield, *The Color of Politics* (New York: New Press, 1977); Richard Iton, *Solidarity Blues* (Chapel Hill: University of North Carolina Press, 2000).

30. Mae M. Ngai, *Impossible Subjects: Illegal Aliens and the Making of Modern America* (Princeton: Princeton University Press, 2014); Mike Davis, *Prisoners of the American Dream* (New York: Verso, 2018); Richard Alba, *Blurring the Color Line* (Cambridge: Harvard University Press, 2009); Matthew Frye Jacobson, *Whiteness of a Different Color* (Cambridge: Harvard University Press, 1998); David R. Roediger, *Working Toward Whiteness* (New York: Basic Books, 2018); Judith Stepan-Norris and Maurice Zeitlin, *Left Out* (New York: Cambridge University Press, 2003).

31. Bruce Nelson, *Divided We Stand* (Princeton: Princeton University Press, 2001); Nelson Lichtenstein, *The Most Dangerous Man in Detroit* (New York: Basic Books, 1995), and the subsequent debate between Lichtenstein and Herbert Hill in *New Politics*.

32. Martin Luther King Jr., *Where Do We Go from Here: Chaos or Community?* (New York: Bantam, 1967), 16. Thomas F. Jackson, *From Civil Rights to Human Rights* (Philadelphia: University of Pennsylvania Press, 2007). Michael K. Honey, *Going Down the Jericho Road* (New York: W. W. Norton, 2007). Michael K. Honey, *To the Promised Land* (New York: W. W. Norton, 2018). For a suggestive analysis of the intersection of what King called the triple interrelated evils which intersects with Du Bois's analysis in *Black Reconstruction*, see Gregory Hooks and Brian McQueen, "The Military-Industrial Complex and the Underdeveloped Welfare State," *American Sociological Review* 75, no. 2, April 2010, 185–204. Ira Katzelson's work has been central in exploring these questions, with his emphasis on the "Southern-influenced mutation of liberalism, brought about by the interlacing of Jim Crow, Wilsonian Progressivism, and the New Deal. This variant-what Katznelson once dubbed a fusion of Sweden and South Africa-has been a particularly engrossing area for his research." Richard M. Vallely, "Ira Katznelson: Toward a Useful Historical Political Science of Liberalism," *PS Online*, 2005, 797. Of course, the US, as Du Bois, King, Katznelson and many others pointed out, veers far from Swedish Social Democracy, and they also sought to bring attention to the importance of the South in the making of this American exceptionalism.

33. William E. Forbath, *Law and the Shaping of the American Labor Movement* (Cambridge: Harvard University Press, 1991); Paul Krause, *The Battle for Homestead, 1880–1892* (Pittsburgh: University of Pittsburgh Press, 1992); Kim Voss, *The Making of American Exceptionalism* (Ithaca: Cornell University Press, 1993).

34. See Richard Franklin Bensel, *Yankee Leviathan* (New York: Cambridge University Press, 1990), especially Chapter 5, "Legislation, the Republican Party, and Finance Capital During Reconstruction," 303–65.

35. Avidit Acharya, Matthew Blackwell, and Maya Sen, *Deep Roots: How Slavery Still Shapes Southern Politics* (Princeton: Princeton University Press, 2018).

36. Michael K. Honey, *Southern Labor and Black Civil Rights* (Urbana: University of Illinois Press, 1993); Michael Goldfield, *The Color of Politics* (New York: New Press, 1997); Elizabeth

Fones-Wolf and Ken Fones-Wolf, *The Struggle for the Soul of the Postwar South: White Evangelical Protestants and Operation Dixie* (Urbana: University of Illinois, 2015); Elizabeth Fones-Wolf and Ken Fones- Wolf, "'Termites in the Temple': Fundamentalism and Anti-Liberal Politics in the Post-World War II South," *Religion and American Culture* 28, no. 2 (2018): 167–205.

37. Glenda Elizabeth Gilmore, *Defying Dixie: The Radical Roots of Civil Rights, 1919–1950* (New York: W. W. Norton, 2008); Eric Schickler, *Racial Realignment* (Princeton: Princeton University Press, 2016). And yet, the failure to focus on labor rights in these struggles make the promissory note of Reconstruction still incomplete. See Risa L. Goluboff, *The Lost Promise of Civil Rights* (Cambridge: Harvard University Press, 2007); Derick Bell, "Progressives' Passion for the Unattainable," *Virginia Law Review* 94, no. 2 (April 2008): 595–20.

38. Schickler, *Racial Realignment*, 237–70. Angie Maxwell and Todd Shields, *The Long Southern Strategy: How Chasing White Voters in the South Changed American Politics* (New York: Oxford University Press, 2019).

39. Bateman, Katznelson, and Lapinski, *Southern Nation*, 401.

40. Glenn Feldman, "Introduction: Has the South Become Republican?," in Glenn Feldman, ed., *Painting Dixie Red* (Tallahassee: University Press of Florida, 2011), 5, quoted in Maxwell and Shields, *The Long Southern Strategy*, 1. Feldman's body of work ought to be on the required reading list of those interested in the legacy of American slavery, the defeat of Reconstruction, and the role of the South in US political development.

41. Ira Berlin, *The Making of African America: The Four Great Migrations* (New York: Penguin, 2010); Davison Douglas, *Jim Crow Moves North* (New York: Cambridge University Press, 2005); Thomas J. Sugrue, *The Origins of the Urban Crisis* (Princeton: Princeton University Press, 2005); Thomas J. Sugrue, *Sweet Land of Liberty: The Forgotten Struggle for Civil Rights in the North* (New York: Random House, 2009); Mike Davis and Jon Wiener, *Set the Night on Fire: L.A. in the Sixties* (New York: Verso, 2020); James N. Gregory, *The Southern Diaspora* (Chapel Hill: University of North Carolina Press, 2005).

42. "The entire edifice of Democratic conservatism, as well as the interlinked corporate and Cold War political alliances which it sustained, ultimately rest on the linchpins of Black disenfranchisement and the poll tax." Mike Davis, *Prisoners of the American Dream* (New York: Verso, 2018), 100, 186; Doug McAdam, "The Surreal Present in Historical Context," Conference on Othering and Belonging, 2017, https://www.youtube.com/watch?v=9yT-9PcF2cA; David S. Meyer and Sidney Tarrow, eds., *The Resistance* (New York: Oxford University Press, 2018).

43. For a compelling analysis, see Mike Davis, "The Great God Trump and the White Working Class," in *US Politics in an Age of Uncertainty*, ed. Lance Selfa (Chicago: Haymarket, 2018), 61–84. For an important analysis contrasting the alliance of labor with Democrats in the New Deal, with that of the evangelical right and the Republican Party, along with a look at the earlier fortunes of abolition-Republicanism, see Daniel Schlozman, *When Movements Anchor Parties* (Princeton: Princeton University Press, 2015). See also Alan I. Abramowitz, *The Great Alignment: Race, Party Transformation, and the Rise of Donald Trump* (New Haven: Yale University Press, 2018), especially Chapter 6, "White Racial Resentment and the Rise of Donald Trump," and Chapter 7, "Negative Partisanship and the Triumph of Trump," 121–74, where he argues for the primacy of white racial resentment (which often framed how voters saw economic issues as well) in Trump's victory in the Republican Presidential primaries, and in the general election, once partisan identification is factored into the latter. Also see Tom Reifer, "The Senator from Wall Street," *Review 31: An Online Literary Journal*, May–June 2016, http://review31.co.uk/article/view/406/the-senator-from-wall-street; along with David G. Blanchflower, *Not Working* (Princeton: Princeton University Press, 2019); E. J. Dionne Jr., Norman J. Ornstein, and Thomas Mann, *One Nation After Trump* (New York: Saint Martin's Griffin, 2018).

44. Doug McAdam and Karina Kloos, *Deeply Divided* (New York: Oxford University Press, 2014), 215; G. William Domhoff and Michael J. Webber, *Class and Power in the New Deal* (Stanford: Stanford University Press, 2011).

45. Dan T. Carter, *The Politics of Rage: George Wallace, the Origins of the New Conservatism, and the Transformation of American Politics* (Baton Rouge: Louisiana State University Press, 1995); Dan T. Carter, *From George Wallace to Newt Gingrich*, Revised Edition (Baton Rouge: Louisiana State University Press, 1999); Glenn Feldman, *The Great Melding: War, the Dixiecrat Rebellion, and the Southern Model for America's New Conservatism* (Tuscaloosa: University of Alabama Press, 2015); Gregory, *The Southern Diaspora.*

46. Walter Dean Burnham argued the 1994 election was probably the most significant midterm election in 100 years, this being the first time the South went Republican, including in Senate and House races, since Reconstruction, as noted in Bateman, Katznelson, and Lapinski, *Southern Nation*, 401. See also Julian E. Zelizer, *Burning Down the House: Newt Gingrich, the Fall of a Speaker, and the Rise of the New Republican Party* (New York: Penguin, 2020).

47. *New York Times*, "What Happened to America's Political Center of Gravity," Sahil Chinoy, 26 June 2019, https://www.nytimes.com/interactive/2019/06/26/opinion/sunday/republican-platform-far-right.html. While polls predicted Trump losing women as a whole, he captured 53 percent of the votes of white women. A breakdown by US regions shows the influence of racism, sexism, evangelical belief and regional Southern identity in support for Republican candidates among white southern voters in particular. In contrast, well over 90 percent of Black women voted against Trump and for Clinton. Thavolia Glymph's scholarship chronicling the struggles of Black women and the intersection of race, class, and gender that led white women to exercise violence against them during slavery and after emancipation, rather than embracing female gender solidarity against patriarchal oppression, is suggestive here. This is part of an increasing body of scholarship that calls for extending Du Bois's insights with that of feminists on intersectionality and the matrix of domination. See Thaviola Glymph, *Out of the House of Bondage: The Transformation of the Plantation Household* (New York: Cambridge University Press, 2008); Patricia Hill Collins, "Pushing the Boundaries or Business as Unusual? Race, Class, and Gender Studies and Sociological Inquiry," in *Sociology in America: A History*, ed. Craig Calhoun (Chicago: University of Chicago Press, 2007), 572–604; Stephanie E. Jones-Rogers, *They Were Her Property: White Women as Slave Owners in the American South* (New York: Cambridge University Press, 2019).

48. Nazita Lejevardi and Marissa Abajano, "How Negative Sentiment Towards Muslim Americans Predicts Support for Trump in the 2016 Presidential Election," *Journal of Politics* 81, no. 1 (January 2019): 296–302; Zoltan L. Hajnal, *Dangerously Divided* (New York: Cambridge University Press, 2020); Marissa Abajano and Zoltan L. Hajnal, *White Backlash* (Princeton: Princeton University Press, 2015).

49. John Sides, Michael Tesler, and Lynn Vavreck, *Identity Crisis* (Princeton: Princeton University Press, 2018); Yochai Benkler, Robert Faris and Hal Roberts, *Network Propaganda* (New York: Oxford University Press, 2018); Erika Lee, *America for Americans: A History of Xenophobia in the United States* (New York: Basic Books, 2019). See also Emily Wilson's introduction to Homer's *The Odyssey* (New York: W. W. Norton, 2018), on the etymology of the term xenophobia.

50. Tyler Anbinder, *Nativism and Slavery* (New York: Oxford University Press, 1992); William H. Frey, *Diversity Explosion* (Washington, DC: Brookings, 2018); Gabriel J. Chin and Rose Cuison Villazor, eds., *The Immigration and Nationality Act of 1965* (New York: Cambridge University Press, 2015); Gwendolyn Mink, *Old Labor and New Immigrants in American Political Development* (Ithaca: Cornell University Press, 1990); Alejandro Portes and Ruben G. Rumbaut,

Immigrant America, 4th ed. (Berkeley: University of California Press, 2014); *Annals of the American Academy of Political and Social Science* 684, Special Editors, Jorge Durand and Douglas S. Massey, July 2019; Seyla Benhabib, *The Rights of Others* (New York: Cambridge University Press, 2004).

51. Mae Ngai, *Impossible Subjects* (Princeton: Princeton University Press, 2014); Katie Rogers and Jason DeParle, "The White Nationalist Websites Cited By Stephen Miller," *New York Times*, 19 November 2019; Southern Poverty Law Center, "Stephen Miller's Affinity for White Nationalism Revealed in Emails," 12 November 2019, https://www.splcenter.org/hatewatch/2019/11/12/stephen-millers-affinity-white-nationalism-revealed-leaked-emails; Bateman, Katznelson and Lapinski, *Southern Nation*, 340–61; Frontline, *Zero Tolerance*, October 22, 2019, https://www.pbs.org/wgbh/frontline/; Daniel Okrent, *The Guarded Gate* (New York: Scribner, 2019); Sarah Churchwell, "American Immigration," *New York Review of Books*, September 26, 2019, 53–55.

52. Eric Rauchway, "Neither a Depression Nor a New Deal," *The Presidency of Barack Obama*, Julian Zeliger, ed. (Princeton: Princeton University Press, 2018), 30–44; Manuel Funke, Moritz Schularick and Christopher Trebesch, "Going to Extremes: Politics After Financial Crises, 1870–2014," *European Economic Review* 88 (2016): 227–60; Alan de Bromhead, Barry Eichengreen and Kevin H. O'Rourke, "Political Extremism in the 1920s and 1930s: Do German Lessons Generalize?," *Journal of Economic History* 73, no. 2 (June 2013): 371–406.

53. James Q. Whitman, *Hitler's American Model: The Nazi State and the Making of Nazi Race Law* (New Jersey: Princeton University Press, 2018); Ira Katznelson, "What America Taught the Nazis," *The Atlantic*, November 2017, https://www.theatlantic.com/magazine/archive/2017/11/what-america-taught-the-nazis/540630/; Alex Ross, "How American Racism Influenced Hitler," *New Yorker*, 23 April 2018, https://www.newyorker.com/magazine/2018/04/30/how-american-racism-influenced-hitler; Robert E. Bonner, "Confederate Racialism and the Anticipation of Nazi Evil," in *The Problem of Evil: Slavery, Freedom, and the Ambiguities of Reform*, eds. Steven Mintz and John Stauffer (Amherst: University of Massachusetts Press, 2007), 115–26.

54. Du Bois, *Black Reconstruction*, 23.

55. Du Bois, *Black Reconstruction*, 23–24.

56. See also Benkler, Faris, and Roberts, *Network Propaganda*.

57. Ibram X. Kendi, *Stamped from the Beginning* (New York: Bold Type Books, 2017), xi.

58. "Freedom had to be secured on every front after the war ended. Freedpeople searched for children and parents lost in slavery and war, affirmed marriages and established churches. Formerly enslaved people of all ages streamed into schools taught at first by devoted teachers from the North and then from among the freedpeople's own community. . . . The enemies of emancipation and Reconstruction drove the revolution forward by their bitter resistance. . . . The opponents of black freedom remained strong after Reconstruction, retreating rather than surrendering after their defeats. The enemies of equality fought for decades to roll back the expansion of America's democracy, eventually undermining the voting and legal rights won in the late 1860s. . . . Even during that long retrenchment, however, advocates of racial equality kept the thin light of freedom alive, determined that it would shine more brightly in a future they could not forsee." Edward L. Ayers, *The Thin Light of Freedom* (New York: W. W. Norton, 2017), xxii–xxiii.

59. Du Bois, *Black Reconstruction*, 24.

60. The Freedom Writers and Erin Gruwell, *The Freedom Writers Diary*, 20th Anniversary edition (New York: Broadway Books, 2019).

61. For a powerful interrogation of these themes, see Ward Moore, *Bring the Jubilee*, (New York: Farrar, Strauss and Young, Inc., with Ballantine Books, 1953), and Mike Davis, "Ward Moore's Freedom Ride," *Science Fiction Studies* 38, no. 115 (November 2011): 385–93.

62. Michael Denning, *The Cultural Front*, 2nd ed. (New York: Verso, 2011); Alexander Saxton, *The Rise and Fall of the White Republic* (New York: Verso, 2003). The important exceptions include the works of critical race scholars and the Sojourner Truth Organization. Michael Staudenmaier, *Truth and Revolution: A History of the Sojourner Truth Organization, 1969–1986* (Oakland: AK Press, 2012).

63. Harold Brackman, "'A Calamity Almost Beyond Comprehension,'": Nazi Antisemitism and the Holocaust in the Thought of W. E. B. Du Bois," *American Jewish History* 88, no. 1 (March 2000); 53–94; George Bornstein, "W. E. B. Du Bois and the Jews: Ethics, Editing, and the Souls of Black Folk," *Textual Cultures* 1, no. 1 (Spring 2006): 64–74; "W. E. B. Du Bois in Warsaw: Holocaust Memory and the Color Line," chapter 4 of Michael Rothberg, *Multidirectional Memory: Remembering the Holocaust in an Age of Decolonization* (Stanford: Stanford University Press, 2009), 111–34; Jenna Weissman Joselit, "Du Bois, the Warsaw Ghetto, and a Priestly Blessing," *Jewish Review of Books*, Summer 2018, https://jewishreviewofbooks.com/articles/3237/du-bois-the-warsaw-ghetto-and-a-priestly-blessing/.

64. *New York Times*, "In Texas Gunman's Manifesto, An Echo of Trump's Language," Peter Baker and Michael D. Shear, 5 August 2019, A1, A15; PBS Frontline, "Targeting El Paso," 2020, https://www.pbs.org/wgbh/frontline/film/targeting-el-paso/; *New York Times*, "Mass Shootings Are Terrorism," 5 August 2019, A1, A15; *New York Times*, "'Replacement Theory,' A Racist, Sexist Doctrine, Spreads in Far-Right Circles," Nellie Bowles, 18 March 2019; "Stephen Miller and White Nationalism," NPR, 14 November 2019, https://www.npr.org/2019/11/14/779208233/stephen-miller-and-white-nationalism. For the long history of such violence, see Monica Muñoz Martinez, *The Injustice Never Leaves You: Anti-Mexican Violence in Texas* (Cambridge: Harvard University Press, 2019); William D. Carrigan and Clive Web, *Forgotten Dead: Mob Violence Against Mexicans in the United States, 1848–1928* (New York: Oxford University Press, 2017). For the rarely discussed realities of immigration, see Noam Chomsky, "Crises of Immigration," United Nations University, November 5, 2016, https://www.transcend.org/tms/2016/11/noam-chomsky-on-the-crises-of-immigration/. Nicholas Confessore and Karen Yourish, "A Fringe Conspiracy Theory, Fostered Online, is Refashioned by the G.O.P.: Replacement Theory, Espoused By the Suspect in the Buffalo Massacre, Has Been Embraced By Some Right-Wing Politicians and Commentators," *New York Times*, 15 May 2022, https://www.nytimes.com/2022/05/15/us/replacement-theory-shooting-tucker-carlson.html

65. Manisha Sinha, *The Slave's Cause: A History of Abolition* (New Haven: Yale University Press, 2017).

66. *New York Times*, "From 280 Tribes, a Protest on the Plains," 11 October 2016, https://www.nytimes.com/interactive/2016/09/12/us/12tribes.html?_r=0.

67. William J. Ripple, et al., "World Scientists' Warning of a Climate Emergency," *Bioscience*, 5 November 2019, https://academic.oup.com/bioscience/advance-article/doi/10.1093/biosci/biz088/5610806; William Steffen, et al., "Trajectories of the Earth System in the Anthropocene," *PNAS* 115, no. 33, https://www.pnas.org/content/pnas/115/33/8252.full.pdf?fbclid=IwAR3nGFgy_sfscBBZJ48HTWemsPQs-gY89IGSGYx7BvsZDp69SsLRjdoDoRo; Martin Oppenheimer, Naomi Oreskes, et al., *Discerning Experts* (Chicago: University of Chicago Press, 2019); Eugene Linden, "How Scientists Got Climate Change So Wrong: Few Thought It Would Arrive So Quickly; Now We're Facing Consequences Once Viewed as Fringe Scenarios," *New York Times*, 9 November 2019, https://www.nytimes.com/2019/11/08/opinion/sunday/science-climate-change.html?action=click&module=Opinion&pgtype=Homepage.

68. Giovanni Arrighi, "World Income Inequalities and the Future of Socialism, *New Left Review* 189, (September/October 1991): 39–66; Jeffrey A. Winters, *Oligarchy* (New York: Cambridge University Press, 2011).

69. William H. Frey, *Diversity Explosion* (Washington, DC: Brookings Institution, 2018). See also the more critical and nuanced work by Richard Alba, *The Great Demographic Illusion: Majority, Minority, and the Expanding American Mainstream* (Princeton: Princeton University Press, 2022).

70. *New York Times*, "A Changing Population Turned Virginia Solid Blue: An Influx of Immigrants Has Turned a State that Was Once the Heart of the Confederacy. And it's Happening Elsewhere," Sabrina Tavernise and Robert Gebeloff, 10 November 2019, https://www.nytimes.com/2019/11/09/us/politics/virginia-elections-democrats-republicans.html?action=click&module=Top%20Stories&pgtype=Homepage.

CHAPTER 3

In Pursuit of Peace Where Freedom Chokes: W. E. B. Du Bois Confronts the Cold War

—Werner Lange

As was the case for 1968, the year 1949 marked a pivotal point in modern world history and the world peace movement. That spring in Paris and Prague, peacemakers from seventy-two nations planted seeds for the World Peace Congress, led in the USA by W. E. B. Du Bois. Within weeks of each other later that fateful year, the Soviet Union succeeded in ending America's monopoly on atomic weapons, and Chinese communists succeeded in creating the world's largest socialist state. In an increasingly militarized and agonized America, war hysteria and the Red Scare reached fever pitch in 1949 as exemplified by the state-instigated violent anticommunist assaults in late summer on a large peace concert in Peekskill, New York, featuring Du Bois's close associate Paul Robeson. The same orchestrated fervor of fear and hate accompanied the historic Cultural and Scientific Conference for World Peace in New York City during late March. Among the main speakers at the embattled conference was the octogenarian W. E. B. Du Bois, who calmly shared his optimistic vision that "the borderland where freedom chokes today may easily, as freedom grows, fade into its more complete realm."[1] That vision was not to be realized, at least not in Du Bois's lifetime. It was the state's chokehold on freedom, not freedom itself, that grew exponentially during the last years of his heroic life as the elderly and seemingly indefatigable peacemaker unrelentingly took on the interlocked forces of war, ignorance, racism, and colonialism. "Two barriers and two alone hem us in and hurl us back today," explained Du Bois at the 1949 conference, "One, the persistent relic of ancient barbarism—war: organized murder, maiming, destruction and insanity. The other, the world-old habit of refusing to think ourselves, or to listen to those who do think. Against this ignorance and intolerance we protest forever. But we do not merely protest, we make renewed demand for freedom in that vast kingdom of the human spirit where freedom has ever had the right to dwell: the expressing of thought to unstuffed ears; the dreaming of dreams by untwisted souls."[2] The twin barriers to freedom's more complete realm, however, proved to be increasingly intransigent and bolstered by the rapid rise of America's military-industrial complex. However, as the peace praxis of Du Bois also demonstrates, the Cold War's fortified barriers to peace were not entirely insurmountable. Du Bois spoke militant truth to militaristic power at the dawn of the Nuclear Age, and his voice in the wilderness, then almost totally muted, now resounds with renewed vigor throughout the world.

Democracy and Freedom under Siege

The gap between the ideal and real America, always a historical reality, was never greater than during the bittersweet last years of Du Bois's residence in the United States. America the Beautiful had morphed into its antithesis in the aftermath of World War II, a radical transformation that left the entire spectrum of progressive social forces and organizations in America in shambles and kept an entire population in ideological shackles within a perpetual state of fear and insecurity. Potent social institutions at all levels and a compliant corporate mass media drove the politics of fear. Americans everywhere were made to believe that the threat of a communist takeover through an external military invasion assisted by internal fifth-column forces was very real and imminent.

To sustain mass fear of the fabricated internal threat, Cold War propagandists and politicians launched a witch hunt of unprecedented proportions nationwide. Typical for witch hunts, the Red Scare in the Cold War fabricated internal nefarious forces in order to smash progressive ones. An avalanche of repressive legislation designed to purge America of its "subversive" citizens and organizations descended on the country with a vengeance, sacrificing democracy and free speech in its wake.[3] An avalanche of a different sort targeted the entire American public, not just suspected subversives. A manipulative mass media and public rituals simulating atomic attacks served daily doses of fear to the general public. Paranoia, induced and sustained by a militaristic power elite, ruled the land.

In the process of this unprecedented repressive onslaught and militarization of society, American democracy was placed under siege; the constitutional rights of citizens were routinely violated; freedom was choked; the world was brought to the brink of nuclear annihilation; and progress toward a more equitable and just society was effectively thwarted. As one astute observer and critic of McCarthyism insightfully assessing the colossal damage inflicted on America during this "Scoundrel Time" and "Nightmare Decade" put it:

> We should keep in mind, however, that McCarthyism's main impact may well have been in what did not happen rather than in what did—the social reforms that were never adopted, the diplomatic initiatives that were not pursued, the workers who were not organized into unions, the books that were not written, and the movies that were never filmed. The most obvious casualty was the American Left. The institutional toll is clear. . . . With their demise, the nation lost the institutional network that created a public space where serious alternatives to the status quo could be presented.[4]

Such was the dismal context in which the elderly Du Bois struggled energetically to keep the hope of peace alive, even though it nearly led to his state-imposed death.

Du Bois under Surveillance

For the last two decades of his long and venerable life, agencies of the US government, primarily the FBI, surveilled Du Bois. The extensive surveillance uncovered absolutely no unlawful behavior; no subversive activities; and no security threats whatsoever. There is, however, a wealth of evidence within the partially released and heavily redacted FBI file (#100-99720, aka W. E. B. Du Bois) that he was indeed guilty of a central feature of the social sciences he helped found in America and an indispensable ingredient of the endangered democracy he helped defend during her darkest days; namely, social criticism. Speaking truth to power was his hallmark.

The first recorded entry in his recently declassified FBI file sets that tone for nearly all of the subsequent hundreds of reports by informants and agents of the FBI regarding Du Bois.

> In subject's writings in this publication [i.e., *The Crisis*], it appears that he leans to the writings and beliefs of the Socialist, also that he is impressed with the success of Russia and of Communism, but at the same time, he criticized the Communist Party of America. He constantly writes of racial discrimination and how his race is oppressed. Further, he believes that there should be social equality between all people, regardless of color, and, although he does not recommend marriage between the black and white races, he demands one's right to do so should he so desire.[5]

The ostensible initial reason that Du Bois became a person of interest to the FBI was his alleged pro-Japanese attitude since, according to an informant, he had made a speech while in Japan during the 1930s in which he allegedly stated that "the Japanese were to be complimented on their progress and especially upon their military prowess . . . and that in the Japanese he saw the liberation of the negroes in America, and that when the time came for them to take over the United

States, they would find they would have help from the negroes in the United States."[6] Such outlandish accusations in his FBI file, including alleged advocacy for a "race war" in America, subsided for a time. After being discontinued for five years, clandestine government surveillance of Du Bois restarted in 1942 and continued unabated until his death in 1963.

It is obvious from several field reports that the FBI defined Du Bois as a communist and treated him as such. An August 1948 entry by the Washington field office accused Du Bois of being a member of the Communist Party. FBI reports repeatedly identified him as a "concealed Communist" from June 1950 until at least August 1958, during the height of McCarthyism when such labels were synonymous with traitor and national security threat. In a revealing 1958 memo to FBI director Hoover, a field officer brazenly identifies Du Bois as "a well known member of the Communist Party of the United States of America—formerly head of Communist front Peace Center in New York City."[7] The operative definitions of the situation, though false, had very real consequences for Du Bois, who was maliciously marginalized in McCarthyite America through state-sponsored character assassination.

Du Bois on Trial

W. E. B. Du Bois was indicted, arraigned, tried, and abruptly acquitted by the US government in one of the most dramatic cases of government repression of peace and free speech in modern American history. The charge against Du Bois was that he was an unregistered agent of a foreign power, a violation of federal law since 1938. The charge was not without its bitter irony. It was nearly fully based on testimony derived from a paid, actual registered agent of the Yugoslavian government (O. John Rogge) and indirectly on statements by a paid, actual agent of the Union of South Africa (Max Yergan). Both men had worked with Du Bois before they felt it necessary to project their own foreign agent status on him. Equally ironic circumstances surround the first official identification of Du Bois and the Peace Information Center (PIC) he directed as agents of a foreign power. It came on August 11, 1950—almost exactly one year after Du Bois prophetically told the House Committee on Foreign Relations that "if anyone questions the power of wealth, wants to build more TVAs, advocates civil rights for Negroes, he is a Communist, a revolutionist, a scoundrel and is liable to lose his job or land in jail."[8] On the very day that his government officially branded him a foreign agent and demanded he agree to the label, Du Bois was in Czechoslovakia as an "unofficial representative" of the American people, a self-appointed status he acknowledged in a speech to the World Council of Peace in Prague that month. In that speech he urged "the insistence even in the United States that persons be given the right and the opportunity to seek and speak the truth."[9] It was precisely that right and opportunity, however, which the US government saw fit to ignore in its contrived case against Du Bois and his associates at the PIC. Upon learning of the government's demand that he register as a foreign agent, Du Bois expressed his outrage from Paris at the false allegation, stating that the PIC's "sole objective is to secure peace, and prevent a third world war," and that

> since there is clearly no justification in fact for the demand by the Department of Justice, I must assume that this action, coming after months of normal activity by our organization is a further move by the Administration to frighten into silence the voices of peace in America . . . to intimidate those working for peace, whether in support of the World Peace Appeal, the Int'l Red Cross Statement calling for banning atomic weapons or the teachings of the Prince of Peace Himself. The desire for peace cannot be made an alien sentiment.[10]

Over the six-month period from the registration demand to the federal indictment, the PIC's chief counsel, Gloria Agrin, repeatedly attempted to clarify her clients' non-foreign affiliation, but to no avail. On February 2nd, the Justice Department ominously told Du Bois that he had been "fully informed" of the "obligations of the Peace Information Center" in regard to registration as a foreign agent. On February 8th, a federal grand jury met in Washington, DC, and hearing only government evidence, returned an indictment against Du Bois and four PIC staff members setting their trial date for April 2nd. The indictment was obviously not intended to destroy the PIC. That goal had already been accomplished by late 1950 through unrelenting slanderous attacks on the World Peace Appeal; incessant demands for registration; and financial difficulties. The indictment was, as Du Bois's major defense committee contended in its publications, designed to permanently silence this elderly voice of peace through death while serving his five-year prison sentence. The contention gains credence when considering the fate of two other victims of government attacks. On April 5th, three days after Du Bois's trial was to originally open, Julius and Ethel Rosenberg were sentenced to death for allegedly sharing atomic secrets with the Soviet Union.

At the core of this case were fundamental human and constitutional rights regarding freedom. However, an exposition and defense of these rights never emerged during the trial, as Du Bois had hoped, since the judge narrowly restricted the case to one single issue: whether or not the defendants acted as unregistered agents of a foreign power. Despite nearly five full days of testimony by government witnesses, the prosecution was utterly unable to establish any direct connection to any foreign power. The presentation by the defense, on the other hand, was limited to less than one day during which Vito Marcantonio, chief counsel for the defense, made an eloquent and successful appeal for an acquittal. The trial itself was rather anticlimactic. None of the sworn depositions of the Defenders of Peace or character witnesses for the defense (including Albert Einstein) were presented at court. Prosecutors only called on seven of its twenty-seven witnesses before resting its case, one which Marcantonio called "one of the most diabolical plots ever pulled."[11] The attempt to silence Du Bois in this legalistic manner failed. That abject failure, however, rested less on what took place inside the courtroom during those five fateful days in November, than it did on the dramatic outpouring of worldwide support for the defendants. Protest messages and petitions from peacemakers across America and throughout the world flooded the US Department of Justice and White House; greetings from every continent on earth poured into the committee organizing a grand celebration for the eighty-third anniversary of Du Bois's birth; and a question at the core of this pivotal case—*Is Peace a Crime?*—marked the title of a pamphlet massively circulated by the National Committee to Defend Du Bois and Associates in the PIC. Among the most impactful press releases issued by his defense committee were ones composed by Du Bois himself, like this one given at a press conference held near the Lincoln Memorial on the day of his arraignment.

> A great demand for peace is being voiced throughout the country. Men and women everywhere are questioning our tragic military adventure in Korea and the prospect of war with China. There is deep apprehension at the thought that an atomic war may be unleashed. In the light of this, the shabby trick of branding those who seek peace as "aliens" and "criminals" will not stem this tide. I am confident that every American who desires peace, Negro and white, Catholic, Jew and Protestant, the three million signers of the World Peace Appeal and the tens of millions more will join us in our fight to vindicate our right to speak for peace.[12]

His confidence was not misplaced. In the months following his arraignment, a groundswell of support for him and his codefendants emerged from within America and abroad. His 1951 speaking tour, sponsored by the Progressive Party, directly brought his poignant message of peace to receptive audiences in over a dozen cities of the West and Midwest. However, unlike news of his indictment, which broadcasted widely, a media blackout prevented his incisive peace message from reaching the fear-ridden public at large—another affirmation of his deep conviction, rooted in America's founding principles, that there can be no peace without freedom.

> For 175 years, this country has struggled toward a full realization of the great principles which gave meaning to its birth. Among those principles was the concept that there is no peace without freedom—of the mind as well as the body.

> My life span encompasses almost half of the history of this nation. In all my work I have been heir to the historic traditions represented by my great-grandfather who struck a blow for freedom of the Negro people and of the inhabitants of this land through service in the revolutionary army.
>
> At this moment of my life, I stand accused by the federal authorities of having acted as an agent of a foreign principal. With me stand my four co-workers in the Peace Information Center and today, in deepest anxiety, the American people search the international horizon for a sign which will tell them whether the problems of this moment will find expression in war—or be resolved through peaceful negotiation.
>
> The defendants in this case declare that in their work for peace through the Peace Information Center, they were acting as Americans for America. The defendants deny that Peace is a foreign idea. They assert that any attempt to curtail free interchange of thought, opinion and knowledge of fact the world over is clearly an interference with the constitutional rights of American citizens. The function of the Center was to give to the citizens of this country those facts concerning the world-wide efforts for peace which the American press for the most part was ignoring or suppressing. The United States has as yet laid no embargo on the importation of ideas, or knowledge of international efforts for social uplift; and surely there can be today no greater need for information than in the peace movement and the effort to remove the horrible threat of a Third World War. Any successful attempt on the part of the Government to suppress and curtail free circulation of ideas among the peoples of the world is monstrous and aimed at making all advocacy of peace and all social reform impossible.[13]

Thousands of Americans openly agreed with Du Bois and came to his defense. "If this indictment of Dr. DuBois and his associates is not defeated by an aroused public opinion," read the concluding sentences of "A Statement to the American People" issued by the National Council of the Arts, Sciences and Professions in June 1951, "no person or organization whose views on the crucial issue of war and peace differ from the administration in power, will be safe from calumny and attack."[14] Over two hundreds Americans signed the statement, mostly in the field of education. The poet Langston Hughes perhaps best captured the nature of the dialectical forces in conflict with each other in this historic struggle for peace incarnated in the indictment and acquittal of Du Bois:

> Somebody in Washington wants to put Dr. DuBois in jail. Somebody in France wanted to put Voltaire in jail. Somebody in Franco's Spain sent Lorca, their greatest poet, to death before a firing squad. Somebody in Germany under Hitler burned the books, drove Thomas Mann into exile, and led their leading Jewish scholars to the gas chambers. Somebody in Greece long ago gave Socrates the hemlock to drink.

Somebody at Golgotha erected a cross and somebody drove the nails into the hands of Christ. Somebody spat upon His garments. No one remembers their names.[15]

Silencing Du Bois Partially

The attempted death of Du Bois through imprisonment after an expected routine court conviction was prevented by a remarkable triumph over the government indictment, a pioneering historic victory that paved the way for the end of official McCarthyism. Nevertheless, the damage to American democracy through political cleansing was done. America emerged from this "Scoundrel Time" with a political landscape largely purged of progressive organizations, particularly those associated with Du Bois. The Council on African Affairs, chaired by Du Bois and Paul Robeson, was charged with subversion in 1953 and consequently forced to disband two years later. The PIC had a shorter organizational longevity; it was forced to cease operations circulating PeaceGrams and the Stockholm Peace Appeal (SPA) within the year of its inception. The Jefferson School of Social Science, which included Du Bois as one of its most prominent lecturers and which attracted thousands of students in the late 1940s, was forced to close its doors in 1956. Du Bois gave several lectures at the California Labor School before the government shut it down in 1956. The US Progressive Party, which ran former US vice president Henry Wallace as its presidential candidate on a peace platform vigorously supported by Du Bois, garnered only about 3 percent of the official vote in 1948 and disbanded completely in 1955. The American Labor Party, formed in 1936 and represented in the US Congress by one member (Vito Marcantonio) from 1938 to 1950, nominated Du Bois as its US Senate peace candidate in 1950; remarkably, he received 220,000 votes statewide, including 12.6 percent of the vote cast in Harlem. The ALP dissolved in 1956.

This sanctioned diminution or disappearance of progressive voices and organizations corresponded in direct correlation with the emergence of embedded militarism and rapid rise of a vast military-industrial complex, which engulfed increasingly large sectors of the economy into massive weapons production feeding the Cold War. To justify large-scale production of costly weapons of mass destruction, threat inflation became as normalized as the permanent war economy and politics of fear. Starting with the 1946 "long telegram" of George Kennan, US ambassador to the USSR, warning US officials of an alleged existential Soviet threat, the Truman's National Security Act of 1947 and the formation of the NATO military alliance in 1949, US foreign policy and practice during the early Cold War was based on containment and mutual assured destruction (MAD). The domestic policy complement of the containment doctrine targeted anyone and any organization perceived as opposed to or even critical of the new militarized order reliant on nuclear weapons. Accordingly, some twelve thousand citizens lost their jobs during this witch hunt, and it is estimated that from 1947 to 1953, nearly five million individuals in America were officially investigated for alleged subversive actions and expressed ideas. Du Bois was one of the few targeted Americans who was also indicted by the government, a testament to the efficacy of his outspoken critique of this new threat to world peace wrought by the advent of the Bomb and the military industrial complex.

The rapidity and ferocity of the assault on Du Bois also provides a clear measure of the extent to which he and a militarized America were on dialectically opposed trajectories. In a highly acclaimed bestseller of the late 1940s, *Inside U.S.A.*, Du Bois is explicitly referenced ten separate times and highly lauded as having a social standing "almost like that of Shaw or Einstein, being the most venerable and distinguished of leaders in his field."[16] A revised 1951 edition of this influential text makes absolutely no mention of Du Bois. The most venerable leader became among the most vilified as the Cold War witch hunt emerged in earnest and Du Bois became, as a recent drama in his honor depicts him, "The Most Dangerous Man in America."[17] An irreversible dialectical divergence between Du Bois and America's militaristic power elite took firm root publicly in the late 1940s and culminated in his departure from the US in the early 1960s. His forced disaffiliation with the NAACP in 1948 announced the onset of a coordinated onslaught that systematically drove Du Bois and his progressive ideas to the margins of American society. Nearly every organization that enjoyed his active participation or support ended up on the attorney general's extensive blacklist of subversive groups. Several of his closest associates, such as Ben Davis and Paul Robeson, were hauled in by the House Un-American Activities Committee and defined and treated as national security threats or dangerous enemies of the American way of life. Upon his own indictment by the government, countless Americans who had previously celebrated his visionary leadership and many accomplishments in progressive social movements abandoned Du Bois. The 1948 celebration of his eightieth birthday, sponsored by Fisk University and the New York Fisk Club, was held in the Hendrik Hudson Room of the Roosevelt Hotel in Midtown Manhattan; by contrast, the postindictment celebration of his eighty-third birthday was forced out of Midtown and held in Harlem, devoid of several scheduled speakers.

Though effectively marginalized, Du Bois was not completely silenced during this bitter time. His clarion call for peace and consistently critical denunciation of America's war policies regularly appeared in the *National Guardian*, *Chicago Globe*, and other limited outlets. As early as 1950, he severely criticized the US role in Indo-China.[18] In a 1950 US Senate campaign speech, he boldly stated that "of all nations on earth today, the U.S. alone wants war," and that he takes his stand "beside the millions in every continent and nation and cry Peace—No More War; end the rule of Brass Hats in our government."[19] Accordingly, it is no surprise that Du Bois held President Truman in utter contempt, asserting that "he ranks with Adolf Hitler as one of the greatest killers of our day."[20] He prophetically identified Vice President Nixon as an "unworthy politician of the lowest order."[21] In explaining why he would not vote in 1956, Du Bois boldly proclaimed that "Democracy is dead in the United States" and that the "present Administration is carrying on the greatest preparation for war in the history of mankind."[22] At the other end of the political spectrum, Du Bois made it clear that he stood for peace and socialism: "I believe in socialism. I seek a world where the ideals of communism will triumph—to each according to his need, from each according to his ability. In this I will work as long as I live. And I still live."[23]

Du Bois lived long enough to witness a vindication, albeit inadvertent and indirect, of his critique of expansive militarism in America from the highest office in the land. In one of the great ironies of US history, it was none other than the man who had presided over much of the militarization of the US government and society during the 1950s, five-star general and US president Dwight Eisenhower, who warned the American public about the dire consequences to our way of life posed by the unprecedented rise of the "military-industrial complex," a term he coined, in his televised farewell address to the nation in early 1961.[24] Later that same year, Du Bois, one of the most persecuted victims and pervasive critics of the military-industrial complex and its many assorted war makers, left the troubled land of his birth to return to a reborn independent land of his ancestors so that "my dust shall mingle with the dust of my forefathers."[25]

However, his explicit identification with his African ancestors and eventual embrace of Ghanaian citizenship certainly does not preclude his quintessential identity as an American, indeed as an American patriot. To identify his highly critical oppositional consciousness as a form of "disidentifactory Americanism"[26] and to assert that his "diasporic identification" rested with the "un-Americanness and exile" of an "autobiographical self forged outside the United States"[27] takes his masterfully articulated concept of double consciousness much too far toward an imposed false consciousness one. Whatever Americanism is, McCarthyism—not Du Bois—was its antithesis. America is certainly not confined to its reactionary and racist reprobates, and progressives err in allowing, even implicitly, the Right to hijack our national symbols and rewrite our revolutionary legacy for its march toward fascism, then or now. Unlike his persecutors, Du Bois never disassociated himself in theory or praxis from the revolutionary Spirit of '76. In fact, he incarnated it over the course of his entire life. In resisting the tyranny and despotism of his times, Du Bois passionately performed his civic duty as defined in none other than the American Declaration of Independence. At the height of his persecution when the negation of that spirit ruled the land, one of his many admirers succinctly captured the qualitative difference between him and his persecutors in a short letter of encouragement: "Good luck. We need more men like you—1951 version of Patrick Henry. We could use less Benedict Arnolds like Joe McCarthy."[28]

Discerning Du Bois Dialectically

The question remains as to why the US government would so viciously pursue, prosecute, and persecute Du Bois, an octogenarian stripped of any significant organizational base. The answer, one that has not been sufficiently addressed by scholars to date, lies in the emergence of a new and ominous force in postwar American society: The military-industrial complex and its congenital bond to the Bomb. Within a few short years following World War II, every segment of the US government and much of the economy was made subservient to the demanding needs of this powerful complex designed to develop and maintain military superiority based on an ever-increasing stockpile of nuclear weapons and repeated at-will military interventions around the globe. Du Bois was caught in its crosshairs. During the last years of his long life and the early years of the Cold War, Du Bois was confined in the crucible of contradictions confronting American society and humanity at the dawn of the Nuclear Age. Though certainly not unscathed, he remained undaunted in his firm commitment to world peace as a militarism of unprecedented proportions firmly gripped US policy as the ruling paradigm. In fact, Du Bois's peace praxis during the critical onset of the Cold War and rise of the military-industrial complex was the functional equivalent of the last movement of a grand symphony dedicated to human harmony. It was his finest hour, an ode to joy and peace.

That, of course, is not the assessment of an assortment of consensus historians and other scholars who totally ignore his peace activism in their myopic biographies, let alone academic publications, which continue to vilify Du Bois. Fortunately, in more recent years, progressive historians and social scientists, ones who were evidently inspired by sociological conflict theory and the "history from below" approach used by Du Bois in his many incisive scholarly works, convincingly refuted the conventional and convenient depiction of the elderly Du Bois as some sorrowful and tragic "prophet in limbo" who had lost his way, if not his mind, in his last years. In his seminal work on Du Bois during the Cold War, Gerald Horne, for instance, envisions Du Bois as the "leader of Gideon's Black Army."[29] Manning Marable places Du Bois, the "Black Radical Democrat" and "stern prophet,"[30] at the forefront of the "transformationist tradition in black political history," the only one who "sensed correctly that a dialectical approach to black activism was needed to overcome the chasm of racial ideologies."[31] Increasingly, progressive scholars also connect the struggle against Jim Crow domestically, a lifelong battle for Du Bois, to the colossal East-West conflict during

SIGN FOR PEACE!

WORLD PEACE APPEAL

• We demand the outlawing of atomic weapons as instruments of intimidation and mass murder of peoples. We demand strict international control to enforce this measure.

• We believe that any government which first uses atomic weapons against any other country whatsoever will be committing a crime against humanity and should be dealt with as a war criminal.

• ***We call on all men and women of good will to sign this appeal.***

HEWLETT JOHNSON, *Dean of Canterbury*:

"A million signatures will annoy the warmongers. . . . 10 million signatures will make them pause. . . . 100 million signatures will wreck their plans and save the world!"

Name ....

Address ....

City.................................... State..........................

Sign this Appeal and mail to the Peace Information Center

• Send for PEACE PETITIONS today—and get your friends, shopmates, neighbors to sign for PEACE today!

For further information write to

PEACE INFORMATION CENTER

DR. W. E. B. DU BOIS, Chairman

222 West 23rd Street, New York 10, N. Y.

or

P.O. Box 349, Grand Central Station, New York City

Peace Information Center "World Peace Appeal" Brochure, 1950. Image appears courtesy of the David Graham Du Bois Literary Trust.

the Cold War internationally, a major battlefield for Du Bois in his last years. An invaluable insight into the crucial link between legalistic breakthroughs in racial desegregation and the anticommunist crusade in the context of the Cold War is afforded by critical race theorists such as Mary Dudziak[32] and Penny von Eschen.[33] Yet while correctly defining the historic US Supreme Court decision in *Brown v. Topeka Board of Education* as a strategic national policy change designed to enhance the international stature of the US in the Cold War struggle, neither exponents of critical race theory nor conflict theory have sufficiently explored or exposed the pivotal role an elderly Du Bois played in openly challenging the rising power of militarism based on nuclear weapons during the waning years of Jim Crow. This longstanding oversight needs to be removed by a comprehensive historiographical analysis that finally and accurately embraces Du Bois as a founder of and pioneering participant in the modern peace movement to abolish nuclear weapons in the mid-twentieth century,[34] just as he was a founder of American social sciences in the late nineteenth century and the founder of the organized civil rights movement in the early twentieth century. The spectrum of his historical contributions to social progress is arguably without its equal.

For his entire life Du Bois consistently and courageously challenged the ruling ideas and practices of the US government, particularly institutionalized racism. However, there was only one challenge that motivated the US government's attempt to permanently silence Du Bois. It was his highly effective promotion of the World Peace Appeal, or Stockholm Peace Appeal, a worldwide effort to abolish nuclear weapons at their genesis during the Cold War's early years. As the most prominent leader of that peace effort in the US, Du Bois stood in direct opposition to the rapid rise of a powerful military-industrial complex and the emergent militarized architecture of the entire US government following the Second World War. A more asymmetrical conflict is hard to imagine.

The ideological content of this dialectical conflict between Du Bois and nuclear militarism is succinctly codified in the language of the SPA and its antithesis, a classified government document known as NSC-68. The text of the SPA is a clear and concise call for the abolition of atomic weapons and a condemnation of their use as a war crime against humanity: "We demand the outlawing of atomic weapons as instruments of intimidation and mass murder of peoples. We demand strict international control to enforce this measure. We believe that any government which first uses atomic weapons against any other country whatsoever will be committing a crime against humanity and should be dealt with as a war criminal. We call on all men and women of good will to sign this appeal."

US government condemnation of the appeal, not atomic weapons, quickly followed. In a widely circulated statement that appeared on the front pages of major papers, Secretary of State Dean Acheson summarily dismissed it as a "propaganda trick in the spurious 'peace offensive' of the Soviet Union."[35]

Warren Austin, head of the US delegation to the United Nations, declared that signers of the appeal were "traitors to their country."[36] Shortly after the outbreak of the Korean War, the State Department issued and strategically distributed an unsigned four-page document, "Moscow's 'Signature for Peace' Campaign," which roundly condemned the appeal as "exclusively a Communist program" designed "to nullify the defensive value of US superiority in the atom weapon both to the United States and its allies by making use of the atom weapon seem morally indefensible."[37] Despite these state-sponsored efforts to discredit the SPA, nearly three million Americans signed it and over five hundred million signed it throughout the world.

By stark contrast to the peace sentiment of the SPA, the official US government policy as contained in the 1950 strategy document (NSC-68) of the National Security Council calls for a vast military build-up to maintain strategic military superiority, particularly in weapons of mass destruction, specifically thermonuclear ones.[38] Accordingly, US military spending during the Cold War dramatically increased from a modest $4.7 billion in 1948 to a yearly average of $109 billion from 1949–1951 and to annual levels never below $143 billion after 1952 (in 1982 constant dollars). During the sixty-five years after WWII, as America transformed into a military empire, taxpayers were forced to spend more on the military than the military spending of the rest of the world combined. In 1939 the US had only the seventeenth largest army in the world with just under 335,000 members of the Armed Forces and only a handful of military bases outside its borders. As a direct result of vastly enhanced militarism during the Cold War and the normalization of perpetual war after it, there are now some eight hundred US military bases or installations in 130 countries and an annual US military budget that nearly equals the entire military budgets of the rest of the world combined.

At the genesis of this gargantuan military empire and permanent war economy courageously stood, in firm opposition, an elderly Black scholar activist and his few associates operating out of the two small rooms of the PIC in a New York hotel. They were, of course, crushed operationally, but not ideologically. The idea of a nuclear-weapons-free world survived and thrived. In 1982, some three decades after Du Bois was indicted for his peace advocacy, over one million peace activists filled the streets of New York City in a massive protest calling for an end to the arms race and the abolition of nuclear weapons.[39] Three decades later, the United Nations General Assembly formally echoed that demand. The determination to rid the world of nuclear weapons continues to resonate, like never before, as does its institutionalized antithesis. The existential battle for peace that embroiled Du Bois at the dawn of the Nuclear Age and into the twilight of his life was not without its casualties; but, to date, civilization was not one. "Peace is the way," declared Du Bois in the midst of the Korean war, "and the only way to civilization."[40]

A Posthumous Victory and Validation

Du Bois will always remain a controversial figure, since it was his genius at the genesis of Jim Crow during his young adulthood and McCarthyism during his advanced senior years that he courageously challenged both forms of institutionalized repression of freedom in America, and consequently contributed substantively to their formal abolition. For those historic accomplishments he was—and continues to be—hailed as a hero and prophet in progressive circles and reviled as a renegade and traitor in their antitheses empowered to this day. However, no one can deny his pivotal and pioneering role in the origins of the movement to Ban the Bomb, a dream whose realization in the form of international law was deferred until well over a half century after his death.

Du Bois's peace praxis, a defining feature of his entire life, reached its most effective forms in McCarthyism's crucible, a widespread witch hunt that succeeded in dismantling the American Left with unprecedented ferocity and rapidity, and whose repressive manifestations are still being painfully felt to this day. It was during those bitter years of the early Cold War and emergence of the military-industrial complex, that the dialectical divergence of Du Bois and America's militaristic power elite also reached unprecedented proportions. Long before the two separated geographically, an admired Du Bois and an America mired deeply in repression and militarism separated ideologically. Evidence of that divergence, some only recently brought to light, abounds. A clear expression of the operative depravity to which America's ruling class had sunk in its quest for world domination through nuclear superiority is the fact that the CIA and FBI employed at least a thousand Nazis, many of whom were known war criminals, as spies and informants during the Cold War. FBI Director Hoover, who pursued Du Bois with a vengeance, was particularly active in having "aggressively recruited one time Nazis of all ranks as secret, anti-Soviet 'assets.'"[41] The same agencies that placed Du Bois, the peacemaker, under surveillance for suspected subversive actions, actively recruited fascist war criminals, ones openly at war with the US a few years earlier, with the manifest function to defend national security but a latent one to finish in a third world war what the Nazi Party started with the second world war. A greater divergence from American ideals is hard to imagine.

Though it certainly must not have seemed so to him at that cruel time, Du Bois's efforts on behalf of peace in a world freed of the scourge of nuclear weapons were not in vain. In 2017, the International Campaign to Abolish Nuclear Weapons received the Nobel Peace Prize. And on July 7th of that watershed year, the Treaty on the Prohibition of Nuclear Weapons, the first legally binding resolution to ban all nuclear weapons and outlaw threats to use them, was adopted by 122 nations of the world at the headquarters of the United Nations, located only a few blocks from the small office of the former PIC headed by W. E. B. Du Bois, the peacemaker, who, in 1950, was instrumental in getting millions of Americans to "demand the outlawing of atomic weapons as instruments of intimidation and mass murder of peoples." As of January 2021, that demand became ratified and codified in international law. Clearly, though his body lies a'moldering in a grave in Africa, his soul and truth go marching on.

NOTES

The World Peace Appeal image on page 73 appears courtesy of the David Graham Du Bois Literary Trust, all rights reserved. The image is in the W. E. B. Du Bois Papers Digital Archive (Identifier mums312-b161-i388).

1. W. E. B. Du Bois, "The Nature of Intellectual Freedom," in *Speaking of Peace: An Edited Report of the Cultural and Scientific Conference for World Peace, New York, March 25, 26 and 27, 1949 under the Auspices of the National Council of the Arts, Sciences, and Professions*, ed. Daniel S. Gillmor (New York City: NCASP, 1949), 78.

2. Du Bois, "The Nature of Intellectual Freedom," 78.

3. The state-orchestrated demonization of the 1949 Cultural and Scientific Conference generated a firm defense of free speech by Du Bois: "I believe that today every American citizen should take pains to make his stand known on freedom of belief and expression in the United States. . . . That the state has right to punish a citizen for personal libel or for actually disturbing the peace. It has no right to suppress belief or curtail its expression . . . This stand is basic to Human Liberty. If we attempt to fight Communism or Capitalism; Catholicism or Protestantism; white oppression of black complaint by overthrow of this fundamental tenet of freedom, we destroy more than the triumph of our ideas can ever gain. On such freedom of opinion all human progress in the last 200 years has been based." In W. E. B. Du Bois Papers, University of Massachusetts Amherst, reel 75, frame 810 (hereafter Du Bois Papers).

4. Ellen Schrecker, *The Age of McCarthyism: A Brief History with Documents* (New York: Bedford/St. Martin's, 1994), 92–93.

5. Anonymous, FBI Field Report on Du Bois (#100-99720), February 8, 1942; FBI Electronic Reading Room, http://foia.fbi.gov./dubois.htm.

6. Anonymous, FBI Field Report on Du Bois (#100-99720), February 29, 1942.

7. Anonymous, FBI Field Report on Du Bois (#100-99720), September 25, 1958.

8. W. E. B. Du Bois, "Statement to US Congress" (August 8, 1949), *Hearings on Mutual Defense Assistance Act of 1949*, 81st Congress, 1st Session, Committee on Foreign Affairs, House of Representatives (Washington, DC: Government Printing Office, 1949), 261–70 (also, in part, in *New Africa*, September 1949).

9. W. E. B. Du Bois, "Address to the World Peace Congress," August 1950, Du Bois Papers, reel 80, frame 1388.

10. "Peace Information Center, Statement by W. E. B. Du Bois, ca. Nov. 1950," Du Bois Papers, reel 65, frame 491.

11. W. E. B. Du Bois, *In Battle for Peace: The Story of my 83rd Birthday with Comment by Shirley Graham* (New York: Masses and Mainstream, 1952), 133.

12. W. E. B. Du Bois, "Statement by Dr. W. E. B. Du Bois, Issued by the National Committee to Defend Dr. W. E. B. Du Bois and Associates at the Peace Information Center; February 8, 1951," Du Bois Papers, reel 67, frame 47.

13. W. E. B. Du Bois, "Statement by W. E. B. Du Bois" April 27, 1951," Du Bois Papers, reel 67, frame 58; and "The Peace Information Center, speech in Philadelphia, April 29, 1951," Du Bois Papers, reel 81, frame 238.

14. "A Statement to the American People, May 1951," Du Bois Papers Digital Archive (Identifier mums312-b134-i189).

15. Langston Hughes, "World Will Wonder," *National Guardian* (October 31, 1951).

16. John Gunther, *Inside the U.S.A.* (New York and London: Harper and Brothers, 1947), 681.

17. Amiri Baraka, *The Most Dangerous Man in America (W. E. B. Du Bois)*, directed by Woodie King, Jr; Castillo Theatre, 543 West 42nd Street, New York City, May 28th–June 28th, 2015.

18. W. E. B. Du Bois, "As the Crow Flies," *Chicago Globe* (17 June 1950).

19. W. E. B. Du Bois, "Harlem in the Campaign," speech delivered at the Golden Gate Ballroom on October 6, 1950, Du Bois Papers, reel 64, frames 833–34.

20. W. E. B. Du Bois, "The Hard-Bit Man in the Loud Shirts," *National Guardian* (January 22, 1953).

21. W. E. B. Du Bois, "Let's Restore Democracy in America Today," *National Guardian* (January 2, 1956).

22. W. E. B. Du Bois, "I Won't Vote," *The Nation* 183, no. 16 (30 October 1956), 324–25.

23. W. E. B. Du Bois, "A Vista of Ninety Fruitful Years," *National Guardian* (February 17, 1958), 7.

24. Dwight Eisenhower, "Farewell Address" in *The Military Industrial Complex*, ed. Carroll Pursell (New York: Harper and Row, 1971), 204–8; originally "Farewell Radio and Television Address to the American People" broadcast on 17 January 1961.

25. W. E. B. Du Bois, "Letter from W. E. B. Du Bois to the Governor General of Nigeria," March 15, 1963. Du Bois Papers Digital Archive (Identifier mums312-b156-i086).

26. Eric Porter, *The Problem of the Future World: W. E. B. Du Bois and the Race Concept at Midcentury* (Durham, NC: Duke University Press, 2010), 165.

27. Bill V. Mullen, *Un-American: W. E. B. Du Bois and the Century of World Revolution* (Philadelphia: Temple University Press, 2015), 6–7.

28. "Letter from Helen Sato to W. E. B. Du Bois, 1951," Du Bois Papers Digital Archive (Identifier mums312-b135-i058).

29. Gerald Horne, *Black and Red: W. E. B. Du Bois and the Afro-American Response to the Cold War, 1944–1963* (Albany: State University of New York Press, 1986).

30. Manning Marable, *W. E. B. Du Bois: Black Radical Democrat* (Boston: Twayne, 1986).

31. Manning Marable, *Beyond Boundaries: The Manning Marable Reader* (Boulder and London: Paradigm, 2011).

32. Mary Dudziak, "Desegregation as a Cold War Imperative" in *Critical Race Theory: The Cutting Edge*, ed. Richard Delgado (Philadelphia: Temple University Press, 1995), 110–21.

33. Penny Von Eschen, "Who's the Real Ambassador? Exploding Cold War Racial Ideology" in *Cold War Constructions: The Political Culture of United States Imperialism, 1946–1966*, ed. by Christian Appy (Amherst: University of Massachusetts Press, 2000), 110–31.

34. A recent publication along these lines—Vincent J. Intondi's *African Americans Against the Bomb* (Stanford: Stanford University Press, 2015)—falls well short of that analysis. While very briefly acknowledging the vital connection Du Bois and other "black leftists" astutely made between colonialism, imperialism, racism, and the Bomb, Intondi relies on highly superficial secondary sources to erroneously and repeatedly identify Du Bois's peace activism as merely part of "the international communist movement" and a "communist-led peace campaign" (24). For an alternative assessment see Werner Lange, *A Voice in the Wilderness: W. E. B. Du Bois on Peace* (Saarbrücken, Germany: Lampert, 2013).

35. Dean Acheson, "Statement of the US State Department on World Peace Appeal," *New York Times* (July 13, 1950).

36. Cited in Horne, 133.

37. Anonymous, "Moscow's 'Signature for Peace' Campaign," Du Bois Papers, reel 65, frames 503–504.

38. Executive Secretary, *NSC-68: A Report to the National Security Council by the Executive Secretary on United States Objectives and Problems for National Security*, April 14, 1950 (marked "Top Secret" and declassified by National Security Advisor Kissinger in 1976).

39. As one of the Ohio organizers of the historic June 12 peace demonstration, I had the pleasure during the march of personally encountering Herbert Aptheker, a very close associate of Du Bois who appointed him in 1946 as his literary executor and asked him what he thought about this massive protest for peace. With a broad smile on his face, he said: "I've been waiting all my life for this to happen."

40. W. E. B. Du Bois, "Peace and War," speech at Golden Gate Ballroom, February 21, 1951, Du Bois Papers, reel 81, frame 150.

41. Eric Lichtblau, "In Cold War, US Spy Agencies Used 1,000 Nazis," *New York Times* (October 26, 2014).

CHAPTER 4

I Am Certainly Not a Conservative: W. E. B. Du Bois, Democratic Socialism, and Black Marxism

–Reiland Rabaka

In a rare 1957 television interview with Al Morgan a world-weary, eighty-nine-year-old W. E. B. Du Bois nonchalantly stated, "I am certainly not a conservative. I should call myself a Socialist, although that isn't a very definite term."[1] Du Bois went further to clarify what he meant by the indefinite term: "I mean I believe in the welfare state. I believe that business should be carried on not for private profit but for public welfare. I believe in many steps which are usually associated with socialism."[2]

Although frequently glossed over, W. E. B. Du Bois's pioneering critique of colonialism was tied inextricably to his critique of capitalism. In some senses we could aver that as he developed his simultaneously sociohistoric and politico-economic analyses, beginning with race and racism and quickly connecting them to colonialism, Du Bois eventually added capitalism to his anti-imperialist agenda as a major target of oppression and exploitation to be eliminated.[3] On the one hand, one of the many things that distinguish his criticisms of capitalism from his criticisms of colonialism involves the fact that from his optic capitalism and colonialism are two very different—albeit intimately interrelated—oppressive and exploitive systems that require specificity in approaching them analytically. On the other hand, another major defining and distinguishing marker of Du Bois's critique of capitalism that he put to use in the Black liberation struggle drew on the fact that some whites, that is to say, some members of *the ruling racial class*, also understood capitalism to be an oppressive and exploitive system and had developed critical theory and radical political praxis traditions. Even though, as Du Bois observed early, most white critics of capitalism focused almost exclusively on capitalism's political and economic exploitative aspects without giving concerted critical attention to how it intersected with and exacerbated racial oppression. This led Du Bois at the outset of his critique of capitalism to simultaneously critique capitalism *and* the white critics of capitalism.[4]

The white critics of capitalism were critical of it for very different reasons than those of their "colored" comrades (to use the parlance of the period). Du Bois was one of the first nonwhite radical theorists to register this difference. As several interpreters of Du Bois have observed, he had a critical and dialectical relationship with the white critics of capitalism, especially Marxist socialist and communist thought and practice. According to Adolph Reed, in *W. E. B. Du Bois and American Political Thought*, "Everyone agrees that Du Bois died a socialist, but few agree on when he became one or on what kind of socialist he was."[5]

In *W. E. B. Du Bois: Negro Leader in a Time of Crisis*, Francis Broderick explained that Du Bois's thought may be difficult to periodize in the manner that many intellectual historians are accustomed to on account of the fact that "his ideas changed constantly, but the major changes came gradually, with a considerable overlap."[6] This is an important point because it speaks to the evolving radical quality and critical character of Du Bois's thought. Consequently, Broderick's comments in this regard deserve further quotation:

> Writing month after month on current events, he [Du Bois] did not, of course, abruptly end one period of intellectual change and begin another. He might drop a hint, then wait twenty years before picking it up for further development. His praise of self-sufficient, segregated Negro communities came at the flood tide of the Niagara Movement. He was making advances to socialism in 1907, although in early 1908 he affirmed his attachment to the principles of the Republican party. Africa had an almost mystical fascination for him even on his twenty-fifth birthday, but thirty years elapsed before the fascination produced a program of action. Even as the hope for alliance with workers and colored men dominated his thought in the 1930s, a minor theme, self-sufficiency for the Negro community, was rising in a crescendo which by the early 1930s would make it dominant. Conversely, as new ideas came to prominence after the World War, the old ones did not disappear: the essence of his lecture "Race Relations in the United States," for the American Academy of Political and Social Science in 1928 could have been written twenty-five years before. His ideas changed constantly, but the major changes came gradually, with considerable overlap.[7]

Du Bois's "socialism," to use this term loosely, may have never been as scientific, dogmatic, or orthodox Marxist as many intellectual historians have claimed, or would like to claim. As he matured, both personally and professionally, his thought took on a chameleonic character, crisscrossing back and forth between the chasms of race and class. His thought often exhibited internal tensions, sometimes appearing race-centered, and at other times seeming overly concerned with class, labor, and economic justice issues. In addition, the complexity and multidimensionality of his thought gave it a contradictory and often confusing character, which his critique of sexism—also a major item on his anti-imperialist agenda right alongside the critique of racism, colonialism, and capitalism—exacerbated. We should therefore distinguish Du Bois's criticisms of capitalism from those of the white critics of capitalism, especially the Marxists, because his criticisms harbored an acute sensitivity to, and critical employment of, subjugated knowledge regarding the ways in which capitalist oppression intersects and interconnects with racial, colonial, and gender domination and exploitation.[8]

Du Bois's Critique of Capitalism

Du Bois's critique of capitalism was not clear-cut or laid out in an easily accessible manner, but rather interspersed throughout his oeuvre and most often surfaced as a result of his critiques of racism and colonialism, which ultimately spawned his discourse on democratic socialism.[9] As early as 1901, six years prior to his so-called "socialist turn" in "The Negro and Socialism" in 1907, and sixteen years before the Russian Revolution in 1917, he argued that the maxim "from each according to his ability—to each according to his needs" embodied the ideal of modern society.[10] His primary problem with capitalism stemmed from what he understood to be its emphasis on individual gain and personal greed. In other words, private profit at any cost. As an economic system, capitalism privileged the wants and whims of the rich minority over the authentic human needs of the poor majority. The situation became much more complex and compounded by the political economy of race and racism.[11]

Du Bois's initial criticisms of capitalism were not radical, but rather reformist.[12] His concept of socialism could be characterized as *evolutionary* as opposed to *revolutionary*, which made it a major point of contention between him and young "New Negro" and Harlem Renaissance radicals.[13] For instance, in his 1921 classic, "The Class Struggle," published in *The Crisis*, Du Bois stated:

> The NAACP has been accused of not being a "revolutionary" body. This is quite true. We do not believe in revolution. We expect revolutionary changes in many parts of this life and this world, but we expect these changes to come mainly through reason, human sympathy and the education of children, and not by murder. We know that there have been times when organized murder seemed the only way out of wrong, but we believe those times have been very few, the cost of the remedy excessive, the results as terrible as beneficent, and we gravely doubt if in the future there will be any real recurrent necessity for such upheaval.[14]

According to A. Philip Randolph and Chandler Owen, the editors of the Black socialist magazine *The Messenger*, Du Bois's "anti-revolutionary" socialist thought was that of the "Old Crowd Negro," and it revealed "Du Bois's ignorance of [Marxist] theory and his inability to advise the Negro in the most critical period of the world's history."[15] Randolph and Owen, representing themselves as "New Negro" radicals, mercilessly criticized Du Bois's early socialism for its emphasis on moderate and moralistic gradual social reform as opposed to all-out social, political, and economic revolution.[16] In "Du Bois on Revolution: A Reply," originally published in 1921, they argued that Du Bois misunderstood revolution because he appeared to almost utterly associate it with violence, or "organized murder," as he put it above.[17] Revolutions need not entail violence, *The Messenger* mused, as the examples of the Copernican revolution and the revolutions in economic and sociological thought of the nineteenth century (à la John Stuart Mill, Adam Smith, Herbert Spencer, August Comte, and Richard Ely) demonstrated. Du Bois, from *The Messenger* editors' point of view, simply did not take seriously the fact that "every notable and worth-while advance in human history has been achieved by revolution, either intellectual, political or economic."[18]

There was much truth to many of Randolph and Owen's criticisms of Du Bois's early socialism. However, because of the longevity of his "unhappy marriage" to Marxism, *The Messenger*'s criticisms are time-sensitive and should not be applied to the whole of Du Bois's work geared toward critiquing capitalism and developing democratic socialism. Manning Marable observed that although Randolph and Owen were initially regarded as the "Lenin and Trotsky" of Harlem, their revolutionary socialism was short-lived.[19] Owen, Marable reported, "became embittered by the racism in the Socialist party and in 1923 withdrew from radical politics."[20] Randolph continued to edit *The Messenger*, although it took a decidedly "more moderate political tone."[21] Of course, Randolph went on to become one of the most acclaimed civil rights leaders in US history, leading and organizing the March on Washington with one of the unsung heroes of civil rights movement, Bayard Rustin.[22] One of Randolph's more noted biographers, Paula Pfeffer, in *A. Philip Randolph: Pioneer of the Civil Rights Movement*, remarked rather earnestly, "Randolph had begun his career as a radical by denouncing Du Bois's conservatism, but by the time of his death, Du Bois had become far more radical than Randolph."[23]

Randolph and Owen's criticisms of Du Bois's socialism help to highlight the important but long-ignored fact that his conception of socialism changed just as twentieth century capitalism and his relationship with Marxism changed. As Marable pointed out, even when Du Bois joined the Socialist Party in 1911, it "did not mark any significant turn to radicalism."[24] Wilson Jeremiah Moses went further to argue that his "early years with *The Crisis* fall into the period when Du Bois toyed with the idea of non-revolutionary white-collar socialism of the

American domestic variety. . . . Even as late as 1912, at the age of forty-four, Du Bois had not become a committed radical, but was still an optimistic Progressive."[25] Marable, Moses, and Reed each note that Du Bois's conception of socialism for a protracted period of time was in line with that of the reformist British Labor Party, which he applauded time and again throughout the pages of *The Crisis*.[26]

In *W. E. B. Du Bois: The Quest for the Abolition of the Color-line*, Zhang Juguo observed that it was Du Bois's four visits to the Soviet Union in 1926, 1936, 1949, and 1958 and his visits to other socialist countries, such as Czechoslovakia, East Germany, and China that quickened, broadened, and "deepened his understanding of socialism."[27] After his 1926 visit to the Soviet Union, Du Bois clearly took a greater interest in the more radical aspects of socialism, although he repeatedly asserted that the Russian Revolution was not the rule. However, he was convinced that Russia "had chosen the only way open to her at the time."[28] He realized early on that there was no blueprint for bringing socialism into being, and that what might work in one country may not work in another.

Partly as a result of the economic depression of the 1930s, and in some degree owing to African Americans' incessant political disenfranchisement and economic exploitation, Du Bois began to seriously engage socialism on his own terms during the last three decades of his career. As a result, he developed one of the first race-based and racism-conscious critiques of capitalism employing a Marxist methodological orientation.[29] In his burgeoning antibourgeois and antiracist view, capitalism was not simply (as many of the white Marxists would have it) a system of economic exploitation, but also a "racial polity," which is to say, a system of racial domination *and* economic exploitation.[30] Race *and* class struggle combined to create the phenomenological dimensions characteristic of Black existence in a simultaneously white supremacist and capitalist society. Moreover, because he found Marxism inadequate for the tasks of theorizing race and racism in both capitalist and colonialist societies, Du Bois created his own—and some of the first—race/class concepts and categories of analysis.[31]

Where the imperialist aspects of colonialism were undeniable from Du Bois's optic—perhaps, ironically, because of his meanderings in Marxism—he believed that capitalism had certain beneficial elements. However, because of the anti-Black racist character of capital in the white supremacist world system, a point Thomas Ehrlich Reifer and Carlton Dwayne Floyd's chapter in this volume explores, whites benefitted greatly and inordinately from capitalism. In 1944 Du Bois asserted:

> Capitalism was a great and beneficent method of satisfying human wants, without which the world would have lingered on the edge of starvation. But like all invention, the results depend upon how it is used and for whose benefit. Capitalism has benefited mankind, but not in equal proportions. It has enormously raised the standard of living in Europe and even more in North America. But in the parts of

> the world where human toil and natural resources have made the greatest contribution to the accumulation of wealth, such parts of the earth, curiously enough, have benefited least from the new commerce and industry. This is shown by the plight of Africa and India today. To be sure Africans and Indians have benefited from modern capital. In education, limited though it be; in curbing of disease, slow and incomplete as it is; in the beginning of the use of machines and labor technique; and in the spread of law and order, both Negroes and Hindus have greatly benefited; but as compared with what might have been done; and what in justice and right should have been accomplished, the result is not only pitiful, but so wrong and dangerous as already to have helped cause two of the most destructive wars in human history, and is today threatening further human death and disaster.[32]

Du Bois's critique of capitalism moved well beyond the Marxists' two-class critique and class struggle thesis. In his sociotheoretical framework there were not only classes but also various races, and the white race was the ultra "ruling class"—were we to refer back to Marx's class theory—*and* the ruling race.[33] For Du Bois, it was not as simple as the bourgeoisie and the proletariat fighting it out until the finish. There was also the obdurate fact of race and racism, and even more, as his comments above accent, *racial* colonialism and *racial* capitalism.[34]

Marx and Engels asserted in *The Communist Manifesto*, "The ruling ideas of each age have ever been the ideas of its ruling class."[35] Du Bois continually questioned: so, what happens when the "ruling class" is for the most part racist? And, what happens when more than white workers compose the proletariat? Along with many orthodox Marxists, Du Bois believed that capitalism had helped to modernize and rationalize the economy. However, in contradistinction to the Marxists, he asserted that there was a racist dimension to the modernization and rationalization associated with capitalism. In addition, he also came to understand capitalist modernization and rationalization to have a sexist (and particularly a patriarchal) dimension.[36]

As Du Bois saw it, capitalism was inextricable from the rise of racism. Therefore, an exclusively Marxist or class analysis only engaged part of the race/class problem. What he and countless others in the Africana tradition of critical theory sought by coupling antiracism and critical race theory with Marxism was to comprehensively understand and develop solutions to both sides of the race/class equation, which is to say, to the problems of racism and capitalism.[37] Perhaps Cornel West's contentions in *Keeping Faith: Philosophy and Race in America* best captures the position of Black Marxists and other race/class theorists: "I hold that Marxist theory as a methodological orientation remains indispensable—although ultimately inadequate—in grasping distinctive features of African American oppression. . . . Marxist theory still may provide the best explanatory account for certain phenomena, but it also may remain inadequate for other phenomena—notably here, the complex of racism in the modern West."[38] The Black Marxist tradition has consistently echoed West's view, although not without reservation and serious criticism.[39]

Here we should earnestly assert that Black nationalism, pan-Africanism, Negritude, Fanonism, Black existentialism, Afrocentricity, and other Africana schools of thought have their theoretic weaknesses as well. Frequently the narrow focus on race in many instances reifies the thought of race theorists, turning what would be race theory into racial ideology. What Africana critical theory proposes is a synthesis of the best (meaning the most emancipatory elements) of both the "race" and "class" schools of thought. Marxism may be "indispensable" when it comes to the critique of capitalism but, as West argued in "Black Strivings in a Twilight Civilization,"

> For those of us interested in the relation of white supremacy to modernity (African slavery in the New World and European imperial domination of most of the rest of the world) or the consequences of the construct of "race" during the Age of Europe (1492–1945), the scholarly and literary works of Du Bois are *indispensable*. For those of us obsessed with alleviating black social misery, the political texts of Du Bois are insightful and inspiring. In this sense, Du Bois is the brook of fire through which we all must pass in order to gain access to the intellectual and political weaponry needed to sustain the radical democratic tradition in our time.[40]

According to West, Marx is "indispensable" for the critique of capitalism, where Du Bois is "indispensable" for the critique of racism. But, even further, as West emphasized in *The American Evasion of Philosophy*, Du Bois was also an innovator in the Marxist tradition.[41] He was not only a pioneer race theorist, but also a pioneer class theorist. His work prefigured and proposed issues that remain on the radical political and critical theoretical agenda. He challenged white Marxists to take seriously the centrality of race and racism to capitalism and European imperialist expansion.[42] The white Marxists shot back that race consciousness is "false consciousness" and a capitalist or bourgeois invention created to divide the workers.

Part of the problem with Du Bois's critique of capitalism involves his contention that capitalism was inequitably creating an enormous amount of wealth and power that was being unjustly distributed on a roughly "whites only" basis. This was compounded by his search for a solution to both the race and class aspects of this issue. The white Marxists, focusing almost exclusively on the class dimension of the problem, found their solution in the proletariat, which is to say, the white working class. Du Bois dismissed the white proletariat, querying, "Why should we assume on the part of unlettered and suppressed masses of white workers, a clearness of thought, a sense of human brotherhood, that is sadly lacking in the most educated [white] classes?"[43] Recollecting the fact that Du Bois is considered one of the great democratic socialists of the twentieth century, it is amazing that he never adequately addressed the question of *who* the revolutionary social agents would be that would crush capitalism and usher in democratic socialism. Also, and of the utmost importance here, is the question of *how* the transition from capitalism to democratic socialism would take place.

It could be that there are no ideal agents of revolutionary social change. Considering the vicissitudes of capitalism one of the things that anticapitalist agents and theoreticians have to bear in mind is that a social faction that may have revolutionary potential in one era may not in the next. This means, then, that as capitalism grows and changes, so too must anticapitalist theory. This is where we come back to Du Bois's evolving critical relationship with Marxist theory. He not only criticized Marxism, but also revised and reconstructed the Marxian tradition by providing new theories, concepts, and categories of analysis—such as race, racism, and antiracist theory, and colonialism and anticolonial theory—that extend and expand Marxism's original intellectual arena and political program. Cedric Robinson's remarks in this regard are extremely insightful: "Du Bois committed himself to the development of a theory of history, which by its emphasis on mass action was both a critique of the ideologies of American socialist movements and a revision of Marx's theory of revolution and class struggle."[44] Further, Robinson continued, Du Bois "possessed no obligation to Marxist or Leninist dogma, nor to the vagaries of historical analysis and interpretation that characterized American communist thought."[45]

All of this is to say that when Du Bois advanced democratic socialism, or communism as he did at the end of his life, he did so from a position independent of mainstream Marxism and Marxist party politics, and often from an optic that stands outside the Marxist tradition altogether. It is in this sense that Moses declared, "Even when he urged Communism, the aging Du Bois did so on black nationalistic rather than on Marxist grounds."[46] Du Bois's concept of democratic socialism highlights and accents several aspects of classical and contemporary social reality that Marx, his disciples, and the members of the Frankfurt School/Institute of Social Research neglected or downplayed in their respective discourses. Du Bois's discourse on democratic socialism provides these assertions with greater weight and gravity.

Du Bois, the Black Radical Tradition, and the Emergence of Black Marxism

Du Bois, indeed, was a "socialist." And he openly admitted as much. But, as many Black and white Marxist theorists have pointed out, what it meant to be a Marxist or socialist prior to the Russian Revolution of 1917 was very different from claiming to be one after that historic event. Prior to the Russian Revolution, socialism generally entailed a belief in nonviolent social revolution or, rather, social reform, trade and industrial unionism, public ownership of utilities and properties, municipal improvement, corporate regulation, and a wide range of other economic and public policies.[47] After the Russian Revolution, socialism became the bane of many social circles in capitalist countries because it was purported to be the transitional state between capitalism and communism, as Karl Marx and his disciples claimed in their theorizations. Obviously, the Russian Revolution was not the prim and proper, prudent nonviolent textbook revolution that so many French, English, and white American socialists had hoped for and long dreamed about.[48]

In fact, according to Roger Gottlieb, in *Marxism, 1844–1990*, although the Russian communists took state power in the spirit of the ideas of Marx and Engels, their interpretation and practice of communism "had virtually nothing in common with Marx's vision of socialism."[49] None of this, of course, stopped the Russian communists' actions and interpretations from staining Marxism and socialism in the American social imagination, as the hysteria of the House Committee on Un-American Activities under the auspices of Senator Joseph McCarthy clearly illustrated.[50] In the final analysis, similar to the terms *race* and *racism*, at the turn of and throughout the twentieth century, *socialism* had a mercurial and malleable meaning, or set of meanings.

Du Bois critically engaged various versions of socialism (and, more generally, Marxism) for many of the same reasons that the Trinidadian triumvirate of C. L. R. James, Oliver C. Cox, and Eric Williams did: because it offered an array of criticisms of capitalism that cut to its core and made visible its obstinately invisible imperialist machinations.[51] However, it must be borne in mind that each of the aforementioned continuously criticized Marxism for its neglect of the racist aspects of capitalist culture and political economy. They were never Marxist in any orthodox or doctrinaire sense because, as Du Bois and James's radical thought regularly reminds us, white trade unions and white labor movements' strides toward economic justice configure Blacks and other nonwhite folk as threats to white workers.[52] Strong strands of racial bias shaped and shaded the white critics of capitalism's theorizations and politics, especially in the socialist and communist parties. This had the effect of placing Du Bois and the other Black critics of capitalism outside of the orthodox Marxist orbit. In a sense, this forced them to develop their own race-centered and racism-conscious critiques of capitalism. It also led many Black radicals to a critical and, at times, volatile relationship with the white critics of capitalism, Marxism, and Marxist party politics.[53]

Just as he had pioneered as an antiracist, pan-Africanist, and anticolonial theorist, Du Bois critically reinterpreted Marxism from perspectives that most often had not been seriously considered by either Marxist or non-Marxist theorists. That is to say, when he critically questioned Marxian theory from an Africana historical, cultural, social, and political frame of reference, or from the position of hyper-raced, "colored," and colonized people generally, he identified several of its theoretic inadequacies. It is the identification of these inadequacies and his development of a distinctly Black (read: race-centered and racism-conscious) critique of capitalism that makes Du Bois's discourse on democratic socialism stand out among Black radical theorists.[54]

Whether they agreed or disagreed with him, few could escape Du Bois's enormous and almost unfathomable influence on Black radicalism during his day. For instance, take perhaps the most noted of the Trinidadian triumvirate, C. L. R. James, who is by many accounts one of the greatest intellectuals the Caribbean has produced.[55] In *C. L. R. James and Revolutionary Marxism*, Scott McLemee argued that although James was highly critical of Du Bois, Du Bois did indeed "deeply influence him."[56] As a matter of fact, in an often-overlooked 1965 tribute to the then recently deceased Du Bois, James wrote,

> There is no need to subscribe to all that Dr. Du Bois has said and done. . . . Only the future can tell to what degree the historical audacities of Du Bois are viable. . . . Dr. Du Bois has always been put forward as one of the great black men and one of the great leaders of the black people. But, I have said that he is one of the great intellectuals—American intellectuals—of the twentieth century, and today and in years to come his work will continue to expand in importance while the work of others declines.[57]

Du Bois's thought appealed to James and other radicals because it was historically nuanced, culturally grounded, critical, and dialectical. In his approach to Marxism, Du Bois consistently demonstrated his ability to distinguish between its progressive and retrogressive elements. Marxism's neglect of the life-worlds and life-struggles of the racially oppressed (his beloved Black folk and other racially colonized folk) was one of the many areas that Du Bois—among many other Black radical theorists—found wanting.[58]

As early as his 1907 essay, "Negro and Socialism," Du Bois detected and detailed deficiencies in the Marxist tradition, which included, among other things, a silence about and/or an inattention to race, racism, and antiracist struggle; colonialism and anticolonial struggle; and the ways in which *both* capitalism and colonialism exacerbate not simply the economic exploitation of nonwhites, but continue (both physical and psychological) colonization beyond the realm of political economy.[59] Du Bois, therefore, laboring long and critically with Marxian theory and methodology, deconstructed it and developed his own original radical democratic socialist theory that simultaneously built on his pioneering work as a critical race theorist, pan-Africanist, and radical anticolonialist; called for the radical transformation of US society and the power relations of the world; was deeply concerned about and committed to world peace and demanded disarmament; and advocated the liberation of all colonized, politically oppressed, and economically exploited people.[60]

Du Bois was well aware of the fact that anyone in the citadel of supercapitalism, the United States, who openly embraced socialism or Marxism in any of its manifestations would quickly become a social and political pariah. But, against a barrage of Black bourgeois and white conservative criticism he sought socialism and a methodical and meticulous understanding of Marxism. In point of fact, Du Bois did not believe that the Russian communists had a monopoly on Marxism any more than he believed that the Marxists put a patent on the critique of capitalism. Marxism was merely one of many tools in Du Bois's ever-evolving critical theoretical framework. Just as the meaning of socialism and Marxism changed as a result of revolutionary praxis and retheorization, so too did Du Bois's relationship with, and critical appreciation or rejection of, certain aspects of Marxism change. It is in this sense that I consider Du Bois a critic of both capitalism *and* Marxism.[61]

Du Bois's Discourse on Democratic Socialism

In one of his later essays on socialism, "The Negro and Socialism" published in 1958, Du Bois argued that a socialist society is a society where there exists the "central idea that men must work for a living, but that the result of their work must not mainly be to support privileged persons," persons who as a result of the labor and economic exploitation of the "colored" masses and working classes have an exponential amount of power and privilege.[62] It is a society where the "welfare of the mass of people should be the main object of government," a society where the government is "controlled by the governed," which is to say, is fundamentally a democratic society.[63] In such a society, Du Bois declared, the "mass of people, increasing in intelligence, with incomes sufficient to live a good and healthy life, should control all government, and . . . they would be able to do this by the spread of science and scientific technique, access to truth, the use of reason, and freedom of thought and of creative impulse in art and literature."[64]

Calculating "seventy-five to ninety percent" of the earth's population to be racially colonized people and living in what he called the "colonies proper: America, Africa, and Asia," Du Bois was critically conscious of the fact that if indeed socialism purported to concern itself principally with "the mass" of "the governed" having a crucial and critical voice in their government, then non-whites should have prominent positions in national and international affairs and policy-making.[65] It could be no other way, he asserted, or else nonwhites ultimately would be led to the "last red alternative of revolt, revenge and war."[66] Where revolution was something he once shied away from, and where war was something that he utterly despised, Du Bois now openly considered both as options for bringing democratic socialism into being. Long gone was the talk of a gradual transition from capitalism to socialism. Additionally, here we also see a significant change in Du Bois's conception of socialism and his strategies and tactics for the realization of a democratic socialist society.[67]

For centuries capitalism has had nonwhites in its clutches. Consequently, from Du Bois's point of view, the "colored" and colonized were justified in their fight against it. Their fight would not only free the racially colonized, but it would also free economically exploited white workers as well. Du Bois reasoned, "The footsteps of the long oppressed and staggering masses are not always straight and sure, but their mistakes can never cause the misery and distress which the factory system caused in Europe, colonial imperialism caused in Asia and Africa, and which slavery, lynching, disenfranchisement, and Jim Crow legislation have caused in the United States."[68] In order to fully realize democratic socialism, Du Bois stated in 1944 that there must be "Freedom." By "Freedom" he meant the "full economic, political and social equality" of all people "in thought, expression and action, with no discrimination based on race or color."[69] "Freedom" is fundamental to democratic socialism, and without the "full economic, political and social equality" of all citizens within a particular society, democratic socialism remains an unrealized project of historical, cultural, social, political, and economic change.

African Americans "were not" and have never been socialists in any great number, contended Du Bois in 1960, "nor did they know what communism was or was doing. But they knew that Negro education must be better; that Negroes must have better opportunity to work and receive a wage which would let them enjoy a decent standard of life."[70] For this reason, socialism, being a "democratic program," could not "contemplate the complete subordination of one race to another."[71] It was to be a "program" or "project" of radical social and historical transformation that sought ultimately to establish "world democracy" so that there might be "world peace."[72] Du Bois queried, "Without democracy, what hope is there of Peace?"[73]

The "essence of democracy," according to Du Bois, "demands freedom for personal tastes and preferences so long as no social injury results."[74] This is important to emphasize because in Du Bois's conception of democracy it was not merely a political project, but a cultural one as well.[75] He explained,

> The vaster possibility and the real promise of democracy is adding to human capacities and culture from hitherto untapped sources of cultural variety and power. Democracy is tapping the great possibilities of mankind from unused and

> unsuspected reservoirs of human greatness. Instead of envying and seeking desperately outer and foreign sources of civilization . . . in these magnificent mountains a genius and variety of human culture, which once released from poverty, ignorance and disease, will help guide the world. Once the human soul is thus freed, then and only then is peace possible. There will be no need to fight for food, for healthy homes, for free speech; for these will not depend on force, but increasingly on knowledge, reason and art.[76]

As long as the "human soul" remained in bondage, so long would the world exist on the brink of "war after war."[77] Under capitalism and colonialism the vast majority of human beings have "for the most part no voice in government."[78] Under these systems it is only the "blood-sucking whites" who "rule and receive large income while others," mostly the "dark" or "native" proletariat, "work and live in poverty."[79] Moreover, capitalism and colonialism, interpreted as two sides of the same coin and two of the greatest impediments to "world democracy," had to be eradicated on the grounds that since their inception they have consistently caused the great mass of human beings, who are (it should be reiterated) "colored," to exist in various states and stages of "slavery, cultural disintegration, disease, death, and war."[80] Moreover, democracy, which for Du Bois was fundamentally predicated on "free discussion," required at minimum the "equal treatment [of] the colored races of the world."[81]

As stated above, a prerequisite for Du Bois's conception of democracy is "freedom," and the "real freedom toward which the soul of man has always striven" is, of course, the "right to be different, to be individual and pursue personal aims and ideals."[82] Long before postmodernist discourse and debate on the politics of difference, Du Bois asserted, the "richness of a culture . . . lies in differentiation."[83] He contended that "Difference" did not necessarily equal "Dangerous," and that once the bare necessities of "food, shelter, and . . . security" were met, then "human friendship and intermingling . . . based on broad and catholic reasoning" could lead to "happier . . . individual and . . . richer . . . social" lives.[84] He continued:

> Once the problem of subsistence is met and order is secured, there comes the great moment of civilization: the development of individual personality; the right of variation; the richness of a culture that lies in differentiation. In the activities of such a world, men are not compelled to be white in order to be free: they can be black, yellow or red; they can mingle or stay separate. The free mind, the untrammeled taste can revel. In only a section and a small section of the total life is discrimination inadmissible and that is where my freedom stops yours and your taste hurts me. Gradually such a free world will learn that not in exclusiveness and isolation lies inspiration and joy, but that the very variety is the reservoir of invaluable experience and emotion. This crowning of equalitarian democracy in artistic freedom of difference is the real next step of culture.

> The hope of civilization lies not in exclusion, but in inclusion of all human elements; we find the richness of humanity not in the Social Register, but in the City Directory; not in great aristocracies, chosen people and superior races, but in the throngs of disinherited and underfed men. Not the lifting of the lowly, but the unchaining of the unawakened mighty, will reveal the possibilities of genius, gift and miracle, in mountainous treasure-trove, which hitherto civilization has scarcely touched; and yet boasted blatantly and even glorified in its poverty. In world-wide equality of human development is the answer to every meticulous taste and each rare personality.[85]

Du Bois's radical democratic theory eschewed the elitism of his "Talented Tenth" thesis, what Moses called the "conservatism of his intellectual origins." Rather, Du Bois based his radical democratic theory on the "inclusion of all human elements," the "richness of humanity," not the "great aristocracies, chosen people and superior races," but on the "throngs of disinherited and underfed men."[86] Du Bois, as radical democratic theorist particularly in his later decades, looked not to the elite, as he once did, but to "disinherited" and "underfed" human beings to bring about the radical socialist transformation of society. In his view, a capitalist society, a so-called "developed society," is to a certain extent a colonized society because it is a society where life and language are not only directed, defined, and deformed by the wants of the ruling class, but inextricable from the exploitation of the racially colonized.[87]

Always and everywhere colonization, like Pandora's box once opened, seeps into every sphere of the life-worlds and life-struggles of both the colonized and the colonizer. It is precisely as Du Bois said it would be, a world of "race war," "racial friction" and "disastrous contradiction."[88] Only in "a free world" where the "problem of subsistence is met and order secured" can human beings arrive at the "great moment of civilization." This "moment," representing perhaps the highpoint in human history in Du Bois's thought, would foster the "development of individual personality," and these "new" individuals, free from the constant pursuit of their basic needs and capitalist greed—similar to Frantz Fanon's "new men" who speak a "new language" to express their "new humanity"—would pride themselves on the "right of variation."[89] In such a world, human beings "are not compelled to be white in order to be free: they can be black, yellow or red; they can mingle or stay separate." The "free world" Du Bois envisioned is a world that puts the premium on the potential of humble, hardworking, ordinary people—folk Fanon referred to as the "wretched of the earth."

Du Bois's concept of democracy, perpetually engaging "power relations," understood, as Michel Foucault did, that "in human relationships, whether they involve verbal communication . . . or amorous, institutional, or economic relationships, power is always present."[90] It exists on "different levels" and in "different forms," but is ultimately a relationship where "one person tries to control the conduct of the other."[91] "Power relations are mobile." Which is to say, "they can be modified" because "they are not fixed once and for all."[92] Power, being omnipresent, mutates, shifts, and changes as human beings and their reality changes, and this makes human beings' relationships to power "mobile, reversible, and unstable."[93]

In fact, Foucault explained that the very notion of a "power relation" is "possible only insofar as the subjects are free."[94] In power relations "there is necessarily the possibility of resistance because if there were no possibility of resistance (of violent resistance, flight, deception, strategies capable of reversing the situation), there would be no power relations at all."[95] In any power relation there exists the possibility of liberation, and "liberation and the struggle for liberation are indispensable for the practice of freedom."[96]

Conquered, colonized, "colored" people must be willing to struggle for liberation and higher levels of human life, and if they are not, they will never know or have the possibility of the "practice of freedom," which for Du Bois rested on *a radicalization of democracy* and *a democratization of socialism*.[97] Du Bois cautiously offered a caveat: "No group of privileged slave-owners is easily and willingly going to recognize their former slaves as men."[98] This means, then, that "former slaves" have as one of their life tasks the reclamation and rehabilitation of their denied humanity. Whether they regain their denied humanity, as Foucault suggested, through "violent resistance, flight, deception, [or any other] strategies capable of reversing the situation," is totally up to them and their specific time and circumstances.

As the "majority of men do not usually act in accord with reason, but follow social pressures, inherited customs and long-established, often subconscious, patterns of action," Du Bois believed that "race prejudice . . . will linger long and may even increase."[99] He charged the racially colonized, and the "black race" in particular, with a special duty, *not*—as Fanon said—to imitate European civilization and culture in "obscene caricature."[100] On the contrary, Du Bois believed that "it is the duty of the black race to maintain its cultural advance, not for itself alone, but for the emancipation of mankind, the realization of democracy and the progress of civilization."[101] Civilization is to progress, and democracy is to be realized (or, rather, *radicalized*), only insofar as the "masses" of human beings gain the "social control" of the "methods of producing goods and of distributing wealth and services. And, the freedom which this abolition of poverty will involve, will be freedom of thought and not freedom for private profit-making."[102]

Du Bois's discourse on democratic socialism, perhaps above all else, is distinguished by its antiracist sociopolitical ethics. It was not simply capitalism and class struggle that impeded the democratization of socialism, but racism, sexism, and colonialism as well.[103] Where he began his adventure in socialism toying with its most conservative, reformist, and gradualist strains, historical happenings on the world scene and the acute and increasing economic exploitation of Blacks and other nonwhites in white supremacist societies led him to couple his critical race and anticolonial theory with Marxist and critical class theory. As a consequence Du Bois developed some of the first race/class theory and criticisms of Marxism from a Black radical frame of reference. Indeed, it was his development of a distinct Black radical frame of reference in the period after he published more noted early works such as *The Philadelphia Negro* (1899), *The Souls of Black Folk* (1903), and "The Talented Tenth" that ultimately enabled him to declare near the end of his life, "I am certainly not a conservative. I should call myself a Socialist, although that isn't a very definite term."[104]

NOTES

1. W. E. B. Du Bois, "Interview with Dr. W. E. B. Du Bois" in *The Seventh Son: The Thought and Writings of W. E. B. Du Bois*, vol. 2, ed. Julius Lester (New York: Vintage Books, 1971), 701.

2. Du Bois, "Interview," 702.

3. Bill Mullen, *W. E. B. Du Bois: Revolutionary Across the Color Line* (London: Pluto Press, 2016), 38–53, 89–104; Eric Porter, *The Problem of the Future World: W. E. B. Du Bois and the Race Concept at Midcentury* (Durham: Duke University Press, 2010), 103–44.

4. David Levering Lewis, *W. E. B. Du Bois: Biography of a Race, 1868–1919* (New York: Henry Holt, 1993), 419–21.

5. Adolph L. Reed, *W. E. B. Du Bois and American Political Thought: Fabianism and the Color Line* (New York: Oxford University Press, 1997), 83.

6. Francis L. Broderick, *W. E. B. Du Bois: Negro Leader in a Time of Crisis* (Palo Alto, CA: Stanford University Press, 1959), 124.

7. Broderick, *W. E. B. Du Bois*, 123–24. See also W. E. B. Du Bois, "Race Relations in the United States," *Annals of the American Academy of Political and Social Science* 140, no.1 (1928): 6–10.

8. For further discussion of Du Bois's critique of sexism, see Cheryl Townsend Gilkes, "The Margin as the Center of a Theory of History: African American Women, Social Change, and the Sociology of W. E. B. Du Bois" in *W. E. B. Du Bois: On Race and Culture*, eds. Bernard W. Bell, Emily R. Grosholz, and James B. Stewart (New York: Routledge, 1996), 111–41; Susan Gillman and Alys E. Weinbaum, eds., *Next to the Color Line: Gender, Sexuality, and W. E. B. Du Bois* (Minneapolis: University of Minnesota Press, 2007); Reiland Rabaka, "'The Damnation of Women': Critique of Patriarchy, Contributions to Black Feminism, and Early Intersectionality," in Reiland Rabaka, *Du Bois: A Critical Introduction* (Cambridge: Polity, 2021), 95–120.

9. Bill Mullen, *Un-American: W. E. B. Du Bois and the Century of World Revolution* (Philadelphia: Temple University Press, 2015), 19–95.

10. W. E. B. Du Bois, "A Memorial to the Legislature of Georgia on Negro Common Schools," in W. E. B. Du Bois, *Pamphlets and Leaflets*, ed. Herbert Aptheker (New York: Kraus-Thomson, 1986), 25.

11. Porter, *The Problem of the Future World*, 21–62.

12. See Kevin K. Gaines, *Uplifting the Race: Black Leadership, Politics, and Culture in the Twentieth Century* (Chapel Hill: University of North Carolina Press, 1996), 152–78; Brian Johnson, ed., *Du Bois on Reform: Periodical-based Leadership for African Americans* (Lanham:

Rowman and Littlefield, 2005); Lewis Perry, *Intellectual Life in America: A History* (Chicago: University of Chicago Press, 1989), 267–72.

13. Lewis, *W. E. B. Du Bois: Biography of a Race*, 143–44.

14. W. E. B. Du Bois, "The Class Struggle," in *W. E. B. Du Bois: A Reader*, ed. David Levering Lewis (New York: Henry Holt, 1995), 555.

15. A. Philip Randolph and Chandler Owen, "Du Bois Fails as a Theorist," in *Black Protest Thought in the Twentieth Century*, eds. August Meier, Elliott Rudwick, and Francis L. Broderick (New York: MacMillan, 1971), 95, 93. On *The Messenger*, see Sondra K. Wilson, ed., *The Messenger Reader: Stories, Poetry, and Essays from* The Messenger *Magazine* (New York: Modern Library, 2000).

16. For further discussion of the "New Negro" and the New Negro Movement, see Ann Elizabeth Carroll, *Word, Image, and the New Negro: Representation and Identity in the Harlem Renaissance* (Bloomington: Indiana University Press, 2005); Erin D. Chapman, *Prove It on Me: New Negroes, Sex, and Popular Culture in the 1920s* (New York: Oxford University Press, 2011); Martin J. Favor, *Authentic Blackness: The Folk in the New Negro Movement* (Durham: Duke University Press, 1999); Barbara Foley, *Spectres of 1919: Class and Nation in the Making of the New Negro* (Urbana: University of Illinois Press, 2003); Henry Louis Gates and Gene Andrew Jarrett, eds., *The New Negro: Readings in Race, Representation, and African American Culture, 1892–1938* (Princeton: Princeton University Press, 2007); Caroline Goeser, *Picturing the New Negro: Harlem Renaissance Print Culture and Modern Black Identity* (Lawrence: University Press of Kansas, 2007); Daphne M. Lamothe, *Inventing the New Negro: Narrative, Culture, and Ethnography* (Philadelphia: University of Pennsylvania Press, 2008); Alain L. Locke, ed., *The New Negro* (New York: Boni, 1925); William J. Maxwell, *New Negro, Old Left: African American Writing and Communism Between the Wars* (New York: Columbia University Press, 1999); Martha Jane Nadell, *Enter the New Negroes: Images of Race in American Culture* (Cambridge: Harvard University Press, 2004); Anna Pochmara, *The Making of the New Negro: Black Authorship, Masculinity, and Sexuality in the Harlem Renaissance* (Amsterdam: Amsterdam University Press, 2011); James Edward Smethurst, *The New Red Negro: The Literary Left and African American Poetry, 1930–1946* (New York: Oxford University Press, 1999).

17. A. Philip Randolph and Chandler Owen, "Du Bois on Revolution: A Reply," in *Voices of a Black Nation: Political Journalism in the Harlem Renaissance*, ed. Theodore G. Vincent (Trenton, NJ: Africa World Press, 1973), 88–92.

18. Randolph and Owen, "Du Bois Fails as a Theorist," 94.

19. Manning Marable, *W. E. B. Du Bois: Black Radical Democrat* (Boston: Twayne, 1986), 109.

20. Marable, *W. E. B. Du Bois*, 110. It is interesting to observe that Owen's resignation from the Socialist Party mirrored Du Bois's short-lived stay in the Socialist Party. According to Marable, "Du Bois became a member of the Socialist party in 1911," but his "commitment to the Socialist party lasted only one year." Du Bois "was fully aware that some of his comrades 'openly excluded Negroes and Asiatics' from their definition of socialism." As a consequence, in November of 1912 "he left the party." Marable quickly quipped, "Du Bois may have resigned from the Socialist party, but he remained a Socialist." Marable, *W. E. B. Du Bois*, 90. See also W. E. B. Du Bois, *Darkwater: Voices from Within the Veil* (New York: Harcourt Brace, 1920), 138.

21. Marable, *W. E. B. Du Bois*, 110.

22. On Randolph, see Jervis Anderson, *A. Philip Randolph: A Biographical Portrait* (New York: Harcourt Brace Jovanovich, 1973); Cornelius L. Bynum, *A. Philip Randolph and the Struggle for Civil Rights* (Urbana: University of Illinois Press, 2011); Andrew Edmund Kersten, *A. Philip Randolph: A Life in the Vanguard* (Lanham: Rowman and Littlefield, 2007); Andrew Edmund Kersten and Clarence Lang, eds., *Reframing Randolph: Labor, Black Freedom, and the*

Legacies of A. Philip Randolph (New York: New York University Press, 2016); A. Philip Randolph, *For Jobs and Freedom: Selected Speeches and Writings of A. Philip Randolph*, eds. Andrew Edmund Kersten and David Lucander (Amherst: University of Massachusetts Press, 2014). On Rustin, see Jervis Anderson, *Bayard Rustin: Troubles I've Seen* (Berkeley: University of California Press, 1998); John D'Emilio, *Lost Prophet: The Life and Times of Bayard Rustin* (Chicago: University of Chicago Press, 2004); Bayard Rustin, *Time on Two Crosses: The Collected Writings of Bayard Rustin*, eds. Devon W. Carbado and Donald Weise (New York: Cleis Press, 2015).

23. Paula F. Pfeffer, *A. Philip Randolph, Pioneer of the Civil Rights Movement* (Baton Rouge: Louisiana State University Press, 1990), 256.

24. Marable, *W. E. B. Du Bois*, 90.

25. Wilson Jeremiah Moses, *The Golden Age of Black Nationalism, 1850–1925* (New York: Oxford University Press, 1978), 139.

26. Marable, *W. E. B. Du Bois*, 109, 112; Moses, *Golden Age*, 140; Reed, *W. E. B. Du Bois and American Political Thought*, 83–89.

27. Zhang Juguo, *W. E. B. Du Bois: Quest for the Abolition of the Color Line* (New York: Routledge, 2001), 137. See also, Mullen, *W. E. B. Du Bois*, 57–72.

28. W. E. B. Du Bois, "Application for Membership in the Communist Party of the United States of America," in *Du Bois: A Reader*, 632.

29. For further discussion of Du Bois's development of one of the first race-based and racism-conscious critiques of capitalism employing a Marxist methodological orientation, see Gerald Horne, *Black and Red: W. E. B. Du Bois and the Afro-American Response to the Cold War, 1944–1963* (Albany: State University of New York Press, 1986).

30. For further discussion of a "racial polity," see Charles W. Mills, *Blackness Visible: Essays on Philosophy and Race* (Ithaca: Cornell University Press, 1998) and Charles W. Mills, "The Racial Polity," in eds. Susan E. Babbitt and Sue Campbell, *Racism and Philosophy* (Ithaca: Cornell University Press, 1999), 13–31.

31. Dan S. Green and Earl Smith, "W. E. B. Du Bois and the Concepts of Race and Class," *Phylon* 44, no. 4 (1983): 262–72; Mullen, *W. E. B. Du Bois*, 73–88; Joe William Trotter, "W. E. B. Du Bois: Ambiguous Journey to the Black Working-Class," in *Reading Southern History: Essays on Interpreters and Interpretations*, ed. Glenn Feldman (Tuscaloosa: University of Alabama Press, 2001), 61–75.

32. W. E. B. Du Bois, "Colonialism, Democracy, and Peace after the War," in W. E. B. Du Bois, *Against Racism: Unpublished Essays, Papers, Addresses, 1887–1961*, ed. Herbert Aptheker (Amherst: University of Massachusetts Press, 1985), 232–33. In "India, the 'Indian Ideology,' and the World Revolution," Bill Mullen asserted that "even more than in his support for the Russian Revolution, Du Bois's dedication to India's twentieth-century struggle for independence bespeaks the widest field of his ideational attachment to the World Revolution concept." See Mullen, *Un-American*, 96. As indicated in Du Bois's quotation above, Mullen argued that India's colonial history and the Indian Revolution played a pivotal role in Du Bois's conception of revolution. Indeed, Mullen's work in *Un-American* deftly demonstrates that by his later years Du Bois was a student of "World Revolution," not merely revolutionary struggles in Europe and North America. For further discussion, see Mullen's "The East Is Red: Supporting Revolutions in Asia" in Mullen, *W. E. B. Du Bois*, 123–35; Kate A. Baldwin, *Beyond the Color Line and the Iron Curtain: Reading Encounters between Black and Red, 1922–1963* (Durham: Duke University Press, 2002), 149–201; W. E. B. Du Bois, *W. E. B. Du Bois on Asia: Crossing the World Color-Line*, eds. Bill V. Mullen and Cathryn Watson (Jackson: University Press of Mississippi, 2005); Robeson Taj Frazier, *The East Is Black: Cold War China in the Black Radical Imagination* (Durham: Duke University Press, 2014), 1–107; Bill V. Mullen, *Afro-Orientalism* (Minneapolis:

University of Minnesota Press, 2004), 1–41; Nikhil Pal Singh, *Black Is a Country: Race and the Unfinished Struggle for Democracy* (Cambridge: Harvard University Press, 2005); Nico Slate, *Colored Cosmopolitanism: The Shared Struggle for Freedom in the United States and India* (Cambridge: Harvard University Press, 2012).

33. Karl Marx and Friedrich Engels, *The Marx-Engels Reader*, 2nd ed., ed. Robert C. Tucker (New York: Norton, 1978), 489.

34. Reiland Rabaka, "*Black Reconstruction*: Critique of Capitalism, Contributions to Black Marxism, and Discourse on Democratic Socialism," in Reiland Rabaka, *Du Bois: A Critical Introduction* (Cambridge: Polity, 2021), 121–56; Reiland Rabaka, "W. E. B. Du Bois: From Pioneering Pan-Negroism to Revolutionary Pan-Africanism," in *The Routledge Handbook of Pan-Africanism*, ed. Reiland Rabaka (London: Routledge, 2020), 187–215; Reiland Rabaka, *W. E. B. Du Bois and the Problems of the Twenty-First Century* (Lanham: Rowman and Littlefield, 2007), 83–135.

35. Marx and Engels, *The Marx-Engels Reader*, 489.

36. Rabaka, "'The Damnation of Women,'" 95–120.

37. On the Africana tradition of critical theory (or, rather, Africana critical theory), see Reiland Rabaka, "Africana Critical Theory of Contemporary Society: The Role of Radical Politics, Social Theory, and Africana Philosophy," in *The Handbook of Black Studies*, eds. Molefi Kete Asante and Maulana Karenga (Thousand Oaks, CA: Sage, 2006), 130–51; Reiland Rabaka, *Africana Critical Theory: Reconstructing the Black Radical Tradition, from W. E. B. Du Bois and C. L. R. James to Frantz Fanon and Amilcar Cabral* (Lanham: Rowman and Littlefield, 2009); Reiland Rabaka, *Concepts of Cabralism: Amilcar Cabral and Africana Critical Theory* (Lanham: Rowman and Littlefield, 2014), 255–308; Reiland Rabaka, *The Negritude Movement: W. E. B. Du Bois, Leon Damas, Aime Cesaire, Leopold Senghor, Frantz Fanon, and the Evolution of an Insurgent Idea* (Lanham, MD: Rowman and Littlefield Publishers, 2015).

38. Cornel West, *Keeping Faith: Philosophy and Race in America* (New York: Routledge, 1993), 258, 267.

39. See Rosemary Cowan, *Cornel West: The Politics of Redemption* (Cambridge: Polity Press, 2003), 79–101; Floyd Hayes, "Cornel West and Afro-Nihilism: A Reconsideration," in *Cornel West: A Critical Reader*, ed. George Yancy (Malden: Blackwell, 2002), 245–60; Clarence Sholé Johnson, *Cornel West and Philosophy: The Quest for Social Justice* (New York: Routledge, 2003), 61–92, 121–46; John P. Pittman, "'Radical Historicism,' Antiphilosophy, and Marxism" in *Cornel West: A Critical Reader*, ed. George Yancy (Malden: Blackwell, 2002), 224–44; Mark David Wood, *Cornel West and the Politics of Prophetic Pragmatism* (Urbana: University of Illinois Press, 2000), 41–86.

40. Cornel West, "Black Strivings in a Twilight Civilization," in Henry Louis Gates and Cornel West, *The Future of the Race* (New York: Alfred A. Knopf, 1996), 55, emphasis added.

41. Cornel West, "W. E. B. Du Bois: The Jamesian Organic Intellectual," in *The American Evasion of Philosophy: A Genealogy of Pragmatism* (Madison: University of Wisconsin Press, 1989), 145–50.

42. Horne, *Black and Red*, passim; Rabaka, "*Black Reconstruction*," 121–56.

43. W. E. B. Du Bois, "The Negro and Radical Thought," in *Du Bois: A Reader*, 533.

44. Cedric Robinson, *Black Marxism: The Making of the Black Radical Tradition* (Chapel Hill: University of North Carolina Press, 2000), 196.

45. Robinson, *Black Marxism*, 228.

46. Moses, *Golden Age*, 140.

47. G. A. Cohen, *Why Not Socialism?* (Princeton: Princeton University Press, 2009); Michael Newman, *Socialism: A Very Short Introduction* (New York: Oxford University Press, 2005); John Nichols, *The S Word: A Short History of an American Tradition . . . Socialism* (London: Verso, 2015).

48. Herbert Marcuse, *Soviet Marxism: A Critical Analysis* (New York: Columbia University Press, 1985; originally published 1958).

49. Roger S. Gottlieb, *Marxism, 1844–1990: Origins, Betrayal, Rebirth* (New York: Routledge, 1992), 77.

50. W. E. B. Du Bois, *In Battle for Peace: The Story of My 83rd Birthday* (New York: Masses and Mainstream, 1952).

51. On C. L. R. James, see Paul Buhle, *C. L. R. James: The Artist as Revolutionary* (New York: Verso, 1988); Kent Worcester, *C. L. R. James: A Political Biography* (New York: SUNY Press, 1995); Aldon Lynn Nielsen, *C. L. R. James: A Critical Introduction* (Jackson: University Press of Mississippi, 1997). On Oliver C. Cox, see Herbert H. Hunter and Sameer Abraham, eds., *Race, Class, and the World System: The Sociology of Oliver C. Cox* (New York: Monthly Review Press, 1987); Christopher McAuley, *The Mind of Oliver C. Cox* (Notre Dame: University of Notre Dame Press, 2004). And, on Eric Williams, see Colin A. Palmer, *Eric Williams and the Making of the Modern Caribbean* (Chapel Hill: University of North Carolina Press, 2009); Selwyn Ryan, *Eric Williams: The Myth and the Man* (Kingston: University of the West Indies Press, 2008); Tanya L. Shields, ed., *The Legacy of Eric Williams: Into the Postcolonial Moment* (Jackson: University Press of Mississippi, 2015).

52. See, for example, W. E. B. Du Bois, *Black Reconstruction in America, 1860–1880* (New York: Harcourt Brace, 1935); C. L. R. James, *C. L. R. James on the "Negro Question,"* ed. Scott McLemee (Jackson: University Press of Mississippi, 1996).

53. Robinson, *Black Marxism*; Charles W. Mills, *From Class to Race: Essays in White Marxism and Black Radicalism* (Lanham, MD: Rowman and Littlefield, 2003); Anthony Bogues, *Black Heretics, Black Prophets: Radical Political Intellectuals* (New York: Routledge, 2003); Rabaka, *Africana Critical Theory*; Rabaka, *The Negritude Movement*.

54. See William Wright, "The Socialist Analysis of W. E. B. Du Bois" (PhD dissertation, State University of New York at Buffalo, 1985) and Ji Yuan, "W. E. B. Du Bois and His Socialist Thought" (PhD dissertation, Temple University, 1998). Because these works are extended studies that focus exclusively on Du Bois's socialist thought, they offer students of Du Bois's socialism some of the best criticism available of his ever-increasing radicalism, as well as intriguing examinations of the myriad meanings of Marxism, socialism, and communism in twentieth-century Black radical discourse.

55. Selwyn Reginald Cudjoe and William E. Cain, eds., *C. L. R. James: His Intellectual Legacies* (Amherst: University of Massachusetts Press, 1994); Grant Farred, ed., *Rethinking C. L. R. James* (Cambridge: Blackwell, 1996); Paget Henry and Paul Buhle, eds., *C. L. R. James's Caribbean* (Durham: Duke University Press, 1992).

56. Scott McLemee, "Afterword: American Civilization and World Revolution: C. L. R. James in the United States, 1938–1953 and Beyond," in C. L. R. James, *C. L. R. James and Revolutionary Marxism: Selected Writings of C. L. R. James, 1939–1949*, eds. Scott McLemee and Paul Le Blanc (Atlantic Highlands, NJ: Humanities Press, 1994), 225.

57. C. L. R. James, "W. E. B. Du Bois," in C. L. R. James, *The Future in the Present: Selected Writings* (London: Allison and Busby, 1977), 202, 211.

58. Cornel West, "Marxist Theory and the Specificity of Afro-American Oppression," in *Marxism and the Interpretation of Culture*, eds. Cary Nelson and Lawrence Grossberg (Chicago: University of Illinois Press, 1988), 17–34; Michael Stone-Richards, "Race, Marxism, and Colonial Experience: Du Bois and Fanon," in *The Cambridge Companion to W. E. B. Du Bois*, ed. Shamoon Zamir (Cambridge: Cambridge University Press, 2008), 102–16; Babacar Camara, *Marxist Theory, Black/African Specificities, and Racism* (Lanham: Lexington Books, 2010).

59. W. E. B. Du Bois, "Negro and Socialism," in W. E. B. Du Bois, *Selections from* The Horizon, ed. Herbert Aptheker (White Plains, NY: Kraus-Thomson, 1985), 6.

60. In "The Socialist Analysis of W. E. B. Du Bois," William Wright declared, "Simply put, Du Bois, in many ways, just went beyond the thinking of his socialist contemporaries, not only in America, but also in Europe, that simply made it difficult for them to follow much of his socialistic thinking or to appreciate it." For instance, Wright continued, "Du Bois was virtually the only American socialist in his day, and one of the few in the Western world, who took a strong analytical interest in the impact that Western expansion, in the form of racism, capitalism, colonialism, and imperialism had on the histories and lives of people in non-Western areas of the world" (ix–x). See also, W. E. B. Du Bois, *Color and Democracy: Colonies and Peace* (New York: Harcourt Brace, 1945); W. E. B. Du Bois, "The World Problem of the Color Line," in W. E. B. Du Bois, *W. E. B. Du Bois on Asia: Crossing the World Color Line*, eds. Bill V. Mullen and Cathryn Watson (Jackson: University Press of Mississippi, 2005), 35–36; W. E. B. Du Bois, "The Negro and Imperialism," in W. E. B. Du Bois, *W. E. B. Du Bois on Asia: Crossing the World Color Line*, eds. Bill V. Mullen and Cathryn Watson (Jackson: University Press of Mississippi, 2005), 37–47; W. E. B. Du Bois, "The American Negro and the Darker World," W. E. B. Du Bois, *W. E. B. Du Bois on Asia: Crossing the World Color Line*, eds. Bill V. Mullen and Cathryn Watson (Jackson: University Press of Mississippi, 2005), 48–55.

61. Du Bois, *In Battle for Peace*; Horne, *Black and Red*; Marable, *W. E. B. Du Bois*, 99–189; Mullen, *W. E. B. Du Bois*, 57–104; Mullen, *Un-American*, 56–95; Rabaka, "*Black Reconstruction*," 121–56; Robinson, *Black Marxism*, 185–240; Wright, "The Socialist Analysis of W. E. B. Du Bois," 280–466.

62. W. E. B. Du Bois, "The Salvation of the American Negro Lies in Socialism," in *Let Nobody Turn Us Around: Voices of Resistance, Reform, and Renewal, An African American Anthology*, eds. Manning Marable and Leith Mullings (Lanham: Rowman and Littlefield, 2000), 410. Originally published as W. E. B. Du Bois, "The Negro and Socialism," in *Toward a Socialist America: A Symposium of Essays*, ed. Helen L. Alfred (New York: Peace Publications, 1958), 179–91.

63. Du Bois, "The Salvation of the American Negro," 410.

64. Du Bois, "The Salvation of the American Negro," 410.

65. Du Bois, "Colonialism, Democracy, and Peace after the War," 230.

66. W. E. B. Du Bois, "On Being Ashamed of Oneself: An Essay on Race Pride," in *Du Bois: A Reader*, 80.

67. W. E. B. Du Bois, "The Negro and Communism," *Crisis* 38, no. 9 (September 1931): 313–15, 318–20; W. E. B. Du Bois, "Karl Marx and the Negro," *Crisis* 40, no. 2 (March 1933): 55–56; W. E. B. Du Bois, "Marxism and the Negro Problem," *Crisis* 40, no. 5 (1933): 103–4, 118; W. E. B. Du Bois, "Our Class Struggle," *Crisis* 40, no. 7 (1933): 164–65; W. E. B. Du Bois, "Negroes and the Crisis of Capitalism in the United States," *Monthly Review* 4 (April 1953): 478–85.

68. Du Bois, "The Salvation of the American Negro Lies in Socialism," 414.

69. W. E. B. Du Bois, "My Evolving Program for Negro Freedom," in *Du Bois: A Reader*, 614.

70. W. E. B. Du Bois, "Socialism and the American Negro," in W. E. B. Du Bois, *Against Racism: Unpublished Essays, Papers, Addresses, 1887–1961*, ed. Herbert Aptheker (Amherst: University of Massachusetts Press, 1985), 304.

71. W. E. B. Du Bois, "A Social Program for Black and White Americans," in W. E. B. Du Bois, *Against Racism: Unpublished Essays, Papers, Addresses, 1887–1961*, ed. Herbert Aptheker (Amherst: University of Massachusetts Press, 1985), 218.

72. Du Bois, "A Social Program for Black and White Americans," 209; W. E. B. Du Bois, "The Future of Europe in Africa," in Du Bois, *Against Racism*, 184. See also Du Bois, *In Battle for Peace*.

73. Du Bois, "Colonialism, Democracy, and Peace after the War," 237.

74. Du Bois, "A Social Program for Black and White Americans," 215.

75. Du Bois, "Colonialism, Democracy, and Peace after the War," 231. See also Du Bois, *Color and Democracy*, 73–99.

76. Du Bois, "Colonialism, Democracy, and Peace after the War," 242–43.

77. Du Bois, "The Future of Europe in Africa," 184.

78. Du Bois, "Colonialism, Democracy, and Peace after the War," 230.

79. Du Bois, "The Salvation of the American Negro Lies in Socialism," 417; Du Bois, "My Evolving Program for Negro Freedom," 616; Du Bois, "A Social Program for Black and White Americans," 216. For further discussion of Du Bois's critique of whites, whiteness, and white supremacy, see W. E. B. Du Bois, "Race Friction Between Black and White," *American Journal of Sociology* 13. no. 6 (1908): 834–38; W. E. B. Du Bois, "Of the Culture of White Folk," *Journal of Race Development* 7, no. 4 (1917): 434–47; W. E. B. Du Bois, "The Superior Race," *Smart Set* 70 (1923): 55–60; W. E. B. Du Bois, "The Souls of White Folk" in Du Bois, *Darkwater*, 29–52; W. E. B. Du Bois, "White Co-Workers," *Crisis* 20, no. 1 (1920): 6–8; W. E. B. Du Bois, "The White World," in W. E. B. Du Bois, *Dusk of Dawn: An Essay Toward an Autobiography of a Race Concept* (New York: Harcourt, Brace and World, 1940), 134–72; W. E. B. Du Bois, "The White Masters of the World," in W. E. B. Du Bois, *The World and Africa: An Inquiry into the Part which Africa Has Played in World History* (New York: Viking Press, 1947), 16–43; Reiland Rabaka, "The Souls of White Folk: W. E. B. Du Bois's Critique of White Supremacy and Contributions to Critical White Studies (Part I)," *Ethnic Studies Review: Journal of the National Association for Ethnic Studies* 29, no. 2 (2006); 1–19; Reiland Rabaka, "The Souls of White Folk: W. E. B. Du Bois's Critique of White Supremacy and Contributions to Critical White Studies (Part II)," *Journal of African American Studies* 11, no.1 (2007): 1–15; Rabaka, *W. E. B. Du Bois and the Problems of the Twenty-First Century*, 35–82; Reiland Rabaka, "'The Souls of White Folk': Critique of White Supremacy and Contributions to Critical White Studies," in Reiland Rabaka, *Du Bois: A Critical Introduction* (Cambridge: Polity, 2021), 64–94.

80. Du Bois, "The Future of Europe in Africa," 196. See also Du Bois, *Darkwater*; Du Bois, *Color and Democracy*; Du Bois, *W. E. B. Du Bois on Asia*.

81. Du Bois, "Socialism and the American Negro," 303; Du Bois, "A Social Program for Black and White Americans," 218.

82. Du Bois, "My Evolving Program for Negro Freedom," 617.

83. Du Bois, "My Evolving Program for Negro Freedom," 617.

84. Du Bois, "My Evolving Program for Negro Freedom," 617.

85. Du Bois, "My Evolving Program for Negro Freedom," 617.

86. Moses, *Golden Age*, 138. On Du Bois's "Talented Tenth" theory, see W. E. B. Du Bois, "The Talented Tenth," in *The Negro Problem: A Series of Articles by Representative American Negroes of Today*, ed. Booker T. Washington (New York: J. Pott, 1903), 33–75. On Du Bois's Marxist-influenced radicalization of his "Talented Tenth" thesis, see W. E. B. Du Bois, "The Talented Tenth Memorial Address," *The Boulé Journal* 15, no. 1 (1948): 3–13.

87. Du Bois, *Darkwater*; Du Bois, *Color and Democracy*; W. E. B. Du Bois, *Africa in Battle Against Colonialism, Racism, and Imperialism* (Chicago: Afro-American Heritage Association, 1960).

88. W. E. B. Du Bois, "The Future of Africa in America," in Du Bois, *Against Racism*, 183, 181; Du Bois, "A Social Program for Black and White Americans," 206.

89. Frantz Fanon, *The Wretched of the Earth*, trans. Constance Farrington (New York: Grove, 1968), 36. See also Reiland Rabaka, *Forms of Fanonism: Frantz Fanon's Critical Theory and the Dialectics of Decolonization* (Lanham: Rowman and Littlefield, 2010), 271–304.

90. Michel Foucault, "The Ethics of the Concern for Self as a Practice of Freedom," in Michel Foucault, *The Essential Works of Michel Foucault, 1954–1984, Volume 1—Ethics: Subjectivity and Truth*, ed. Paul Rabinow (New York: New Press, 1997), 292.

91. Foucault, "The Ethics of the Concern for Self as a Practice of Freedom," 292.

92. Foucault, "The Ethics of the Concern for Self as a Practice of Freedom," 292.

93. Foucault, "The Ethics of the Concern for Self as a Practice of Freedom," 292.

94. Foucault, "The Ethics of the Concern for Self as a Practice of Freedom," 292.

95. Foucault, "The Ethics of the Concern for Self as a Practice of Freedom," 292.

96. Foucault, "The Ethics of the Concern for Self as a Practice of Freedom," 284.

97. W. E. B. Du Bois, "Socialism and Democracy," *American Socialist* 4, no. 1 (1957): 6–9.

98. Du Bois, "My Evolving Program for Negro Freedom," 616.

99. Foucault, "The Ethics of the Concern for Self as a Practice of Freedom," 618.

100. Fanon, *The Wretched of the Earth*, 315.

101. Du Bois, "My Evolving Program for Negro Freedom," 618. See also Du Bois, "The Negro and Imperialism," 37–47; W. E. B. Du Bois, "We Fight for a Free World . . . This or Nothing!," *Chicago Defender* (September 26, 1942): 4; W. E. B. Du Bois, "Prospect of a World Without Race Conflict," *American Journal of Sociology* 49, no. 5 (1944); 450–56.

102. Du Bois, "The Future of Europe in Africa," 197–98.

103. Reiland Rabaka, *Du Bois: A Critical Introduction* (Cambridge: Polity, 2021).

104. W. E. B. Du Bois, *The Philadelphia Negro: A Social Study* (Philadelphia: University of Pennsylvania Press, 1899); W. E. B. Du Bois, *The Souls of Black Folk: Essays and Sketches* (Chicago: A. C. McClurg, 1903); Du Bois, "The Talented Tenth."

PART II

Identity and Culture

CHAPTER 5

Democracy in America Is Impossible: The Pessimistic Prophecy of W. E. B. Du Bois in "Why I Won't Vote"

–Andre E. Johnson

In its November 1917 edition, the NAACP official organ *The Crisis* published an editorial titled, "The Oath of the Negro Voter."[1] As one of "Earth's Disowned," Black voters pledging allegiance to the oath were to "swear to hold" the ballot as the "sacred pawn of Liberty for all mankind and for my prisoned race." They were to "accept no price" for their vote and to make "first and foremost" the aim of their voting the "enfranchisement of every citizen, male and female. Adherents to this oath also promised not to accept any office they could not fill and would "judge all officials by their service to the common weal" and would not "regard the mere giving of Office to my friends as payment for my support of any party." They promised to "judge all Political Parties not by their past deeds or their future promises but simply by the present acts of the Officials who represent them" and to "scan carefully the record of every candidate . . . learning what manner of man each is, how he has carried out his trust and what pledges he makes in general."

The oath further charged adherents to have a "firm faith in Democracy, despite its mistakes and inefficiency, knowing that in no other way can the common Experience, Want and Will be pooled for the common good, and that no Despot or Aristocrat can ever be wise or good enough to rule his fellowmen." It closed by asking oath takers to "entrust the National Association for the Advancement of Colored People and its local branches with the investigation and co-operation necessary to the listing of suitable candidates for each election and for like-minded individuals to send their names to the editor of *The Crisis*," which Du Bois edited at the time. Led by Du Bois's efforts, this editorial was one in a long line of writings to get African Americans to use their right to vote and participate in democracy as fully fledged citizens of America.

Almost forty years later, however, Du Bois's positions had changed. For example, he eventually believed that the "talented tenth" could no longer lead African Americans because they too had "capitulated to the rapacious capitalism" that harmed Blacks. This prompted Du Bois to offer "international socialism" as a program that would benefit Blacks more. Even his position on "scientific inquiry and education" as elements that would solve the "race problem" underwent alteration and he no longer saw a world "without race conflict." Additionally, while he saw in the First World War an opportunity for peace and prosperity, he later would become antiwar—arguing that war came from capitalists wanting to "stem the worldwide tide toward socialist democracy."[2]

One of Du Bois's most significant philosophical adjustments, however, came in the area of voting. He championed the ballot box as the great equalizer at obtaining rights for African Americans earlier in his career. However, as time went on and electoral politics did not provide the panacea for Black folks he had hoped, Du Bois's enthusiasm for voting began to wane. As his support for candidates switched from Republican to Democrat to third party and independent, frustration with electoral politics led Du Bois to become apostate when it came to voting.

In this chapter, I chart this change by examining Du Bois within the African American prophetic tradition. I argue that Du Bois's rhetorical trajectory[3] from advocating voting to his decision to abstain from voting in the 1956 election coincided with his shift from a mission-oriented prophet to a pessimistic one. To demonstrate this shift to a pessimistic prophet, I offer a close reading of his "Why I Won't Vote" editorial published in 1956. I argue that while Du Bois's hope in American institutions and the democratic process had waned during this time in his life, he was not hopeless or nihilistic. On the contrary, Du Bois continued to believe in "democracy." I suggest that it was the use of the lament tradition within this pessimistic prophecy that gave Du Bois hope to keep speaking, writing, and visioning a better day.

The African American Prophetic Tradition

Before I turn to the African American prophetic tradition, I define prophetic rhetoric. It is

> discourse grounded in the sacred, rooted in a community experience that offers a critique of existing communities and traditions by charging and challenging society to live up to the ideals they espoused while offering celebration, encouragement and hope for a brighter future. It is a rhetoric "characterized by a steadfast refusal

> to adapt itself to the perspectives of its audience" and a rhetoric that dedicates itself to the rights of individuals. Located on the margins of society, it intends to lift the people to an ethical conception of whatever the people deem as sacred by adopting, at times, a controversial style of speaking.[4]

There are two primary traditions in which critics seek to situate prophetic rhetoric—apocalyptic and the jeremiad.[5] While there are many studies on prophetic rhetoric drawing from the two traditions mentioned above until recently, not many of them focus primarily on the African American tradition. Created in the crucible of slavery and formed in segregation, this tradition has given voice to many African Americans and provided a level of comfort and reassurance. This tradition has "expressed black people's call for unity and cooperation, as well as the community's anger and frustrations." Further,

> It has been both hopeful and pessimistic. It has celebrated the beauty and myth of American exceptionalism and its special place in the world, while at the same time damning it to Hell for not living up to the promises and ideals America espouses. It is a tradition that celebrates both the Creator or the Divine's hand in history—offering "hallelujahs" for deliverance from slavery and Jim and Jane Crow, while at the same time asking, "Where in the hell is God?" during tough and trying times. It is a tradition that develops a theological outlook quite different at times from orthodoxy—one that finds God very close, but so far away.[6]

It is also a tradition that does not exclusively reside in the aforementioned examples of the discourse because "contextual restraints and rhetorical exigencies have not always allowed for an apocalyptic or jeremiadic appeal."[7] For example, traditionally, in apocalyptic rhetoric, the world is a bad place, and the speaker argues that God (or some divine action) will cause a cataclysmic event and bring about a new age. In the jeremiad, the speaker appeals to some prearranged covenant to call back the audience to a right relationship with the Divine. However, what if a speaker who adopts a prophetic persona does not believe that God or some divine action will cause a cataclysmic event that will bring in a new age? What if a speaker does not appeal to a covenant—or for that matter, does not believe the covenant is available to the people? What if the covenant itself is the problem?

This is the position in which many African Americans find themselves when addressing audiences. Therefore, to adopt prophetic personas, many African American prophets adopt other rhetorical nuances within the prophetic tradition. In my work on Bishop Henry McNeal Turner, I identify at least four types of prophetic rhetoric found primarily, but not exclusively in the African American Prophetic Tradition—celebratory prophecy, disputation, mission-oriented prophecy, and pessimistic prophecy.[8] For the purposes of this essay, it is to pessimistic prophecy that we now turn.

Pessimistic Prophecy

The notion of a pessimistic prophecy on the surface may contradict my earlier definition of prophetic rhetoric's hope and encouragement. However, I argue that it does not because, as I attempt to demonstrate later, pessimistic prophecy is simultaneously pessimistic and hopeful. As I wrote previously, it is in this tradition that the "prophet's primary function is to speak out on behalf of others and to chronicle their pain and suffering as well as their own. By speaking, the prophet offers hope and encouragement to others by acknowledging their sufferings and letting them know that they are not alone."[9]

In addition, African American orators adopt a prophetic persona—realizing racism is too entrenched and the American covenant ideals not realistic for Black Americans to ascertain and become wailing and moaning prophets within the *lament tradition of* prophecy. Laments are "expressions of grief and pain that are in search of an outlet." The one "practicing lamentation understands that nothing will change about her or his situation (at least not immediately), but the chance to express oneself and to speak one's mind becomes therapeutic for the person and abates, at least for a while, the frustration the person feels about the situation." Lamentation "helps a person continue with the struggle, and while not understanding the 'why' questions, the person is still able to function and maintain, thankful that at least the Divine hears her or his cry."[10]

Moreover, when one who adopts a prophetic persona does this, "she invites all who hear (or read) her words to understand the frustration and pain that the community shares. The aim at proclaiming the message is "simply *to speak and to get the audience to hear*." By doing this, the prophet offers a record that chronicles the "pains and sufferings of the people the prophet claims to represent and to give voice to the voiceless."[11]

Drawing from the work of Cornel West, I located this type of prophecy in the frustration of the prophet to fight and resist racism and racist practices. However, this aggressive pessimism, as West has called it, has a way of "awakening a new zeal" and "restores for African Americans the courage to renew their struggle to appropriate the hegemonic traditions and to resist those societal forms that simply do not make sense to them, namely, those that exclude them, that predict and label them, and that sonorously silence them. In short, aggressive pessimism helps speakers deal with those insurmountable obstacles placed in front of them, thereby becoming a coping strategy that staves off communal nihilism and self-destruction."[12]

I argue that Du Bois adopted a pessimistic persona and engaged in prophetic pessimism in his editorial "Why I Won't Vote." Earlier in his career, Du Bois was an optimistic prophet, and while editor of *The Crisis* magazine he grounded much of his rhetoric within a mission-oriented prophecy.[13] During this time, Du Bois was hopeful that America would live up to the ideals espoused in its covenant of freedom and democracy. He understood the importance of citizenship and argued that if African Americans neglected their duties, their rights would always be in danger. This led him to urge African Americans to support the war effort. His notions of rights and duties led him to argue that "this is our country . . . it is our war" because while not perfect, America was the hope of "mankind and of black mankind."[14]

Du Bois's optimistic view of American democracy also led him to support women's suffrage. In 1914, he published an editorial, "Votes for Women," where he challenged African Americans to "bring it to pass." He reasoned that extending democracy involved a "discussion of the fundamentals of democracy," which further led Du Bois to contend that if it is "acknowledged to be unjust to disenfranchise a sex, it cannot be denied that it is absurd to disenfranchise a color."[15]

Even when Du Bois was critical of America, African Americans, and particularly the church, he typically ended his editorials with hope and encouragement to his readers. He consistently challenged African Americans to "gird up [their] loins," because a "great day is coming." He suggested that while things were tough at the present moment, he argued that African Americans would not "endure it forever" because one day society would grant the rights of citizenship to all Americans.[16]

However, by the time Du Bois wrote "Why I Won't Vote," he had shifted from an optimistic to a pessimistic prophet. Pessimistic prophecy typically has a three-part rhetorical structure. First, the prophet often "recalls past events to lay claim on the present conditions of the people the prophet represents." Second, within this framework, the prophet then "chronicles the sufferings of the people, offering the prophetic lament." Finally, the prophet "encourages the people that while nothing will change in the present, the people are not alone—the prophet hears and will represent the voice of the voiceless and remind others that not all is well."[17]

In his column, Du Bois follows this rhetorical structure. First, he recalls events by offering a history of his voting and the theory behind his selections. Second, by detailing why he will not vote in the 1956 presidential election, he chronicles and laments the failings of trusting in electoral politics. Third, while he takes a prophetic stand not to participate in the election because he argues it would make little difference, he also, by speaking of society's ills, offers reassurance to his audience that he too stands with them.

"Why I Won't Vote"[18]

Du Bois opened his essay, "Since I was twenty-one in 1889, I have in theory followed the voting plan strongly advocated by Sidney Lens in The Nation of August 4, i.e., voting for a third party even when its chances were hopeless if the main parties were unsatisfactory; or, in absence of a third choice, voting for the lesser of two evils." This opening served two primary purposes. First, he wanted his audience to know that up until this writing, he had consistently voted since he was twenty-one or voting age. Second, he also wished his audience to know that he always had "in theory" followed the voting plan outlined by labor leader and peace activist Sidney Lens. While Lens may have come to his "third party" position or voting for the "lesser of two evils" theory in 1956, Du Bois wanted his audience to know that he had consistently voted in such a way.

The reason for Du Bois's position on voting earlier in life had to do with his understanding of candidates' "attitude towards the Negro." Du Bois grounded his vote in his own self-interest and what he believed a candidate would do for African Americans as a whole. However, he had not always had the opportunity to vote. He reminded his audience that in the twenty-three years he spent in the South teaching at Atlanta University, his "voting choice" was not asked of him because of disfranchisement either by "law" or "administration." In short, Du Bois wanted his readers to know that even when he attempted to vote and put his "theory" to the test, in the South, at least, he could not.

Du Bois then shifted to his time "in the North." Starting in the 1912 presidential election, he wrote that he "wanted to support Theodore Roosevelt, but his Bull Moose convention dodged the Negro problem." Therefore, he "tried to help elect (Woodrow) Wilson as a liberal Southerner." However, for Du Bois, Wilson was a bitter disappointment. He wrote, "Under Wilson came the worst attempt at Jim Crow legislation and discrimination in civil service that we had experienced since the Civil War." Therefore, in 1916, during the reelection of Wilson, Du Bois supported "(Charles Evans) Hughes as the lesser of two evils" even though he promised, "Negroes nothing and kept his word." In 1920, Du Bois supported (Warren G.) Harding because he promised to "liberate Haiti," and in 1924, he "voted for (Robert M.) La Follette," although he knew "he could not be elected."

In 1928, Du Bois argued that "Negroes faced an absolute dilemma. Neither Hoover nor Smith wanted the Negro vote, and both publicly insulted us." This led him to vote for "Norman Thomas and the Socialists," although, according to Du Bois, the "Socialists had attempted to Jim Crow Negro members in the South." In 1932 Du Bois wrote, "I voted for Franklin Roosevelt since (Herbert) Hoover was unthinkable and Roosevelt's attitude toward workers most realistic." Upon returning to the South again, from 1934 until 1944, Du Bois reminded his audience, "Technically I could vote, but the election in which I could vote was a farce. The real election was the White Primary." Upon returning to the North, Du Bois "found a party to my liking." Therefore, in 1948, Du Bois voted for the "Progressive ticket" and again in 1952.[19]

Du Bois's narrative history of his voting history helps him shape the next part of the essay. By sharing the story of how he went to the polls and his frustrations even then with voting, Du Bois could definitively declare that in 1956 he "shall not go to the polls" and that he had "not registered." By adding that he had "not registered," he signals to anyone thinking he may have a change of heart that even if he does, he could not vote because he was not registered to vote in this presidential election. In short, he communicated the finality of his decision—and since it is final, he now shifts to tell his audience that after all the years he advocated participation in the electoral process, why he now has a change of heart.

Du Bois did not believe that democracy existed in the United States—and since there was no democracy, no two evils could exist. "There is but one evil party with two names, he wrote, and "it will be elected despite all I can do or say." Du Bois had a reason for his pessimism. Promoted by both Democratic (Truman) and Republican (Eisenhower) administrations, the frenzy surrounding the Cold War's "Red Scare" led to laws that subverted American democracy. Unsubstantiated congressional investigations into communism, outlawing the Communist Party from electoral participation, the banning of free speech, and the charging and arrest of people on suspicion of being communists all led to Du Bois's belief that there was no reason to vote in the 1956 presidential election.[20]

Framing it this way, Du Bois also highlighted the problem of the pessimistic prophet. He wrote that he would not vote because there was no real choice for voters. However, "it will be elected" despite what he "could do or say." While this may have been true for Du Bois, it did not stop him from writing this essay or speaking out about what he believed to be a flawed system. In short, part of the prophetic pessimistic persona is that the prophet does not quit or give up because they do not think anything will change. Yet, it is despite that; the prophet continues to address problems facing the community.

For Du Bois, the problem voters faced was that there was no third party for voters to choose. Mentioning that the "Socialist" party would appear on some presidential ballots in some states, Du Bois argued that "few will hear its appeal because it will have almost no opportunity to take part in the campaign and explain its platform." However, he maintained that if a "voter organizes or advocates a real third-party movement, he may be accused of seeking to overthrow this government by "force and violence" or, even worst, called a "Communist."

Du Bois, however, sought to place the communist charge within the framework of what a third party would have to advocate. For Du Bois, a third party would have to support such things as "government ownership of the means of production; government in business; the limitation of private profit; social medicine, government housing and federal aid to education; the total abolition of race bias; and the welfare state."

Further, he laments why initiating a "real" third-party movement is challenging. First, a third party must "discuss and advocate" the very issues that would lead to a charge of "communism or socialism." Second, if one advocates them, they are also at the risk of "losing their job, surrendering his social status and perhaps landing in jail." Third, people would stand against those who would start a third party, even though, for Du Bois, they may be "liars, insane, or criminals. According to Du Bois, they even may be in the "pay of the United States Government."

Du Bois wants his audience to understand why it is hard to start a third-party movement in America. He also wants them to know that the reason is that the government may have a hand in establishing a system that is hostile to third-party starts. He closes this part of the speech by critiquing would be liberal or progressive movements. "'A.D.A.'s' (Americans for Democratic Action) and 'Liberals' are not third parties; they seek to act as tails to kites. But since the kites are self-propelled and radar-controlled, tails are quite superfluous and rather silly." In short, for Du Bois, there are no real progressive movements in the country—especially ones that would seriously challenge the hegemonic forces of capitalism and the ills that it causes. At best, they are just ornamentation that looks quite "silly." Moreover, by stating that there are no real third-party movements in America, the current Socialist Party, which Du Bois would have been sympathetic to, does not constitute a real third party.

Du Bois then shifts to a stinging critique of the Eisenhower administration. First, not only is the administration "carrying on the greatest preparation for war in the history of mankind," but he also argues that the "weight of our taxation is unbearable and rests mainly and deliberately on the poor." For Du Bois, there is a reason for this. He maintains that the "administration is dominated and directed by wealth and for the accumulation of wealth." He claims that it "runs smoothly like a well-organized industry and should do so because industry runs it for the benefit of industry."

Du Bois continues his critique by noting that while "corporate wealth profits as never before in history," the country seemingly cannot find the funds for "education, health or housing." Further, he writes, "Our crime, especially juvenile crime, is increasing. Its increase is perfectly logical; for a generation, we have been teaching our youth to kill, destroy, steal and rape in war; what can we expect in peace?" Then he switches back to electoral politics. He argues, "It costs three times his salary to elect a Senator and many millions to elect a President. This money comes from the very corporations, which today are the government. This in a real democracy would be enough to turn the party responsible out of power. Yet this we cannot do."[21]

Du Bois then turns to what he calls the "other" party and levels critiques at them as well. He sees no difference in (Adlai) Stevenson and Eisenhower in domestic affairs—outside the observation that Stevenson has a "sly humor" whereas Eisenhower "has none." He argues that "Stevenson stands on the race question in the South not far from where his godfather Adlai stood sixty-three years ago, which reconciles him to the South," and he suggests that Stevenson does not have a "clear policy on war or preparation for war; on water and flood control; on reduction of taxation; on the welfare state." Probably the strongest critique from Du Bois comes from his belief that Stevenson (and his party) "wavers on civil rights." Du Bois states,

> His party blocked civil rights in the Senate until (Senator Paul) Douglas of Illinois admitted that the Democratic Senate would and could stop even the right of Senators to vote. Douglas had a right to complain. Three million voters sent him to the Senate to speak for them. His voice was drowned and his vote nullified by (Senator James) Eastland, the chairman of the Senate Judiciary Committee, who was elected by 151,000 voters. This is the democracy in the United States which we peddle abroad.

By comparing both leading candidates and their parties and presenting them unworthily, Du Bois attempts to do two things. First, he bolsters his argument for not voting. If the policy on both sides is terrible and unacceptable, the right thing to do—even the moral thing to do, is to abstain from voting. Du Bois proclaims to his audience that he will not participate in his own oppression by not voting. Second, in highlighting the differences between the candidates and parties, Du Bois also frames them as the same. Though Du Bois approaches governing in different ways, "Stevenson and Eisenhower" are essentially the same—therefore, there is no real choice for Du Bois to make in this election. For him, when there is no real choice to make, genuine democracy does not exist.

Du Bois then focuses on the African American voter in the 1956 presidential election and wonders where they will cast their votes. He asks, "What have the Republicans done to enforce the education decision of the Supreme Court?" He further asks, "what has the Administration done to rescue Negro workers, the most impoverished group in the nation, half of whom receive less than half the median wage of the nation, while the nation sends billions abroad to protect oil investments and help employ slave labor in the Union of South Africa and the Rhodesians?" After suggesting that the Democratic Party of "(Herman) Talmadge, Eastland and (Allen J.) Ellender" will not do any better than the Republicans if African Americans return them to office, he closes by writing, "I have no advice for others in this election. Are you voting Democratic? Well, and good; all I ask is why? Are you voting for Eisenhower and his smooth team of bright ghostwriters? Again, why? Will your helpless vote either way support or restore democracy to America?"

By framing his argument using rhetorical questions, Du Bois invites African Americans to reflect on their vote and even their voting patterns over time. He reminds them that not only has the Republican Party not done anything to "rescue" African Americans from the segregated conditions in which they live, but even the decisions that seem progressive—such as the "education decision"—lack steadfast Republican support. Further, by framing his argument this way, Du Bois invites his audience to see that, at least for African Americans, no matter who they vote for and support, the end remains the same. Therefore, voting for the Republican or Democratic parties will not support or "restore democracy to America."

In the next part of the essay, Du Bois asks, "Is the refusal to vote in this phony election a counsel of despair?" By way of hypophora,[22] he responds, "No, it is dogged hope. It is hope that if twenty-five million voters refrain from voting in 1956 because of their own accord and not because of a sly wink from Khrushchev, this might make the American people ask how much longer this dumb farce can proceed without even a whimper of protest." However, he seems to understand the limits of this type of protest because; in his following sentence, he reminds his audience, "Yet if we protest, off the nation goes to Russia and China." In short, Du Bois reasons that a nonvote protest may lead some in America to criticize nonvoters as communists.

Du Bois then turns his attention to a recent open letter issued by "fifty-five American ministers and philanthropists" asking the Soviet Union "to face manfully the doubts and promptings of their conscience."[23] Noting the letter's hypocrisy, he asks, "Cannot these do-gooders face their own consciences? Can they not see that American culture is rotting away: our honesty, our human sympathy; our literature, save what we import from abroad?" Further, Du Bois lamented, "our manners are gone and the one thing we want is to be rich—to show off. Success is measured by income. University education is for income, not culture, and is partially supported by private industry. We are not training poets or musicians, but atomic engineers. Business is built on successful lying called advertising. We want money in vast amount, no matter how we get it. So, we have it, and what then?"

Du Bois ends his essay by asking, "Is the answer the election of 1956?" He argues that whoever it is, America will be in the "same mess." He writes that while he will be "no party to it," he also recognizes that his protest nonvote "will make little difference." He also acknowledges that people who will "bravely march to the polls," and their vote "also will make no difference." He advises Americans to stop giving advice about Russia and China when "we cannot rule ourselves decently." He closes the essay with a charge to America.

> Stop yelling about a democracy we do not have. Democracy is dead in the United States. Yet there is still nothing to replace real democracy. Drop the chains, then, that bind our brains. Drive the money-changers from the seats of the Cabinet and the halls of Congress. Call back some faint spirit of Jefferson and Lincoln, and when

again we can hold a fair election on real issues, let's vote, and not till then. Is this impossible? Then democracy in America is impossible.

Real democracy for Du Bois is dead in the United States. Invoking the New Testament prophet Jesus, Du Bois suggests that the remedy to resurrect democracy would involve driving the "money changers from the seats of the Cabinet and the hall of Congress." He also challenges America to look towards Jefferson and Lincoln as exemplars of democracy. However, he also does not dismiss voting ever again—only when America can "hold fair elections of real issues"—should Americans vote. Until then, he suggests withholding the vote. If this is not possible, he concludes, then democracy is impossible.

A little over two weeks later, on November 6, over sixty million people went to the polls. The popular incumbent, Dwight D. Eisenhower, soundly defeated his Democratic opponent Adlai Stevenson with both Electoral College and popular-vote victories. In addition, because of his grassroots campaign targeting African Americans, Eisenhower secured an estimated 36 percent of the African American vote. Indeed, instead of not voting, many African Americans switched their vote to the Republican candidate for the first time in twenty years.[24]

Therefore, one could argue correctly that Du Bois's rhetoric failed to achieve its goal. However, persuasion was not his aim, and to judge a piece of prophetic rhetoric by its persuasive effects is to misjudge the function of the rhetorical enterprise. As Robert Terrill notes, there are "other conceptions of rhetoric." One of those conceptions is to "understand that action does not necessarily have to happen after the speech—that the very rhetoric itself is an action." Rhetoric addressing the "consciousness of the audience even if the audience rejects the political action that the speaker calls for—still allows the audience to act in the way they see fit."[25]

Many have followed Du Bois in his seeming condemnation of electoral politics. For instance, during the election between Obama and Romney in 2012, Pastor Thabiti Anyabwile argued that the "vote for the lesser of two evils" is not a good enough reason to vote. He wrote, "a vote for the 'lesser evil' is still a vote for evil. I can't make that vote. I know there are no perfect candidates, but I do know there are perfect principles."[26]

In the 2016 presidential election between major party nominees Donald Trump (Republican) and Hillary Clinton (Democrat), many Black activists, religious and opinion leaders, and public intellectuals also invoked Du Bois's column as a reason why African Americans should not vote in that election. Many lifted themes similar to those in Du Bois's column.

Ahmad Greene-Hayes, writing for *The Root*, echoed the "two evils" frame. He argued that both Trump and Clinton were "two faces of the same coin." While one is the "lesser evil, and the other is (the) greater evil," he writes, "evil is still evil. And amid rampant anti-black racial animus, settling for the lesser evil will not stop bullets, put an end to mass incarceration, end poverty, abolish prisons, and bring back to life the countless black and brown people taken by state-sanctioned violence."[27]

Arica L. Coleman, writing for *Time* magazine, argued that many Black voters view the "right not to vote as a democratic exercise of conscience that reimagines a politics unchained from the mere act of casting a ballot"[28] while others supported the #IAintVoting campaign; a campaign aimed at getting activists not to participate in the two-party system.[29]

However, Princeton professor and public intellectual Eddie Glaude gained much attention during the 2016 presidential campaign. In his debate with Michael Eric Dyson[30] and his op-ed in *Time* magazine,[31] Glaude questioned the validity of African Americans not only voting for Clinton but voting in the presidential election at all. He wrote that he would "vote down ballot, focusing his attention on "congressional, state, and local elections." However, at the top of the ticket, Glaude wrote that he would "leave the presidential ballot blank." He reasoned that neither Clinton nor Trump would address issues pertinent to African Americans and poor people of all races and grounded this reasoning within the Du Boisian tradition that rejected the "lesser of two evils" argument.[32]

While similar in many ways, I suggest a close reading of Du Bois's essay would reveal something more than trying to persuade people not to vote. What Du Bois calls for in his essay is a moral revolution of what it means to vote. When he asks African Americans, "Will your helpless vote either way support or restore democracy to America?" he seeks a higher ethical consideration to voting. For Du Bois, one should only vote in the 1956 election if that vote would support or restore democracy to America. For him, democracy is the sacred ideal that he holds up for his audience to emulate. Du Bois here makes a moral argument for democracy by not participating in what he believes is a sham. If only the people would "drop the chains that bind our brains," we can see that not only is democracy dead, but there is nothing to replace "real democracy."

Therefore, Du Bois's rhetoric here is not meant to persuade. It is intended to bear witness to the truth he proclaims. Moreover, as in prophetic rhetoric in general—but more explicit in prophetic pessimism—the initial audience may not be the primary audience that the speaker has in mind. When a speaker *bears witness*, she or he moves beyond the constraints of an immediate audience to speak to what Edwin Black calls an implied audience.[33] In other words, when speakers adopt a prophetic persona, part of the rhetoric typically is to cast a vision of the world as it should be. Since the immediate audience cannot hear the prophet and cannot see the vision, it is up to future audiences (generations) to pick up the mantle and begin to live out the truth proclaimed previously by the prophet.

While many have picked up Du Bois's mantle and desire to act prophetically, they forget about the context that gave utterance to the prophetic action. The issues and problems in 2016 were not the same as in 1956, and a failure to see that makes any proclamation fall woefully short. In short, context matters, and we would do well to see the signs of our own times.

NOTES

1. W. E. B. Du Bois, "The Oath of the Negro Voter," *The Crisis* (November 1917): 7.

2. Andre E. Johnson, "To Make the World So Damn Uncomfortable: W. E. B. Du Bois and the African American Prophetic Tradition," *Carolinas Communication Annual* (XXXII/2016).

3. I use rhetorical trajectory as Dionisopoulos et. al uses it, as "the progression or curve of development that a speaker establishes as he or she attempts to turn a vision into reality." See George N. Dionisopoulos, Victoria J. Gallagher, Steven R. Goldzwig, and David Zarefsky, "Martin Luther King, the America Dream and Vietnam: A Collision of Rhetorical Trajectories," *Western Journal of Communication* 56 (Spring 1992): 91–107.

4. Andre E. Johnson, *The Forgotten Prophet: Bishop Henry McNeal Turner and the African American Prophetic Tradition* (Lanham, MD: Lexington Books, 2012), 7.

5. Johnson, "To Make the World," 22. See also Johnson, *The Forgotten Prophet.*

6. Johnson, "To Make the World," 22.

7. Johnson, "To Make the World," 22

8. Johnson, *The Forgotten Prophet*, 14; Andre E. Johnson, *No Future in This Country: The Prophetic Pessimism of Bishop Henry McNeal Turner* (Jackson: University Press of Mississippi, 2020), 15–18.

9. Johnson, *The Forgotten Prophet*, 14; Johnson, *No Future in This Country*, 16.

10. Johnson, *The Forgotten Prophet*, 14.

11. Johnson, *The Forgotten Prophet*, 14.

12. Johnson, *No Future in This Country*, 16.

13. Johnson, "To Make the World."

14. W. E. B. Du Bois, *Writings*, ed. Nathan Huggins (New York: Library of America, 1975), 160.

15. Du Bois, *Writings*, 80.

16. Du Bois, *Writings*, 17.

17. Johnson, *The Forgotten Prophet*, 15; Johnson, *No Future in This Country*, 16.

18. W. E. B. Du Bois, "Why I Won't Vote," *The Nation*, October 20, 1956, https://www.thenation.com/article/i-wont-vote/.

19. Du Bois voted for Henry Wallace in 1948 and Vincent Hallinan in 1952. The 1952 election is noteworthy because Hallinan selected as his running mate Charlotta Bass—making her the first African American woman nominated for Vice President.

20. Manning Marable, *W. E. B. Du Bois: Black Radical Democrat* (New York: Routledge, 2016).

21. Du Bois, "Why I Won't Vote."

22. A rhetorical device in which the speaker raises a question and then immediately precedes to answer the question.

23. "An Appeal to Conscience," *New Outlook: A Digest of Ideas and Ideals* (Vol 9, No. 9, 1956): 4.

24. See Lincoln Fitch, "Throwing the Switch: Eisenhower, Stevenson and the African American Vote in the 1956 Election," *Student Publications* 219 (2014), http://cupola.gettysburg.edu/student_scholarship/219.

25. Johnson, *The Forgotten Prophet*, 4–5.

26. Thabiti Anyabwile, "W. E. B. Du Bois Will Not Vote in this Election," *The Gospel Coalition*, October 3, 2021, https://www.thegospelcoalition.org/blogs/thabiti-anyabwile/w-e-b-dubois-would-not-vote-in-this-election/.

27. Ahmad Greene-Hayes, "#Election2016: Trump Ain't New, and Clinton Ain't Savior," *The Root*, July 28, 2016, https://www.theroot.com/election2016-trump-aint-new-and-clinton-aint-savior-1790856201.

28. Arica Coleman, "The W. E. B. Du Bois Argument for Not Voting in a 'Phony Election,'" *Time*, August 18, 2016, https://time.com/4443840/web-du-bois-not-voting/.

29. Hawk Newsome, "White American Deserves Donald Trump," *PRLOG*, August 11, 2016. https://www.prlog.org/12579379-black-lives-matter-leader-hawk-newsome-white-america-deserves-donald-trump.html.

30. "Michael Eric Dyson vs. Eddie Glaude on race, Hillary Clinton and the Legacy of Obama's Presidency," *Democracy Now!*, July 28, 2016, https://www.democracynow.org/2016/7/28/michael_eric_dyson_vs_eddie_glaude.

31. Eddie S. Glaude Jr., "My Democratic Problem with Voting for Hillary Clinton," *Time*, July 12, 2016, http://time.com/4402823/glaude-hillary-clinton/.

32. Glaude Jr., "My Democratic Problem with Voting for Hillary Clinton."

33. Edwin Black, "The Second Persona," *Quarterly Journal of Speech* 56, no. 2 (April 1970).

CHAPTER 6

The Dharma of Socialism: How Hindu Thought Influenced W. E. B. Du Bois's Vision for Afro-Asian Solidarity

–Murali Balaji

As the Harlem Renaissance was at its peak, W. E. B. Du Bois was undergoing a period of intellectual restlessness. After having helped to get rid of his rival Marcus Garvey, Du Bois began to doubt the efficacy of the NAACP's vision for integration and equality. By the late 1920s, Du Bois was slowly beginning to embrace the idea that revolution—and a coalescing of the masses around economic equality—was the only way for African Americans to achieve full suffrage. His discomfort with the NAACP growing, Du Bois found refuge in the writings by and correspondences with anticolonial leaders from other parts of the world.

Through these correspondences, Du Bois began looking overseas for intellectual inspiration. Shortly after World War I ended, he was already engaged in healthy correspondences with Indian luminaries such as Sarojini Naidu and Rabindranath Tagore, both of whom had inspired him to think of civil rights as more than an American struggle. Even as he tired of NAACP executive secretary James Weldon Johnson's calls for working within the American legal framework to achieve equality and integration, Du Bois used *The Crisis*, which he still had as his own platform within the organization, to promote other causes. In 1922, Du Bois hailed Mahatma Gandhi's satyagraha movement in India, writing that his Hindu- and Jain-inspired nonviolent protest "kills without striking its adversary."[1]

For all of Du Bois's praise for Gandhi, it was the Mahatma's erstwhile rival who grew to have an outsized influence on Du Bois. Lala Lajpat Rai, an Indian nationalist leader and one of the leading voices of Arya Samaj, a reform movement in Hinduism that called for a return to living life according to the Vedas, became Du Bois's inspiration and counsel over the course of the 1920s.

Du Bois's friendship with Rai wasn't just a correspondence between two men who saw a common bond between their struggles. For Du Bois, Rai's faith—and his willingness to sacrifice himself for a cause greater than himself—profoundly stirred a newfound political awakening. Moreover, the Hindu concept of *dharma*, or righteous action, which Rai and Gandhi claimed as an underpinning their approaches to resisting British imperialism, influenced Du Bois in his own thinking about a future merging of his ideals of anticolonialism and socialism. While much has been written about how Du Bois envisioned an Afro-Asian alliance, including Mullen's recent works[23] on his worldview, as well as Horne's[4] work on African Americans' view of India, there has not been a deeper interrogation of how Hinduism as a religion impacted his works and changing politics.

This chapter examines how Hindu leaders such as Rai and Gandhi influenced Du Bois, particularly in his quest for a new Afro-Asian world order, and how those relationships helped him question the Christian-centric worldview he had tacitly accepted.

Du Bois at a Philosophical Crossroads

To better understand how Du Bois became drawn to India and its influential Hindu leaders, it is important to provide the context from which Du Bois had long shaped his own politics. As biographers such as David Levering Lewis write, he had come to realize that any hope that Blacks had in their own suffrage would rest with tying their fortunes to other suffrage movements across the globe, including India's. Similarly, Mullen and Rampersad add that Du Bois had joined a growing group of Black intellectuals who drew inspiration and common cause with internationalism, a sharp break from a previous generation of civil rights advocacy that focused on the plight of African Americans. Indeed, while Du Bois had famously noted the problem of the color line in *The Souls of Black Folk* and participated in the 1911 First Universal Races Congress in 1911, he had not seriously immersed himself in internationalism until the early 1920s.

In 1920, Du Bois published *Darkwater: Voices from Within the Veil*, which shifted his position from racial equality to a more pronounced attack on class privilege. It was also his first open call for a more unified struggle of darker races against white oppression. In "The Souls of White Folk," Du Bois wrote, "A belief in humanity is a belief in colored men. If the uplift of mankind must be done by men, then the destinies of this world will rest ultimately in the hands of darker nations."[5] It was perhaps the first explicit attempt by Du Bois to think of a unified struggle that involved more than African Americans' connection to Africa (which, like many African American intellectuals, Du Bois idealized and orientalized).

Still, Du Bois saw this unification as abstract until the early 1920s, when he encountered a fierce activist from Punjab, India, whose passion for Indian freedom would inspire many outside of India. The next several years would not only shape Du Bois profoundly but establish the frameworks from which Black internationalism would develop in subsequent decades.

The Lion of Punjab Meets the Doctor

From a distance, it would seem that a friendship between Rai and Du Bois was unlikely, given how different their philosophies were. Rai, whose confrontational style landed him in British jails and on the receiving end of beatings from colonial authorities, fiercely advocated for an Indian society based on Hindu values. He was a follower of nineteenth-century Hindu reformer Swami Dayanand Sarasvati, whose Arya Samaj movement gained hundreds of thousands of followers for its adherence to Vedic principles and its eschewal of caste. The Arya Samaj movement argued that India's caste system—which had become a formal and legal part of Indian life after the 1850 British census—was contrary to Hindu philosophy. Though Gandhi and other Indian leaders, including Dalit leader B. R. Ambedkar, argued the same thing, Arya Samaj leaders were almost militant in their rejection of any form of social practice not mentioned in the four Vedas. Their adherence to the Vedic lifestyle, for example, also meant their rejection of the common Hindu practice of worshiping multiple deities. While some scholars claim that the movement also intensified tensions between Hindus and Muslims, as well as with Sikhs, Arya Samaj devotees were also seen as being part of the frontlines of the Indian independence movement, giving them high visibility among Hindus and non-Hindus.[67]

Rai became the editor of the sect's newspaper, *Arya Gazette* in 1907, but he slowly began to embrace a more confrontational political style. He would later also establish and edit the publication, *Young India*. Like his contemporaries, freedom fighters Aurobindo Ghosh and Bipin Chandra Pal, Rai became disillusioned with the Indian National Congress, arguing that their approach to independence was too moderate. Moreover, Rai opposed an independent India that swayed too far from its Hindu identity, contending that Indian National Congress leaders were doing too much to appease Muslims and non-Hindus in the name of communal unity. Rai's criticism of the Indian independence struggle included his disagreements with Gandhi on the best approaches to achieve liberation, and he became more and more enthralled by the idea of a revolutionary struggle against British imperialism. In 1917, Rai visited the United States, founding the India Home Rule League in New York. During his three-year stay, which was extended because British officials denied him a return passport to India, he met leaders of the Ghadar Party—a radical Indian independence outfit based in California—and championed a style of resistance that rejected the norms of Gandhi and Indian National Congress leaders. As he became more involved in the freedom struggle, Rai believed one's body should be sacrificed for a greater good. It was that belief that would land him on the receiving end of British brutality over the next decade.

Du Bois, on the other hand, was not an activist. He did not join the frontlines of protests and was more comfortable writing in his office and keeping a comfortable distance from the marchers he so often claimed to speak for in his works. Historian and African American studies scholar Molefi Asante argued that Du Bois's resistance to being a militant activist stemmed from his decidedly Eurocentric views. Many Afrocentric scholars also have been critical of Du Bois for his attacks on Garvey.

But Du Bois, whose upbringing in the First Congregational Church of Great Barrington often clashed with his ardent secularism as an adult, was not entirely dismissive of religion, nuanced yet divergent points Christopher Cameron and Phillip Luke Sinitiere address in this volume. In fact, given the outsized influence of Quakers, Unitarians, and Jews on civil rights in the first part of the twentieth century, Du Bois did not have dramatically different views than leaders such as Mary White Ovington or Joel Spingarn. Du Bois was also deeply influenced by Harold Lasky, the British Labour leader who embraced socialism even as he remained steadfastly Jewish. Du Bois's own musings on religion tended to reflect his own philosophical changes, especially as he moved from a liberal Republicanism to a more open embrace of socialism by the mid-1920s and more specific communist convictions towards the end of his life.

While Du Bois met Rai during his three-year stay in the United States, the correspondences between the two men after Rai returned to India were more instrumental in changing Du Bois's global outlook. Even as he admired Rai and Gandhi for their fight for Indian suffrage, Du Bois was slowly drawn to the idea of revolution, even as he remained at an arm's length from calling for one in the United States. His trip to the Soviet Union in 1926 bolstered this realization, where Du Bois saw the effects of a societal revolution firsthand. Similarly, Rai's own fascination with nineteenth-century Italian revolutionary Giuseppe Mazzini fueled his impatience with the Indian National Congress.

The Du Bois–Rai correspondences shed light on both men's philosophical transformations, but also the way Du Bois began to see the world. He took a deep interest in Hinduism[8] and responded in kind when Rai asked Du Bois about "the cruelties inflicted on your people by the whites of America."[9] For Du Bois, it was the sort of relationship he craved with an international leader whose own struggles with white oppression forged a common cause. In Rai, he saw someone not beholden to organizational fidelity, a quality Du Bois himself appreciated through his numerous tussles with the leadership of the NAACP during and after World War I and World War II.

Dark Princess

Even as Du Bois became more intellectually drawn to the Indian freedom struggle, Rai's militant opposition to the British grew. He defied British authorities by speaking Punjabi and Urdu instead of English during ceremonies that involved colonial officials. Like other Indian freedom leaders, he also saw the inside of jail cells with frequency, often because of phony or spurious charges.

Like other African Americans, Du Bois visited the Soviet Union in 1926, drawn to the idea of a country that promoted integration of all its peoples. While Du Bois was not as enamored with the USSR as Paul Robeson and William L. Patterson (who would later become one of the leaders of the Communist Party USA), he was more interested in how the Soviet Union would support anticolonial movements in other parts of the world, including India. Fresh with ideas about a global emancipation effort of darker peoples, Du Bois began writing *Dark Princess*, which he envisioned as a manifesto wrapped into a fictional romance. In the fall of 1927, Du Bois wrote to Rai that he was "going to write a novel in the spring. It touches upon India incidentally in the person of an Indian princess."[10] He asked Rai for feedback, particularly on issues such as caste and color, which the latter provided. While he likely did not intend for the novel to become a response to Katherine Mayo's *Mother India*, broadly seen as a racialized attack on Indians and a Christian's diatribe against Hinduism, *Dark Princess* would ultimately take on issues that Mayo brought up in the book. In *Mother India*, Mayo passionately argued *against* Indian self-rule, claiming that Hindus were unable to govern independently and needed the Christian civilizing mission of the British to be redeemed.

> Given men who enter the world out of bankrupt stock, rear them through childhood in influences and practices that devoir their vitality; launch them at the dawn of maturity on an unrestrained outpouring of their whole provision of creative energy in one single direction; find them, at an age when the Anglo-Saxon is just coming into full glory of manhood, broken-nerved, low-spirited, petulant ancients; and need you, while this remains unchanged, seek for other reasons why they are poor and sick and dying and why their hands are too weak, too fluttering, to seize or to hold the reins of government?[11]

The book drew the immediate rebuke of leaders like Gandhi, who argued that Mayo's attacks would actually serve to strengthen the Indian Home Rule movement.

Rai, whose movements were becoming increasingly surveilled and restricted by the British, was infuriated by the book and published a response, *Unhappy India*, in which he lambasted Mayo and criticized the more moderate leaders of the Indian independence movement.

> Now it is quite plausible to argue that we Indians have by our disunion and foolishness invited foreign rule, and must blame ourselves if that rule has dwarfed our stature, emasculated our bodies, made us incapable of initiative, blocked our way to progress and national efficiency. If such were Miss Mayo's argument, we would admit its force. In fact, it is because this argument is so strong that we want to throw off the foreign yoke and be free to develop to our full stature as a nation.
>
> But Miss Mayo seems to argue in quite a different way. To her, political environment has nothing to do with national inefficiency and helplessness. Are initiative and enterprise in a nation wholly independent of its political environment? Are literacy, health, national efficiency in no way influenced by those who run the legislative and administrative machinery? Are these things dependent wholly on social custom, as Miss Mayo would have us believe? Are not, on the other hand, even social customs largely determined by the political conditions prevailing in a country and the literacy of her people?[12]

Du Bois himself had a searing critique of Mayo, which he published in *The Crisis*. He wrote, "Katherine Mayo, white American, declares that brown India is sexually immoral. Thus the pot calls the kettle black."[13] With more than just a vigorous rebuttal of Mayo needed, Rai encouraged Du Bois to use *Dark Princess* as a way to promote an image of India that transcended tropes of poverty and despair. Du Bois took the words to heart, as the final draft of *Dark Princess* handled issues like widowhood and caste, two of the topics of Mayo's attacks, with sensitivity. Du Bois also rebuked Mayo through his interactions between his protagonist (and imagined ideal) Matthew Townes and the princess Kautilya, whom Du Bois seemed to exoticize as the ideal "Other." Du Bois saw the book as a coming together of what he saw as the subjugated races, though he included the Japanese as protagonists in his plot.

We can in some ways interpret the premise of *Dark Princess* as how Du Bois idealized the world, especially when it came to Blacks' connections to other colonized/oppressed groups. As some Du Bois biographers note, it was partially the product of his Orientalist fantasy, woven together with his recollections of the First Universal Races Congress, where he met Indian freedom struggle leader Bhikaji Cama (whom many Du Bois biographers believe was the inspiration for Kautilya).[14] Cama, a Parsi woman who was lauded for her charisma and ferocity as an advocate for independence, likely mesmerized Du Bois during the conference. While the language Du Bois used could be described as orientalizing, paternalistic, and in some ways naive about the dynamics of non-European cultures, the book was empathetic to the struggles of colonized peoples in a way that made *Dark Princess* arguably unique in its perspective. Scholars like Rampersad take a much more nuanced view of the book, arguing that "Du Bois is well aware of the pariah status of black Americans and blacks in the eyes of the rest of the world, including India. . . . The novel interrogates both India and black America on the questions of class and caste"[15]

Rampersad, Mullen, and Levering Lewis have more complete summaries of the novel's plot, but the plotline is often secondary to Du Bois's intentions in the book. The book's hero, Matthew Townes, escapes Chicago—and imminent charges for working for a corrupt politician—and finds himself in an international gathering of the darker races. It is there he meets Kautilya, the daughter of an Indian maharaja, who seeks to bring a select group of thinkers together to fight white subjugation. Eventually, Townes falls in love with Kautilya, who teaches him about the glory of the darker races and the need to restore them to their rightful place in history. She even points to Matthew's own legacy as a son of the goddess Kali, the Hindu deity. Even as the novel's heroes face their own shaming (Matthew is sent to jail while Kautilya is stripped of her royalty), the redemption lies in their son becoming a crown prince of the darker nations. As she tells Matthew, "God lives forever—Brahma, Buddha, Mohammed, Christ—all His infinite incarnations. From God we came, to God we shall return. We are eternal because we are God."[16] Kautilya's exclamation mirrors the Advaita school of Hindu philosophy, premised on the idea that the soul and God are one, but it also reflects one of the central premises of Hinduism, exemplified in the Rig Veda verse: "The Truth is one; the wise call it by many names."[17] These theological reflections are overlooked in subsequent analyses of the novel, but provide a glimpse into Du Bois's more advanced understanding of Hindu philosophy than he was given credit for. Du Bois[18] also expresses his discomfort with Gandhi's approach as well, and the interactions between Matthew and Kautilya suggest his desire for a more confrontational approach to the problem of colonialism. Kautilya, for example, tells Matthew that "the strongest group among us believe only in force."[19]

While the novel received largely negative reviews, it was an important social and political commentary reflecting his worldview. As Mullen notes, "It marks a continuation and departure in the history of African American intellectual engagement with the discourse of orientalism, an engagement crucial for later generations of African American radicals and intellectuals."[20] Moreover, Du Bois engaged in the paradigm of shared struggle that would come to dominate Marxist and other left-leaning progressive movements in subsequent decades. As Rampersad writes, "Du Bois emphasizes a link between African blood and Indian blood."[21] Indeed, the novel reflected Du Bois's own perplexity over the disconnect between Indians and Blacks, and vice versa. "The Negroes taught in American schools and reading books and articles by American writers, have almost no conception of the history of India," he lamented. "On the other hand, the knowledge which educated Indians have of the American Negro is chiefly confined to the conventional story spread by most white American and English writers."[22]

Unfortunately, Rai would never see Du Bois to give him a personal critique of the final book. After being beaten severely by British authorities during a protest in October 1928, Rai died several weeks later. His death devastated Du Bois, who had found a kindred spirit in activism. In later years, he would lament the lack of knowledge many Indians had about the struggle of Blacks in the United States, noting that "unless they are as wise and catholic as my friend . . . Lajpat Rai, they are apt to see little and know less of the 12 million Negroes in the America."[23]

Dharma and Socialist Thought

Dark Princess, while a critical failure, would become one of the works Du Bois most fondly recollected in later years, and provided at least a template by which African American thinkers could engage with international issues. It also marked both the epitome of and his shift away from "Afro-Orientalist" perspective, which, as Mullen writes, "generally depended on an exotic essentializing of Afro-Asian vitality, usually associated with the feminine and an uncritical glorification of black antiquity."[24] What made the work prescient was that the Bandung Conference in 1955 touched on many of the same topics Du Bois imagined in the novel. But even as Du Bois became more skeptical of organized religion, and in later years would grow critical of India (particularly after Jawaharlal Nehru's violent putdown of a Marxist rebellion), *Dark Princess* reflected an indelible mark left by Rai. Indian anticolonialists, especially since many of the rank-and-file independence fighters were deeply religious, embraced to varying degrees Rai and Gandhi's belief in dharma as a guiding principle of the Indian state. The idea of a Hindu socialist state, which Rai favored, was consistent with other socialist movements across the world that did not eschew religion as a guiding force. Du Bois was arguably more sympathetic to Rai's position because he viewed all Indians as Hindus, a common belief held among his contemporaries at the time. As many scholars note, the term Hindoo or Hindu was a racialized term describing anyone of Indian origin, though Rai's influence on Du Bois made the latter somewhat more informed than his peers.

For at least the several years of correspondence between Rai and Du Bois, Du Bois did not view religion as necessarily an obstruction to the socialist project. Like Lasky, he was sympathetic to the idea that religion could be compatible with the state, and Rai likely impressed on him the importance of culture and religion not suppressed by the state or capitalism. This was not a common view among thinkers of the Left, and Du Bois likely struggled to negotiate with Rai's overtly political Hinduism with his own deep-seated concerns about the emancipatory potential of religion, even in fighting state oppression. However, Rai's death left Du Bois with few who would share that view, and he slowly drifted towards the Popular Front of the 1930s, thanks in part to his growing friendship with Paul Robeson. What made Du Bois's engagement with Hinduism through Rai and Gandhi more ironic was that Indian freedom leaders like Nehru and Krishna Menon, both friends of Robeson, embraced a staunchly secular socialism in later years. Even as practicing Hindus, Nehru and Menon believed that a free India could not exist with an official religion, or even have its core principles guided by it. Their views would eventually dominate the Indian nationalist movement, even as leaders like Gandhi and Sardar Patel (whom Du Bois distrusted because of Patel's sympathy for capitalism) pushed for a state guided by Hindu principles of dharma.

However, the efforts to partition India along religious lines, with a country for Muslims and one for Hindus, effectively ended the quest for a unified India guided by dharmic principles. It also ended any of Gandhi's hopes for an India guided by *ahimsa*, the dharmic concept of nonviolence. But the long-term consequences of India's failure to accommodate the spiritual underpinnings of its majority with its socialist state-building would be felt for decades to come, especially as communal tensions bubbled over into violence, highlighted by a Sikh separatist movement in Punjab, an Islamic insurgency in Muslim-majority Kashmir, and several communal riots that left thousands dead.

As scholars such as Doniger note, the absence of spirituality—namely Hinduism—in India's postindependence state-building would create an unnecessary chasm between a rational commitment and an emotional commitment to sustaining democracy. Nehru's rejection of Gandhi's paradigm, which was arguably more similar in practice to that for which Rai advocated, came at the expense of India's secularism, which was eroded as a result of a failure to connect with Indians' spiritual ties. She writes, "Emotion and religious or quasireligious commitment played a large part in Gandhi's movement, as in his thought about what Indian democracy should be. But mistrust of these forces on the part of India's subsequent leaders led to their neglect, and the Hindu Right quickly seized this opportunity, filling a cultural void with resonant appeals to nationalistic emotion and to exclusivist ideas of the polity"[25]

Conclusion: The Legacy of a Friendship

It might seem that the correspondence between Rai and Du Bois did not have a lasting impact, particularly in creating the template from which socialism could coexist with religion in the darker worlds. Additionally, Du Bois became disenchanted with India's role as a leading voice for the "darker races," particularly for African Americans. By the end of his life, he had come to view Mao's China as the model of a socialist ideal and had distance himself from Nehru's India.

But upon closer inspection, what Du Bois managed to do was engage with a paradigm that had been largely out of the view for many American civil rights leaders. His friendship with Rai, coupled with his own understandings of India and Hindu society, pushed him to support closer relations between two oppressed peoples, a preoccupation of Du Bois's latter decades. As Rampersad and Mullen note, Du Bois in many ways had become as passionate an advocate for India as he had for the rights of African Americans. While the postscript might seem that in Du Bois's eyes that India had failed him and African Americans, it likely understated the scope of influence India and its philosophies had on him. Perhaps that is why Du Bois felt so disenchanted. He had come to believe in the providence of an outcome similar to the one he envisioned in *Dark Princess*, and that leaders like Nehru would follow in the footsteps of Rai in their concern for African Americans. When that did not happen, or when life did not emulate the idealized fiction of Du Bois's dreams, his disillusionment was profound. Yet he paved the way for an African and African American appreciation for Hindu thought—in conjunction with a form of socialism—that never been previously possible. The Rev. Martin Luther King Jr. used Mahatma Gandhi's life—particularly his call for using the *Bhagavad Gita* as a life guide for righteous action—as a template for how he would make *ahimsa* the central part of the civil rights movement. King, who sympathized with socialism as a governing concept, viewed Gandhi in the same way as Du Bois viewed Rai: a man of faith who put righteousness above his own well-being. In South Africa years later, Nelson Mandela looked to Hindu philosophy as an inspiration to deal with his imprisonment at Robben Island.

While Du Bois might not have been able to appreciate the magnitude of his friendship with Rai and the connections it would inspire later, in some ways, *Dark Princess* would prove prophetic. As Kautilya tells Matthew, "In 1952, the Dark World goes free—whether in Peace and fostering Friendship with all men, or in Blood and Storm—it is for Them—the Pale Masters of today—to say."[26] Much of South Asia achieved its independence in the late 1940s, and most of Africa had achieved independence by the 1960s.

More than fifty years after Du Bois's death, Indian prime minister Narendra Modi, a staunch Hindu conservative who had risen to power on a message of right-wing populism, visited the Martin Luther King Jr. memorial in Washington, DC. He stood in silence with his friend, US president Barack Obama, who in many ways was the scion of the internationalism that Du Bois had lived for. While they represented opposite ideological perspectives, both men, knowingly or not, embodied the legacy of a friendship from nearly a century earlier. Modi and Obama, much like Rai and Du Bois, embraced a vision of the world that looked outward and sought cooperation among the formerly oppressed nations. And, as if a nod to the legacy of an Afro-Asian spiritual lineage, the *Black Panther* comic series—made into a worldwide smash hit film in 2018—makes frequent references to the Jobari tribe, which worships the Hindu deity Hanuman.[27] It was a fitting postscript to a novel that might have been too far ahead of its own time, but a case of life finally catching up to art.

NOTES

1. W. E. B. Du Bois, "Gandhi and India," *The Crisis* (March 1922): 203–7.

2. Bill V. Mullen, *Un-American: W. E. B. Du Bois and the Century of World Revolution* (Philadelphia: Temple University Press, 2015).

3. Bill V. Mullen, *W. E. B. Du Bois: Revolutionary Across the Color Line* (London: Pluto Press, 2016).

4. Gerald Horne, *The End of Empires: African Americans and India* (Philadelphia: Temple University Press, 2008).

5. W. E. B. Du Bois, *Darkwater: Voices from Within the Veil* (New York: Harcourt Brace, 1920), 49.

6. Norman G. Barrier, "The Arya Samaj and Congress Politics in the Punjab, 1894–1908," *The Journal of Asian Studies* 26, no. 3 (1967): 363–79.

7. Dhanpati Pandey, *The Arya Samaj and Indian Nationalism, 1875–1920* (New Delhi: S. Chand, 1972).

8. Murali Balaji, *The Professor and the Pupil: The Politics and Friendship of W. E. B. Du Bois and Paul Robeson* (New York: Nation Books, 2007).

9. Lala Lajpat Rai to W. E. B. Du Bois, October 6, 1927, W. E. B. Du Bois Papers, reel 22, frame 1261.

10. W. E. B. Du Bois to Lala Lajpat Rai, November 9, 1927, W. E. B. Du Bois Papers. Correspondence obtained with prior permission from David Graham Du Bois. File retrievable at, http://credo.library.umass.edu/view/pageturn/mums312-b040-i436/#page/1/mode/1up.

11. Katherine Mayo, *Mother India* (New York: Harcourt Brace, 1927), 32.

12. Lala Lajpat Rai, *Unhappy India* (Calcutta: Banna Publishing Company, 1928), 5.

13. W. E. B. Du Bois, "As the Crow Flies," *The Crisis* (November 1927): 293.

14. Bill V. Mullen, "W. E. B. Du Bois, *Dark Princess*, and the Afro-Asian International," in *Left of the Color Line: Race, Radicalism, and Twentieth-Century Literature of the United States*, eds. Bill V. Mullen and James Smethurst (Chapel Hill: University of North Carolina Press, 2003), 87–106.

15. Arnold Rampersad, "Du Bois's Passage to India," in *W. E. B. Du Bois on Race and Culture*, eds. Bernard W. Bell, Emily R. Grosholz, and James B. Stewart (New York: Routledge, 1996), 161.

16. W. E. B. Du Bois, *Dark Princess*, ed. with introduction by Claudia Tate (Jackson: University Press of Mississippi, 1995), 297.

17. *Rig Veda* Hymn 1.164.44.

18. Du Bois, *Dark Princess*, 297.

19. Du Bois, *Dark Princess*, 297.

20. Mullen V. Mullen, "Du Bois, Dark Princess, and the Afro-Asian International," *positions: east asia cultures critique* 11, no. 1 (2003): 219.

21. Rampersad, "Du Bois's Passage to India," 172.

22. W. E. B. Du Bois, "The Clash of Colour," *Aryan Path*, March 1936.

23. Du Bois, "The Clash of Colour."

24. Mullen, "WEB Du Bois, Dark Princess, and the Afro-Asian International."

25. Wendy Doniger, introduction to *Pluralism and Democracy in India: Debating the Hindu Right*, edited by Wendy Doniger and Martha Nussbaum (New York: Oxford University Press, 2015), 5.

26. Du Bois, *Dark Princess*, 297.

27. In both the comic and the film, Hanuman is depicted as a gorilla. In Hindu iconography, he is generally represented as a monkey with some human physical features.

CHAPTER 7

W. E. B. Du Bois and African American Humanism

—Christopher Cameron

On January 10, 1956, W. E. B. Du Bois wrote a letter to his good friend, fellow Marxist, and literary executor Herbert Aptheker that briefly explored his notions on the existence of "Absolute Truth" and his faith in human beings' ability to use science and reason to change the world. Du Bois noted that he gave up the search for absolute truth at a fairly young age because he did not think current research methods would provide a fruitful means to apprehend it, thus causing him to turn toward scientific hypothesis as a means of approximating truth as much as possible. When beginning his well-known sociological studies at Atlanta University in the early twentieth century, Du Bois "began to count and classify the facts concerning the American Negro and the way to his betterment through human action. I assumed that human beings could alter and re-direct the course of events so as to better human conditions." Du Bois recognized that the environment, inheritance, and natural law would always limit human agency, but he nevertheless retained his faith in humanity. He "did not rule out the possibility of some God also influencing and directing human action and natural law." Du Bois responded, however, that he "saw no evidence of such divine guidance. I did see evidence of the decisive action of human beings."[1]

In these few lines, W. E. B. Du Bois articulates some of the central themes of African American humanism, a system of thought that has recently gained many more adherents but that has been present in the United States since the mid-nineteenth century. While there is no hard-and-fast definition of African American humanism, there are a number of basic principles it includes. First, African American humanists believe that human beings are responsible for their own condition and for changing the world. This belief squares well with Du Bois's statement that he saw no evidence of God influencing human life but saw plenty of evidence that human beings had done so. Second is a claim that human beings have evolved over time from lower life forms and constitute an intrinsic part of the natural world. African American humanists also share an appreciation for Black culture, a responsibility to help better the world, and optimism that such change is possible. Many if not most African American humanists are nonbelievers, and such was the case with Du Bois, who had already become an agnostic by the time he started his position at Atlanta University in 1897.[2]

Despite Du Bois's many professions of disbelief and harsh criticism of Black and white Christianity for decades, many scholars have downplayed his religious skepticism. Manning Marable, for example, argued that Du Bois "was simultaneously an agnostic and Anglican, a staunch critic of religious dogma and a passionate convert to the black version of Christianity." This is despite the fact that Du Bois wrote in 1938 that the Black church "has built up a body of dogma and fairy tale, fantastic fables of sin and salvation, impossible creeds and impossible demands for ignorant unquestioning belief and obedience." These words hardly sound like those of a "passionate convert" to the old-time religion, but Marable nevertheless insisted that Du Bois's commitment to Blacks meant that he could never fully reject African American Christianity. Edward Blum refers to Du Bois as a prophet and one of the central African American spiritual figures of the twentieth century, someone who prefigured both liberation and womanist theology by decades. Du Bois's use of religious language, sociological studies of Black religion, knowledge of the Bible, and periodic involvement with religious institutions, according to Blum, clearly demonstrate a level of religiosity that other scholars have either ignored or dismissed.[3]

Many scholars have of course recognized and discussed Du Bois's religious skepticism, including David Levering Lewis, Phil Zuckerman, and Brian L. Johnson, but none place Du Bois's thought within the context of a broader African American humanist movement, nor do they explore at any length the connection between his religious skepticism and political radicalism. This essay attempts to broaden the scholarly understanding of Du Bois and religion by doing exactly those two things. I argue that becoming and being a humanist and a freethinker were central components of Du Bois's identity and ones that significantly influenced his political ideology and activity. Just as scholars often point to an individual's conversion to a particular religion as a critical moment in their lives and one that informs much if not most of their worldview, so too did Du Bois's "conversion" to secular humanism influence the course of his life in significant ways, especially his acceptance of Marxism later in his career. In embracing humanism, Du Bois became part of a growing movement of Black artists, intellectuals, and political activists, including figures such as Louise Thompson Patterson, Hubert Harrison, and Harry Haywood, that denied the existence of God, an afterlife, and other central teachings of American Christianity. By rejecting the supernatural, embracing human potential, and working to transform their world through science and reason, African American humanists such as Du Bois laid the foundations for one of the most significant streams of twentieth-century Black thought and culture.[4]

Du Bois's humanism represents another central component of his conception of freedom. Numerous essays in this volume discuss Du Bois's political thought, as does this chapter. But this piece also argues that Du Bois's embrace of communism was closely tied to his agnosticism. His critiques of both white and Black Christianity and his dogged nonbelief in God throughout his life represent another aspect of "freedom of soul" and "freedom of thought" that he believed were crucial to the Black freedom struggle. While Du Bois certainly demonstrated ambivalence toward Black Christianity and a nuanced perspective on religion in general, as Phillip Luke Sinitiere's essay points out, sometimes praising its potential and other times condemning religion's ties to racism, the main thrust of his personal writings on the topic situate him squarely in the ranks of twentieth-century Black freethinkers.

Becoming a Humanist

Before he enrolled in college, Du Bois adhered to the theological tenets of the First Congregational Church, the congregation he attended in Great Barrington, Massachusetts. David Levering Lewis notes that during his teenage years, his beliefs "were superficially orthodox and anchored in the rigorous Calvinism of New England Congregationalism." This Calvinism posited that humans were sinners by nature, sinners were doomed to spend eternity in hell, salvation came only through faith in Jesus, and the Bible should be interpreted literally. Had Du Bois grown up in the same town one hundred years earlier, he likely would have also believed in predestination, which held that humans could do nothing to influence their spiritual fate. Indeed, Du Bois did seemingly subscribe to a different aspect of predestination, namely that of the Elect, the small percentage of the world that God deemed worthy of salvation. On a practical level, church attendance represented an opportunity for Du Bois to practice and show off his Greek language skills and to demonstrate his facility with biblical interpretation during Sunday school. While he eventually abandoned his adherence to Calvinism, Lewis argues that it continued to influence Du Bois throughout his life, although it became secularized. Instead of salvation coming from faith in God, it would come from the social sciences. Damnation awaited all those who lived morally dissolute lives or wasted their talents, and the Elect transformed into the Talented Tenth for Du Bois, at least early in his career.[5]

In 1885, Du Bois began attending college at Fisk University and in short order threw off the religiosity of his youth to embrace secularism. This embrace started not because of revelations in science or philosophy courses, as would be the case with later Black freethinkers, but because of what he saw to be the religious hypocrisy of those around him. Du Bois joined the college church and even began teaching Sunday school. He soon gave up this latter endeavor, however, after a dispute with an older student named "Pop" Miller. Pop was an official in the school's Congregational Church and he had Du Bois and other students brought up on charges for dancing. These charges were astonishing to Du Bois, who had danced all his life, and represent the differences between northern and southern variants of Congregationalism. What made Du Bois even more incensed was that the teachers admitted to him that his dancing may be innocent but still disciplined him because of the negative example it might set. During the dispute, Du Bois notes, "the teachers intervened and tried to reconcile matters in a way which for years made me resentful and led to my eventual refusal to join a religious organization."[6]

Du Bois was also put off by the school's attempt to enforce Christian orthodoxy by making all students read George Frederick Wright's *The Logic of Christian Evidences*. Wright, an amateur geologist and historian, worked as a professor of New Testament language and literature at Oberlin Theological Seminary while Du Bois was a student at Fisk. Administrators there hoped that reading Wright's text would bolster religious orthodoxy among the students. For Du Bois, it had the opposite effect. He notes that *The Logic of Christian Evidences*, which presented standard ideas such as God's rulership of the world, Christ's love, and punishment for sinners, "affronted my logic" and "was to my mind, then and since, a cheap piece of special pleading." So just at the time when many young men and women were becoming strengthened in their faith, Du Bois began to move away from his. The situation with Pop Miller and being forced to imbibe Wright's ideas set Du Bois on "an intellectual journey that would end, after a very short time, in serene agnosticism," according to David Levering Lewis.[7]

Du Bois's path toward secular humanism continued after he left Fisk University. Within short order he threw off his faith in God and replaced it with a faith in humanity. As he noted in the foreword to Reverdy Ransom's *The Negro, the Hope or the Despair of Christianity*, "I have little faith that Christianity can settle the race problem, but I have abiding faith in men." This faith in men began to flower during the 1890s. Du Bois graduated from Harvard College in 1890 with a bachelor of arts in philosophy and then traveled to Germany in 1892 to work on his doctorate. It was in Germany, Du Bois states, that he "became a freethinker." So just what did freethought mean to him? It certainly wasn't participating in polemical wars with Christians as prominent freethinkers of the time such as Robert Ingersoll engaged in. Nor was it writing for freethought periodicals such as the *Truth Seeker*. Du Bois's freethought was somewhat public but not as open as many self-professed atheists and agnostics. In 1894, for example, Du Bois accepted a teaching position at the Methodist school Wilberforce University where he refused to lead students in prayer and refused to participate in religious revivals. He notes of his time there that "it took a great deal of explaining to the board of bishops why a professor at Wilberforce should not be able at all times and sundry to address God in extemporaneous prayer." He believed that the only thing that prevented him from getting fired was the fact that his hiring had been widely advertised and that he possessed an extraordinary work ethic, as he regularly taught five classes a semester while pursuing his research. Indeed, by the mid-1890s, Du Bois had come to believe that in his work ethic "lay whatever salvation I have achieved." His humanist perspective thus informed both his semipublic stances on religion as well as his private beliefs.[8]

Agnostic Pulpit

After a brief stint at the University of Pennsylvania and a fifteen-year stint teaching at Atlanta University, Du Bois moved to New York City to work for the NAACP and in short order launched *The Crisis*, a magazine that historian Brian Johnson refers to as Du Bois's "agnostic pulpit." *The Crisis* was to be a monthly periodical performing multiple functions: reporting on issues around the world relevant to African Americans, reviewing new and significant works of literature, publishing articles on race relations in the United States and globally, and advocating for civil and human rights for African Americans. The magazine was also an outgrowth of his early notion of the Talented Tenth, or his belief that a small cadre of Black intellectual elites bore the responsibility for improving the fortunes of the race. His idea of the Talented Tenth, which he largely abandoned after becoming a communist later in life, likely drew from his Calvinist background but was a secular philosophy that argued education, manners, morality, refinement, and culture were necessary for any leadership class. Du Bois felt that these qualities were lacking in Black leadership of the time, which consisted primarily of ministers. So, *The Crisis* would become his "agnostic pulpit" and his tool for "disseminating a newfangled version of reform for the African American community that would not be grounded in unknowable dogma but in knowable scientific study."[9]

Du Bois's evolving humanist perspective was on full display when, in 1912, he published a scathing indictment of the Black Church in *The Crisis*. He started his piece "The Negro Church" softly, noting that Black churches had instilled morals, strengthened family life, provided opportunity for community, and even contributed to success in business. The tone of the piece quickly became negative, however. He argued that Black religious leaders were by and large uneducated and immoral. "The paths and the higher places are choked with pretentious, ill-trained men," he posited. "And in far too many cases with men dishonest and otherwise immoral. Such men make the walk of upright and business-like candidates for power extremely difficult. They put an undue premium upon finesse and personal influence." Harkening back to his college days at Fisk University and his punishment for dancing, Du Bois also decried the fact that Black churches were "still inveighing against dancing and theatergoing, still blaming educated people for objecting to silly and empty sermons, boasting and noise." To top it off, in his view, was churches' practice of raising exorbitant sums of money for new church buildings while many Black people in the country remained homeless or in need of school buildings.[10]

Du Bois's denunciations of Black religious leaders might lead one to believe he saw no place for religion or religious institutions, but that was not the case. Rather than advocating for Black people simply to abandon their faith or their churches, Du Bois called for reform, demonstrating his complex engagement with Black religion that would characterize his life. He argued that Black churches needed to begin addressing their problems by electing honest and upright leaders and incorporating more positive educational and social uplift programs. He likewise urged Black religious institutions to stop trying to compel religious orthodoxy and to focus less on belief and more on behavior. For him, effective Black churches would be ones that bent "every effort to make the Negro church a place where colored men and women of education and energy can work for the best things regardless of their belief or disbelief in unimportant dogmas and ancient outwork creeds." The Black church, then, would be an institution open to including people like him who had no faith in God but did have faith in men and a desire to improve human life in this world.[11]

Du Bois's humanist perspective was informed by his views of the Black church as well as his views of American Christianity writ large. In his 1913 article "The Church and the Negro," Du Bois argued that from the founding of the nation, white Christian churches "aided and abetted the Negro slave trade" by justifying slavery on the grounds that it would bring the gospel to Africans. He likewise stated that "the church was the bulwark of American slavery; and the church today is the strongest seat of racial and color prejudice." His comments here are reminiscent of the nineteenth-century freethinker Frederick Douglass's critiques of white Christianity in the well-known speech "What to the Slave Is the Fourth of July?" There Douglass had similarly posited, "The church of this country is not only indifferent to the wrongs of the slave, it actually takes side with the oppressors. It has made itself the bulwark of American slavery, and the shield of American slavehunters." It is hard to believe that Du Bois had not read Douglass, and it appears that Du Bois adopted, nearly wholesale, Douglass's perspective on American Christianity. He ended the piece by noting that wherever Black people fought for civil and economic rights, "the church gaily tosses him stones for bread."[12]

Du Bois's animus for American Christianity seemed to grow stronger with each passing year and cemented his secular humanist perspective. In a 1929 essay for *The Crisis* entitled "The Color Line and the Church" he built on and extended many of the critiques from his 1913 article. Du Bois began by referencing the fact that one Reverend Blackshear of the Episcopalian Church in Brooklyn was in the process of kicking Blacks out of his congregation, a practice that Du Bois notes had been standard in the nation for 250 years. This situation led Du Bois to conclude that "the American Church of Christ is Jim Crowed from top to bottom. No other institution in America is built as thoroughly or more absolutely on the color line." The dilemma that American churches faced, in Du Bois's estimation, was whether they would be worldly institutions that reinforced economic disenfranchisement and racism, or whether they would live up to their claims to divine inspiration and try to undermine social injustices. For Du Bois, it was clear that the majority of American religious institutions were choosing the former. This was especially true of white churches. "When the church meets the Negro problem," Du Bois proclaimed, "it writes itself down as a deliberate hypocrite and systematic liar. It does not say 'Come unto me all ye that labor'; it does not 'love its neighbor as itself'; it does not welcome 'Jew and Gentile, barbarian, Scythian, bond and free'; and yet it openly and blatantly professes all this." Demonstrating his deep knowledge of scripture, despite his skepticism of its veracity, Du Bois decries the hypocrisy of white churches and the fact that "the church had opposed every great modern and social reform," including the labor movement, universal education, women's rights, the spread of democracy, and abolitionism.[13]

Along with his own critiques of religion, Du Bois opened up the pages of *The Crisis* to other humanists and freethinkers desirous of a venue in which to air their thoughts on Christianity. One contributor to the magazine was the skeptic Franz Boas, an anthropologist at Columbia University, who served as a mentor to another significant Black freethinker of the era, Zora Neale Hurston. Boas's colleague at Columbia University, John Dewey, likewise contributed to the magazine, an inclusion that was significant because he was widely recognized as a leading humanist during the 1920s and an individual who "completely discards all supernatural forces and entities and regards mind as an instrument of survival and adaptation developed in the long process of evolution," according to the humanist and philosopher Corliss Lamont. Another skeptic and anthropologist at Columbia University who wrote for *The Crisis* was Livingston Farrand, as did Clarence Darrow, the famous lawyer from the 1926 Scopes Trial that dealt with the teaching of evolution in schools. Darrow's presence in *The Crisis*, along with Du Bois's own public critiques of religion, served to scandalize many people in the Black community and led to angry letters written to the magazine.[14]

In more than twenty years editing *The Crisis*, Du Bois demonstrated his contempt for American Christianity and his growing commitment to secular humanism. The magazine became his outlet for what were at times incredibly harsh denunciations of both Black and white Christianity. Of the former, he argued that the church was too focused on enforcing right belief and restricting harmless behaviors such as dancing and theatergoing. And his views on the latter were that white churches were profoundly racist and unlikely to reform themselves any time soon. As an advocate of science, Du Bois believed in Darwinian evolution and invited skeptics who believed in it as well to write pieces for *The Crisis*. Lastly, the magazine became an outlet for a new generation of Black freethinkers to share their work, including writers and artists such as Langston Hughes and Zora Neale Hurston. Du Bois left his position as editor of the magazine in 1933 and his positions on religion and politics would become even more radical over the next few decades.[15]

Communism, Religion, and African American Humanism

Du Bois's humanism early in his career very likely had a direct influence on his acceptance of communism in the latter part of his life. This was partially because secularism and Marxism arose out of similar social and economic conditions, namely urbanization and industrialization during the nineteenth and twentieth centuries. The rise of cities and the onset of the Industrial Revolution significantly affected religious belief in a number of ways. For one, man-made structures now towered over nature and God's creation, diminishing their importance in the eyes of many. Also, with the growth of large cities such as New York and Chicago, "Bible stories, built from the metaphors and folkways of a pastoral and agrarian people, lost their immediate emotional resonance," according to James Turner. It is not the case that urbanization necessarily causes secularization. While urban life may push people toward religious skepticism, others might try and find community and kinship through participation in religious life, as was the case with thousands of migrants during the Great Migration. But for many people, including intellectuals such as Du Bois, urban life helped foster religious skepticism.[16]

Du Bois's first encounter with socialism came at the same time that he said he became a freethinker, namely while he was a student in Germany. While there he periodically attended meetings of the Socialist Democratic Party, although he was unable to actually engage in organizing activities because he was a foreign student. Back in the United States, Du Bois had actually joined the Socialist Party in the early 1910s but soon left it and became a Democrat, as he believed that Woodrow Wilson's Progressivism would best help African Americans achieve civil rights. For the next two decades, Du Bois would be ambivalent toward socialists and communists. He supported America's entry into World War I in 1917, for example, because he believed that it might inaugurate a socialist revolution that would undermine the twin influences of capitalism and racism in the world. But in a 1921 *Crisis* editorial, he rejected the Bolshevik Revolution because he thought change would best occur not through revolution but through reason, proper education, and human sympathy. Then he switched gears and supported the Socialist A. Phillip Randolph's organizing of Pullman Porters into the Brotherhood of Sleeping Car Porters union in 1925.[17]

At the end of the 1920s he expressed positive views of socialism, noting that he believed it to be "an attempt to rearrange work and industry, wages and income on a basis of reason, need and desert, rather than leaving it to chance and the rule of the strong." He likewise changed his tune on the Russian Revolution, claiming "if what I have seen with my eyes and heard with my ears in Russia is Bolshevik, I am a Bolshevik." When the communists emerged as the primary activists in the fight to save the Scottsboro Boys from the death penalty in the early 1930s, however, Du Bois was troubled and argued that the NAACP would be better suited to the task. His growing acceptance of Marxism as an ideology remained colored by the continual racism of the white working class and unions, as there were 2.5 million Blacks employed in nonagricultural work in 1928, yet only sixty-six thousand were allowed in white unions such as the American Federation of Labor. As he wrote in 1926, "if we could count on the cooperation of the white working classes nothing could stop the advance of both. We cannot count upon that. The mass of the white workers are our deliberate enemies."[18]

Multiple trips to Russia helped to quell the ambivalence Du Bois felt about communism and indicate his views on religion were intimately tied to his political radicalism. The first of these trips came in 1926, less than a decade after the Russian Revolution, and Du Bois left unimpressed, observing that the nation "was handicapped by 90 percent illiteracy among her peasants, and nearly as much among her working classes; by a religion led by a largely immoral priesthood, dealing in superstition and deception, and rich with the loot of groveling followers." He went back a decade later and his feelings shifted drastically. "This was no longer a people struggling for survival," he recalled. "It was a nation sure of itself. . . . The golden domes of churches were not so numerous and tall office buildings were taking their place. Few priests were visible, and few beggars." The juxtaposition of priests and beggars indicates that Du Bois had come to see religion not only as something that promoted racism and justified slavery in the United States but also as something that reified class distinctions around the world. In order for economic justice to prevail, the place of religion in a society must be scaled back. The Soviet Union was now prosperous in large part because it was no longer as religious, and this prosperity marked it as a useful model for what the United States could become should Americans accept Marxism.[19]

Du Bois was one of many Black humanists during this era whose worldviews were significantly expanded by traveling to the Soviet Union. Louise Thompson was one such freethinker. She had grown up primarily in small white towns out West such as Walla Walla, Washington, and Bend, Oregon. Experiencing racism at an early age turned her away from organized religion. She had few opportunities to attend Black churches and while in Bend she tried to attend a Sunday school class in a local white church "but they would not admit me into their 'house of God,'" she recalled with contempt. Thompson eventually graduated from the University of California in 1923. While enrolled there, she heard Du Bois give a talk and dedicated herself to working for the race. Within a few years she had moved to Harlem and Du Bois would become a lifelong mentor. She was first exposed to Marxism by her future husband William Patterson and had leftist leanings before her first pilgrimage to the Soviet Union in June 1932, after which she returned to the United States as a committed revolutionary. Historian Erik S. McDuffie posits that this trip to the Soviet Union helped both Thompson and other Black female communists "come to think critically about gender, race, and class in a global context." Thompson was pleasantly surprised by the greater freedom that women enjoyed in the country, including the right to get abortions and opportunities to do work that were only open to men in the United States. She likewise saw an acceptance of Black people to an extent that was unimaginable in America. Her travels in the early 1930s and throughout her life fostered a commitment to radical leftist politics that went hand in hand with her religious skepticism.[20]

The combination of religious skepticism and commitment to Marxism that both Du Bois and Thompson displayed was common among other Black socialists and communists dating back to the early 1910s. Hubert Harrison, a Caribbean migrant to Harlem in the early twentieth century, was among the first Black radical thinkers to embrace both freethought and Marxism. Just one year after his arrival in New York City, Harrison had abandoned orthodox and institutional Christianity, a process that came about after his reading of Thomas Paine, Voltaire, and Jean Jacques Rousseau. He replaced his belief in God with "a new belief—Agnosticism. I said belief: what I did mean was philosophy-of-life, point-of observation, attitude-towards things." Early on, Harrison notes, he was not a "dogmatic *dis*believer" along the lines of Robert Ingersoll. That is, he did not feel the need to proselytize his nonbelief or try to convince others to reject religion.[21]

By the early 1910s, this attitude had shifted, and Harrison began to participate in the broader freethought movement and attempt to bring other African Americans into the freethought fold. At a Thomas Paine commemoration dinner held in 1911, for example, Harrison posited "it is this dual aspect of Paine—militant unbelief and democratic dissent—that is most truly representative of him in the thought of our time." Harrison saw himself in the same vein, namely an advocate of socialism, which he would have viewed as akin to democratic dissent, and militant unbelief. Harrison also appreciated Paine's methods of spreading his secularism. "Paine popularized the arguments against Christianity," he claimed, "and brought them down to the level of the democracy, and this broadened and quickened the advance of freethought." Harrison believed that freethought and radical politics were intimately intertwined, and that African Americans especially should become advocates of both. "It should seem that Negroes, of all Americans would be found in the Freethought fold," he proclaimed in 1914, "since they have suffered more than any other class of Americans from the dubious blessings of Christianity."[22]

Like Du Bois, Harrison also argued that religion and global capitalism were together largely responsible for imperialism in Africa and among other darker peoples. "The Nineteenth Christian Century saw the international expansion of capitalism . . . and its establishment by force and fraud over the lands of the colored races," he claimed. Events in the United States could not be separated from those across the Atlantic. A riot in East St. Louis in 1917, which saw the destruction of 244 buildings and $373,000 in property damage, was a prime example. Harrison saw this event as "simply the climax of a long series of butcheries perpetrated on defenseless Negroes which has made the murder rate of Christian America higher than that of heathen Africa and of every other civilized land." Imperialist wars were the "natural and inevitable effect of the capitalist system, of what (for want of a worse name) we call 'Christendom.'" Capitalism and Christianity, then, represented twin systems of oppression that activists must combat simultaneously if they were to achieve their goals of elevating the working class and ending white supremacy.[23]

Du Bois's friends and comrades in the Communist Party, James and Esther Cooper Jackson, were similarly nonbelievers. James's father had opposed World War I because he thought it was another imperialist land grab by Western nations. His father was also an atheist "in the sense that he had a scientific view of things" rather than someone who simply did not go to church. The same was true of James's uncle, a railroad clerk whom he notes was an authority on both Thomas Paine and Robert Ingersoll. Esther Cooper Jackson's father was also an atheist, and she directly attributes his nonbelief to her political radicalism, noting that "I think it makes you revolutionary to have a father life that." James likewise believed that his irreligious upbringing was closely tied to his political views. In one interview, David Levering Lewis asked him "with this background, an atheistic uncle and father, and moving into the political circles you did really was not that big a departure perhaps?" James replied simply that it was not. By the age of sixteen, he had joined the Communist Party and organized the first Marxist Club while a student at Virginia Union University. He met Esther Cooper while they were both organizing Black workers for the Southern Negro Youth Congress in Birmingham, Alabama, and the two would go on to become some of the leading Black communists in the country during the following decades.[24]

Like Thompson, Harrison, and the Jacksons, W. E. B. Du Bois came to believe that religion and capitalism had been and were still intimately tied to colonialism, imperialism, and racism around the world. In a 1945 address delivered to the East and West Association, Du Bois argued that "the first impulsive recoil of religion and humanity from this horror of the slave trade to America was, in the face of the new wealth in crops, manufacture and commerce, quickly *rationalized* into a new defense of poverty. The rich were envisaged as the white nations of the earth, armed with a new and miraculous technique; the congenital poor were the peoples of the tropics born to be slaves and fulfill their destiny and the glory of God by working for the comfort and luxury of the whites." Christianity had historically been the primary justification for slavery and was also responsible for drawing racial lines in early America. "New patterns of contempt for human beings," he claimed, "were based on a doctrine of the inferiority of most men, which was announced as a scientific law and spread by the education of youth and the teachings of religion." These patterns prevalent in the colonial era were still present in the twentieth century and until all people had enough food and the basic necessities of life, true democracy would never be able to thrive. This would not happen with religious philanthropy or pity but rather when reasonable people came together to insist on four important truths: poverty can be alleviated; economies should be planned; good should be distributed according to reason and need, not birth and privilege; and education and healthcare should be free.[25]

Du Bois believed that the Soviet Union had come closest to achieving these goals, in large part because the nation had by and large discarded the religious beliefs and institutions that had caused so much trouble around the world. Education in the Soviet Union was a case in point, as he claimed, "the greatest gift of the Soviet Union to modern civilization was the dethronement of the clergy and the refusal to let religion be taught in the public schools." Once people began receiving an adequate education, Du Bois was sure they would discard their beliefs in miracles, the veracity of scripture, and a benevolent God who ruled the world. In fact, Du Bois strongly believed that one of the worst threats to modern societies were individuals who "allow their children to learn fairy tales and so-called religious truth, which in time the children come to recognize as conventional lies told by their parents and teachers for the children's good. One can hardly exaggerate the moral disaster of this custom." Instead of a religious education teaching children orthodox Christian creeds, Du Bois called for both the state and the church to foster "hearty research into real ethical questions." These included queries such as: "When is it right to lie? Do low wages mean stealing? Does the prosperity of a country depend upon the number of its millionaires?" These ideas that Du Bois articulated from the late 1930s to the 1950s represent both his growing disenchantment from Christianity and increasing identification as a communist. As David Levering Lewis observes, by the late 1930s "Du Bois's distaste for the vibrant evangelism of black religious observance was so palpable that he might well have invented the lag line about religion being the opiate of the people had not Marx supplied it." He still continued to identify as an agnostic, but it was an agnosticism with no significant differences from atheism.[26]

Following the Great Depression and the failure of the Double V campaign during World War II to bring about any significant improvement in Black life, Du Bois came to believe that socialism and communism offered the best opportunity for African Americans to improve their economic and political situations. When the Depression first hit "and thousands of workers, black and white, were starving in the 30's," he notes, "I began to awake and see in the socialism of the New Deal, emancipation for all workers, and the labor problem, which included the Negro problem." No longer was the problem of the twentieth century solely the problem of the color line, as he had proclaimed in *The Souls of Black Folk* in 1903. It was now also the problem of class and, as he argued in 1958, African Americans must recognize that "no system of reform offers such real emancipation as socialism. The capitalism which so long ruled Europe and North America was founded on Negro slavery in America, and that slavery will never completely disappear so long as private capitalism continues to survive."[27]

Du Bois knew there would be challenges in spreading socialism among the Black population from both established civil rights groups and from Black churches. After forced retirement from Atlanta University in 1944, Du Bois returned to the NAACP and hoped this might be an effective vehicle for advancing his political agenda but was disappointed. With some people charging the organization as being a communist front and the Cold War in its earliest stages, Walter White and Roy Wilkins exercised increased vigilance over the organization and would not let it be dragged into support of communism. In the late 1940s and early 1950s, Du Bois's opposition to the Marshall Plan, NATO, and the Korean War "as instruments of capitalist imperialism were heresies" that most contemporary Black leaders could not get behind. Moreover, Du Bois hoped that African Americans would be at the forefront of spreading worldwide socialism because of their greater educational opportunities but "'philanthropy,' disguised in bribes, and 'religion' cloaked in hypocrisy, strangled Negro education and stilled the voices of prophets. The yellow, brown, and black thinkers of Asia had forged ahead." As both Du Bois and his fellow African American humanist thinkers had stated many times before, religious dogma and religious institutions remained one of, if not the, primary obstacles in extending democracy to the economic realm.[28]

On October 3, 1948, at the age of eighty years old, Du Bois received a letter from E. Piña Moreno asking him if he believed in God. A little over a month later he replied "if by being 'a believer in God,' you mean a belief in a person of vast power who consciously rules the universe for the good of mankind, I answer No;

I cannot disprove the assumption, but I certainly see no proof to sustain such a belief, neither in History nor in my personal experience." While he did not believe in a personal God, he did leave room for "a vague Force which, in some uncomprehensible way, dominates all life and change." He likely had Mother Nature, Natural Law, or the universe in mind as this vague force, although he did not object to calling it God, he noted. Du Bois's mention of history as a primary reason for his nonbelief places him squarely within the tradition of African American humanism that dates back to Frederick Douglass. For Black humanists and freethinkers, the history of the slave trade and racism in America clearly demonstrated that there could not possibly be a just and benevolent deity who cared and loved for all people on Earth. It was either the case that God did not exist, that God was dead, or that perhaps God was a racist, "a pale, bloodless, heartless thing," as Du Bois speculated in "A Litany of Atlanta," penned shortly after the bloody race riot in that city.[29]

Since they believed they could not rely on assistance from the Almighty, African American humanists such as Du Bois took it upon themselves to work for the betterment of humanity in any way they could. Writers such as Zora Neale Hurston used their talents to display the beauty of Black culture and offer an implicit refutation of racist arguments prevalent throughout American culture. Langston Hughes used poems such as "Song for a Dark Girl" and "Litany" to critique police brutality and draw attention to the lack of economic opportunities and other social problems that Blacks faced on a daily basis. Louise Thompson Patterson became a leading Black female Marxist thinker during the 1920s and 1930s and helped to formulate the "triple oppression" paradigm that became a staple of Black feminism by the 1970s. W. E. B. Du Bois had a hand in nearly all these efforts, supporting the work of Harlem Renaissance writers, becoming an early and staunch advocate of feminism, and working tirelessly to spread socialism and communism during the 1930s to the end of his life. His efforts mark him not only as a pioneering radical political thinker but also as one of the most important African American humanists of the twentieth century.[30]

NOTES

1. "W. E. B. Du Bois to Herbert Aptheker," 10 January 1956 in Herbert Aptheker, ed. *The Correspondence of W. E. B. Du Bois Volume III: Selections, 1944–1963* (Amherst: University of Massachusetts Press, 1978), 395–96.

2. My definition of African American humanism comes from Anthony B. Pinn. See his *African American Humanist Principles: Living and Thinking Like the Children of Nimrod* (New York: Palgrave Macmillan, 2004), 7; also see Carol Wayne White, *Black Lives and Sacred Humanity: Toward an African American Religious Naturalism* (New York: Fordham University Press, 2016), 3–4.

3. Manning Marable, *Black Leadership* (New York: Columbia University Press, 1998), 60, 66; W. E. B. Du Bois, "The Revelation of Saint Orgne the Damned" in Philip S. Foner, ed. *W. E. B. Du Bois Speaks: Speeches and Addresses, 1920–1963* (New York: Pathfinder Press, 1960), 111; Edward J. Blum, *W. E. B. Du Bois: American Prophet* (Philadelphia: University of Pennsylvania Press, 2007), 7–12.

4. David Levering Lewis, *W. E. B. Du Bois: Biography of a Race, 1868–1919* (New York: Henry Holt and Company, 1993); Phil Zuckerman, ed. *Du Bois on Religion* (Walnut Creek, CA: AltaMira Press, 2000), 4, 8–9; Brian L. Johnson, *W. E. B. Du Bois: Toward Agnosticism, 1868–1934* (Lanham, MD: Rowman and Littlefield, 2008).

5. Lewis, *W. E. B. Du Bois: Biography of a Race*, 48–50.

6. Lewis, *W. E. B. Du Bois: Biography of a Race*, 65; W. E. B. Du Bois, *The Autobiography of W. E. B. Du Bois: A Soliloquy on Viewing My Life from the Last Decade of Its First Century* (New York: International Publishers, 1968), 111.

7. W. E. B. Du Bois, *The Autobiography of W. E. B. Du Bois*, 127; George Frederick Wright, *The Logic of Christian Evidences* (Andover, MA: Warren F. Draper, 1883); Lewis, *W. E. B. Du Bois: Biography of a Race*, 65.

8. Meyer Weinberg, ed. *The World of W. E. B. Du Bois: A Quotation Sourcebook* (Westport, CT and London: Greenwood Press, 1992), 167; *The Autobiography of W. E. B. Du Bois*, 285, 186–87, 183; Lewis, *W. E. B. Du Bois: Biography of a Race*, 66.

9. Lewis, *W. E. B. Du Bois: Biography of a Race*, 409–10; Johnson, *W. E. B. Du Bois: Toward Agnosticism*, 66, 84.

10. W. E. B. Du Bois, "The Negro Church," *The Crisis: A Record of the Darker Races* 4, no. 1 (May 1912): 24.

11. W. E. B. Du Bois, "The Negro Church," 25.

12. W. E. B. Du Bois, "The Church and the Negro," in Zuckerman, ed. *Du Bois on Religion*, 99, 100; Frederick Douglass, "What to the Slave Is the Fourth of July," in David W. Blight, ed. *Narrative of the Life of Frederick Douglass, An American Slave: Written by Himself, with Related Documents*, 2nd ed. (Boston and New York: Bedford/St. Martin's, 2003), 164.

13. W. E. B. Du Bois, "The Color Line and the Church," in Zuckerman, ed. *Du Bois on Religion*, 169, 170.

14. Johnson, *W. E. B. Du Bois: Toward Agnosticism*, 111; Corliss Lamont, *The Philosophy of Humanism* (1949; New York: Continuum, 1990), 36, 37.

15. For Hurston's freethought see Christopher Cameron, "Zora Neale Hurston, Freethought, and African American Religion" *Journal of Africana Religions* 4, no. 2 (2016): 236–44.

16. James Turner, *Without God, Without Creed: The Origins of Unbelief in America* (Baltimore and London: The Johns Hopkins University Press, 1985), 119.

17. Lewis, *W. E. B. Du Bois: Biography of a Race*, 143–44, 525–26; David Levering Lewis, *W. E. B. Du Bois: The Fight for Equality and the American Century, 1919–1963* (New York: Henry Holt and Company, 2000), 195–96.

18. Weinberg, ed. *The World of W. E. B. Du Bois*, 158, 92; Lewis, *W. E. B. Du Bois: The Fight for Equality and the American Century*, 262, 250–51.

19. *The Autobiography of W. E. B. Du Bois*, 30, 31–32.

20. Louise Thompson Patterson, Memoirs, Chapter 1, draft b "Childhood/West," 23–25, Folder 16, Box 19, Louise Thompson Patterson Papers, Manuscripts, Archives, and Rare Book Library, Emory University, Atlanta, Georgia; Erik S. McDuffie, *Sojourning for Freedom: Black Women, American Communism, and the Making of Black Left Feminism* (Durham and London: Duke University Press, 2011), 63.

21. Hubert Harrison to Frances Reynolds Keyser, 20 May 1908 in Jeffrey B. Perry, ed. *A Hubert Harrison Reader* (Middletown, CT: Wesleyan University Press, 2001), 37–38.

22. Hubert Harrison, "Paine's Place in the Deistical Movement" *Truth Seeker* 38, no. 6 (11 February 1911): 87; Hubert Harrison, "The Negro a Conservative: Christianity Still Enslaves the Minds of Those Whose Bodies It Has Long Held Bound" *Truth Seeker* 41 (12 September 1914): 583.

23. Hubert Harrison, "The White War and the Colored Races" in Perry, ed. *A Hubert Harrison Reader*, 204, 206.

24. "Tapes #14 and #15, Interview with Esther and James Jackson," David Levering Lewis Papers, University of Massachusetts Amherst; Robin D. G. Kelley, "The Jacksons" in David Levering Lewis et al., eds. *Red Activists and Black Freedom: James and Esther Jackson and the Long Civil Rights Revolution* (London and New York: Routledge, 2010), 5–9.

25. W. E. B. Du Bois, "Human Rights for All Minorities," in Foner, ed. *W. E. B. Du Bois Speaks*, 181.

26. *The Autobiography of W. E. B. Du Bois*, 285, 43; Du Bois, "The Revelation of Saint Orgne the Damned," 111; Lewis, *W. E. B. Du Bois: The Fight for Equality and the American Century*, 306, 307.

27. *The Autobiography of W. E. B. Du Bois*, 305; W. E. B. Du Bois, "The Negro and Socialism," in Foner, ed. *W. E. B. Du Bois Speaks*, 307.

28. Lewis, *W. E. B. Du Bois: The Fight for Equality and the American Century*, 496–98, 526, 555; Du Bois, "The Negro and Socialism," 309, 299.

29. "W. E. B. Du Bois to E. Piña Moreno," 15 November 1948 in Aptheker, ed. *The Correspondence of W. E. B. Du Bois Volume III*, 223; W. E. B. Du Bois, "A Litany of Atlanta," in Henry Louis Gates Jr. and Nellie Y. McKay, eds. *The Norton Anthology of African American Literature* (New York and London: W. W. Norton and Company), 611.

30. For more on the ties between socialism, communism, and freethought among African Americans, see Christopher Cameron, *Black Freethinkers: A History of African American Secularism* (Evanston, IL: Northwestern University Press, 2019), Ch. 3.

CHAPTER 8

Blessed Are the Peacemakers, for They Shall Be Called Communists: W. E. B. Du Bois and American Religious Culture, 1935–1963

–Phillip Luke Sinitiere

> The Bible was as much a guide to class struggles as Marx and Engles' *Communist Manifesto*; rank-and-file black Communists and supporters usually saw nothing contradictory in combining religion and politics.
> —Robin D. G. Kelley

The year 1951 turned out to be a critical moment for eighty-three-year-old W. E. B. Du Bois. It was a time of great difficulty and enormous stress; it was also a year during which he more resolutely expressed convictions about peace and democracy. As Du Bois was a target of anti-Black, anticommunist Cold War surveillance, the FBI devoted substantial attention to his writings and tracked his movements. In February, the US government indicted Du Bois and several colleagues associated with the Peace Information Center for failing to register as foreign agents, presumably agents who did Moscow's bidding. Arraigned in Washington, DC, officials fingerprinted and handcuffed him. Although he eventually posted bail, Du Bois described this experience as "brusque and unsympathetic. We were not treated as innocent people whose guilt was to be inquired into, but distinctly as criminals whose innocence was to be proven, which was assumed to be doubtful." The trial was set for November. Du Bois awaited these proceedings by commencing extensive fundraising speaking tours. He received support from community groups, labor unions, and fellow activists, even as former friends wilted amidst the heat of anticommunist hysteria. The NAACP also failed to side with its founder. In the end, Judge Matthew McGuire acquitted Du Bois and his comrades. In his written account of the trial, a 1952 book titled *In Battle for Peace: The Story of My 83rd Birthday*, an example of counter propaganda in response to prevailing political trends that demonized leftist radicals, Du Bois rang a note of profound gratitude: "Without the help of trade unionists, white and black, without the Progressives and radicals, without Socialists and Communists and lovers of peace all over the world, my voice would now be forever stilled." Echoing a line from Jesus Christ's Sermon on the Mount and narrating his persecution using religious rhetoric, Du Bois wrote, "Blessed are the Peacemakers for they shall be called Communists."[1]

Du Bois's provocative reinscription of the Sermon on the Mount at a signal moment in his life and career—and in the midst of severe anticommunist persecution—opens a pathway to examine what I call the prophetic propaganda during his final three decades. This phrase centers Du Bois's dynamic notion of propaganda while it pursues greater clarity on his materialist, dialectical analysis of American religion and culture. His materialist concerns about American religion focused on the social impact and economic consequences of religious ideas and teachings; in other words, whether it concerned Protestantism or Roman Catholicism, Du Bois believed that deeds should align with one's stated belief in religious creeds. As a result, his dialectical analysis of American religion analyzed how religious ideas and practices simultaneously spawned oppression and instigated liberation.

In this chapter "prophetic" refers to Du Bois's opposition to white supremacy; his Africana outlook on society, politics, and culture; and how he expressed the notion of ultimate justice in the moral and ethical idioms of the Christian tradition. When Du Bois addressed religion, he primarily focused on Protestantism, while at times his work engaged Roman Catholicism. Propaganda denotes Du Bois's capacious conception of how translating social scientific research into popular artistic, aesthetic reflections might contribute to white supremacy's defeat while simultaneously promoting Black self-determination. This chapter burrows deep into Du Bois's archives to explore the ways that he artfully highlighted religion's political impact through spiritual parables he wrote for Black newspapers. It examines how his extensive correspondence during the New Deal and early Cold War periods documents an abiding attention to spiritualized anticommunism that used religion to silence dissent and subvert freedom. Finally, this chapter records Du Bois's solidarity with individuals I call "socialist saints," fellow leftists and radicals who, like Du Bois, endured anticommunist repression.

This essay is not an exploration of Du Bois's personal religious convictions. Nor does it advocate a particular position with respect to his religiosity or lack thereof, a compelling interpretation that Christopher Cameron's chapter in this volume presents. It is a study that uses his literary writings, correspondence, and speeches as sites of analysis to explore how he understood the interrelationship of religion and culture in the United States from the 1930s to the early 1960s. It is an essay that discloses ways that Du Bois, through thoughtful considerations of religion and culture, conceptualized and practiced freedom at a critical stage of his late-career life.

As an inquiry into Du Bois and American religious culture, this chapter engages several historiographical conversations that strand together the insights of American religious history and African American studies. First, it expands the historical assessment of Du Bois, Black culture, and religion beyond the early twentieth century by focusing on his latter decades. Works by scholars such as Edward Blum, Jonathon Kahn, Brian Johnson, and Gary Dorrien, among others, track the intellectual and cultural history of Du Bois's religious thought in modernity during his early career as a professor, author, and activist with the NAACP.[2] Second, this chapter's dialectical evaluation of Du Bois's understanding of religion and culture relates to recent work on class and American religion. In concert with studies that examine the working class's radical, leftist, and socialist Christianity by scholars like Jarod Roll, Alison Collis Greene, Heath W. Carter, Janine Giordano Drake, and Elizabeth and Ken Fones-Wolf, it shows that Du Bois's Marxism did not include an ideological, defiant rejection of religion.[3] Instead, this study contends that his materialist perspective produced creative, idiosyncratic, and nuanced evaluations of religion and culture. Third, this chapter draws on scholarship of the Cold War's cultural and religious history, what Andrew Preston calls "the religious Cold War."[4] The dialectical analysis of spiritualized anticommunism coupled with the religious thought of socialists and communists that this chapter features fleshes out Jonathan P. Herzog's notion of America's "spiritual-industrial complex."[5] Similarly, this chapter's centering of cultural history tracks with Paul Boyer's emphasis on a "counter-discourse" of religion and politics during the Cold War that held space for those like Du Bois whose religious ideas did not equate to conservative Christian anticommunist convictions.[6] By speaking collectively to specific historiogaphies, this chapter offers fresh perspectives that reconfigure the intellectual history of Du Bois's cultural and social analysis of religion across several key junctures of his twentieth-century life.

Prophetic Propaganda: Midcentury Spiritual Parables

Du Bois's most famous comments about propaganda date to 1926, when in *The Crisis* magazine he published an essay titled "The Criteria of Negro Art." For Black artists, he wrote that creative endeavors must work as a form of propaganda that performs political resistance through aesthetic presentations of truth, beauty, and goodness. Cognizant of the long history of white supremacy's anti-Black aesthetics, Du Bois's efforts of protest and propaganda shifted over time throughout his career depending on social and political conditions. While he generally viewed propaganda as less scientific than scholarship, his conception of propaganda always considered the political stakes of translating scholastic social science and history into creative expressions accessible to a wider public. Recognizing the assumed meanings of propaganda assigned to it by whichever group possessed political clout or social capital, Du Bois defended as a political strategy the idea of assembling scientific facts and analytical argument with creative endeavor and artful expression.[7]

Du Bois featured his prophetic propaganda in *The Crisis*. Between 1910 and 1934, when he was the magazine's editor, he published over a dozen fictional stories of a Black Christ who visited America in the early twentieth century. Du Bois set these parables in the urban North and the rural South; in some stories, the Christ figure was a labor radical who inspired insurgency through teachings on economic equality. In other accounts, a mob captured the subversive savior and lynched the radical Christ. Readers and subscribers to *The Crisis* took notice. In response to these stories, typically published in either April or December to coincide with Easter and Christmas, during the 1920s and early 1930s Du Bois received letters that speculated about his religious beliefs. Some lauded his depiction of Jesus as a communist, laborer, and social radical. Others scoffed at his apparent atheism, since the miracles of Du Bois's Black Christ involved economic justice and political liberation instead of divine healing or turning water into wine.[8]

Although Du Bois left the NAACP and the editorship of *The Crisis* in 1934, congruent with his early career he continued to use prophetic propaganda by composing spiritual short stories for *Amsterdam News* and the *Pittsburgh Courier*. During his stint with the *Pittsburgh Courier* between 1936 and 1938, Du Bois mixed his "Forum of Fact and Opinion" columns with political analysis, historical reflection, and creative expression. In December 1937, he retooled Jesus's teaching on the talents in "A Christmas Parable: The Gospel According to Saint Matthew XXV: 14, 15." Du Bois told the story of three characters, one of whom was white, the other Chinese, the other Black. The white character in the story who received the five talents "had undoubtedly a splendid start in the world; he was white." A man from China possessed two talents; resourceful and hardworking, he was healthy, stable, and content. The Black character in the story had one talent, "was not a bit thankful," and squandered it by frequenting "pool rooms and drink[ing] bad liquor and gambl[ing] when he had anything to gamble with and ran with whores. He fell fatally ill in his twenties, almost before he had lived." In the midst of economic calamity, Du Bois composed this Depression-era parable as a commentary on race, class, and privilege. While the impoverished Black character in the story did not reflect Du Bois's own bourgeoisie experiences, his parable spotlighted the stark racial and economic disparities in New Deal America.[9]

In December 1940, the second year of a five-year relationship with *Amsterdam News*, in his "As the Crow Flies" column Du Bois offered a Christmas tale titled "A Revision of the Gospel According to Saint Luke." The story began with the famous edict from Caesar to take a census, except in 1940 Du Bois wrote that "a decree from Washington" went out declaring "that everybody should be taxed." Traveling north from Richmond, Virginia, Joseph and Mary Johnson, "being great with child," headed north to New York City to pay their taxes. While there Mary gave birth, wrapped the child in swaddling clothes, but "laid him in an alley because they did not rent rooms to colored people in the hotel." Rather than keeping watch over sheep in the fields, the shepherds collected taxes. While in the alley, an angel appeared to Joseph, Mary, and the child. The angel attempted to calm their fears and had a major announcement: "Fear not! For behold I bring you good tidings of great joy. For unto you is born this day in the city of New York a Saviour which is Christ the Lord." And with a multitude of heavenly host the angel continued, "Glory to God in the highest and on earth peace, good-will to men!" Hearing the divine announcement, the shepherds asked, "Is he a Jew?" The angel queried, "Do you mean [good will] to all white men?" Upon finding the holy family huddled in the alley, the shepherds then shouted, "My God! He's black, let's get out of here!" Revising the familiar Christmas account of Christ's birth to emphasize the contemporary economic and political situation, Du Bois also pointed out that Jim Crow infected institutionalized religion—white folks absolutely shuttered at the Black Christ.[10]

Du Bois continued these religious reflections in another *Amsterdam News* column in January 1942. In "The Missionaries" Du Bois told the tale of three African Episcopal missionaries who traveled to New York in order to preach the gospel to the United States. They were also on official business to the US: the Archbishop of Canterbury sent a letter they were to deliver to the local rector at St. Bartholomew Church in Harlem. The round, white rector read the letter and said, "If I get the implication of His Grace's letter, you are here to convert . . . America to Christianity? . . . do you not consider us Christians already?" The missionary sheepishly skirted around a direct answer. "You see we are humble followers of the Great Missionary, who came to us in Africa from America, years ago," the missionary said. "We want simply to preach Christianity to poor, dear America, for no reward—just to convert them."[11]

Pressing further, the rector now swelled with a sense of white privilege anchored in religious authority: "And why do you and the Archbishop of Canterbury think us heathen?" the rector raged. The lead missionary then asked his colaborer Brother Iguenye to preach. Referencing Christ's Sermon on the Mount, the missionary said,

> Blessed are the meek; for they shall inherit the earth . . . Blessed are the peacemakers: for they shall be called the children of God . . . Ye have heard it hath been said, An eye for an eye and a tooth for a tooth . . . but whosoever shall smite thee on thy right check, turn to him the other also.[12]

Hearing this, the rector turned red, and exclaimed "We are at war[!]" making reference to the United States' December 1941 entry into World War II. Not flinching at all, the missionary proclaimed, "War is terrible, is it not? And I am afraid it is unchristian, Christ said!" Adding fuel to the raging fires of white supremacy, Brother Iguenye continued his sermon: "Ye have heard that is has been said, Thou shalt love thy neighbor and hate thine enemy. But I say unto you, Love your enemies, bless them that curse you, do good to them that hate you, and pray for them which despitefully use you, and persecute you." Livid, the rector stood up and attempted to silence the missionaries, reminding the visitors that there were American laws against sedition. The missionary replied that he was aware of such statues, saying, "They crucified Christ" for such offenses. Du Bois ended the story with the rector demanding the missionaries' exit. To this, the missionaries responded in a posture of prayer: "Our Father, which art in Heaven, Hallowed be Thy Name—Thy Kingdom come."[13]

Du Bois's use of religion as political commentary reflected his keen analysis about Christianity, colonialism, and decolonization even as it proclaimed his solidarity with Japan and commitment to pacifism. The themes in this story not only gestured to Du Bois's internationalism, but also anticipated his continued framing of national social and political concerns in global perspective.[14]

Finally, in an unpublished story, "The Reverend Mr. Bond's Assistant," Du Bois designed a narrative about a wealthy, white suburban church in New York that tackled race, class conflict, gender, and the social gospel. In the parable a diminutive Reverend Bond clashes constantly with a domineering female church member named Mrs. Durant. She incessantly complained to the pastor about church visitors who don't "fit into our church people at all," and openly expressed her disdain for African Americans. The composite of a tragic wealthy, liberal white Christian in a bourgeoisie congregation, Mrs. Durant willingly doled out charity to the less fortunate but insisted on maintaining racial and economic dominance. "Nobody approves more than I do of helping the deserving poor," Durant remarked to Reverend Bond, "but in these days none of them seem to know their place anymore." She feared that "they're all socialists, every one of them, just given over to upsetting things."[15]

Wearied from the demands of church work, Reverend Bond took a two-week vacation. At a summer camp in the Adirondacks, he witnessed men drinking beer and women puffing on cigarettes. To the pastor's surprise he found them "honest, virile, and earnest, and they talked of mighty things: new tenements on the East Side, the proposed factory inspection, children's work, sweat shops, Negro peons, Mexican slaves, Russian revolutionists." Although Reverend Bond "winced at their religion," he "loved their devotion" since they accepted the pastor "at face value—asked few questions, let him alone and never neglected him."[16]

Reverend Bond's respite, however, wasn't a vacation after all. Mrs. Durant pestered him while he was away and sent him a letter saying that all hell had broken loose at First Presbyterian Church. "I am sure you will feel it your duty to come home immediately when I tell you that your strange assistant [pastor] is acting in an incomprehensible manner," her letter began, "Literally, we are upside down and I think the climax was reached today when a Negro was taken into church and an Italian baby from the West Side baptized." Such actions by an "unwashed mob," Mrs. Durant continued, "desecrated" the church, ruined the carpets and pews, and caused the "respectable people" to leave. Hearing the Reverend Bond's assistant preach, Mrs. Durant stated, "His talk sounds to me anarchistic" and "I saw him stop in the public street to talk with a woman of no character and when I ventured to point out the impropriety of this in a clergyman, he said things to me which I will not repeat." She pleaded with Pastor Bond to "return at once and let us get rid of this person before our church is ruined." The radical assistant was holding "popish vespers and the whole town is cramming itself into the church—into <u>our</u> church, Mr. Bond, think of it: shop girls, clerks, dirty section hands, servants—a perfect mob of ill-smelling people."[17]

Upon his return, Reverend Bond met with his assistant minister, a "tall dark figure with sallow gleaming face." "You had a large meeting today," Bond commented, "What was your text?" The Black assistant pastor replied, "Come unto me all ye that labor and are heavy laden and I will give you rest." This unsettled Bond, as he intended to preach on this text many times. He never did, he told his assistant, because such a message would "drive away the best people in the church." "I came to call sinners to repentance," the assistant stated, "I am the Way; And the Truth; And the Life. He that believeth in me, though he were dead, yet shall he live again! And he that liveth and believeth in me shall never die."[18]

Similar to many of Du Bois's *Crisis* short stories and his columns in *Pittsburgh Courier* and *Amsterdam News*, this unpublished tale depicted white liberals as racist, reactionary, and utterly unwilling to embrace a message of equality and justice for all people. More interested in preserving class status and social capital, white religious liberals distributed charity with a colonizer's mindset. On the other hand, the Christ figure in the story, a clergyperson of color, bolstered his religious creed by his deeds of liberating the poor, oppressed, and marginalized. The Black Christ mingled with the proletariat, welcomed Black folks into the church, and even baptized immigrants. Du Bois expressed his criticism of institutional religion by depicting a Christ figure whose religious message was so politically radical that it resulted in expulsion from the church.

Considered collectively, the midcentury parables Du Bois composed expressed prophetic propaganda because they explicitly contested dominant images of an Anglo Jesus purveyed across America's cultural landscape at the time, such as the ubiquitous *Head of Christ* (1941) by Warner Salman. They opposed white supremacy through ethical idioms of the Christian tradition, often in aesthetic alignment with other Black artists such as William Henry Johnson's depictions of a Black Jesus in *Mount Calvary* (1939), *Jesus and the Three Marys* (1939), *Come Unto Me Little Children* (1943), and *Lamentation* (1944). The political parables on African missionaries preaching Christianity to the United States registered a provocative pan-African view that assaulted a smug religious American nationalism amplified during wartime. Finally, each parable revealed how Du Bois's dialectical understanding of American religion in the New Deal era showed the ruling class deploy religious teachings to uphold its privilege while workers and radicals found from Christian teachings tools for economic democracy and political emancipation.

Faith and Letters: W. E. B. Du Bois's Correspondence

Not unlike the early decades of his career, readers and observers of Du Bois's work in his later years responded vigorously to the voluminous amount of political reflection that employed religious phrases, concepts, and terminology. Numerous laypeople and religious professionals, both Protestant and Catholic, exchanged letters with Du Bois throughout the 1930s, 1940s, and 1950s. Letters solicited Du Bois's advice on religious publications, while others sought his counsel on religion and race relations. Priests criticized Du Bois's opinions about the Roman Catholic Church, and one clergy member asked directly about his opinion on Jesus Christ.

Writing from Tennessee in 1932, a religious teacher named J. S. Dailey sent Du Bois a letter informing him about an essay competition held for high school students at Shiloh Presbyterian Church. Dailey sent Du Bois her student's prize-winning paper, three pages of biographical facts and details about the Black intellectual. The student, a young scholar named Cleveland Tate, compared the material impact of Du Bois's life to the political nature of Jesus Christ's teachings. "DuBois is hated by the white race because he has the courage to stand up at any time on any occasion that opportunity presents and portray the white man's injustice to the black," Tate wrote. "He exposes it in such a way that it eats to his very soul making him angry and miserable, showing him his bad points, letting him know that though he claims the Christian religion his policies are the exact opposite of the teachings of the Master. Mr. Du Bois stirs the heart of the white man as did Jesus Christ the hearts of the Scribes and Pharisees." This letter reveals that Du Bois's work figured into church educational curriculum and voices the impact of his scholarship in the language of the Christian tradition.[19]

In August 1939, a white Presbyterian minister from West Virginia wrote to Du Bois about southern churches and African Americans, querying his "opinion regarding the effect of the Negro Race of the Failure of White Southern Christians to measure up to Christian standard of dealing with the Negro; and what we can do now to meet our responsibilities." Du Bois replied four days later.

Before recommending the works of African American Presbyterian ministers Matthew Anderson and Francis Grimke, he commented extensively about the failings of white supremacist Christianity and moralized about actions that contradicted faith claims. Du Bois indicted white Presbyterian Christians with holding a "double standard of truth" where professions of faith undercut "actual conduct." Highlighting political dimensions of religious faith, he commented to Crowe, "the fundamental fact [is] that your church is an expression of economic organization, a group for social purposes with members composed of persons for the most part who receive an income above the average and whose primary solicitude is to protect that interest." In plain language Du Bois's materialist analysis of a congregation's, or denomination's, resources pinpointed where a religious institution's class privilege mattered more than putting into practice the moral or religious claims of human equality. He continued: "Whatever ethical action does not interfere with that income is permissible and encouraged and often exceedingly well done. On the other hand, any action or program that threatens income has little chance for recognition and none for adoption." While Du Bois answered Crowe's question for materials on religion, his reply underscored an emphatic understanding of religious bodies not just as spiritual communities, but also as economic institutions and political organizations.[20]

Shortly after Atlanta University retired Du Bois in 1944 as a professor of sociology, he received a letter from John R. Timpany, SSJ, a white Catholic priest from Tyler, Texas. He praised Du Bois's chapter in Rayford Logan's *What the Negro Wants* (1944) and commented specifically about his references to the church as a social uplift organization. In addition to his writing, the Josephite priest had the state of Du Bois's soul in mind. "I write this letter to urge you not only to consider the Catholic Church but to urge you to join her. Maybe I am wrong and you are already Catholic but nevertheless I seem to see in your writing that you expect a great deal from the church." Timpany offered an honest assessment of the church's attitude toward African Americans, writing that, "The Catholic Church in the United States has not given the Negro all that she can and should do." Acknowledging the difficulties of Du Bois's activism and expressing some knowledge of his work, Timpany believed that the Catholic Church would "be able to give you greater strength and courage to carry on your life work. She will help you when men fail you." Timpany concluded his letter with positive comments about the decrease of race prejudice, again claiming the Catholic Church had much to offer Du Bois.[21]

Du Bois responded to Timpany's letter, remarking that he had "great sympathy with the Catholic Church and know something of its history" especially since his granddaughter at the time attended a private Catholic elementary school in Baltimore. Nevertheless, he registered critical comments about the church for its posture towards race. Du Bois contended that "the human friendship and intellectual fellowship" of the Roman Catholic Church fell far below his standard. "There are separate white and Negro congregations in the South," he pointed out. "The Catholics refuse to receive colored students in a large number of their schools and their training of Negro Catholic priests in America has been ridiculously below the demand." For Du Bois deeds validated creeds as the test of faith. Commenting about personal belief, Du Bois patently refused "as a scientist" to adhere "to any creed which demands that I accept on faith the elaborate doctrine and dogma of the Catholic Church" since "I am perfectly aware that there are some things in this world we must accept on faith so long as we rigorously test them by the data of experience. Beyond that I cannot go."[22] Not only is Timpany's evangelistic appeal in this exchange quite remarkable, but it is also equally interesting to observe in the midst of Du Bois's later career that a priest held out that possibility that Du Bois perhaps was religious. The Timpany–Du Bois exchange also highlights how Du Bois maintained a materialist perspective on religious matters, linking his conception of religion's impact to documented developments and data-driven analysis.

While working with Paul Robeson at the Council on African Affairs, in 1948 Du Bois exchanged letters with a Cuban pastor. Their conversation addressed the very significance of Jesus Christ himself. "I am writing this letter to ask a favor of you," wrote cleric E. Piña Moreno to W. E. B. Du Bois on October 3, 1948, "I would like to know if you are a believer in God, [and] also[,] what is your opinion about the Lord Jesus." Slightly over a month later, Du Bois wrote, "If by being 'a believer in God,' you mean a belief in a person of vast power who consciously rules the universe for the good of mankind, I answer No," he admitted. "I cannot disprove this assumption, but I certainly see no proof to sustain such a belief, neither in History nor in my personal experience." Du Bois stated further, "If . . . you mean by 'God' a vague Force, which, in some incomprehensible way, dominates all life and change, then I answer, Yes; I recognize such Force, and if you wish to call it God, I do not object." This is the only known exchange between Du Bois and Moreno. It is plausible they met in 1941 when Du Bois traveled to Cuba.[23] Similar to Timpany's query about Du Bois's personal faith, Moreno's direct question during his twilight years about Du Bois's religious subjectivity runs against the notion that his radical, materialist orientation extinguished critical religious inquiry.

In a remarkably candid letter dated September 11, 1950, a Catholic laywoman from St. Louis named Monica Morrison petitioned Du Bois's advice for a religious history text she wished to write titled *Betrayal of the Cloth*. Part of Morrison's aim was "to show how in America, which is spoken of as a [C]hristian country, th[at] churches have practiced and upheld white supremacy." As an "active member" of the Catholic Church, Morrison told Du Bois of her educational background and her research forays in St. Louis. Morrison also claimed to know "many Negroes [who] have lost the faith." She related a story about her grandparents, faithful folks who absented themselves from communal worship "because they could not see Christ in the Catholic Church." Morrison also spent three paragraphs explaining several situations in St. Louis that exemplified systemic racism in the Church, including local efforts to remove a racially progressive white archbishop. On another occasion, a priest removed her son as an altar boy due to the color of his skin. "Today my son is a crushed and confused [C]atholic boy," Morrison lamented to Du Bois, "yet daily we are asked to pray to crush communism but if this was done what would become of all the colored races whose only hope depends on it since [C]hristianity (as lived) has failed." Morrison displayed an understanding of the global implications of racism and the religious sanction of white supremacy. To cope with these realities Morrison told Du Bois that she and her family read *The Souls of Black Folk* and *Black Reconstruction* and that "it help[ed] them." Du Bois's short reply one week later commended Morrison's book but failed to comment on her proposed outline. Nevertheless, he encouraged Morrison's literary efforts to "write it out frankly and fearlessly." He promised to forward her letter to the Catholic magazine *America* in order to see what advice they could offer. In reply to Du Bois's letter, anticommunist editor Robert C. Hartnett commented that Morrison's hope in communism—and by extension Du Bois's—revealed "considerable confusion in thought."[24]

Not only did Du Bois's private correspondence reveal numerous conversations with laypeople and religious leaders, but also newspaper articles throughout the 1940s and 1950s. He brought several of these conversations to public attention. For instance, in the February 27, 1941, issue of *Amsterdam News* Du Bois publicly replied to a letter from a Jesuit educator Father J. E. Coogan, a sociology professor from the University of Detroit. Coogan wrote that he had "for a long time been interested in your mighty efforts to better American racial conditions." This inspired Coogan to read *Dusk of Dawn* (1940). He found troubling Du Bois's criticisms of religion, his commentary on the significance of Paul the Apostle, and Du Bois's argument that the Catholic Church had in most instances supported slavery. Du Bois wrote to Coogan that he had "the deepest respect for religious convictions" but "when I must express myself I try to express what I believe is true." Du Bois praised "the forward movement in labor relations undertaken by Father LaFarge and others, but in general the struggle of the black man in America is for recognition of his manhood." He adamantly claimed that "Notwithstanding the work of the individual priests and occasional general pronouncements, the Catholic Church defended the slavery of Negroes for four hundred years." Du Bois continued: "Even today a black man in Uganda has a better chance to enter the priesthood of the Catholic Church than an American Negro and this will still be the truth as long as the Irish hierarchy dominates. . . . I am sorry to offend your convictions by these statements but I am a student of the truth and not a missionary of religion."[25]

Father Coogan continued to follow Du Bois and his work. Seven years later, he again took issue with the way Du Bois covered religion, this time in *Phylon*. Three years removed as editor, Du Bois published a short chronicle of publications on race relations in which he mentioned Protestant interracial initiatives but failed to discuss anything about the Roman Catholic Church. Citing this article Coogan accused Du Bois of being "habitually less than fair to the Catholic Church." According to Coogan, Du Bois's article gave "little inkling of what has been happening in the Catholic Church in America" with respect to racial justice. Du Bois's communist convictions and support for Russia also troubled Coogan. The priest promised to continue his subscription to *Phylon* but wished "to find it at least grudgingly fair to the Catholic Church."[26]

Du Bois's exchanges with ordinary people religious leaders document a wide engagement with his intellectual labor during the early Cold War. His work as a scholar, activist, and public intellectual provoked both protest and praise, all of which responded to Du Bois's nuanced, scientific, and historically based opinions on religion's cultural and political work. Time and time again in his work emerges a dialectical analysis of religion's historical and material meaning in American society.

Black and Red Religion: W. E. B. Du Bois's "Socialist Saints"

The years surrounding Du Bois's 1951 McCarthy trial further solidified an already resolute commitment to racial justice and economic democracy. In his speeches and publications throughout the 1950s the Black scholar fashioned himself and other marginalized radicals in the mold of persecuted prophets. In a righteous rage about racist, religious anticommunism, looming nuclear threats, and the steady beating drum of procapitalist propaganda, Du Bois invoked religious language in his steadfast support of midcentury radicals I call "socialist saints." Whereas some of his speeches offered general pronouncements about churches or clergy coupled with critical economic analysis or brimming with political insight, other speeches focused on specific individuals, namely persons caught in anticommunist dragnets. Du Bois effusively praised socialist saints for their willingness to analyze American political power or offer vocal support of socialism or communism.

In 1953, the author Dashiell Hammett sent a letter inviting Du Bois to attend a dinner in New York City in honor of V. J. Jerome, a leader in the Communist Party. Citing fatigue from extensive travel, Du Bois's March 9 reply declined the offer; however, he included the text of a statement he wished to have read at the dinner. Hammett read the speech.[27] Du Bois's comments about Jerome were at once religious and political; it was the prophetic performance of a fellow traveler and the public protest of propaganda. "Of all sins against the Holy Ghost," Du Bois began, "the stopping of Thought, the silencing of the Thinker is the worst." He believed deeply in utilizing social scientific thought to analyze and solve the world's problems: "than this there is no surer salvation," he contended. "The vicious and utterly unjustifiable persecution of our greatest Marxist philosopher, V. J. Jerome, is more than unjust, it is obscene; it is sacrilegious," cried Du Bois. Continuing to use starkly religious language, Du Bois wrote that such actions end up "crucifying an artist and writer . . . in futile effort to keep Truth hidden." To inhibit, arrest, malign, murder, or discredit someone whose ideas could improve the welfare of human life, whose ideas could bring liberation, particularly for those on the margins, fueled Du Bois's principled rage.[28]

Similarly, the context of the Cold War prompted Du Bois to praise the actions of another socialist saint: Paul Robeson. Du Bois's comments about Robeson in his *Autobiography* echoed the support for Jerome. Speaking at Robeson's birthday celebration in 1958, he said, "The persecution of Paul Robeson by the government and people of the United States during the last nine years has been one of the most contemptible happenings in modern history. Robeson has done nothing to hurt or defame this nation." Echoing a passage from the Hebrew scripture of Isaiah, Du Bois then wrote, "Yet [Robeson] fought the good fight; he was despised and rejected of men; a man of sorrows and acquainted with grief and we hid as it were our faces from him; he was despised and we esteemed him not."[29]

Although he delivered no speech on behalf of William Howard Melish, Du Bois considered the Brooklyn preacher a socialist saint.[30] He resolutely praised the Episcopal minister's stand during his own season of persecution. In 1938, Melish began to collaborate with his father, John Howard Melish, as assistant rector of Church of the Holy Trinity in New York City. Melish's support for civil rights and his work on behalf of the National Council of American-Soviet Friendship drew the attention of anticommunist crusaders both within the United States and within the hierarchy of the Episcopal Church. Ecclesiastical leaders pressured the pastors to relinquish their radicalism.[31]

Due to Melish's unflagging commitments to justice and his unfettered support for interracial Christian fellowship, Du Bois considered him "one of the few Christian clergymen for whom I have the highest respect."[32] It is likely that Melish's public persecution, after an ecclesiastical inquisition during the early 1950s, reminded Du Bois of his own and roused deep solidarity for the minister. Although in his *Autobiography* Du Bois pointed out that he did not share Melish's belief in "Christian dogma," he described the minister as "a young man of ideal character, of impeccable morals" who worked "for guidance of the young, for the uplift of the poor and ignorant, and for the betterment of his city and his country."[33] Du Bois's second wife Shirley Graham Du Bois, who along with her husband attended Melish's congregation, remarked affectionately that the church welcomed a diverse assembly of people that consisted of "Negroes, Puerto Ricans, the foreign-born and the poor. Holy Trinity thus became a community church in the truest sense of the word."[34]

There was a mutual respect and affinity between the two socialist saints. Melish invited Du Bois to speak at Holy Trinity's Negro History Week celebrations. In February 1955, the "world-famous historian-scholar" lectured on "Africa and Afro-America." The speech, a version of which Du Bois gave the previous year at a Council on African Affairs event, delineated precolonial African history to the Transatlantic Slave Trade followed by the Civil War and Reconstruction. He covered imperialism in Africa, then discussed contemporaneous developments of decolonization, commenting that the future of freedom in Africa connected to African American liberation at home.[35]

Holy Trinity's 1958 Negro History Week meeting also featured Du Bois. On the occasion of his ninetieth birthday Alphaeus Hunton lectured on the Black intellectual's scholarly accomplishments and devotion to freedom. He praised Du Bois's commitment to economic education and consistently drawing global connections between African American and African history. And lauded "his unflinching persistence in speaking the truth, in his undiminished vigor of utterance, stronger indeed today than it was at any time before." Hunton concluded by saying, "His life and his work illustrate and exemplify that which he has tried to tell us who believe in peace and justice and freedom—has told us over and over again—'Stand up and be counted!'"[36] Following Hunton's address Du Bois commented briefly that across the years he had witnessed a "mighty change between capitalism and socialism." He stated that Holy Trinity's 1958 Negro History Week event was not a birthday "celebration of what I have done, but rather a reminder of what is still to do."[37]

The Du Bois-Melish alliance extended further. Du Bois requested that Melish deliver his eulogy. In 1963, the Brooklyn minister traveled to Ghana. An autobiographical reflection titled "Du Bois, Nkrumah and Ghana" revealed Melish's profound gratitude at being able to summarize the life of and honor such a noted, inspirational figure. He detailed the "Reformation songs" Du Bois wanted played, including Martin Luther's "A Might Fortress" as well as the post-funeral dinner and commemoration of Du Bois. Melish's eulogy covered Du Bois's life biographically, commenting on his influence both in the United States and across the world. "Into thy hands, O most loving Father, we entrust thy servant, William Edward Burghardt Du Bois, whom we shall ever recall with thankfulness, for the faith he held in life," prayed Melish. "God, our Father, give to the peoples of the world a new heart of comradeship," he continued, "renewed in knowledge, to strengthen and to serve the brethren; that every people may bring its tribute of excellence to the common treasury, without fear, and without the lust of domination; and that all the world may go forward in the new and living way which he hath consecrated for us; who now liveth and reigneth with thee and the Spirit of truth, one God, world without end."[38] Melish's concluding meditation celebrated Du Bois's life and called for a fuller realization of freedom in honor of his deceased comrade.

An unpublished manuscript from Du Bois's late career also featured his dialectical assessment of religion. Titled "Russia and America: An Interpretation," this text presented an expansive analysis of how he conceptualized freedom in the form of economic democracy, free expression of ideas, and speech, and the purposeful pursuit of peace. "Russia and America" is a 324-page, eight-chapter manuscript that Harcourt, Brace & Company reviewed in 1950 but ultimately rejected. Publisher Robert Giroux wrote that the press did not find the manuscript "the balanced interpretation we had hoped it would be and, in honesty, we could not publish it with conviction. It seems an uncritical apologia for Soviet Russia and an excessive condemnation of the United States."[39] While this text remains unpublished at present, it has increasingly become part of the scholarship on Du Bois's later career.[40]

The book's final chapter addresses religion in Russia and the United States. Du Bois framed a question directed at US, anticommunist readers: "Does the Soviet Union suppress religion?" He answered the question by pointing out that atheism and agnosticism were the preferred convictions in Russia. Du Bois saw this not as evidence of antireligious fervor but instead perspectives influenced by modern science, technology, and rationalistic thinking. Du Bois wrote, "Russia represents today that emancipation from dogmatic religion which Western Europe has professed since the Protestant revolt, but which has been only partially realized; indeed today Europe and America can praise the Soviet Union for establishing actual freedom of religious belief."[41] He contrasted the situation of religion and Russia with American religious culture of the Cold War period. He commented on how Christian nationalism rendered a view of US history as a distinctly Christian nation, a perspective emphatically proclaimed during the 1940s and 1950s. Again, Du Bois turned his materialist analysis of religion to focus on the relationship between deeds and creeds. He presented a contrast between freedom of religious belief (or a choice to not believe) and societies in which a religious fundamentalism pressured free expression while demanding spiritual conformity, thus actually curbing the practice of freedom. Du Bois asked why it was that "in lands which profess the most intimate relations with the Almighty" like South Africa or the United States that "there is and has been the most cruel denial of basic human rights."[42] Sometimes, Du Bois suggested, the most vocally religious nations in history were the most racist where local and national leaders wielded religion as a tool of oppression. Yet, as this chapter also demonstrates, there were places and times in which radicals viewed religion and practiced belief in ways that spurred human dignity and liberation.

In addition to speeches and writings, Du Bois turned to poetry to valorize socialist saints. Writing about the execution of Julius and Ethel Rosenberg in

1953, Du Bois penned a poetic lamentation. In this poem, he condemned racial, political, and religious injustice in the United States. He fashioned the account with apocalyptic overtones using imagery drawn from the Hebrew scriptures and from the New Testament.

"The Rosenbergs" began with the word "Crucify," a reference to those who perished unjustly.[43] Du Bois's use of the term crucify signaled a religious reference to an unjust death while it simultaneously condemned the United States for injustice. In a specific reference to the death of Jesus Christ, Du Bois wrote of hammering nails, pressing down on a crown of thorns, and the bloody mess of crucifixion. The poem's second stanza called judgment on the United States, and specifically on the anticommunist, antisocialist segments of American society. It depicted warmongers as evil and likened the Rosenberg's execution to a lynching. Referring to the McCarthy trials, Du Bois intoned: "We are the murderers hurling mud/We are the witchhunters, drinking blood." In this stanza, he also focused his rage on religious elites, people who regularly received his criticism, for their unwillingness to denounce oppression and injustice during the Second Red Scare. This is not merely anticlericalism, but a disgust with religious leaders who failed to align their religious creeds with deeds that supported justice and equality.[44] Later in the poem Du Bois imagines an unfolding apocalypse where the "Father and Mother" of the universe sat on the "Great Black Throne," an allusion to judgment in the New Testament book of Revelation. They sent pall bearers—a group of Du Bois's socialist saints—to the Rosenberg's funeral to "raise the crucified aloft." The pall bearers included early twentieth-century anarchists Sacco and Vanzetti, nineteenth-century abolitionist John Brown, and Willie McGee, a Black man from Mississippi executed in 1951 for allegedly raping a white woman.[45]

In the next stanza, Du Bois envisioned other socialist saints welcoming the Rosenbergs in paradise. With heaven weeping and "its tears" raining down, "drops . . . a staircase from the Sun," a line reminiscent of Jacob's ladder, a famous story from the Hebrew Bible. Around this staircase congregate world historical figures such as the Buddha, Muhammed, the prophet Isaiah, Jesus Christ, Abraham Lincoln, Toussaint Louverture, Savonarola, and Joan of Arc. These notables "and all the other millions" greeted the Rosenbergs with song and celebration.[46]

It is significant that Du Bois mentioned fifteenth-century religious figures Savonarola and Joan of Arc in the same line. While Joan of Arc has traditionally been cast as a courageous heroine, Du Bois depicted her as the kind of assertive and independent female he often praised in his work. Savonarola's story also resonated with Du Bois. The civic leader and religious radical lived in Renaissance Florence and traveled widely throughout Italy. A popular preacher, fiery orator, and fierce critic of the Medici's economic policies, Savonarola preached truth to power and called religious officials to account when their actions did not exhibit the ethics of Jesus. After a career of prophetic preaching and advocacy on behalf of Florence's working classes, in 1498 church officials hanged Savonarola and burned his body.[47]

In a striking final stanza, Du Bois made clear who was on the side of justice: those who had been part of what he called the "Red Resurrection" and welcomed into a figurative utopian paradise. The poem served as a kind of rallying cry for the socialist saints still living. It was a sacred liturgy for political radicals, and a prayer for the oppressed.[48]

In the 1950s, Du Bois witnessed countless injustices and often sided with radicals who suffered political persecution. In speeches, writings, and creative work during this period, he lamented the problematic nature of capitalism and praised the virtues of socialism. Given how Du Bois used a religious framework to imagine and reimagine particular historical moments, "The Rosenbergs" exemplifies his religious rendering of the early Cold War in overtly apocalyptic terms, a counter-discourse to anticommunist visions of the same period.

The religious Cold War of Du Bois's twilight years explains the decision to express his support of leftist radicals in religious terms of prophetic propaganda because in America's spiritual-industrial complex anticommunists framed a midcentury divided world of good versus evil. Rhetorically, conservative politicians and religious leaders associated communism with God's archenemy Satan and expressed fears about "apostles of deceit" infiltrating religious institutions. According to historian Angela M. Lahr, the "polarization paradigm" by which evangelicals operated underwrote their worldview's bipolarity.[49]

Several examples illustrate how evangelical Protestants deployed such language. In Houston, a pastor named R. B. Thieme Jr. developed a sermon from Matthew 22 that spiritualized allegiance to God, to the independent "local church"—and not the National Council of Churches, a liberal coalition he denounced—and only to political philosophies that promoted individual freedom "which is represented . . . in states['] rights."[50] "There is no true Bible Christianity which can co-exist with communism!" he exclaimed, "Socialism in any form is anti-biblical!"[51] Elsewhere, Michigan pastor Lehman Strauss used apocalyptic Bible prophecy speculations to interpret communism as a current spirit of the age. He called it a "satanically inspired . . . false atheistic doctrine" in "an all-out war against God." Using New Testament parables about wealth and an accumulation of material resources as points of reference, Strauss's acute fears predicted that communist infiltration across the United States would produce materialism, immorality, and apostasy or rejection of God.[52] In a similar fashion, Thomas O. Kay, a professor at Wheaton College, wrote the National Association of Evangelicals 1962 booklet *The Christian Answer to Communism*. In it Kay warned against communist influence in education, labor activism, and within "minority groups" whom the radical leftists had "exploited . . . and used to play on the emotions" associated with economic and racial inequality.[53] Author and professor Roy B. Zuck wrote the study guide to Kay's volume in which he echoed the evangelical contention that communism is a mortal threat to Christianity because it is a "demonic force" that "challenges organized religion" and "opposes Christianity's missionary outreach."[54]

Billy Graham was one of the most emblematic voices of Christian anticommunism during the Cold War period. Spiritual advisor to both presidents and pew-sitters and coming of age during the 1940s, the Southern evangelist led preaching crusades all over the United States and abroad. As one of the leaders of midcentury Protestant evangelicalism, with other religious leaders like Carl F. H. Henry and Harold John Ockenga, Graham helped to birth the evangelical periodical *Christianity Today*, where in a 1954 article he called communism "Satan's religion." Many of Graham's fellow evangelicals followed suit with a strident religious anticommunism, as did mainline Christians. Norman Vincent Peale, for instance, most famous for his Cold War bestseller *The Power of Positive Thinking* (1952) and pastor at New York City's Marble Collegiate Church, spoke out against communism—once calling it a "virus"—in sermons and through his magazine *Guideposts*.[55]

While J. Edgar Hoover exacted his anticommunist animus ruthlessly through the arms, eyes, and ears of the FBI, evangelical Christians gave him a literary platform to propagandize through the pages of *Christianity Today* magazine. He believed clergy played a crucial role in a kind of moral defense of the nation through anticommunist sermonizing. "Ministers of America are truly on the front lines of the battle for freedom," Hoover wrote in 1958. "On their shoulders, in large measure, depends the future of our nation."[56] His "rhetorical tactics" echoed evangelical denunciation of communism's assumed antireligious character and penchant for extreme manipulation.[57] He wrote that communism "works to weaken the tenets of religion" and "attack the believers of God" because it is "atheistic, utterly denying God."[58]

Hoover's rhetorical campaigns performed anticommunist propaganda so well that ordinary Americans wrote thousands of letters to the Bureau inquiring about the loyalty of particular institutions and individuals.[59] In 1963, he received a letter about W. E. B. Du Bois. In Du Bois's voluminous FBI file, an unnamed Methodist laywoman queried the director about the radical Black intellectual. She wrote:

> Dear Sirs:
>
> Could you please give me any information on "William Edward Dubois" in connection with Communis[t] activities in America[?]. It is my understanding that he no longer lives in America. I'm a housewife with four children and some of this man's material was used in our Bible school sessions for Junior children in our Methodist church and it would help me to know about this man. I know you are very busy with all the fine work you are doing and maybe you can't advise me; but I don't know who to ask about it, but you. Very Sincerely,
>
> [redacted][60]

Hoover replied to this unidentified woman with a form letter that characteristically neither admitted nor denied it had any information on Du Bois. However, the director enclosed a number of pamphlets, including his own speech titled "Communist Illusion and Democratic Reality" and a column he published in *Christianity Today* titled "The Communist Menace: Red Goals and Christian Ideals." This letter reveals the stature that Du Bois still had among ordinary Black people. However, it also displays how in some cases anticommunism aimed to spoil the reception of his ideas. Moreover, Hoover's enclosures indicate the religious zeal that informed anticommunism and demonstrate his active attempts through religious propaganda to influence public discussions about communism as subversive. Du Bois put in his intellectual crosshairs the kind of religious anticommunism with which Hoover replied to the unidentified Methodist laywoman.

Protestants were not the only Christians who bolstered a religious anticommunism. Among Roman Catholic ecclesiastical leaders, the monk Thomas Merton, Cardinal Francis Spellman, the Jesuit John Courtney Murray, intellectuals like William F. Buckley, and leading publications such as *The Catholic World* and *National Review* regularly invoked religion to condemn communism. In the early 1940s, Archbishop Francis Beckman spoke of "Christ-haters of Moscow." Many lay Catholics held similar convictions, some of which the leading Bishop-televangelist, Fulton Sheen, helped to foster. His 1950s television show, *Life is Worth Living*, often featured biting criticism of communism. "As the Communists perverted the notion of brotherhood into world imperialism," Sheen stated on a broadcast, "so, too, have they perverted the sense of diffused guilt by denying God, denying morality, denying conscience, but keeping confession and guilt. The only guilt that any person can be guilty of in their theology is to sin against the revolutionary philosophy." In an era not only of anticommunism but rife anti-Catholicism, Sheen forged a middle path that sought to make Catholicism more affable to American Protestants while assuring his audiences that he was a respectable critic of atheistic communism.[61]

One of the most notorious examples of religious anticommunism from the early Cold War era was fundamentalist evangelical preacher Billy James Hargis. Born in Texarkana, Texas, in 1925, the Great Depression and Protestant Christianity defined Hargis's childhood. In his early twenties, Hargis began preaching a religious message of anticommunism, patriotism, segregation, and Christian nationalism both in churches and across the radio. In 1950, Hargis founded Christian Crusade, an activist organization devoted to the elimination of communism and the support of free-market principles. He published a magazine, *Christian Crusade*, and wrote books that presented communism in as viciously evil. Hargis's 1963 harangue *Communism: The Total Lie!* fashioned the Cold War as a "spiritual war" of apocalyptic proportions. For Hargis "Communism has been conceived in the brains of the devil, spawned in hell, and receives its inspiration and direction from Satan."[62]

The 1950s and 60s witnessed an increasing intensity in Hargis's anticommunist and anti-Black rhetoric. Billed as an evangelistic tour, in the 1960s Hargis traveled to South Africa and visited Rhodesia. He met and interviewed Ian Smith and praised the leader for "educat[ing] the Negroes, [and] almost completely stamp[ing] out cannibalism and 'ritual murders.'" About the rest of the continent, Hargis described Kenya a haven of "savages and cannibals" that British colonization eliminated. "Such people," Hargis continued about Africans, "are not capable at this point of self-government." Relatedly, Hargis stated that the transatlantic slave trade "may have been a blessing in disguise to future generations of blacks because it introduced them to Western civilization." Such dismissive, ludicrous, and racist descriptions of Africans also shaped his perspectives on Black people in the Americas, especially leftists like Du Bois. However, Hargis praised and forged alliances with conservative, anticommunist African Americans such as J. H. Jackson of the National Baptist Convention. Jackson even published an essay in Hargis's *Christian Crusader* promoting national security and domestic peace.[63]

For Hargis, Black radicals were of particular concern, especially Du Bois, whom he targeted specifically. After Du Bois joined the Communist Party in 1961, Hargis blasted him and the NAACP. "W. E. B. Du Bois has long been one of the top idols of those who follow the NAACP line of racial agitation," he wrote in his newsletter *For and Against*. "Informed Americans know that Dr. Du Bois has been neck deep in operations of the communist conspiracy for years," wrote Hargis, citing Du Bois's columns in radical newspapers and his classes at the New York City's Jefferson School in the 1950s. He claimed that Du Bois had "been associated with over 75 communist fronts and causes" and described him as an "agent of the communist conspiracy." Hargis tagged the Black intellectual's book *Black Reconstruction* and noted Du Bois's associations with Herbert Aptheker and Paul Robeson. Most disturbingly, Hargis stated, Du Bois's plans for world revolution and African liberation included piercing criticism of Christianity and institutional religion.[64]

This chapter remaps the intellectual contours of Du Bois's social and cultural analysis of religion across key moments of his twentieth-century life. During the New Deal and early Cold War periods as Marxism rendered a clearer materialist direction in his thought, his dialectical analysis of American religion and culture revealed how religion produced oppression and inspired liberation. The documentary record shows that in his closing decades, whether in political parables, correspondence, speeches, or poems, Du Bois turned frequently to religious ideas and religious language to analyze an America intoxicated with power built on white supremacy. In a nation stridently devoted to fostering consumer culture, and obsessed with eradicating "godless Communism," Du Bois's prophetic propaganda during this period produced a counter-discourse maintaining that leftist radicals lived within an equally valid moral universe that prized peace, antinuclear convictions, cooperative economics, and pacifism. For Du Bois this was a world in which he resolutely supported socialist saints by boldly proclaiming, "Blessed are the Peacemakers for they shall be called Communists."

NOTES

As this chapter materialized, I presented portions of it at the Baylor Symposium on Faith and Culture, the African American Intellectual History Society Workshop at Mississippi State University, and the Center for Marxist Education in Boston. I thank Tommy Kidd and Darrin Davis for making my travel to Waco possible and for Lauren Louise Anderson and Keisha Blain's invitation to discuss my work in Starkville. For helpful feedback, questions, and comments at these venues and in others, I thank Mark Eaton, Alan Scot Willis, Edward Carson, Lerone Martin, Ed Blum, Suren Moodliar, Christopher Cameron, Greg Childs, Keisha Blain, Brandon Byrd, Ashley Farmer, Kami Fletcher, Alison Collis Greene, Emily Owens, and John Wilsey.

1. W. E. B. Du Bois, *In Battle for Peace: The Story of My 83rd Birthday* (New York: Oxford University Press, 2007 [1952]), 48, 108, 111; cf Gerald Horne, *Black and Red: W. E. B. Du Bois and the Afro-American Response to the Cold War, 1944–1963* (Albany: State University of New York Press, 1986), 151–82; 201–21; David Levering Lewis, *W. E. B. Du Bois: The Fight for Racial Equality and the American Century, 1919–1963* (New York: Henry Holt, 2000), 163–78; Manning Marable, *W. E. B. Du Bois: Black Radical Democrat*, Updated Edition (Boulder, CO: Paradigm, 2005), 190–217; Eric Porter, *The Problem of the Future World: W. E. B. Du Bois and the Race Concept at Midcentury* (Durham: Duke University Press, 2010), 145–78; Shawn Leigh Alexander, *W. E. B. Du Bois: An American Intellectual and Activist* (Lanham: Rowman and Littlefield, 2015), 111–32; Bill V. Mullen, *W. E. B. Du Bois: Revolutionary Across the Color Line* (London: Pluto Press, 2016), 107–22.

2. Edward J. Blum, *W. E. B. Du Bois: American Prophet* (Philadelphia: University of Pennsylvania Press, 2007); Jonathon S. Kahn, *Divine Discontent: The Religious Imagination of W. E. B. Du Bois* (New York: Oxford University Press, 2009); Edward J. Blum and Jason R. Young, eds., *The Souls of W. E. B. Du Bois: New Essays and Reflections* (Macon, GA: Mercer University Press, 2009); Brian L. Johnson, *W. E. B. Du Bois: Toward Agnosticism, 1868–1934* (Lanham, MD: Rowman and Littlefield, 2008); and Gary Dorrien, *The New Abolition: W. E. B. Du Bois and the Black Social Gospel* (New Haven: Yale University Press, 2015). Additional scholarship covers religion and Du Bois's early career: Herbert Aptheker, "W. E. B. Du Bois and Religion: A Brief Reassessment," *Journal of Religious Thought* 39, no. 1 (Spring–Summer 1982): 5–11; Manning Marable, "The Black Faith of W. E. B. Du Bois: Sociocultural and Political Dimensions of Black Religion," *Southern Quarterly* 23, no. 3 (Spring 1985): 15–33; Don Hufford, "The Religious Thought of W. E. B. Bu Bois," *Journal of Religious Thought* 53/54 (1997): 73–94; Curtis J. Evans, "W. E. B. Du Bois: Interpreting Religion and the Problem of the Negro Church," *Journal of the American Academy of Religion* 75, no. 2 (June 2007): 268–97; Barbara Diane Savage, "W. E. B. Du Bois and the 'Negro Church,'" *Annals of the American Academy of Political and Social Science* 568 (March 2000): 235–49; J. Kameron Carter, "An Unlikely Convergence: W. E. B. Du Bois, Karl Barth, and the Problem of the Imperial God-Man," *New Centennial Review* 11, no. 3

(Winter 2012): 167–224; Phillip Luke Sinitiere, "Of Faith and Fiction: Teaching W. E. B. Du Bois and Religion," *History Teacher* 45, no. 3 (May 2012): 421–36; Christopher Buck, "The Interracial 'Baha'i Movement' and the Black Intelligentsia: The Case of W. E. B. Du Bois," *Journal of Religious History* 36, no. 4 (December 2012): 542–62; Guy Emerson Mount, "A Troubled Modernity: W. E. B. Du Bois, 'The Black Church,' and the Problem of Causality," in *'Abdu'l-Bahá's Journey West: The Course of Human Solidarity*, ed. Negar Mottahedeh (New York: Palgrave Macmillan, 2013), 85–110; Shirley A. Waters White, "A Consideration of African-American Christianity as a Manifestation of Du Boisian Double-Consciousness," *Phylon* 51, no. 1 (Fall 2014): 30–41; and Phillip Luke Sinitiere, "W. E. B. Du Bois's Prophetic Propaganda: Religion and *The Crisis*, 1910–1934," in *Protest and Propaganda: W. E. B. Du Bois,* The Crisis, *and American History*, eds. Amy Helene Kirschke and Phillip Luke Sinitiere (Columbia: University of Missouri Press, 2014), 190–207. While not a primary concern of this chapter, it is important to note that social scientists and social theorists find in Du Bois's pioneering research at the turn of the twentieth century a leading figure in the sociology of religion. See Phil Zuckerman, "The Sociology of Religion of W. E. B. Du Bois," *Sociology of Religion* 63, no. 2 (2002): 239–53; Phil Zuckerman, ed., *Du Bois on Religion* (Walnut Creek, CA: AltaMira, 2000); Robert A. Wortham, "Du Bois and the Sociology of Religion: Rediscovering a Founding Figure," *Sociological Inquiry* 75, no. 4 (October 2005): 433–52; Robert A. Wortham, "W. E. B. Du Bois, the Black Church, and the Sociological Study of Religion," *Sociological Spectrum* 29, no. 2 (February 2009): 144–72; and Reiland Rabaka, *Against Epistemic Apartheid: W. E. B. Du Bois and the Disciplinary Decadence of Sociology* (Lanham, MD: Lexington, 2010), 223–63. Also useful are editorial introductions to Du Bois's *The Negro Church*, published in 1903. See W. E. B. Du Bois, *The Negro Church*, introduction by Phil Zuckerman, Sandra L. Barnes, and Daniel Cady (Walnut Creek, CA: AltaMira, 2003), vii–xxvi, and W. E. B. Du Bois, *The Negro Church*, introduction by Alton B. Pollard III (Eugene, OR: Cascade Books, 2011), ix–xxxii.

3. On class and American religion more generally, see Sean McCloud, *Divine Hierarchies: Class in American Religion and Religious Studies* (Chapel Hill: University of North Carolina Press, 2007). For studies that address religion, class, and race across the early twentieth century, see among others, Alison Collis Greene, *No Depression in Heaven: The Great Depression, the New Deal, and the Transformation of Religion in the Delta* (New York: Oxford University Press, 2016); Jarod Roll, *Spirit of Rebellion: Labor and Religion in the New Cotton South* (Urbana: University of Illinois Press, 2010); Erik Gellman and Jarod Roll, *Gospel of the Working Class: Labor's Southern Prophets in New Deal America* (Urbana: University of Illinois Press, 2011); Elizabeth Fones-Wolf and Ken Fones-Wolf, *Struggle for the Soul of the Postwar South: White Evangelical Protestants and Operation Dixie* (Urbana: University of Illinois Press, 2015); Christopher D. Cantwell, Heath W. Carter, and Janine Giordano Drake, eds., *The Pew and the Picket Line: Christianity and the American Working Class* (Urbana: University of Illinois Press, 2016). While neither book addresses religion in a central way, Robin D. G. Kelley's *Hammer and Hoe: Alabama Communists during the Great Depression*, 25th Anniversary Edition (Chapel Hill: University of North Carolina Press, 2015), and Glenda Elizabeth Gilmore's *Defying Dixie: The Radical Roots of Civil Rights, 1919–1950* (New York: W. W. Norton, 2008) discuss where religion intersects with Communist political resistance. Kelley, as the epigraph to this chapter suggests, details how attendees at Party meetings in Alabama revised gospel songs and spirituals with overtly political contents (*Hammer and Hoe*, 107–8). Gilmore identifies the influence of social gospel theology on members of the CPUSA (*Defying Dixie*, 175, 212, 245).

4. Andrew Preston, "Introduction: The Religious Cold War," in *Religion and the Cold War: A Global Perspective*, ed. Philip Muehlenbeck (Nashville: Vanderbilt University Press, 2012), xi–xxii; cf. Andrew Preston, *Sword of the Spirit, Shield of Faith: Religion in American War and Diplomacy* (New York: Penguin, 2012), Part VII.

5. Jonathan P. Herzog, *The Spiritual-Industrial Complex: America's Religious Battle Against Communism in the Early Cold War* (New York: Oxford University Press, 2011).

6. On Boyer's invocation of "counter-discourse" see his review of William Inboden, *Religion and American Foreign Policy, 1945–1960: The Soul of Containment* (Cambridge: Cambridge University Press, 2008) in *Church History* 78, no. 4 (December 2009): 935–38, and relatedly, the counter-discourse he explores in *By the Bomb's Early Light: American Thought and Culture at the Dawn of the Atomic Age* (New York: Pantheon Books, 1985), 129–30, 196–203, 219–40, 344–48.

7. Portions of this paragraph follow a longer discussion of Du Bois and propaganda in Phillip Luke Sinitiere, "The Black Futures of W. E. B. Du Bois," in Philip Reed-Butler, ed. *Critical Black Futures: Speculative Theories and Explorations* (New York: Palgrave Macmillan, 2021), 19–36. The phrase protest and propaganda comes from Kirschke and Sinitere, eds., *Protest and Propaganda: W. E. B. Du Bois,* The Crisis, *and American History*. On Du Bois and propaganda, see W. E. B. Du Bois, "The Criteria of Negro Art," *The Crisis*, November 1926, 290–97; W. E. B. Du Bois, *Black Reconstruction in America: An Essay Toward a History of the Part Which Black Folk Played in the Attempt to Reconstruct Democracy in America, 1860–1880* (New York: Oxford University Press, 2007 [1935]), 582–97; W. E. B. Du Bois, "Phylon Science or Propaganda," *Phylon* 5, no. 1 (1st Quarter, 1944), 5–9. See also Arnold Rampersad, *The Art and Imagination of W. E. B. Du Bois* (Cambridge: Harvard University Press, 1976); Keith Byerman, *Seizing the Word: History, Art, and Self in the Work of W. E. B. Du Bois* (Athens: University of Georgia Press, 1994); Herman Beavers, "Romancing the Body Politic: Du Bois's Propaganda of the Dark World," *Annals of the American Academy of Political and Social Science* 568 (March 2000): 250–64; Robert W. Williams, "W. E. B. Du Bois and Positive Propaganda: A Philosophical Prelude to His Editorship of *The Crisis*," in *Protest and Propaganda: W. E. B. Du Bois,* The Crisis, *and American History*, 16–27.

8. Sinitiere, "W. E. B. Du Bois's Prophetic Propaganda," in *Protest and Propaganda*; cf. Edward J. Blum and Paul Harvey, *The Color of Christ: The Son of God and the Saga of Race in America* (Chapel Hill: University of North Carolina Press, 2012), 141–204.

9. W. E. B. Du Bois, "Forum of Fact and Opinion," *Pittsburgh Courier*, December 25, 1937, in W. E. B. Du Bois, *Newspaper Columns by W. E. B. Du Bois, Volume 1: 1883–1944*, ed. Herbert Aptheker (White Plains, NY: Kraus-Thomson, 1986), 260–61.

10. W. E. B. Du Bois, "Christmas, 1940: A Revision of the Gospel According to Saint Luke," *Amsterdam News*, December 21, 1940, in *Newspaper Columns by W. E. B. Du Bois*, 349–50.

11. W. E. B. Du Bois, "The Missionaries," *Amsterdam News*, January 17, 1942, W. E. B. Du Bois Papers Digital Archive (Identifier mums312-b217-i157). My narration of this story follows closely with my short summary of it in "Of Faith and Fiction."

12. Du Bois, "The Missionaries."

13. Du Bois, "The Missionaries."

14. Du Bois's praise of Japan in the internationalist religious parable "The Missionaries" is a creative expression of what historian Yuichiro Onishi calls Du Bois's "Afro-Asian philosophy of world history." See Yuichiro Onishi, *Transpacific Antiracism: Afro-Asian Solidarity in 20th Century Black America, Japan, and Okinawa* (New York: New York University Press, 2013), 54–93.

15. W. E. B. Du Bois, "The Reverend Mr. Bond's Assistant," 1–4, W. E. B. Du Bois Papers Digital Archive, http://credo.library.umass.edu/view/full/mums312-b235-i051. Unpublished and undated, it is likely that Du Bois composed this short story during the 1920s or 1930s. Its creative details about the entanglement of race, religion, and class correspond to the concurrent publication of his nonfiction journalistic writings such as his 1931 *Christian Century* article "Will the Church Remove the Color Line?," in *W. E. B. Du Bois on Religion*, 173–79.

16. Du Bois, "The Reverend Mr. Bond's Assistant," 8–9.

17. Du Bois, "The Reverend Mr. Bond's Assistant," 9–12.

18. Du Bois, "The Reverend Mr. Bond's Assistant," 13–15.

19. Mrs. J. S. Dailey to W. E. B. Du Bois, July 14, 1932, Box 57, Folder 25, W. E. B. Du Bois Collection, Fisk University.

20. William Crowe Jr. to W. E. B. Du Bois, August 5, 1939; W. E. B. Du Bois to William Crowe Jr., August 9, 1939, *The Correspondence of W. E. B. Du Bois, Volume II: Selections 1934–1944*, ed. Herbert Aptheker (Amherst, MA: University of Massachusetts Press, 1976), 194–95.

21. John R. Timpany, S. S. J. to W. E. B. Du Bois, December 10, 1944, *The Correspondence of W. E. B. Du Bois, Volume III: Selections 1944–1963*, ed. Herbert Aptheker (Amherst, MA: University of Massachusetts Press, 1978), 26–27.

22. W. E. B. Du Bois to John R. Timpany, S. S. J., January 17, 1945, *The Correspondence of W. E. B. Du Bois, Volume III: Selections 1944–1963*, 27.

23. E. Piña Moreno to W. E. B. Du Bois, October 3, 1948; W. E. B. Du Bois to E. Piña Moreno, November 15, 1948, *Correspondence, Volume III*, 221–23; Lewis, *W. E. B. Du Bois: The Fight for Racial Equality and the American Century, 1919–1963*, 485.

24. Monica Morrison to W. E. B. Du Bois, September 11, 1950; W. E. B. Du Bois to Monica Morrison, September 18, 1950, *Correspondence, Volume III*, 291–92. For Harnett's reply see America National Catholic Weekly to W. E. B. Du Bois, September 22, 1950, W. E. B. Du Bois Papers Digital Archive (Identifier mums312-b127-i049).

25. W. E. B. Du Bois, "As the Crow Flies," *Amsterdam News*, February 27, 1941, W. E. B. Du Bois Papers Digital Archive (Identifier mums mums312-b217-i121). The "forward movement" about which Du Bois wrote referenced LaFarge's work on interracial religious alliances and labor activism. On LaFarge, see David W. Southern, *John LaFarge and the Limits of Catholic Interracialism, 1911–1963* (Baton Rouge: Louisiana State University, Press, 1996), and Phillip Luke Sinitiere, "Interracialism and American Christianity," *Oxford Encyclopedia of Religion in America* (December 2017), http://religion.oxfordre.com/abstract/10.1093/acrefore/9780199340378.001.0001/acrefore-9780199340378-e-499?rskey=3GCZU4&result=42.

26. J. E. Coogan, S. J., "*Phylon* Unfair to Catholic Church!," *Phylon* 9/4 (1948): 390–92.

27. W. E. B. Du Bois to Dashiell Hammett, March 9, 1953, *Correspondence, Volume III*, 344.

28. W. E. B. Du Bois to Dashiell Hammett, March 9, 1953, *Correspondence, Volume III*, 345.

29. W. E. B. Du Bois, *The Autobiography of W. E. B. Du Bois: A Soliloquy on Viewing My Life from the Last Decade of Its First Century* (New York: Oxford University Press, 2007 [1968]), 256.

30. For the larger context of the period of Du Bois's Brooklyn residence, which mentions briefly the Melish-Du Bois friendship, see David Levering Lewis, "Exile in Brooklyn: W. E. B. Du Bois's Final Decade," in *Citizen of the World: The Late Career and Legacy of W. E. B. Du Bois*, ed., Phillip Luke Sinitiere (Evanston, IL: Northwestern University Press, 2019), 187–99; Blum, *W. E. B. Du Bois: American Prophet*, 188–89, 209.

31. Francis Henry Touchet, "The Social Gospel and the Cold War: The Melish Case" (PhD dissertation, New York University, 1981).

32. Du Bois, *Autobiography*, 271–72.

33. Du Bois, *Autobiography*, 271–72.

34. Shirley Graham Du Bois, *His Day is Marching On: A Memoir of W. E. B. Du Bois* (Philadelphia: Lippincott, 1971), 232–35; cf, Blum, *W. E. B. Du Bois: American Prophet*, 187–88.

35. "Church of the Holy Trinity Bulletin," February 6, 1955, Box 282, Folder 21, W. E. B. Du Bois Papers; W. E. B. Du Bois, "Africa and Afro-America," February 20, 1955, W. E. B. Du Bois Papers Digital Archive (Identifier mums mums312-b205-i022).

36. Alphaeus Hunton, "Tribute to Dr. W. E. B. Du Bois," February 9, 1958, Box 1, Folder 21, James Aronson-W. E. B. Du Bois Collection, University of Massachusetts Amherst.

37. "Church of the Holy Trinity Bulletin," February 9, 1958, Box 15, Folder 2, John Howard Melish, William Howard Melish and Protestant Episcopal Church of the Holy Trinity Collection, Brooklyn Historical Society.

38. William Howard Melish, "Du Bois, Nkrumah and Ghana," and "Address Delivered by the Rev. William Howard Melish at the Memorial Service of the Late Dr. W. E. B. Du Bois at the Aggrey Memorial Church, Achimota College, Accra, Ghana, on Sunday 29th September, 1963," Box 14, Folder 6, John Howard Melish, William Howard Melish and Protestant Episcopal Church of the Holy Trinity Collection, Brooklyn Historical Society; cf, Blum, *W. E. B. Du Bois: American Prophet*, 214–15.

39. See Harcourt Brace & Company to W. E. B. Du Bois, October 17, 1949, https://credo.library.umass.edu/view/full/mums312-b124-i318 and "Harcourt Brace & Company to W. E. B. Du Bois," July 13, 1950, https://credo.library.umass.edu/view/full/mums312-b128-i296, WEBD Papers Digital Archive.

40. Kate A. Baldwin, *Beyond the Color Line and the Iron Curtain: Reading Encounters Between Black and Red, 1922–1963* (Durham: Duke University Press, 2002), 149–80; Vaughn Rasberry, *Race and the Totalitarian Century: Geopolitics in the Black Literary Imagination* (Cambridge, MA: Harvard University Press, 2015), 187–237; Bill V. Mullen, "Russia and America: An Interpretation of the Late W. E. B. Du Bois and the Case for World Revolution," in *Citizen of the World*, 49–66.

41. W. E. B. Du Bois, "Russia and America: An Interpretation," 279, W. E. B. Du Bois Papers Digital Archive, https://credo.library.umass.edu/view/full/mums312-b221-i082.

42. Du Bois, "Russia and America," 281.

43. W. E. B. Du Bois, "The Rosenbergs," in *Creative Writings by W. E. B. Du Bois: A Pageant, Poems, Short Stories, and Playlets*, ed. Herbert Aptheker (White Plains: NY: Kraus-Thomson, 1985), 42.

44. Du Bois, "The Rosenbergs," 42.

45. Du Bois, "The Rosenbergs," 43.

46. Du Bois, "The Rosenbergs," 43–44.

47. Lauro Martines, *Fire in the City: Savonarola and the Struggle for the Soul of Renaissance Florence* (New York: Oxford University Press, 2006).

48. Martines, *Fire in the City*, 44.

49. Michael J. McVicar, "Apostles of Deceit: Ecumenism, Fundamentalism, Surveillance, and the Contested Loyalties of Protestant Clergy During the Cold War," in Sylvester A. Johnson and Steven Weitzman, eds., *The FBI and Religion: Faith and National Security before and after 9/11* (Princeton: Princeton University Press, 2017), 85–107; Markku Ruotsila, " "Russia's Most Effective Fifth Column": Cold War Perceptions of Un-Americanism in US Churches," *Journal of American Studies* 47/4 (November 2013): 1019–41; and Angela M. Lahr, *Millennial Dreams and Apocalyptic Nightmares: The Cold War Origins of Political Evangelicalism* (New York: Oxford University Press, 2007), 37.

50. Rev. R. B. Thieme, "The Christian's Responsibility to the Church and the State," July 1, 1956, 10, Church and State Vertical File, College of Biblical Studies Special Collections.

51. Thieme, "The Christian's Responsibility," 6.

52. Lehman Strauss, *Communism and Russia in Bible Prophecy* (Findlay, OH: Dunham Publishing Company, 1959), 7–12, 16, Prophecy Vertical File, College of Biblical Studies Special Collections.

53. Thomas O. Kay, *The Christian Answer to Communism* (Grand Rapids: Zondervan, 1961), 58–60, Communism Vertical File, College of Biblical Studies Special Collections.

54. Roy B. Zuck, *Communism and Christianity: Leader's Guide for an Adult Study Courser* (Wheaton, IL: Scripture Press Publications, 1962), 6, Communism Vertical File, College of Biblical Studies Special Collections.

55. On conservative religion and anticommunism see Eric R. Crouse, "Popular Cold Warriors: Conservative Protestants, Communism, and Culture in Early Cold War America," *The Journal of Religion and Popular Culture* 2 (2002), http://www.usask.ca/relst/jrpc/article-popcoldwar.html; Eric R. Crouse, "Responding to the Reds: Conservative Protestants, Anti-Communism, and the Shaping of American Culture, 1945–1965," Canadian Society of Church History *Historical Papers* (2002): 97–109; and Thomas Aiello, "Constructing 'Godless Communism': Religion, Politics, and Popular Culture, 1954–1960," *Americana: The Journal of American Popular Culture* 4/1 (Spring 2005), http://www.americanpopularculture.com/journal/articles/spring_2005/aiello.htm; Carol V. R. George, *God's Salesman: Norman Vincent Peale and the Power of Positive Thinking* (New York: Oxford University Press, 1993), 103–27.

56. J. Edgar Hoover, "The Challenge of the Future," *Christianity Today*, May 26, 1958, 3–4. I thank Lerone Martin for numerous enlightening conversations on Hoover, religion, and the FBI.

57. Dianne Kirby, "J. Edgar Hoover, the FBI, and the Religious Cold War," in *The FBI and Religion: Faith and National Security before and after 9/11*, 67–84.

58. J. Edgar Hoover, "Communism: The Bitter Enemy of Religion, *Christianity Today*, June 22, 1959, 3–5; J. Edgar Hoover, "Communist Propaganda and the Christian Pulpit," *Christianity Today*, October 24, 1960, 5–6.

59. McVicar, "Apostles of Deceit," 97–100.

60. William E. B. DuBois, FBI file. See Part 15 of Du Bois's file from William Maxwell's *F.B. Eyes Digital Archive*, http://digital.wustl.edu/fbeyes/.

61. Patrick N. Allitt, "Catholic Anti-Communism," InsideCatholic.com (April 4, 2009) http://insidecatholic.com/Joomla/index.php?option=com_content&task=view&id=5744&Itemid=48; Christopher Owen Lynch, *Selling Catholicism: Bishop Sheen and the Power of Television* (Lexington, KY: University Press of Kentucky, 1997), 152–53; Anthony Burke Smith, "Prime-Time Catholicism in 1950s America: Fulton J. Sheen and 'Life Worth Living,'" *U.S. Catholic Historian* 15/3 (Summer 1997): 57–74; Irvin D. S. Winsboro and Michael Epple, "Religion, Culture, and the Cold War: Bishop Fulton J. Sheen and America's Anti-Communist Crusade of the 1950s," *Historian* 71/2 (2009): 209–33. The quote from Sheen comes from his *Life is Worth Living* (Fort Collins, CO: Ignatius Press, 1999), 92–97.

62. On Billy James Hargis see John Harold Redekop, *The American Far Right: A Case Study of Billy James Hargis and Christian Crusade* (Grand Rapids, MI: Eerdmans, 1968), 51–64; Randall Balmer, "Billy James Hargis," *Encyclopedia of Evangelicalism*, Revised and Expanded Edition (Waco, TX: Baylor University Press, 2004), 321–22; Charles Lippy, ed., "Billy James Hargis," *Twentieth-Century Shapers of American Popular Religion* (Westport, CT: Greenwood, 1989), 193–96; and Lahr, *Millennial Dreams and Apocalyptic Nightmares*, 40–48.

63. See Billy James Hargis, "My Fact-Finding Mission to Rhodesia, South Africa and Greece," *Christian Crusade* (March 1968): 9–16, 18–21; Billy James Hargis, *The Total Revolution* (Tulsa: Christian Crusade, 1972), 62; and J. H. Jackson, "The Strength of the Nation the Security of Her Citizens," *Christian Crusader* (April 1968): 11–15, Box 94, Billy James Hargis Folder, William Martin Collection, Woodson Research Center, Rice University.

64. Billy James Hargis, "Dr. Du Bois and the Communist Conspiracy," *For and Against* (1961), Box 56, Folder 47, Billy James Hargis Papers, University of Arkansas; Billy James Hargis, *The Facts about Communism and Our Churches* (Tulsa: Christian Crusade, 1962), 34–37.

PART III

Literature and Legacy

CHAPTER 9

The Mutual Comradeship of W. E. B. Du Bois and Radical Black Women, 1935–1963

—Charisse Burden-Stelly

On October 1, 1961, shortly before permanently relocating to Accra, Ghana, William Edward Burghardt Du Bois applied for membership in the Communist Party of the United States of America (CPUSA).[1] In his application he exhorted, "Communism—the effort to give all men what they need and to ask of each the best they can contribute—this is the only way of human life. . . . The path of the American party is clear: It will provide the United States with a real Third Party and thus restore democracy to this land."[2]

Leftists[3] who knew him best at the end of his life have differing opinions about why he made this bold move. Some contended that his CPUSA membership crystallized his longstanding commitment to leftwing politics, particularly socialism. Doxey Wilkerson, for example, asserted that Du Bois understood "this system had to go, had to be changed, and so there was no other course."[4] James E. Jackson made the similar argument that because Du Bois became a card-carrying Red only after serious study, contemplation, and experimentation, it "was the consummated act of commitment to the social forces which the people can command to forge and fashion for all mankind a bright and joyous future."[5] Herbert Aptheker, who, along with Shirley Graham Du Bois, was the "sole charge" of Du Bois's files,[6] and whom Du Bois regarded as a son,[7] tended to agree with Wilkerson and Jackson. Aptheker's assessment is of particular interest insofar as he was one of Du Bois's trusted advisors on and a key source of information about Marxism-Leninism,[8] as the latter cemented his belief in the ideology. In 1964, Aptheker concluded that Du Bois saw CPUSA membership as "embodying the best in the radical and liberating tradition of this country and the best in the egalitarian and militant traditions in humanity . . . joining the party symbolized his convictions as to what was true and what was necessary."[9]

By contrast, other of Du Bois's acquaintances, including Lloyd Brown and St. Clair Drake, argued that he joined the CPUSA to make a statement, to spite and condemn the country that had blacklisted and denigrated him because of his radicalism, and to punctuate his solidarity with those who had been persecuted and repressed by the US government.[10] For the radical Puerto Rican doctor Ana Livia Cordero, who offered care to Du Bois throughout his time in Accra, his joining the CPUSA specifically was symbolic. "It wasn't really that he became a Communist in his old age. It was a gesture against the U.S. Government," she opined. "Not that it was out of character. . . . as you know, he was Socialist. [But] why join the American Communist Party? . . . He was thumbing his nose . . . at the whole white structure, and at imperialism in a broader sense."[11] Expanding on his earlier interpretation, Aptheker agreed in 1996 that Du Bois joined the CPUSA to protest the government's attempts to discredit, isolate, and persecute him, and because "he knew that those who wanted the Cold War as a key to advancing domestic poverty and racism could not ignore his action. He wanted this gesture to be one of defiance."[12]

Other of Du Bois's comrades and confidants, like Bernard Jaffe, attributed this "thumbing his nose" interpretation to the perfidious refusal—especially of African Americans—to accept that Du Bois had undergone a fundamental ideological conversion. Jaffe averred, "It was not . . . an act of bravado, nor some kind of gesture. . . . He had decided that the appropriate thing for him to do in terms of where he stood in the world was to join the Communist party and identify himself with that Party. . . . I know a lot of people think that it was an act of personal defiance. I am inclined to doubt that."[13] Abbott Simon split the difference, insisting that in joining the CPUSA, Du Bois demonstrated both rebellion and resolve: "It was . . . an act of defiance in which the word defiance was throwing down the gauntlet. . . . I would say it was an act of courage . . . that he had his joining of the Communist party made public, as he did . . . by choosing this moment to make people realize that he was a Communist."[14]

While Du Bois had been a "socialist of the path" since the beginning of the twentieth century,[15] he joined the CPUSA at a time when a number of his contemporaries—Ralph Bunche, Max Yergan, Mary McLeod Bethune, Langston Hughes—had raced to the center or to the right in the midst of Cold War anticommunist hysteria,[16] and despite the fact that not a few Black radicals, including Audley Moore, Doxey Wilkerson, and Harry Haywood, had exited (or been expelled from) the CPUSA in the previous decade given the party's inconsistent commitment to racial justice and the explosive "Khrushchev revelations" of 1956.[17] Notwithstanding these trends, Du Bois's move toward the CPUSA seems to reflect the connections he made after World War II between communism, freedom for racialized and oppressed people at home and abroad, and international peace. Stated differently, he understood the US government's unrelenting repression of the CPUSA, and organizations linked to it—under the guise of national security—as inseparable from the continued denial of civil rights and liberties to African Americans, increased militarism against nations on the darker side of the color line, and accelerated US imperialism. He was particularly sensitive to the US government's use of the "communist threat" to rationalize all these forms of domination. Likewise, while Du Bois was targeted for his radicalism in the United States, in communist nations, namely China and the USSR, his politics were valued, venerated, and celebrated.[18] Thus, his 1957 proclamation that, "[Negroes'] main interest lies in stopping this senseless fear of Socialism and Communism and the crazy idea that we can control human thought and effort by endless war," was a harbinger for his formal affiliation with the CPUSA four years later.[19]

Du Bois's move to the left was not merely autodidactic; after the Second World War, he was increasingly in conversation and communion with radical Black women and men who were committed to extirpating capitalist immiseration. As Du Bois became a steadfast believer in the conjuncture of socialism, peace, and progress, and became more acquainted with leftist organizations like the United Office and Professional Workers of America (a largely female union) and the Greater New York Negro Labor Council, radical Black women were a constant in his life.[20] Bill V. Mullen argues that comrades including Shirley Graham Du Bois, Claudia Jones, and Vicki Garvin helped to "gender" Du Bois's analysis by emphasizing the importance of women to the proliferation of world peace, the elevation of the working class, and the forging of international proletarian alliances.[21]

Such influence is evident in his 1949 unpublished essay entitled "The American Negro Woman," in which he argues that the Black woman's role as worker, head of household, and leader in cultural development has been essential to the progression of American culture, and provides the key to resolving the central problem of the "woman question"—economic dependence.[22] The essay not only refines his position on Black women presented in "The Woman in Black" (1913) and "The Freedom of Womanhood" in *The Gift of Black Folk* (1924), but also dovetails with the arguments of Louise Thompson Patterson in "Toward a Brighter Dawn" and Claudia Jones in "An End to the Neglect of the Problems of the Negro Woman!"[23] Both of these essays center not only the triple exploitation of Black women—"as workers, as women, and as Negroes"—but also the leading role of Black women's activism in combatting the structures of unfreedom in which their oppression and domination inhered. Likewise, whereas in previous writings Du Bois emphasized Black women's spiritual strength and the idealism of Black womanhood, in "The American Negro Woman" he attempted to outline the importance of Black women, given their unique structural and material conditions, to proletarian struggle and to the potential resolution of the exploitation of the working class. This shift in emphasis was consonant with Herbert Aptheker's assessment that "the greatly developed militance and political maturity of Negro people (putting them in the forefront of the American progressive battle) has owed very much to the Negro woman," especially radicals like Ada B. Jackson, Charlotta A. Bass, Shirley Graham, and Moranda Smith.[24]

Du Bois's courage and commitment likewise inspired many progressive Black women. Lorraine Hansberry sums it up with her declaration that his consistent condemnation of oppressive forces, tireless attention to the "genuine needs of humankind," outright rejection of racism in all its forms, and sincere dedication to the realization of a global socialist society, made him a "fact," "bulwark," and "institution" of radical Black culture and society.[25] Such an indelible impact undoubtedly motivated these women to work tirelessly on Du Bois's behalf when antiradical persecution reared its ugly head. The work of peace activist and labor organizer Thelma Dale is one such example. In raising money and organizing meetings for Du Bois's defense after he was indicted for being an agent of a foreign power in 1951, she wrote, "I never had a more pleasant and rewarding assignment. I only wish I were working full-time so that I could really see the full fruits of Labor."[26] When he was acquitted, she penned an article in *New Aspects* arguing that the dismissal of the case against him represented a victory for lovers of freedom and peace throughout the world.[27] Hansberry and Dale are representative of the cadre of progressive Black women who engaged in a feedback loop of affection, protection, and struggle with Du Bois as they challenged racism, capitalism, and militarism head-on. These mutually supportive relationships infused their strivings for freedom with forms of love and care that made it easier to face down statist backlash.

This chapter explores a phenomenon I call "mutual comradeship"[28] during Du Bois's "radical period," which spans roughly 1935–1963. Mutual comradeship can be understood as an affective practice of freedom constituted by the enduring commitment to, advocacy for, and protection of those engaged in radical political struggle. It also entails radical African descendants' ethical practice of collaboration, reciprocal care, and learning in community rooted in political work on behalf of the racialized, colonized, and oppressed. It is articulated through dedication of time, energy, and resources to radical causes; mutual support for radical organizations, institutions, and periodicals; the provision of jobs and income for persons whose politics deemed them undesirable as employees; and protection from and defense against state repression. Mutual comradeship also includes the lateral and intergenerational practice of legacy maintenance—including archiving, commemoration, public remembrance, and truth-telling—predicated on an allegiance to those who, because of their radical praxis, are intentionally erased, obscured, distorted, displaced, silenced, or hidden from memory.

Mutual comradeship explicates the ways that Du Bois, through his leadership, activism, and intellectual production, influenced a generation of leftist Black women to fight anti-Blackness, colonialism, imperialism, fascism, misogynoir, and war—women who in turn motivated, supported, and defended Du Bois in his latter, more militant years. Particular attention is given to the Sojourners for Truth and Justice, Shirley Graham (Du Bois), and Louise Thompson (Patterson), who were not only freedom fighters in their own right but who were also deeply concerned with the plight, safety, and success of their partners and leftwing leaders who had been subjected to the violence of the Cold War state. These women's protracted engagement with economic democracy, durable peace, and Black internationalism shaped and were shaped by W. E. B. Du Bois. This mutual comradeship traversed a multitude of leftist organizations, including the Southern Negro Youth Conference,[29] the National Negro Congress, the Civil Rights Congress, and the Council on African Affairs. It endured a deluge of anticommunist indictments and trials, including those of Claudia Jones, William Patterson, and the Peace Information Center. Moreover, it withstood the dragnet of statist repression, most manifest in the Smith Act (the Alien Registration Act of 1940) and the McCarran Act (the Internal Security Act of 1950).[30]

"Our Cup Truly Runneth Over!": Black Progressive Women in the Defense of Black Life and Leadership

The relationship between Du Bois and the Sojourners for Truth and Justice (STJ) captures the essence of mutual comradeship.[31] Louise Thompson Patterson explained that the group was formed in part to protest the curtailment of radical Black leaders' freedom, including Du Bois's "indict[ment] in handcuffs," and the incarceration of Paul Robeson, W. Alphaeus Hunton Jr., William Patterson, and Benjamin J. Davis Jr.[32] Founded in September 1951 by a cadre of militant Black women located throughout the nation,[33] STJ sought to "rally Black women to defend their men" and to organize wives and mothers "of the legally lynched . . . of those imprisoned and threatened with prison . . . widowed by police brutality . . . [and] who mourn [their] sons dead in foreign wars" against the US government's insults, humiliations, indignities, and repression.[34] In other words, the organization was deeply concerned about the US state's quest to crush radical Black freedom dreams. Prior to the formation of STJ, many of the future members fortified their political position through the fierce and unrelenting battle for the freedom of Rosa Lee Ingram, a Black sharecropper and widowed mother of twelve who, in 1948, had been convicted, along with two of her sons, of killing a white man who assaulted her.[35] Months later, Du Bois modeled the solidarity and support that he would later receive during his period of anticommunist duress by writing a petition, at the request of these Black leftist women, to the United Nations Commission on Human Rights demanding that the General Assembly take up the Ingram case.[36]

Du Bois's involvement in the Ingram case was part of a long history of insisting on justice for Black women, especially their safety from "racialized sexual violence," which dovetailed with the concerns of STJ.[37] His sponsorship of the Committee for Equal Justice for Mrs. Recy Taylor in 1944 is a case in point. The Federal Bureau of Investigation (FBI) considered his support for Mrs. Taylor, who had been gang raped by six white men who were never charged for the crime, to be part of his extensive "Communist Front activity." This was because the Committee was linked to the International Labor Defense, an organization that had been deemed a "communist front."[38] The bad faith characterization of radical Black mobilization against the ravages of white supremacy, capitalist exploitation, inexorable indignity, and racialized sexual violence as subversive—and the disregard of basic civil liberties that often accompanied this label—helps to explain why mutual comradeship was a practice of freedom that was so important to the Left generally, and leftist African descendants particularly.

When the full weight of the Justice Department's anticommunist fanaticism descended on Du Bois on February 9, 1951, in the form of indictment for failing to register the Peace Information Center (PIC) under the Foreign Agents Registration Act of 1938,[39] STJ organized a sojourn to Washington, DC, from September 29 to October 1, 1951, in part to demand his release and freedom. They also raised money for his defense, attended his trial, and used his plight to protest other injustices suffered by Black people. The combination of Du Bois's noxious indictment and his invaluable activism undoubtedly inspired STJ to demand that the US government drop "all persecution and prosecution of our great leaders, that they may be free to carry on the fight for full freedom of our people unhampered."[40] In addition to defending Du Bois against state repression, the group worked closely with a number of leftist entities including the Civil Rights Congress, the National Negro Labor Council, and the Progressive Party (for which STJ cofounder Charlotta Bass was the 1952 vice-presidential candidate) to condemn various forms of subjection. These included anti-Black violence, as evidenced in the bombing murder of NAACP activist Harry T. Moore and his wife in Mims, Florida;[41] warmongering and aggression against other nations, exemplified by the Korean War and the conscription of their sons into it; and the reign of McCarthyism and McCarranism, as manifested in Du Bois's prosecution and the revocation of Paul Robeson's passport.[42] Du Bois's participation in these and other freedom struggles fortified his bond with the members of STJ and militant Black women like them.

"A Two-Person United Front": The Comrade Love of Shirley Graham and W. E. B. Du Bois[43]

The Black progressive with whom Du Bois shared the most significant form of mutual comradeship during his "radical period" was Shirley Graham,[44] who was considered by some to be one of the most remarkable women in world history, given her international influence.[45] John Henrik Clarke, who knew Graham both before and after her marriage to Du Bois, stressed that she was more than simply a "useful and most worthy companion."[46] It was she, he asserted, who incited Du Bois's move to the Left.[47] Ethel Ray Nance agreed that many persons "blamed" Graham for his membership in the CPUSA, because she surrounded him with radicals, leftists, and outright communists.[48] While it is unclear whether Graham formerly joined the CPUSA, her devotion to the Left is unmistakable.[49] Indeed, she had been accused of promoting "communist propaganda" since the early 1930s, and she was thinking about revolution of the Soviet variety by 1943.[50] Based on information provided by career informant Louis Budenz, she was the subject of an Internal Security investigation starting in July 1950 (though she had been under FBI surveillance at least since "the critical year of 1948"), which resulted in the preparation of her security index card in 1951.[51]

Of particular interest to the government was her affiliation with a multitude of ostensible communist fronts, including the Jefferson School of Social Science, the Council on African Affairs, the American Labor Party, and the National Council of Arts, Sciences, and Professions[52]—organizations in which Du Bois was also active. Her FBI file also copiously documented her association with purported CPUSA members, fellow travelers, and otherwise subversive persons, namely Eslanda and Paul Robeson, Ethel and Julius Rosenberg—over whose children Graham gained trusteeship after their execution on June 19, 1953[53]—Ben Davis, and of course, Du Bois. The Du Boises freedom struggles for socialism, peace, and other left-wing causes resulted in brazen surveillance, curtailment of civil rights, and the confiscation of their passports. In a gross invasion of privacy, their office was burgled, with files and financial records were stolen; Graham held the FBI responsible for the robbery.[54]

Graham had known Du Bois for most of her life because he was friends with her father and had been a guest at her parents' home in Colorado Springs, Colorado. She was in constant contact with Du Bois from 1935 onward—even sending him her master's thesis—regularly seeking his advice, approval, and aid.[55] Graham claims that when she was a young woman in college, Du Bois invited her to his educational lectures, and over time, he advised her on employment; recommended her for prestigious positions; loaned her money; utilized his extensive networks to obtain information for her; helped her get published; took her to important events (like a reception at the United Nations); and served as her advisor, mentor, and confidant.[56] Around April 1936, Du Bois shifted from calling her "Ms. Graham" to the more familiar "Shirley," and her biographer Gerald Horne infers that it was around that time that they started having an "illicit affair."[57] The two had developed an unbreakable bond by this point, despite the fact that Du Bois was married and Shirley Graham had multiple suitors.[58] Not long after the death of Du Bois's first wife, Nina Gomer, the couple, who "love[d] the same kind of people,"[59] married on Valentine's Day in 1951, just as Du Bois became a codefendant in *United States v. Peace Information Center*, et al.[60] While Lloyd Brown and Marvel Cooke claimed that Graham had "always wanted to marry Dr. Du Bois," "had set her cap" for him, and had gained a lot from their marriage,[61] Esther Cooper Jackson and Ana Livia Cordero contended that it was Graham who protected him and assured that he was properly taken care of, remunerated fairly, and was able to earn a living after joining the CPUSA.[62]

The assistance, advancement, and appeasement Du Bois afforded to Graham in the early phase of their exchange were returned in later years. Transforming her "'mothering' skills into a political weapon . . . [to] defen[d] race men,"[63] she became her husband's most ardent advocate. In 1948, she headed the Emergency Committee for Dr. W. E. B. Du Bois and the NAACP, which was organized to challenge Du Bois's ouster from the National Association for the Advancement of Colored People at the end of his contract on December 31, 1948. He was ostensibly let go for unsanctioned political activity, although the likely reason was his criticism of Walter White for accepting an appointment from Harry Truman's administration, which, for Du Bois, represented alignment with "the reactionary war mongering colonial imperialism of the present administration." According to his FBI file, however, he was terminated "for urging the Wallace line too strongly," a reference to his support for Henry Wallace, the Progressive Party's presidential candidate.[64] By 1951, the new Mrs. Du Bois had set her career aside to immerse herself in the defense of the PIC (for which she was a member of the advisory council) and her new husband's peace politics in general. Her work on this front, and their collaborative relationship more broadly, is conveyed in her postscript comments throughout Du Bois's understudied manifesto, *In Battle for Peace: The Story of My 83rd Birthday*.[65] She also dedicated herself to protecting and perpetuating her husband's life and legacy against vitriolic anticommunist criticism after his death in 1963.[66] Emblematic of the latter effort is *His Day Is Marching On: A Memoir of W. E. B. Du Bois*, Graham's 1971 biography of her husband, in which she "poignantly relates her role and feelings . . . as a wife in making a home for him in New York City, [and] as a companion in standing beside him through the difficulties of his trial and subsequent impediments to foreign travel placed upon them by the State Department." The global impact of Du Bois, one reviewer noted, became more "fully understood" and "illuminated" through "the efforts of Shirley Graham Du Bois," whose work rendered him "more alive, more comprehendible, more relevant to the issues and style of our struggle."[67] Thus, while her marriage was not an "exemplar of feminism," it was nonetheless an affective practice of freedom that embodied reciprocal care and consideration—in other words, mutual comradeship—that made possible protracted struggle on behalf of the racialized, colonized, exploited, and abjected.

"I . . . Shall Do Anything I Can to Help You": Quotidian Comradeship and Radical Black Care

The mutual comradeship of Du Bois and Louise Thompson was both political and practical. It had at its foundation the cornerstone of any sustainable radical Black freedom struggle: reciprocal responsibility, encouragement, and connection.

It was after seeing Dr. Du Bois lecture when she was a student at the University of California that Louise Thompson decided to dedicate her life to eradicating racial oppression. She determined that New York was an ideal place to start this work, especially because Du Bois lived there.[68] Thus, after graduating in 1923, she reached out to him for employment opportunities, advice, and guidance, to which he responded favorably.[69] The two stayed in consistent contact when she joined the faculty at Hampton University later that year. Already disgusted with white philanthropy and racial conservatism,[70] she was sympathetic to and supportive of the student strike that erupted at the historically Black university in 1927. As an act of solidarity with militant students, she wrote Du Bois on October 17 of that year to provide details about the two-week strike, to encourage him to editorialize about it in *The Crisis*, and to seek advice on how she should proceed. She explained that she and others who were "not afraid to think for [themselves] even at the risk of personal security" had taken it upon themselves to support the students' protest of Hampton's "hypocrisy, racial prejudice, and backwardness."[71] She excoriated the white female teachers who, because they could not understand why Black students would be anything but gracious and obsequious toward them, attempted to appease unrest with sewing bees and tea parties while ignoring the earnest student demands. She enjoined the "Negro world" to see the "justice in the students' stand," and beseeched Du Bois to meet with her in New York the upcoming weekend to help decide her next steps. (Interestingly, it was during that trip that she met her future husband, the communist stalwart William L. Patterson, though they did not marry until 1941.)[72]

Du Bois assured Thompson that he would do all he could to help her, suggesting that she apply for an Urban League scholarship using his name, and advising her to remain at Hampton only if she could endure reactionary forces. A few months later he wrote her a letter of recommendation for the scholarship, which she received and quickly abandoned due to the Urban League's condescending and oppressive attitude toward the poor, and agreed to meet with her in New York in June 1928.[73] These exchanges between the two progressives throughout the 1920s—especially their mutual support for the Hampton strikers' struggle for freedom from white supremacy and Black bourgeois despotism[74]—foreshadowed a long and fruitful comradeship.

Thompson continued to move to the left throughout the 1930s. She played a prominent role in the "Free the Scottsboro Boys" march on Washington on May 8, 1933, which portended the STJ sojourn two decades later; joined the CPUSA that same year and became a member of the Central Committee by 1938; and travelled to the Soviet Union in 1934.[75] The antiracist freedom struggle that constituted Patterson's involvement in the Scottsboro Case also shaped her trip to the USSR in that she, Langston Hughes, and other Black Americans were especially interested in visiting Central Asia to get a sense of how the Bolsheviks were treating "people who were browner than [they] were." As a result of her experience in the "colored" region of the Soviet Union, she returned in 1939 and opined that its phenomenal development could serve as a model for Africa.[76] Patterson's leftist racial militancy and Black communist internationalism became a hallmark of her activism and resulted in her membership in a multitude of organizations, including the National Negro Congress, for which, according to a confidential FBI informant, she was one of the original organizers;[77] the Council on African Affairs, which she joined in 1949 and served as the director of organization until 1952; and STJ, which was formed at her New York apartment and for which she served as chairman and executive secretary.[78]

In these organizations, Patterson worked closely with or on behalf of Du Bois on issues that combined the mundane and the deeply political. This familiarity certainly aided in her decision to help initiate, and serve as acting secretary for, the Committee to Defend W. E. B. Du Bois and Associates in the Peace Information Center. The committee was organized in March 1951 to encourage persons to write the US president "urging the dismissal of the indictment" and for "immediate" and "urgent" fundraising so that the defendants could retain counsel. She drafted letters and circulars, recruited members to the committee, and handled the correspondence.[79] Du Bois appreciated her hard work and dedication to his cause.[80] He returned the favor by lending his name to the formation of the National Committee to Defend the Civil Rights of William L. Patterson, organized in July 1954.[81] These decades-long comrades stayed in contact until Du Bois's departure to Ghana in 1961, when the Pattersons sent him off with the following message: "Your tremendous contributions will live forever . . . live long . . . the world ahead is beautiful to contemplate."[82]

Robbie Lieberman's assertion that "the government saw voices for peace and freedom, especially those of black leftists, as a serious threat to national security"[83] is especially true in the case of W. E. B. Du Bois. The more he connected Black freedom to socialism and durable peace, the more the US government perceived him as threatening and antagonistic. This was because his politics inhered in anticolonial, antiracist, egalitarian, and anti-imperial analysis and linkage, and fomented international coalition building. His freedom strivings fundamentally contested the reactionary underpinnings of US policy and practice. Du Bois's defense of peace over the "American way of life" effectively rendered him, in the eyes of the government, a subversive who, through the PIC, was acting on behalf of a "foreign principal."[84] In reality, his work in the PIC, and scores of other organizations, was for the betterment of all persons who suffered under the yoke of racist, capitalist, and militaristic domination.

As Du Bois paid the price for his politics, a host of leftist Black women, including Lorraine Hansberry, Thelma Dale, Shirley Graham Du Bois, and Louise Thompson Patterson, fortified him against antiradical attack. They operationalized the strength and inspiration they gained from his activism over several decades to not only deepen their own resolve, but also to protect and defend other organizers who were essential to the radical freedom struggle. Their efforts did not go unacknowledged; Du Bois wrote in 1951, "Women have played a great role in my life . . . [as] faithful companion[s] and help-mate[s] of my last years, sustaining and helping me in my last thoughts and efforts . . . [they have been] friends and helpers in many times and places who worked with me and whom I loved for their belief and sacrifice."[85] Radical Black women, whose mutual comradeship helped to shape Du Bois's leftist politics in the second half of his life, were especially deserving of that tremendous accolade.

NOTES

1. Lester Abelman, "Du Bois, Long Red Pal, Goes Whole Hog at 93," *New York News*, November 19, 1961; Peter Kihss, "Dr. Du Bois joins Communist party at 93," *New York Times*, November 23, 1961; "Dr. Du Bois joins the Communist party," *People's World*, November 25, 1961; "Du Bois announces his great decision," *People's World*, December 2, 1961.

2. James E. Jackson, "W. E. B. Du Bois to Gus Hall: 'Communism Will Triumph. I want to Help Bring that Day,'" *The Worker*, November 26, 1961; "'My Mind's Settled,' Says Du Bois," *Pittsburgh Courier*, December 2, 1961.

3. "Radical," "leftist," and "progressive" are used interchangeably throughout this chapter.

4. Doxey Wilkerson, interview by David Levering Lewis, October 1986, interview 19, transcript, David Levering Lewis Papers (MS 827), Robert S. Cox Special Collections & University Archives Research Center, W. E. B. Du Bois Library, Amherst, MA (Subsequently, DLL Papers). Interviews by David Levering Lewis accessed in July and August 2017 before they were formally organized and processed.

5. James Jackson, "Tributes," in *Black Titan, W. E. B. Du Bois: An Anthology by the Editors of Freedomways*, eds. John Henrik Clarke et al. (Boston: Beacon Press, 1970), 19.

6. W. E. B. Du Bois to John W. Parker, January 12, 1953, W. E. B. Du Bois Papers (MS 312), Robert S. Cox Special Collections & University Archives Research Center, W. E. B. Du Bois Library, Amherst, MA (subsequently Du Bois Papers).

7. Herbert Aptheker and Fay Aptheker, "Personal Recollections on W. E. B. Du Bois: The Person, Scholar, and Activist," in *Herbert Aptheker on Race and Democracy*, eds. Eric Foner and Manning Marable (Urbana: University of Illinois Press, 2006), 211.

8. See e.g., W. E. B. Du Bois to Herbert Aptheker, September 19, 1950; W. E. B. Du Bois to Herbert Aptheker, December 21, 1954; Herbert Aptheker to W. E. B. Du Bois, December 24, 1954, Du Bois Papers.

9. Herbert Aptheker, "Du Bois Joined CP at 94," *National Guardian*, February 20, 1964.

10. Lloyd Brown, interview by David Levering Lewis, October 1986, interview 18, transcript; St. Clair Drake, interview by David Levering Lewis, August 1987, interview 8A, transcript, DLL Papers.

11. Ana Livia Cordero, interview with David Levering Lewis, May 1988, interview 3.2, transcript, DLL Papers.

12. Aptheker and Aptheker, "Personal Reflections," 238.

13. Bernard Jaffe, interview with David Levering Lewis, September 1986, interview 6, transcript, DLL Papers.

14. Abbott Simon, interview with David Levering Lewis, August 1986, interview 6, transcript DLL Papers.

15. See Charisse Burden-Stelly and Gerald Horne, *W. E. B. Du Bois: A Life in American History* (Santa Barbara: ABC-CLIO, 2019), 45.

16. See Charisse Burden-Stelly, "Black Cold War Liberalism as an Agency Reduction Formation during the Late 1940s and Early 1950s," *International Journal of Africana Studies* 19, no. 2 (Fall–Winter 2018): 77–130.

17. Audley Moore, interview with Mark Naison, December 23, 1981, interview 2, Oral History of the American Left, http://digitaltamiment.hosting.nyu.edu/s/cpoh/item/4071; Doxey Wilkerson to Sidney Stein, November 25, 1957, Box 2, Folder 47, James Aronson Papers (MSS 1062), Division of Library, Archives, and Museum Collections, Wisconsin Historical Society, Madison, WI; Harry Haywood, *Black Bolshevik: Autobiography of an Afro-American Communist* (Chicago: Liberator Press, 1978), 622–28; Michael Dobbs, "Khrushchev's 'Secret Speech' Printed," *Washington Post*, April 6, 1989.

18. Burden-Stelly and Horne, *W. E. B. Du Bois*, 185–88.

19. W. E. B. Du Bois, "Negroes and Socialism," *National Guardian*, April 29, 1957.

20. W. E. B. Du Bois to United Office and Professional Workers of America, May 11, 1950, and July 21, 1950; United Office and Professional Workers of America to W. E. B. Du Bois, May 16, 1950, and June 14, 1950; Greater New York Labor Council to W. E. B. Du Bois, May 1952; W. E. B. Du Bois to Vicki Garvin, June 12, 1952; Greater New York Labor Council to W. E. B. Du Bois, December 22, 1953, February 11, 1954, and January 7, 1955; W. E. B. Du Bois to Greater New York Labor Council, December 31, 1953, Du Bois Papers.

21. Bill V. Mullen, *Un-American: W. E. B. Du Bois and the Century of World Revolution* (Philadelphia: Temple University Press, 2015), 156–57.

22. W. E. B. Du Bois, "The American Negro Woman" (unpublished), ca. 1949, Du Bois Papers.

23. Louise Thompson Patterson, "Toward a Brighter Dawn," *Woman Today*, April 1936; Claudia Jones, *An End to the Neglect of the Problems of the Negro Woman!* (New York: National Women's Commission CPUSA, 1949). It is unclear whether Du Bois's "The American Negro Woman" draft preceded or followed Jones's article.

24. Herbert Aptheker, "The Negro Woman," in *Herbert Aptheker on Race and Democracy*, eds. Eric Foner and Manning Marable (Urbana: University of Illinois Press, 2006), 126–27.

25. Lorraine Hansberry, "Tributes," in *Black Titan*, 17.

26. Thelma Dale to W. E. B. Du Bois, September 26, 1951, Du Bois Papers.

27. Thelma Dale, "Dr. Du Bois Victory: A Victory for All," *New Aspects* 1, no. 1 (Spring 1952): 17–18.

28. Burden-Stelly and Horne, *W. E. B. Du Bois*, 207–8.

29. For a thorough treatment of Du Bois's important relationship with the Southern Negro Youth Conference, see Lindsey R. Swindall, *The Path to the Greater, Freer Truer, World: Southern Civil Rights and Anticolonialism, 1937–1955* (Gainesville: University Press of Florida, 2014), 1–11, 50–61, 110–80.

30. Charisse Burden-Stelly, "The Modern Capitalist State and the Black Challenge: Culturalism and the Elision of Political Economy" (PhD Dissertation: University of California, Berkeley, 2016), 55.

31. See Carole Boyce Davies, *Left of Karl Marx: The Political Life of Black Communist Claudia Jones* (Durham: Duke University Press, 2007), 35–37, 82–84; Claudia Jones, "Sojourners for Truth and Justice," *Daily Worker*, February 10, 1952; Erik McDuffie, "A 'New Freedom Movement of Negro Women': Sojourning for Truth, Justice, and Human Rights during the Early Cold War Period," *Radical History Review* 101 (Spring 2008): 81–106; "Sojourners for Truth and Justice," in *Encyclopedia of the African Diaspora: Origins, Experiences, and Culture, Vol. 3*, ed. Carole Boyce Davies (Santa Barbara: ABC-CLIO, 2008), 845–48; *Sojourning for Freedom: Black Women, American Communism, and the Making of Black Left Feminism* (Durham: Duke University Press), 160–82; Gerald Horne, *Communist Front? The Civil Rights Congress, 1946–1956* (London: Associated University Press, 1988), 208.

32. Louise Thompson Patterson, interview with David Levering Lewis, June 1987, interview 17A, transcript, DLL Papers.

33. The STJ initiating committee comprised Charlotta Bass (California), Alice Childress (New York), Shirley Graham (New York), Josephine Grayson (Virginia), Dorothy Hunton (New York), Sonora B. Lawson (New York), Amy Mallard (Georgia), Rosalie McGee (Mississippi), Bessie Mitchell (New Jersey), Louise Thompson Patterson (New York), Beulah Richardson (Mississippi), Eslanda Robeson (Connecticut), Pauline Taylor (Ohio), and France Williams (California). Other notable members and affiliates included Lorraine Hansberry, Claudia Jones, Audley Moore, and Angie Dickerson. The FBI contended that all of the officers of STJ were either in the CPUSA or CPUSA "front organizations," that the STJ was "Communist Party sponsored," and that the STJ followed the Communist Party line. STJ insisted that the Communist Party was not backing the organization. File 66–35 Sub 264-SA, October 15, 1951, Cleveland Federal Bureau of Investigation.

34. Patterson, interview; File 66–35 Sub 264-SA, May 14, 1952, Cleveland Federal Bureau of Investigation.

35. "A Call to Negro Women for an Eastern Seaboard Conference of the Sojourners for Truth and Justice," File 66–35 Sub 264-SA, May 14, 1952, Cleveland Federal Bureau of Investigation. Ingram and her sons were released in 1959 due to overwhelming national and international pressure. See Horne, *Communist Front?*, 210–11.

36. McDuffie, "A 'New Freedom Movement,'" 85.

37. McDuffie, "A 'New Freedom Movement,'" 87.

38. File 100–99129–32, September 4, 1951, Federal Bureau of Investigation.

39. Five officers of the Peace Information Center—Du Bois, Elizabeth Moos, Kyrle Elkin, Abbott Simon, and Sylvia Soloff—were indicted.

40. "Proclamations of the Sojourners for Truth and Justice," File 66–35 Sub 264-SA, May 14, 1952, Cleveland Federal Bureau of Investigation.

41. STJ released a statement about the Christmas Day murder of the Moores that ended with the following: "We will not be quieted until the death of our sister Harriett Moore and her husband Harry T. Moore is avenged, and until every man, woman and child can walk this land from Florida to Maine, from Virginia to California, in full dignity." They also referenced other cases in which Black folk suffered at the hands of the state and the police, including the Martinsville Seven, Willie McGee, Samuel Shepard, and Walter Lee Irvin. Another document expressed that the Sojourners "mourned" the death of the Moores and were grief-stricken and outraged by the Rosa Lee Ingram Case and the "violation" of Mrs. Lula Mae Artis by four white paratroopers. They issued a call to action to "Negro women everywhere, widowed by lynching, war casualties, police killing and jailings, and yet denied opportunities to earn their own living in industry and shop," to attend their Eastern Seaboard Conference in New York on March 23, 1952. "Our Cup Runneth Over" and "A Call to Negro Women for an Eastern Seaboard Conference of the Sojourners for Truth and Justice," File 66–35 Sub 264-SA, May 14, 1952, Cleveland Federal Bureau of Investigation; McDuffie, "A 'New Freedom Movement,'" 89–90.

42. File NY 100-24624, July 3, 1958, New York Federal Bureau of Investigation; File 66–35 Sub 264-SA, May 14, 1952, Cleveland Federal Bureau of Investigation.

43. Gerald Horne and Margaret Stevens, "Shirley Graham Du Bois: Portrait of the Black Woman Artist as Revolutionary," in *Want to Start a Revolution? Radical Women in the Black Freedom Struggle*, eds. Dayo F. Gore et al. (New York: New York University Press, 2009), 103. I borrow the term "comrade love" from Alyssa Adamson's conference paper entitled, "The Tragic Comrade Love of Toussaint L'Overture and General Etienne Laveaux Read through CLR James's Decolonial Humanism," presented at the Caribbean Philosophical Association XIV, June 23, 2017.

44. Horne and Stevens, "Shirley Graham Du Bois," 31–32, 115–16.

45. Jaffe, interview; Bernard Jaffe, Sylvia Soloff Steinberg, Abbott Simon (Peace Information Center), interview with David Levering Lewis, October 1994, interview 16B, DLL Papers; Gerald Horne, *Race Woman: The Lives of Shirley Graham Du Bois* (New York: New York University Press, 2000), 30.

46. Andrew Paschal, "The Spirit of W. E. B. Du Bois," *Black Scholar* 2, no. 2 (October 1970): 28.

47. John Henrik Clarke, interview with David Levering Lewis, June 1988, interview 7, transcript, DLL Papers.

48. Ethel Ray Nance, interview with David Levering Lewis, March 1986, interview 25, transcript, DLL Papers.

49. Louise Thompson Patterson claimed that Graham was brought into the Party by Howard Fast, while Bernard Jaffe suggested that she never formally joined the Party, though she was supportive of Du Bois's choice to do so. A confidential informant told the FBI that she had been a "staunch member of the CP" at least since 1944 or 1945. Historian Gerald Horne, who has written the only book-length biography of Graham, asserts that she joined the party after the death of her son Robert, though she was not "forthcoming or expansive" about her membershipshe joined the party after the death of her son Robert, though she was not "forthcoming or expansive" about her membership. He explains that even her son David was not certain about her CPUSA membership, writing in a letter to Horne, "I do not know for certain whether my mother was a member of the Party or not . . . if she was, it was Howard [Fast] who recruited her." Patterson, interview; File 100–87531, October 3, 1950, Federal Bureau of Investigation; Horne, *Race Woman*, 30, 280 fn. 79, 115; Horne and Stevens, "Shirley Graham Du Bois," 103.

50. Horne and Stevens, "Shirley Graham Du Bois," 100, 102.

51. Horne, *Race Woman*, 115–16.

52. In 1949, the California Un-American Activities Committee listed Graham as "a person known to have affiliated with from one to ten communist fronts." "Summary," File 100-370965-2, September 10, 1950, Federal Bureau of Investigation; Horne, *Race Woman*, 31, 281 fn. 85.

53. Esther and James Jackson, interview with David Levering Lewis, October 1986, interview 7, transcript, DLL Papers; Horne and Stevens, "Shirley Graham Du Bois," 105; Robert Meeropol and Michael Meeropol, *We Are Your Sons: The Legacy of Julius and Ethel Rosenberg* (Boston: Houghton Mifflin, 1975).

54. Horne and Stevens, "Shirley Graham Du Bois," 104; Jackson and Jackson, interview; Shirley Graham Du Bois, *His Day Is Marching On* (Philadelphia: Lippincott, 1971), 115.

55. Cordero, interview; Kathy A. Perkins, "The Unknown Career of Shirley Graham," *Freedomways* 25, no. 1 (1985): 12; Horne, *Race Woman*, 123; Paschal, "The Spirit of W. E. B. Du Bois," 27; Shirley Graham to W. E. B. Du Bois, May 16, 1935, and September 9, 1935, Du Bois Papers.

56. Paschal, "The Spirit of Du Bois," 28; W. E. B. Du Bois to Shirley Graham, November 17, 1943; W. E. B. Du Bois to Julius Rosenwald Fund, December 10, 1937; Shirley Graham to W. E. B. Du Bois, September 20, 1939, and November 30, 1942; W. E. B. Du Bois to Rayford Logan, January 4, 1945; W. E. B. Du Bois to Shirley Graham, October 20, 1947; W. E. B. Du Bois to Walter White, October 20, 1937; Shirley Graham to W. E. B. Du Bois, January 20, 1943, Du Bois Papers; Horne, *Race Woman*, 124–33.

57. W. E. B. Du Bois to Shirley Graham, April 8, 1936, Du Bois Papers. On January 17 of that year, Du Bois was still using the more formal "My Dear Miss Graham." Also see Gerald Horne, *Race Woman*, 125.

58. Horne, *Race Woman*, 128.

59. On December 12, 1950, Graham wrote to Roselyn Richards, describing her engagement and upcoming marriage to Du Bois: "I will have a 'position' to maintain but we both love the same kind of people and have not the slightest concern about what certain other kinds of people think about us." Cited in Horne, *Race Woman*, 122.

60. Du Bois was arrested for being an "unregistered foreign agent" and indicted on February 9, 1951, under the Foreign Agent Registration Act of 1938 for failing to register the Peace Information Center. The case was ultimately dismissed on November 20, 1951.

61. Brown, interview; Marvel Cooke, interview with David Levering Lewis, October 1986, interview 21, transcript, DLL Papers. According to Louise Thompson Patterson, Du Bois had women admirers who were "downright jealous" when he married Graham; as she recalls, "They said, 'She finally got him. She hung on all this time, and she finally made it' . . . Shirley was a very ambitious woman." This is more or less consistent with the contention of Brown and Cooke that Graham had intentions to marry Du Bois for quite some time. Patterson, interview.

62. Jackson and Jackson, interview; Cordero, interview.

63. Horne and Stevens, "Shirley Graham Du Bois," 98.

64. "Committee Is Set up to Defend Dr. Du Bois," *New York Times*, September 29, 1948; John Hudson Jones, "Du Bois Ousted by NAACP Board as Research Head," *Daily Worker*, September 15, 1948; File NY 100–20789, April 12, 1955, April 30, 1955, Central Intelligence Agency; Horne and Stevens, "Shirley Graham Du Bois," 103–4.

65. W. E. B. Du Bois, *In Battle for Peace: The Story of My 83rd Birthday* (New York: Oxford University Press, 2007 [1952]).

66. W. E. B. Du Bois, *The Autobiography of W. E. B. Du Bois* (New York: International Publishers, 1968), 378; Perkins, "The Unknown Career," 16; Horne, *Race Woman*, 123; Paschal, "The Spirit of W. E. B. Du Bois," 27–28. Also see Phillip Luke Sinitiere, "Leadership for Democracy and Peace: W. E. B. Du Bois's Legacy as a Pan-African Intellectual," in *Leadership in Colonial*

Africa; Disruption of Traditional Frameworks and Patterns, ed. Baba G. Jallow (New York: Palgrave Macmillan, 2014), 159–62.

67. Ronald Walters, "Review: *His Day Is Marching On: A Memoir of W. E. B. Du Bois* by Shirley Graham Du Bois," *Journal of Negro History* 58, no. 1 (January 1973): 107–9.

68. Patterson, interview; McDuffie, *Sojourning for Freedom*, 63.

69. In 1926 she sent him her résumé to solicit employment in New York. Louise A. Thompson to W. E. B. Du Bois, July 13, 1926, Du Bois Papers.

70. McDuffie, *Sojourning for Freedom*, 64.

71. Louise A. Thompson to W. E. B. Du Bois, October 17, 1927, Du Bois Papers; Patterson, interview.

72. Patterson, interview.

73. McDuffie, *Sojourning for Freedom*, 64; W. E. B. Du Bois to Louis A. Thompson, April 15, 1928, and May 9, 1928; W. E. B. Du Bois to Eugene K. Jones, May 9, 1928, Du Bois Papers.

74. W. E. B. Du Bois, "The Hampton Strike," *Nation*, November 2, 1927.

75. McDuffie, *Sojourning for Freedom*, 66–76.

76. Patterson, interview; McDuffie, *Sojourning for Freedom*, 86–88. Also see Meredith L. Roman, *Opposing Jim Crow: African Americans and the Soviet Indictment of U.S. Racism, 1928–1937* (Lincoln: University of Nebraska Press, 2012), 133, 147–49; Kate Baldwin, *Between the Color Line and the Iron Curtain: Reading Encounters between Black and Red, 1922–1963* (Durham: Duke University Press, 2002), 86–148.

77. File 100–4092, May 29, 1943, Chicago Federal Bureau of Investigation.

78. File NY 100–24624, July 3, 1958, New York Federal Bureau of Investigation.

79. Louise T. Patterson to E. Franklin Frazier, n.d.; Louise T. Patterson to P. L. Prattis, March 27, 1951; Council on African Affairs to Carl Murphy, March 27, 1951; Council on African Affairs to Nathan Otto, March 27, 1951; National Committee to Defend Dr. W. E. B. Du Bois and Associates in the Peace Information Center to Joint Board Fur Dressers' and Dyers' Unions, March 27, 1951; National Committee to Defend Dr. W. E. B. Du Bois and Associates in the Peace Information Center to Mary Van Kleeck, March 29, 1951; Louise T. Patterson to Sandra Ray, March 29, 1951, Du Bois Papers.

80. W. E. B. Du Bois to Louise T. Patterson, April 10, 1951, Du Bois Papers.

81. Louise T. Patterson to W. E. B. Du Bois, July 21, 1954; W. E. B. Du Bois to Louise T. Patterson, July 23, 1954, Du Bois Papers.

82. William and Louise Thompson Patterson to W. E. B. Du Bois, March 3, 1961, Du Bois Papers.

83. Robbie Lieberman, "'Another Side of the Story': African American Intellectuals Speak Out for Peace and Freedom during the Early Cold War Years," in *Anti-Communism and the African American Freedom Movement*, eds. Robbie Liberman and Clarence Lang (New York: Palgrave MacMillan, 2009), 37–38.

84. W. E. B. Du Bois, "The Trial," in *W. E. B. Du Bois: A Reader*, ed. David Levering Lewis (New York: Henry Holt and Company, 1995), 777–78.

85. W. E. B. Du Bois, "Greetings to Women," July 1951, Du Bois Papers.

CHAPTER 10

Martin Luther King Jr. and the Legacy of W. E. B. Du Bois

—Robert Greene II

"Tonight we assemble here to pay tribute to one of the most remarkable men of our time."[1] This was the opening line to Martin Luther King Jr.'s tribute to W. E. B. Du Bois, given in New York City on what would have been Du Bois's one hundredth birthday, February 23, 1968. Martin Luther King Jr.'s turn towards the American Left—and away from the comforts of Cold War American liberalism—was complete by this point. Bereft of most of his liberal allies, a pariah in the eyes of most mainstream civil rights leaders, and deeply unpopular with many Americans, King nonetheless knew he still had receptive audiences on the Left. Among those was an audience of writers (including James Baldwin),[2] editors, and supporters of *Freedomways* magazine, the leading organ of the African American radical tradition in the nineteen sixties. His speech about Du Bois's legacy on that day offered King an opportunity to opine about both a personal hero of his and the larger currents of radical thought that were at the heart of the antiwar, Black freedom, and economic justice movements of the late sixties.

This chapter examines the rhetorical and ideological relationship between the two men. Though they were inexorably bonded by their shared passions for advancing the cause of equal rights, the links between Du Bois and King go even deeper. Du Bois and King's careers bracket the "long civil rights era" described by Nikhil Pal Singh and Jacquelyn Dowd Hall—that period of American history stretching from the New Deal of the 1930s until the twilight of American liberalism in the late sixties.[3] Both men were giants in American society's long-running debates about racism, and by the later years of their lives both were largely ostracized by an America gripped with fear about communism and the rise of nonaligned African and Asian nations.

King's recognition of Du Bois's importance to the civil rights movement—not to mention larger movements of social and economic justice—comes through in his speech. This chapter contextualizes the speech. In this case, context means not just the year 1968 or King's turn towards the Left that was apparent late in his life. For our purposes, the context is also the larger legacy of the Black Radical Tradition, written about so extensively by Cedric Robinson.[4] A tradition dedicated to the freedom of Black peoples everywhere, the Black Radical Tradition looked beyond borders for solidarity and inspiration. This certainly applied to King and Du Bois. King's speech recognized the centrality of the radical tradition, and the legacy of Du Bois, to the rapidly changing political and social state of American society.

The relationships of Shirley Graham Du Bois and Herbert Aptheker to both W. E. B. Du Bois and Martin Luther King Jr. are also an important element of this story. Both individuals kept alive the legacy of Du Bois at the end of his life and through the 1960s, as historians began to turn back to Du Bois's writings to make sense of the intersections of civil rights agitation at home and the rise of decolonization movements abroad. The importance of both to preserving Du Bois's radical writings in the late 1960s cannot be underestimated—nor can it be downplayed in relation to King's own use of Du Bois's writings and works in his own changing ideology.

Contextualization also considers King's earlier writings and statements about Du Bois, as well as Du Bois's commentary about the rise of King shortly before the inimitable scholar's death in 1963. While from different backgrounds, both men occupied a critical position within the Black freedom struggle and the larger worldwide struggle against oppression in the twentieth century. King recognized this. He used his speech, and the nearly mythical figure of Du Bois, to rally the American Left during a time when white backlash to civil rights, the Vietnam War, and economic inequality threatened to end once and for all King's dream of a "beloved community."

Du Bois on King, King on Du Bois

It should not be forgotten that, before his passing in 1963, W. E. B. Du Bois lived long enough to observe the rise of Martin Luther King Jr. to national prominence in the late 1950s. By that point in the decade, Du Bois was virtually persona non grata among mainstream civil rights activists, a broader point about his life with which this volume is concerned. His continued backing for the Soviet Union, and a broader policy of peace and an end to the Cold War, made Du Bois a problem for the NAACP and other activists. His alliance with Paul Robeson—another avowed opponent of the Cold War and, like Du Bois, a staunch supporter of communism—also isolated him from African American liberals.

At that same time, Martin Luther King Jr. had just gained national attention for his leadership in the 1955 Montgomery Bus Boycott. Made an international star by the campaign, King was catapulted into the same leadership strata as leaders of the NAACP, the Congress for Racial Equality, and other groups. King's preaching of civil disobedience and nonviolence—without rocking the boat on America's central Cold War values—made him the kind of mainstream leader and activist that Du Bois, by the late fifties, was no longer capable of being.

No one, at that time, assumed that within a decade King would go from a nationally respected civil rights icon to an isolated radical. What is more intriguing about the two men in the fifties is that they interacted several times via mail, with Du Bois offering King support after the Montgomery Bus Boycott. King, in return, would express his admiration for the doctor. For example, after Du Bois sent King a short stanza from the poem "Battle Hymn" by Gustavus Adolphus showing his support for the boycott, King's church office responded with a word of thanks.[5]

Du Bois would also devote considerable column space in the late fifties to writing about King and the new phase of the civil rights movement. He praised the Montgomery bus boycott in a *National Guardian* column from February 11, 1957. Praising the working-class background of the people boycotting Montgomery's public transit, Du Bois reserved special praise for King. "These folk, led by a man who had read Hegel, knew of Karl Marx, and had followed Mohandas Karamchand Gandhi, preached: 'Not by Might, nor by Power, but by My Sprit,' saith the Lord."[6] However, Du Bois's column also contained considerable concern about what the movement in Montgomery accomplished. He argued that the South had to be changed for the sake of humanity. "If we cannot civilize the South," he argued, "or will not even try, we continue in contradiction and riddle."[7]

Du Bois's critique of King continued with his review of the Lawrence Reddick biography of Martin Luther King Jr. titled *Crusader Without Violence*. Here Du Bois argued that while the approach of civil disobedience was a noble attempt at facing discrimination, he worried that more was not being done and planned by King and his cohorts. "In Montgomery hundreds of Negroes have suffered and lost their jobs because of the strike. What program have King and his followers to offset this?"[8] The economics of civil rights struggle, as Carlton Dwayne Floyd and Thomas Ehrlich Reifer's and Reiland Rabaka's essays in this book tackle, were of paramount importance to Du Bois. He worried, in this column, that King and his allies had not yet created a broad-based program to handle the very real problems of economic violence inherent in any movement for social justice. This should be kept in mind when considering the later evolution of King's Poor People's Campaign of 1968.

Further, Du Bois expressed reservations about the utility of civil disobedience in an American setting. He critiqued King and offered support to Robert F.

Williams in their debate over nonviolence versus self-defense. "I was sorry to see King," wrote Du Bois, "lauded for his opposition to the young colored man in North Carolina who declared that in order to stop lynching and mob violence, Negroes must fight back."[9] We should recall that Du Bois understood the necessity of self-defense, arming himself during the height of the Atlanta race riot of 1906—and, no doubt, having never forgotten the terror of that moment.

King, meanwhile, offered up numerous critiques of communism during the late fifties and early sixties. His critiques of Marx and communism need to be seen in proper context. King set himself firmly within the safe confines of Cold War liberalism for tactical reasons. As we know from works such as Thomas J. Jackson's *From Civil Rights to Human Rights*, King entertained leftist sympathizes much earlier than his public left-wing shift in the late sixties.[10] Nonetheless, King's critiques of communism need to be taken seriously, especially in contrast with Du Bois's mostly unapologetic support for worldwide communism. In addition, much of the intellectual heart of these critiques comes from King's own training as a Christian minister. The nuance within the critiques should also be understood too—for they show King, even well before his public turn towards the Left in the late sixties, wrestling with the limits of freedom within a capitalistic system.

For example, King's 1962 sermon "Can a Christian Be a Communist?" serves as a distillation of his criticisms of communism. There, he argued that it was impossible for a Christian to be a communist due to its "avowedly secularist and materialist" worldview. However, King saw communism as a challenge to Christians due to communism's stringent answers for social problems in modern life. If the church did not answer the call, argued King, then communism would only gain more adherents. "A passionate concern for social justice," he argued, "must be a concern of the Christian religion." King's critique of the church's continuing inability to forcefully challenge injustice became a meditation on modern capitalism, a comparative point Phillip Luke Sinitiere offers throughout his chapter in this volume on Du Bois's analysis of Cold War–era American Christianity. King argued, "I'm afraid that there are too many people in America concerned about making a living rather than making a life." King, in other words, was willing to criticize the church in America, communism, *and* the limits of modern capitalism.[11]

While King never effusively praised the Soviet Union or communist China the way Du Bois did, he was also unafraid of offering a stinging critique of America's actions abroad. When King formally announced his opposition to the Vietnam War on April 4, 1967, he referred to the United States government as "the greatest purveyor of violence in the world today."[12] These are words that Du Bois, who spent decades criticizing American imperialism and, later, American actions during the Cold War, would likely have agreed with. After his "Beyond Vietnam" speech, King found himself ostracized by liberals and conservatives alike. For conservatives, King was never a hero—merely someone who had made trouble.

To liberals, however, King seemed to have betrayed them. By speaking out so forcefully against Lyndon Johnson's war in Vietnam and his weak attempts at home to prosecute a War on Poverty, King alienated the very liberals who once saw themselves as his most estimable allies.

In other words, his career trajectory had taken a similar path to Du Bois's. With his only allies being on the American left, King's final year found him taking stock of the limits of the civil rights movement's gains. By raising his voice more on American foreign policy and economic inequality, King reached a position of critiquing American society from a political position that Du Bois would have found familiar—and commendable.

King and the Left, 1967–1968

When King gave his speech in February 1968, he faced not only a divided nation but a fractured civil rights movement. In April of 1967, King's Riverside Church address, where he formally and forcefully came out against the Vietnam War, split him from more moderate members of the movement. For leaders such as strategist Bayard Rustin and NAACP president Roy Wilkins, loyalty to President Lyndon Johnson overrode whatever concerns they had about war in Southeast Asia. Believing President Johnson's accomplishments in civil rights and antipoverty efforts to be worth silencing dissent on foreign policy, Rustin, Wilkins, and much of the African American press criticized King for this antiwar stance.[13]

The antagonistic relationship between King and African American liberals in the final years of his life paralleled the battles between Du Bois and African American leaders in the NAACP in the 1930s through the 1950s. For both men, a shift towards the Left meant they went to a place where mainstream civil rights organizations could not go. While it meant they had ostensible freedom of thought, their radical solutions for racial and economic problems also cut them off from the resources and prestige of groups such as the NAACP. King's Southern Christian Leadership Council struggled for support during King's final years due to this move left.

The rise of the Black Power movement also gave King and other activists pause. Sparked by Stokely Carmichael's call for "Black Power" in 1966 and fueled by the concerns of young African Americans living in northern and western cities, the Black Power movement alienated older civil rights leaders. For the older generation of activists and intellectuals, it appeared Black Power threatened to undo the hard work they'd put into campaigning for racial equality under the law.

King was present at the "creation" of Black Power, being one of the leaders of the "March Against Fear" campaign in Mississippi where Carmichael coined the phrase Black Power. He, like other older civil rights leaders, was critical of both the phrase and what it purportedly stood for. But, by the middle of 1967, King's stance on Black Power began to change. Still offering criticism of the movement when he felt it was warranted, King nonetheless understood the position—and anger—of many young Black Power activists. In trying to wrestle with the phrase, King tried to forge a genuine bridge between the mostly young Black Power activists and the rest of the civil rights and left-liberal coalition members to whom he still had ties.

"First, it is necessary to understand that Black Power is a cry of disappointment," he wrote in *Where Do We Go from Here?*[14] He also noted that most of the members of the Black Power Movement—indeed, its most faithful adherents—had been, not too long before, the most stalwart members of numerous nonviolent campaigns on behalf of civil rights. But King continued to critique Black Power as well, fearing that the understandable anger palpable within that branch of the Black freedom struggle threatened to overwhelm any potential coalition building in the future. He made this clear in his speech honoring Dr. Du Bois.

The speech became a clearinghouse for King's continued concerns about the fate of Black Power. He noted that Du Bois was Black Power personified. "He symbolized in his being his pride in the black man. He did not apologize for being black and because of it, handicapped."[15] King, of course, had in mind subsets of the Black Power Movement that emphasized pride in black hair, appearance, and culture. But he also throws up a caution warning here, in the next section:

> And yet, with all his pride and spirit he did not make a mystique out of blackness. He was proud of his people, not because their color endowed them with some vague greatness but because their concrete achievements in struggle had advanced humanity and he saw and loved progressive humanity in all its hues, black, white, yellow, red and brown.[16]

This entire section warrants a full quote, for two reasons. First, King warned his audience away from going too far with Black nationalistic pride. After all, King was well aware of white and Black liberal concerns about Black Power being a cover for "Black supremacy," which was argued as soon as the phrase Black Power took off in the summer of 1966. More importantly, however, it shows that King is thinking deeper than ever about the concerted need for Black American activists to form, and work hard to lead whenever necessary, multiracial coalitions dedicated to helping all Americans. As he prepared to take the Poor People's Campaign to Washington, DC, King could not help but note W. E. B. Du Bois's lifelong dedication to interracial cooperation and organizing.

King argued that Du Bois could be an example to all Black activists—but only if they were willing to learn from him. "The educated Negro who is not really part of us, and the angry militant who fails to organize us have nothing in common with Dr. Du Bois. He exemplified black power in achievement and he organized black power in action. It was no abstract slogan to him."[17] King wanted to help the Black Power movement. However, to do so, he felt critique was as important as defending them from conservative and liberal critics. The occasion to remember the Du Bois's life became his last prominent public forum in which to do so.

His move towards an open antiwar stance in 1967 was applauded by young activists, although most thought it was a belated shift. This was part of King's own broadening thinking about the status of Black people within an international system of oppression and militarism. His antiwar stance came to be tied with an international solidarity. King had already begun to speak of such solidarity in the late fifties, speaking fondly of seeing Ghana's independence ceremonies in 1957. His sermon "Birth of a New Nation" expressed pride in seeing the creation of a new, unmistakably Black country but also sounded notes that Du Bois—himself having expressed pride in African liberation movements—would have understood and appreciated.[18]

Ghana, of course, was also the nation where Du Bois would spend his final days. Well before the fifties Du Bois supported the Pan-African Congresses, attending several of them. At the height of America's Cold War attempts to romance newly decolonized nations to the banner of the West, Du Bois wrote to Kwame Nkrumah, the first prime minister of Ghana, in 1957. He argued for the need for Ghana to lead the rest of Africa for the foreseeable future. Linking Ghana's problems with those of the rest of the "colored world," Du Bois argued, "All the former barriers of language, culture, religion, and political control should fall before the essential unity of race and descent, the common suffering of slavery and the slave trade and the modern color bar."[19] Du Bois desired for Ghana to lead a sub-Saharan Black Africa not tied to either Cold War power but an independent entity deserving of respect on the international stage.

However, King's views on international solidarity had, by 1968, been shaped profoundly by the Vietnam War. He argued that Du Bois would have been right there with the antiwar movement, calling for an end to America's war in Southeast Asia. King argued that Du Bois "would readily see the parallel between American support of the corrupt and despised Thieu-Ky regime and northern support to the southern slavemasters in 1876."[20] He makes that connection between Vietnam in 1968 and the Reconstruction-era South of 1876 not only due to Du Bois's own scholarship on Reconstruction—developed more fully below—but to make his audience understand that, across time *and* space, solidarity was paramount.

King's worldview was always more expansive than the United States. Traveling to India and Ghana in the fifties, winning a Nobel Peace Prize in 1964, and advocating an end to the Vietnam War by 1967 meant that King always thought internationally. He joined such intellectuals and activists as Du Bois, Frederick Douglass, Malcolm X, Angela Davis, and Coretta Scott King as Black American leaders who embodied what Nick Bromell thought of as a "reimagining of nation, demos, and citizenship," a way to see shared worldwide struggles against oppression as central to Black American worldviews.[21]

The search for an alternative to civil rights liberalism or Black Power radicalism was at the heart of King's campaigns in 1967–68. Pushing back against the brutality of the Vietnam War, the assumed orthodoxy of the Cold War, the inadequate gains of the War on Poverty, *and* the rapidly rising tide of white backlash threatening to overtake the political sphere of the 1968 election, King was besieged on many sides. His speech on the legacy of Du Bois must be understood in that context. King used the speech, in fact, to talk to a generally sympathetic audience about his concerns on all these ideological fronts.

King also made clear his opposition to virulent anticommunism. For King, too many great thinkers had been communists at some point in their lives to merely dismiss the ideology as too radical to be entertained. Putting Du Bois in the same light as Pablo Neruda and Sean O'Casey, King argued, "Our irrational obsessive anti-communism has led us into too many quagmires to be retained as if it were a mode of scientific thinking."[22] He linked together an American reluctance to entertain radical solutions to fundamental problems with the nation's deepening commitment to conflict in Southeast Asia. King acknowledged Du Bois's turn towards communism late in his life, and his flirtation with the Left in general for most of his life, with no shame at all—"we cannot talk of Dr. Du Bois without recognizing that he was a radical all of his life" he uttered.[23] This was a friendly audience to which King spoke. *Freedomways*, after all, was both a journal of the Black Left and one that had been founded, in part, by Du Bois in 1961. That King felt comfortable saying this in public at all, however, is indicative of both how far left he had staked his ideological flag and how little he cared about currying favor with mainstream pundits.

At the same time, the ways in which Du Bois and King's public careers in the United States ended contain similarities, which bear further thinking through the longer Black Radical Tradition. Du Bois, out of favor by the 1950s due to his pro–Soviet Union stance and harsh criticisms of America during the early Cold War years, found the new nation of Ghana far more amenable to him and his political beliefs than the United States. Leaving the place of his birth for what he saw as a type of homeland for African Americans, Du Bois was relieved to have left behind a nation that, for his entire life, discriminated against him simply for the color of his skin. He was no longer considered a major leader of the civil rights movement, having been (like King after him) marginalized for challenging American liberal orthodoxy on race, class, and foreign policy issues.

King, perhaps, found a kindred spirit in Du Bois. Both men were thrust into national prominence at relatively young ages. They both spent a considerable amount of time in the South—specifically, in the racially divided city of Atlanta. Both men, in the twilight of their lives, found themselves ostracized by former allies and forced to turn Left to find erstwhile allies on a wide range of ideological battles against white supremacy and militarism. But both men also found one refuge in particular—Black history.

Du Bois and King on Black History

The two men were united on one subject: their shared love for African American history. For both Du Bois and King, the subject of African American history gave them an opportunity to both excite fellow activists and to inspire African Americans who weren't already engaged in the struggle for freedom. To both men, history was not just something written down in books to be read and discussed by only a few people. Du Bois and King alike knew the importance of history in the larger battle of ideas that was being waged during the entirety of the civil rights movement. They grasped history's power as an intellectual practice of freedom. Public remarks and books written by both men show how they both took history seriously. King's speech honoring Du Bois was, in many ways, a tribute to Du Bois as an activist, intellectual, and historian.

The tradition of Black Americans using history as a weapon in the fight for justice was a long one. Vincent Harding, historian and confidant to Dr. King, argued that proper knowledge of Black history was essential to understanding American history. However, for Harding—as well as for Du Bois and for King—knowing Black history was also integral to the building of a more free and equal United States. "For there will be no new beginnings for a nation," Harding wrote, "that refuses to acknowledge its real past."[24] This was the intellectual milieu in which Du Bois wrote for his entire career, and it was in this ideological context that King gave his speech.

Du Bois's lengthy career as an academic was launched with the writing of his dissertation on the Atlantic Slave Trade.[25] From there, the inimitable intellectual spent a career upending popular arguments about American history. Striking back against the "Dunning School" of Reconstruction historiography, for his entire public career Du Bois argued that the brief era of Black political power in the South represented the best example of democracy ever seen on America's shores. Its sudden and violent end was, in Du Bois's estimation, the greatest tragedy to befall the American Republic.

The culmination of this was Du Bois's 1935 magnum opus, *Black Reconstruction*. An over seven-hundred-page work, Du Bois labored to make the American public understand the ways in which the Reconstruction era in Southern history represented American democracy at its best. The book came at the height of new considerations of the Reconstruction by radical historians—what Bruce E. Baker has referred to as a "radicals' Reconstruction." It was, argued Baker, an attempt to change how people remembered Reconstruction "to further social and political change in the South and in the United States as a whole."[26] In *Black Reconstruction*, as he had done many times before—and would continue to do so until his dying days—Du Bois sought to use history to challenge public perceptions of the past and the present in the United States. He argued that the interpretation of Reconstruction was a disaster, and proof of African Americans being unsuitable for American citizenship, was propagated by a white historical profession that had brought discredit to itself and the very "science" of history. "It is propaganda like this," Du Bois argued, "that has led men in the past to insist that history is 'lies agreed upon'; and to pint out the danger in such misinformation."[27] He understood the value of teaching an American history that put front and center the story of African Americans, enslaved and free.

Du Bois made clear to audiences after 1935 that his interpretation of Reconstruction was meant to be a clarion call for progressive forces in the South. In his "Behold the Land" speech given in Columbia, South Carolina, to the Southern Negro Youth Congress in 1946, Du Bois tied the failure of Reconstruction to the continuing need for activists to fight against both segregation and the rapidly growing anticommunist strain already damaging left-wing activism in America. "Slowly but surely the working people of the South, white and Black, must come to remember that their emancipation depends upon their mutual cooperation," Du Bois argued, repeating the argument for interracial solidarity he made in *Black Reconstruction* and also forwarded by leftists during the Great Depression.[28] In his "Behold the Land" speech and other writings and public addresses, Du Bois reminded his audience of the failure of Reconstruction—and, within it, the lessons that were necessary to reshape American society.

Time and again, Du Bois would press the importance of Black history to understanding—and changing—the United States for the better. As he wrote in a later note for a national radio address on the need for Negro History Week (later Black History Month), "It is not merely a matter of entertainment or information: it is part of our necessary spiritual equipment for making this a country worth living in."[29] Du Bois would use such Negro History Week speeches and addresses to talk both about African American history and current affairs, often linking the two together. Remarking on the progress made by African Americans through the winter of 1960, Du Bois told his audience that the celebration of Negro History Week was "a measure of reward" of everything accomplished by people of African descent since arriving on the shores of North America.[30] When referring to Du Bois as an "agitator-prophet," Herbert Aptheker argued that Du Bois's career as a historian was as much about serving all of Black America as it was about meticulous scholarship.[31] The two, after all, went hand in hand.

The relationship between Herbert Aptheker, Shirley Graham Du Bois, and Dr. King should be considered in this context of African American history and memory. Graham Du Bois, the second wife to W. E. B. Du Bois, was critical to the later years of Du Bois's writing and research. Marrying Du Bois in 1951, at the height of his persecution by the United States government during the Cold War, Shirley Graham became one of the few confidants Du Bois had during a tumultuous 1950s.[32]

Graham was instrumental in helping found the magazine *Freedomways* in 1961. An organ of the African American Left that replaced such newspapers as *Freedom* from the 1950s, *Freedomways* was the latest attempt to craft a magazine that would speak to the experience of the entire African Diaspora from a leftist perspective. W. E. B. Du Bois served as one of its founding editors in 1961 and wrote an essay on Africa for the first issue of the magazine. As the twilight of Du Bois's life and career wound down, both Graham and historian Herbert Aptheker worked to keep alive his legacy. She would forcefully argue over who should have memorialized Du Bois before and after the *Freedomways* sponsored memorial service put on in his honor shortly after his death. In the process, Graham Du Bois argued with Esther Cooper Jackson and other key leaders among the African American Left in the early 1960s. She argued that, as a result of not only being Du Bois's spouse but also being close to him for two decades, she understood his legacy in a way even other leftists could not: "Every plan I make now—every detail of my work . . . every word I write—every action or dream or hope is carried out in close communion with him."[33] Graham Du Bois published several works on Du Bois's life in the 1970s, including *Du Bois: A Pictorial Biography*. Filled with images that showed Du Bois not only at work but sometimes at play, Graham Du Bois tried to humanize her late husband and, at the same time, make clear his lifelong struggle on behalf of people of color around the world.[34]

Aptheker and Du Bois alike had a similar viewpoint of the importance, and utility, of history. Herbert Aptheker published numerous works of "radical" history, often emphasizing the stories of those previously left out of critical narratives—especially showcasing the African American experience in many of his histories. Eschewing any sense of an "ivory tower" in how they both viewed history and academia more broadly, both Aptheker and Du Bois strongly believed in their activism and scholarship not only intertwining but being very much one in the same. When Aptheker wrote about Du Bois after the latter's death, he referred to the historian and sociologist as "an agitator-prophet." It was within this vein that Aptheker labored to make sure Du Bois's later writings—especially those that demonstrated a use of Marxist ideology to diagnose the intractable problems of race and class in American society—were widely available. "Du Bois," wrote Aptheker, "saw the neglect of, or prejudice against, the Negro in American historiography as an aspect of a prevailing elitism in dominant history writing in general." In other words, the very act of writing about African Americans as historical subjects, worthy of study, was itself radical in the early to mid-twentieth century.[35]

Aptheker would be asked by Du Bois to take on the role of his literary executor in 1946, just as Du Bois was increasingly on the outs with the mainstream civil rights movement. This put Aptheker in a unique position to curate the voluminous works of Du Bois, and to determine what would be most important to future generations of would-be Du Bois scholars. This decision by Du Bois was born not only by their personal friendship, but also by Aptheker's keen understanding of the centrality of African American history to the American experience.[36]

This utilization of African American history was one that Martin Luther King Jr. certainly understood. King repeatedly used history in his sermons, public addresses, and the books he wrote during his career. Time and again, King would argue that American history showed how important Black Americans were to the nation—and that the nation needed to do right by them. "My grandfather and my great-grandfather did too much to build this nation for me to be talking about getting away from it," King argued in an August 1967 sermon titled "Why Jesus Called a Man a Fool." He told his audience that before the Declaration of Independence was written, before the landing of the Pilgrims at Plymouth Rock, "We were here."[37] Such arguments about the centrality of Black Americans to the long history of the United States—stretching back to well before the founding of the nation—were nothing new for Black audiences to hear from speakers such as King, Malcolm X, or years before, W. E. B. Du Bois.

King recognized the importance of Du Bois as a historian. In his speech, he called attention to that critical aspect of Du Bois's career. *Black Reconstruction* received special attention. "Dr. Du Bois confronted this powerful structure of historical distortion and dismantled it," King said of *Black Reconstruction.* "He virtually, before anyone else and more than anyone else, demolished the lies about Negroes in their most important and creative period of history."[38] This is not surprising: by 1968, historians had already begun to take a new look at the arguments of Du Bois's work, and a reframing of the Reconstruction historiography was taking place. For example, his work on the Freedman's Bureau in 1901—decades before *Black Reconstruction*—merited attention. Lamenting the many times members of the Dunning School ignored Du Bois and other African American scholars already doing pioneering reinterpretations of Reconstruction, Daniel Walden wrote, "If they had eyes to see with . . . eyes unclouded by prejudice," then historians could have uncovered a different version of the post–Civil War period much sooner.[39] Within the academy, a new appreciation of Du Bois's *Black Reconstruction* was followed by books such as Kenneth Stampp's *The Era of Reconstruction*, which sought to rethink the Dunning School interpretation of Reconstruction.[40]

This new look at Reconstruction took place in the public too. Articles published in places such as *Ebony* magazine, with historian Lerone Bennett at the helm, helped to change public perceptions of the Reconstruction period. Bennett's own views on the Reconstruction era, unsurprisingly, were shaped by Du Bois's *Black Reconstruction*. His series on the political history of African Americans during the Reconstruction period—titled "Black Power"—began in the November 1965 issue of *Ebony*. This series, which would include an essay in each issue of *Ebony* until January 1967, emphasized both the growth of Black political power during the age, and the inevitable backlash of white supremacy. "The long-term effects" of the end of Reconstruction "were disastrous, not only to the black man but to the South and to America," wrote Bennett.[41]

Of course, the interest in Reconstruction in the sixties was tied not just to changes in academic discourse, or the centennial of the American Civil War and Reconstruction. Comparisons between the Reconstruction of the 1860s and the "Second Reconstruction" of the 1960s caused civil rights leaders, American politicians, and intellectuals to all look back to the tumult of the previous century's fleeting experiment with African American citizenship.[42] Reminding white Americans of a Blacker, more accurate history of Reconstruction, King argued that they owed Du Bois a great deal: "White America, drenched with lies about Negroes, has lived too long in a fog of ignorance. Dr. Du Bois gave them a gift of truth for which they should eternally be indebted to him."[43]

As King rose to give his speech in February of 1968, he likely knew his crowd was aware of the burgeoning interest in African American history across the nation. Television programs on the major networks devoted to African American history were already being broadcast by 1968. Where the call for "Black Power!" provided ratings, television networks were also more than willing to create programming around African American history. This was the world in which King gave his speech—one that was not only experiencing an upsurge in white, conservative backlash against the still-indeterminate gains of the civil rights movement and the burgeoning Black Power Movement but, paradoxically (or perhaps in reaction to), also a world in which the slogan "Black is Beautiful" and learning about Black history had never been more popular.

Conclusion: King's Speech, Du Bois, and the Black Radical Tradition of the 1960s

King's own writings and sermons utilized an understanding of American, and especially African American, history that was inspired by W. E. B. Du Bois's own trailblazing path. What should be taken away from King's speech is that he was indebted to Du Bois in ways that were almost incalculable. By February 1968, King understood the isolation of Du Bois's later years. Both men, fired by the fight against racism, imperialism, and economic exploitation, were willing to go from being at the heart of the popular struggle for civil rights to being forced to its margins by Black and white liberals, uncomfortable with both men's tying of militarism and economic injustice to racial discrimination.

By the time King's memorial address for Dr. Du Bois was published in the pages of *Freedomways*, King himself was also dead. Assassinated on April 4, 1968, King's death made him yet the latest martyr in a decade full of them. The spring issue of *Freedomways* went from being a tribute to Du Bois to being a tribute to King—as well as a tribute to three young Black men killed in Orangeburg, South Carolina, during unrest there in January 1968, and five Black Africans executed by the Ian Smith regime in Rhodesia.[44]

In this issue, indeed in all the issues of *Freedomways*, several traditions of the Black left embodied by both Du Bois and King always came to the fore. The magazine, cofounded by Du Bois in 1961, would remain a mainstay of Black left-wing thought throughout the Black diaspora until its closing in 1985. Dedicated to political agitation, historical education, and international solidarity, *Freedomways* was the periodical personification of what both King and Du Bois stood for during the bulk of their lives.

Immediately after King's assassination, the centrality of Du Bois to King's, and other leaders,' thinking on fighting racism was made clearer by fellow Black intellectuals. Vincent Harding wrote as much in 1969. He argued that Du Bois "was likely the most significant voice to prepare the way for this current, newest age of Blackness. He is the proper context for an adequate understanding of Malcolm, of Fanon, of Stokely Carmichael and Martin Luther King."[45] It is telling that Harding united these men—divided in some ways by ideology and geography—under one powerful intellectual umbrella. Without Du Bois, Harding argued, none of these other giants of the twentieth-century Black diaspora could have ascended to the heights that they did.

Martin Luther King Jr. knew this. His speech was both a clarion call to the American left and a tribute to one of his intellectual heroes. The connections between the two men appear, at times, to be guided by more than the random chance of history. Du Bois died the day of King's "I Have a Dream Speech," on August 27, 1963. One of King's last public speeches was this very tribute to Du Bois. But, in fact, the two men were always linked together—as civil rights leaders, dreamers of the Left, and tribunes of the Black diaspora.

NOTES

1. "Honoring Dr. Du Bois," *Freedomways* 8, no. 2 (Spring 1968): 104. All quotations from Dr. King's speech will be derived from the reproduction of the speech in this issue of *Freedomways*.

2. James Baldwin would also give a speech at the same event as King. Titled "A Letter to Americans," the speech was originally a letter that had been written to both the *New York Times* and *London Times*. Neither published it. The letter was also published in the same

Freedomways issue which published Dr. King's speech. "A Letter to Americans," *Freedomways* 8, no. 2 (Spring 1968): 112–16.

3. Nikhil Pal Singh, *Black is a Country: Race and the Unfinished Struggle for Democracy* (Cambridge: Harvard University Press, 2004), 6. See also, Jacquelyn Dowd Hall, "The Long Civil Rights Movement and the Political Uses of the Past," *Journal of American History* 91, no. 4 (March 2005): 1233–63.

4. Cedric Robinson, *Black Marxism: The Making of the Black Radical Tradition* (London, Zed Press, 1983; Chapel Hill, University of North Carolina Press, 2000).

5. "To W. E. B. Du Bois," March 19, 1956, The Martin Luther King Jr. Papers Project, Stanford University, http://okra.stanford.edu/transcription/document_images/Vol03Scans/180_19-Mar-1956_To%20W%20E%20B%20Du%20Bois.pdf.

6. W. E. B. Du Bois, "Will the Great Gandhi Live Again?" in *W. E. B. Du Bois: A Reader*, ed. David Levering Lewis (New York: Henry Holt and Company, 1995), 359. Originally published in *National Guardian*, February 11, 1957.

7. *W. E. B. Du Bois: A Reader*, 360.

8. W. E. B. Du Bois, "Crusader Without Violence," in *W. E. B. Du Bois: A Reader*, 361. Originally published in *National Guardian*, November 9, 1959.

9. *W. E. B. Du Bois: A Reader*, 361.

10. Thomas F. Jackson, *From Civil Rights to Human Rights: Martin Luther King, Jr. and the Struggle for Economic Justice* (Philadelphia: University of Pennsylvania Press, 2007).

11. Martin Luther King Jr. "Can a Christian Be a Communist?" Delivered on September 30, 1962, The Martin Luther King Jr. Papers Project, Stanford University, https://kinginstitute.stanford.edu/king-papers/documents/can-christian-be-communist-sermon-delivered-ebenezer-baptist-church, accessed June 2, 2022.

12. Martin Luther King Jr. "Beyond Vietnam." Delivered on April 4, 1967, https://www.americanrhetoric.com/speeches/mlkatimetobreaksilence.htm, accessed on June 2, 2022.

13. Daniel Lucks, *From Selma to Saigon: The Civil Rights Movement and the Vietnam War* (Lexington: University Press of Kentucky, 2014), is the best single-volume monograph on this split. In addition, fractures within the division have been chronicled by, among others, David C. Carter, *The Music Has Gone Out of the Movement* (Chapel Hill: University of North Carolina Press, 2009).

14. Martin Luther King Jr., *Where Do We Go from Here: Chaos or Community?* (Boston: Beacon Press, 1994 [1968]), 33.

15. King, 108.

16. King, 109.

17. King, 109.

18. Martin Luther King Jr., "The Birth of a New Nation," Delivered April 7, 1957, The Martin Luther King Jr. Papers Project, Stanford University, https://kinginstitute.stanford.edu/king-papers/documents/birth-new-nation-sermon-delivered-dexter-avenue-baptist-church, accessed April 30, 2022.

19. W. E. B. Du Bois, "Letter from W. E. B. Du Bois to Kwame Nkrumah," February 7, 1957, W. E. B. Du Bois Papers Digital Archive, University of Massachusetts Amherst, http://credo.library.umass.edu/cgi-bin/pdf.cgi?id=scua:mums312-b146-i353.

20. King, 110.

21. Nick Bromell, *The Time Is Always Now: Black Thought and the Transformation of U.S. Democracy* (New York: Oxford University Press, 2013), 85.

22. King, 109.

23. King, 109.

24. Vincent Harding, "The Uses of the Afro-American Past," *Negro Digest* 17, no. 4 (February 1968): 5.

25. W. E. B. Du Bois, *The Suppression of the African Slave-Trade to the United States of America, 1638–1870* (New York: Longmans, Green, and Co., 1896).

26. Bruce E. Baker, *What Reconstruction Meant: Historical Memory in the American South* (Charlottesville, VA: University of Virginia Press, 2007), 110.

27. W. E. B. Du Bois, *Black Reconstruction in America: 1860–1880* (New York: The Free Press, 1992 [1935]), 714.

28. W. E. B. Du Bois, "Behold the Land," Delivered on October 20, 1946, in Columbia, South Carolina. Reprinted in *Freedomways Reader: Prophets in Their Own Country*, edited by Esther Cooper Jackson (Westview Press: Boulder, CO, 2000), 7.

29. W. E. B. Du Bois, "Negro History Week," January 27, 1949, W. E. B. Du Bois Papers Digital Archive, University of Massachusetts Amherst, http://credo.library.umass.edu/cgi-bin/pdf.cgi?id=scua:mums312-b199-i038.

30. W. E. B. Du Bois, "The American Negro," February 19, 1960, W. E. B. Du Bois Papers Digital Archive, University of Massachusetts Amherst, http://credo.library.umass.edu/cgi-bin/pdf.cgi?id=scua:mums312-b206-i046.

31. Herbert Aptheker, "Du Bois as Historian," *Negro History Bulletin* 32, no. 4 (April 1969), 6.

32. David Levering Lewis, *W. E. B. Du Bois: A Biography* (New York: Henry Holt, 2009), 690.

33. Gerald Horne, *Race Woman: The Lives of Shirley Graham Du Bois* (New York: New York University Press, 2000), 218–19.

34. Shirley Graham Du Bois, *Du Bois: A Pictorial Biography* (Chicago: Johnson Publishing Company, 1978). For more on the importance of the *Pictorial Biography*, see Britt Russert, "Shirley Graham Du Bois's Labor of Love," *Black Perspectives*, March 12, 2019, https://www.aaihs.org/shirley-graham-du-boiss-labor-of-love/.

35. Herbert Aptheker, *Afro-American History: The Modern Era* (Secaucus, NJ: Citadel Press, 1971), 47–51.

36. Christopher Lehmann-Haupt, "Herbert Aptheker, 87, Dies; Prolific Marxist Historian," *New York Times*, March 20, 2003, https://www.nytimes.com/2003/03/20/us/herbert-aptheker-87-dies-prolific-marxist-historian.html.

37. Martin Luther King Jr. "Why Jesus Called a Man a Fool," delivered at Mount Pisgah Missionary Baptist Church, Chicago, Illinois, August 27, 1967, https://www.youtube.com/watch?v=6CENN9f12yQ, accessed June 2, 2022.

38. King, 107.

39. Daniel Walden, "W. E. B. Du Bois: Pioneer Reconstruction Historian," *Negro History Bulletin* 26, no. 5 (February 1963): 159.

40. Kenneth Stampp, *The Era of Reconstruction, 1865–1877* (New York: Vintage Books, 1965).

41. Lerone Bennett, "Black Power IX: America at the Crossroads," *Ebony*, January 1967, 122.

42. C. Vann Woodward referred to a "Second Reconstruction" in his book, *The Strange Career of Jim Crow*, in 1955. It is notable that Martin Luther King Jr. referred to this book as "the historical Bible of the Civil Rights Movement."

43. King, 109.

44. *Freedomways* included an advertisement, titled "In Memoriam to the Martyrs," dedicated to the two groups of young people killed fighting for black freedom on both sides of the Atlantic. "In Memoriam to the Martyrs," *Freedomways* 8, no. 2 (Spring 1968), 103.

45. Vincent Harding, "W. E. B. Du Bois and the Messianic Vision," *Freedomways* (Winter 1969), 57.

CHAPTER 11

W. E. B. Du Bois's UnAmerican End, Reconsidered

—Jodi Melamed and Tyler Monson

> The treatment of the Negro is America's greatest and most conspicuous scandal. For the colored peoples all over the world, whose rising influence is axiomatic, this scandal is salt in their wounds. . . . [However,] the American Negro is thoroughly American in his culture and whole outlook on the world. He is loyal to America, and there is no danger that he will betray it. . . . America, for its international prestige, power, and future security, needs to demonstrate to the world that American Negroes can be satisfactorily integrated into its democracy.
> —Gunnar Myrdal, *An American Dilemma: The Negro Problem and Modern Democracy* (1944)

> I believe in communism. I mean by communism a planned way of life in the production of wealth and work designed for building a state whose object is the highest welfare of its people and not merely the profit of a part. . . . Who now am I to have come to these conclusions? . . . This is the excuse for this writing which I call a Soliloquy.
> —W. E. B. Du Bois, *The Autobiography of W. E. B. Du Bois: A Soliloquy on Viewing My Life from the Last Decade of Its First Century* (written 1958–1960, first international publication 1963, first US publication 1968)

The following essay interprets W. E. B. Du Bois's late witness for communism in his final, major work, *The Autobiography of W. E. B. Du Bois*, as a strategy for memorializing a critical consciousness of race in the history of capitalism during the early Cold War, at a time when this critical consciousness was being criminalized precisely by associating economic critiques of race and racism with communism. From the hindsight of the twenty-first century, this confluence reveals how much the "American Creed" of racial liberalism coming into dominance in the postwar period—the belief that American values of individualism, abstract equality, and freedom were the proper framework for racial justice and African American inclusion—was already oriented towards an economic or capitalist understanding of these terms, familiar to our neoliberal era. Returning to Du Bois's *Autobiography*, we can limn the long arc of how discourses of Black loyalty and disloyalty to the US nation connect to the material history of racial capitalism in the US after World War II.

The essay was originally written in 2006[1], during the George W. Bush administration and at the height of the influence of neoliberal multiculturalism, a kind of postracialism that equates free trade and free markets with the end of the relevance of race in global modernity, or rather, with the reduction of racial difference to a cultural commodity or a human-resource factor for global corporations. Against the presumption that multiculturalism was the spirit of neoliberalism, Du Bois's witness for the shape and force of racial capitalism at the beginning of the Cold War seemed important for developing critical strategies for recognizing neoliberal political economy as racial capitalism (from the rise of mass incarceration in the US as a "solution" to racialized economic precarity to free trade zones, often called new slave zones to emphasize the impunity with which governments have facilitated the exploitation of Black and brown bodies). Turning back to the essay in the Trump era, it is the criminalization of Du Bois for his witness for communism—and thus, according to the protocol of his witness in the *Autobiography*, for his critical consciousness of racial capitalism—that stands out. Once again, criminality and accusations of disloyalty are being used to silence writers, activists, and intellectuals of color who limn the political expressions of racial capitalism in our times, from defenders of the Boycott, Divestment and Sanctions movement (such as Steve Salaita) to those helping us understand the Black Lives Matter movement as a response to austerity and other forms of neoliberal governance (prominently Keeanga-Yamahtta Taylor). How can the story Du Bois tells in the *Autobiography*, of coming into a critical consciousness about the role of race in capitalism, inform contemporary struggles to actualize antiracial capitalist thinking and politics? For one, it testifies once again that the "freedom" envisioned by Black freedom struggles is fully exorbitant to the "freedom" of US patriotism and the "freedom" of the market. In this way, it helps us refuse to finesse this distinction in the manner of racial liberalism and other "loyal" versions of state-sanctioned antiracisms.[2]

The Witness for Communism

During and after World War II, as liberation struggles and the costs of war undermined the system of territorial colonialism employed by European powers, US neocolonialism emerged as the ascendant form of international hegemony, one that superseded colonial methods of direct rule with political and economic domination and a preponderance of military strength. As postcolonial countries achieved a negotiated independence, they found themselves facing the effective control of the United States, which sought to manage global decolonization through a discourse of anticommunism and a transnational capitalist system that included the unprecedented penetration of US capital and goods into formerly restricted economies. The presence and power of the Soviet Union, however, meant that the subordination of formerly colonized states to US hegemony remained contingent to a degree. The Soviet Union sought to undermine consent for US influence in Asia and Africa by publicizing acts of racial violence and segregation in the United States, claiming these acts as evidence that white supremacist doctrine suffused the world-ordering ambitions of the US and the social relations of international capitalism. Central to the postwar rise of US neocolonialism, therefore, was the necessity to manage the racial contradictions that gave rise both to decolonization in formerly colonized states and to antiracist movements in the US.

Because it proved capable of managing such contradictions, racial liberalism emerged as a central political ideology and mode of social organization in postwar US society. In contrast to white supremacy, racial liberalism acknowledged racial inequality to be a problem and secured a liberal symbolic framework for resolving racial antagonisms centered on legal equality, African American attainment of possessive individualism, and inclusive civic nationalism. The watershed document of racial liberalism, *An American Dilemma: The Negro Problem and American Democracy* (1944), a social scientific study of US race relations spearheaded by Swedish social scientist Gunnar Myrdal, dominated the rationality and politics of race in the United States until the mid-1960s.[3]

In the first epigraph above, *An American Dilemma* calls for a liberal, nationalist antiracism that was to become a tenet of Cold War ideological battles: "The treatment of the Negro is America's greatest and most conspicuous scandal. For the colored peoples all over the world, whose rising influence is axiomatic, this scandal is salt in their wounds. . . . America, for its international prestige, power, and future security, needs to demonstrate to the world that American Negroes can be successfully integrated into its democracy" (Myrdal 1021). Although the study takes it to be self-evident that decolonization and the ascendancy of the United States have elevated race to a global symbol and that the visibility of racial inequality compromises US dominance, this situation does not invalidate US claims to global leadership. Instead, the "Negro Problem" becomes an opportunity, the grounds for a new American exceptionalist narrative. Linking domestic race reform to the moral legitimation of US global power, *An American Dilemma* defines a nationalist imperative for liberal race reform: the key to the nation's achievement of its international manifest destiny was to be the visible integration of African

Americans into American democracy. As Mary Dudziak has demonstrated, this narrative was to become a governing statement for mainstream civil rights activism and State Department propaganda during the early Cold War (47–79).

In the first part of this essay, we investigate how liberal nationalist antiracist discourse, in positioning the "American Negro" as "America's witness," elevated control over narratives of African American lives to an ideological imperative. We consider how the narrative was policed by the generative and repressive force of the postwar nation-state and through the agency of racial liberal intellectuals, social scientists, and culture workers. To witness for America, African American existence had to demonstrate identity with a liberal nationalist rendering of white American patriotism, cultural values, and normativity. Folded into the context of the Cold War, *An American Dilemma*'s conclusion that the "American Negro" is "loyal to America, and there is no danger he will betray it" became an anchor for disciplinary violence. Black people in the United States were enjoined to prioritize an identification with America above all other identifications, racial, antiracist, internationalist, or diasporic. Those who refused to subordinate such alternate identifications faced repression as "UnAmerican subversives." Such was the case with Paul Robeson, W. Alphaeus Hunton, C. L. R. James, Claudia Jones, Richard Wright, Benjamin Davis, and W. E. B. Du Bois.

In the second part of the essay, we reconsider Du Bois's neglected final autobiography, *The Autobiography of W. E. B. Du Bois: A Soliloquy on Viewing My Life from the Last Decade of Its First Century*. We suggest that reconstructing the political centrality of the narrative of the "American Negro" as "America's witness" lets us read the *Autobiography* as an important intervention into the global politics of race in the period, one that strove against the grain of liberal representations to renarrativize the story of the "American Negro" as a witness against US neocolonialism and leadership of transnational capitalism. In the second epigraph above, Du Bois's refusal to witness for America could not be clearer: "I believe in communism. I mean by communism a planned way of life in the production of wealth and work. . . . Who now am I to have come to these conclusions? . . . This is the excuse for this writing which I call a soliloquy" (*Autobiography* 57–58).

Rather than reading here a dogmatic pledge of allegiance to the Soviet Union, we contend that if we situate these lines within the geopolitics of Blackness as a global symbol during the era of decolonization, then we can read them to be a rhetorically, politically, and theoretically sophisticated attempt by Du Bois to refashion his life story as a countersymbol that might rupture American exceptionalist representations of African American racial formation as a symbol for the probity of US-led global capitalism. Du Bois locates his life story in the history of the international development of capitalism and imperialism to call for an ethico-economic revolution in human relations more robust than liberal nationalism. In so doing, he reconceives the Black witness as a means to orchestrate desire for an antiracism responsive to the history and present of racial capitalism.[4] Du Bois's witness becomes all the more poignant when viewed against the context of the struggle between liberalism and radicalism in Du Bois's own career. By the early 1940s, Du Bois had renounced his earlier understanding of a "Talented Tenth" and distanced himself from his formulation of double consciousness in *The Souls of Black Folk*, concepts allied with the liberalism of his coleaders at the NAACP and eventually incorporated into midcentury racial liberalism. Ironically, Du Bois wrote the *Autobiography* from a position of radical opposition to a liberal nationalist integrationism that had mainstreamed his prescient liberal thinking.

In reconsidering the *Autobiography*, we hope to contribute to the ongoing scholarly effort to recover suppressed African American critiques of Cold War civil rights thinking from the time of its emergence. In scholarship by Kate Baldwin, Brent Edwards, Roderick Ferguson, Nikhil Singh, and Penny Von Eschen, we find a restoration of the importance of Black intellectual work rendered marginal by Cold War historiography.[5] This direction has been developed further in major scholarship by Amy Bass, Bill V. Mullen, and Eric Porter. Directly discussing the racial and cultural politics of representing Du Bois's legacy, this work illuminates the significance and persistence of Du Bois's commitments to economic justice against the grain of post–World War II liberal antiracisms.

Witnesses for Freedom

"American Negroes are becoming American. But what then is America to become?" (quoted in Von Eschen, *Race* 87). Voiced in the late 1950s, Du Bois's question short-circuits the causal logic of liberal race narratives: he remarks on the successful invention of a racially inclusive American nationality but refuses to see this nationality as a guarantee that United States global power will become more benign. Instead, he hints grimly that the sublation of the contradiction between "American" and "Negro" opens the door for the United States to exert its force with greater impunity. How is it that for 1950s liberal discourse, the skepticism in Du Bois's question could not be entertained? We briefly examine nodal points in liberal discourse during the early Cold War that demonstrate how the "Americanness" of African American lives became increasingly important for ideologies of US nationalism and international manifest destiny. One example: we take the heading for this section from Rebecca Chalmers Barton's widely read study of African American autobiography *Witnesses for Freedom* (1948). In an unironic act of rhetorical transference, Barton claimed that African American life narratives featuring personal battles for "freedom" from American racism counted for the Cold War as witnesses for the superiority of American "freedom" over Soviet communism. Eric Porter beautifully captures the dark side of this discourse in his study of Du Bois's thinking in the 1940s and 1950s: "Du Bois implicitly defined Cold War politics as a racial project that subverted black rights claims via the litmus test of loyalty while simultaneously using a potential black disloyalty to foment a sense of political crisis, thereby justifying other trajectories of political repression or inaction" (Porter 158).

We open with a close consideration of Myrdal's *An American Dilemma* and its project of remaking white racial identity to align with a more racially inclusive liberal nationalism. Incorporating antiracism into postwar Americanism, *An American Dilemma* portrayed white Americans as moral heroes who, in ridding themselves of racial prejudice, would prove the American nation to be a model for universal human aspiration. Anchoring the narrative of a universal nation redeemed by confronting racism was a regulative narrative that ideologically fixed African Americans as passive witnesses to, rather than agents of, white America's redemptive transformation. We see the extreme irony of the representation of Black passivity when we recognize that *An American Dilemma* popularized a racial liberalism that some Black Americans had spent more than thirty years trying to promote through political activism (such as that of the NAACP and the National Urban League) and intellectual activism, including the work of prominent thinkers such as E. Franklin Frazier, Ralph Bunche, and Du Bois himself, whose original research and analysis Myrdal appropriates and reframes in *An American Dilemma*.

An American Dilemma begins with two propositions: that "the Negro Problem is a moral issue which has its existence in the [white] American mind" and that white racial prejudice is in fatal contradiction with the "American Creed," a presumed national social ethos whose "main norms . . . as usually pronounced are centered in the belief in equality and in the rights to liberty" (Myrdal lxxix, 8). According to the study, racial prejudice occurs because white Americans are constantly forced to recognize a contradiction between their identification with the American Creed and their participation in the material and social practices of racial inequality. To compensate for this contradiction, white Americans indulge in racial prejudice, invent racist doctrine, and develop a skewed sense of reality. The solution the study proposes is a comprehensive national program of education to result, hopefully, in the conversion, on a national scale, of prejudiced white Americans into liberal white Americans who would apply the American Creed in their attitudes and actions towards African Americans. At the same time, the full substantialization of the American Creed in American life would enable the US to fulfill its postwar international manifest destiny:

> If America should follow its own deepest convictions, its well-being at home would be increased directly. At the same time America's prestige and power abroad would rise immensely. The century old dream of American patriots, that America could

> give the entire world its own freedoms and its own faith, would become true. . . . America saving itself becomes savior of the world. (1022)

Thus, the study interweaves race reform with the ubiquitous evangelical strand of US nationalism portraying America as the world's best hope for advancement and salvation, linking America's salvation from its racial dilemma to the salvation of the world. It depicts the conversion of prejudiced white Americans into white racial liberals to be an act of heroic moral conversion on which the realization of American dreams of international manifest destiny rest. Instead of rhetorically disconnecting US liberal democracy from white privilege, however, *An American Dilemma* continually coordinates the meaning of US nationalism, troped as universal human aspiration, with the meaning of liberal whiteness, metaphorized as the unmarked "American" subject, as we see in the passage above. Even as the goal of antiracism engages with the conventional narrative of American manifest destiny, "America" maintains its exclusive associations with whiteness.

While *An American Dilemma* grants white Americans the agency to transform themselves and rejuvenate the country for international leadership, it fixes African Americans as objects of certain knowledge. The study's project of white public enlightenment depends, in the first place, on knowing the "truth" of African American racial formation. Because its goal is ultimately to argue that African Americans are part of the social community to which the American Creed applies, it is not surprising that the "truth" of African American existence and consciousness is its national character. In the quote below, Myrdal construes African American culture to be the same as (white) national culture in most respects and as much as possible under conditions of racial inequality. "In his allegiances the Negro is characteristically an American. He believes in the American Creed and in other ideals held by most Americans, such as getting ahead in the world, individualism, the importance of education and wealth. He imitates the dominant culture as he sees it and in so far as he can adopt it under the conditions of his life" (928). Where the study does not "nationalize" African American culture—that is to say, where it does recognize cultural difference—it pathologizes it. Rather than evaluating cultural forms that are distinctly Black to indicate the existence of a separate epistemology or a distinct culture, Myrdal judges that "in practically all its divergences, American Negro culture is not something independent of general American culture. It is a distorted development, or a pathological condition, of the general American culture" (928). In other words, where Black American culture is not "thoroughly American," *An American Dilemma* concludes that racial oppression has distorted it.

Ultimately, the positing of the "American Negro" as "America's witness" to the world depends on this binary taxonomy of African American culture as either just like "the general American culture" or "a pathological condition" of it. This taxonomy becomes the basis of a progress narrative: because all differences from the "general American culture" are seen to be the "pathological" results of racial inequality, the more American that Black Americans (are allowed to) become, the more proof that white Americans are shedding themselves of racist beliefs and that the US is ready to fulfill its messianic mission of giving "its own freedoms and own faith" to the world (Myrdal 1022).

This inference constructs a passive witness around the figure of "the American Negro." According to its terms, Black Americans do not have to testify that US racist state practices have ended. Instead, a certain set of conditions and behaviors supposedly exhibited in African American lives count as evidence of US legitimacy in and of themselves. The passivity of the witness constructed around the figure of the "Negro" becomes particularly obvious at the end of *An American Dilemma* in a section entitled "America at the Crossroads": If America in actual practice could show the world a progressive trend by which the Negro finally became integrated into modern democracy, all mankind would be given faith again . . . and America would have gained a spiritual power many times stronger than all her financial and military resources. . . . America is free to choose whether the Negro shall remain her liability or become her opportunity (1022; original emphasis). According to the witness constructed here, "America" meaning "white Americans" are the active agents "free to choose" whether or not to bring about the conditions for progress against racial inequality. That is, white Americans are "free to choose whether the Negro shall remain [America's] liability or become her opportunity." "The Negro," on the other hand, although established as the witness for America, actually witnesses only passively, like the weathervane that shows which way the wind is blowing or the mercury that indicates a rise in temperature.

While racial liberalism incorporated the idea of the "American Negro" as "America's witness" into consciousness-raising projects designed to produce a racially inclusive liberal nationalism, the Truman and Eisenhower State Departments deployed the narrative as propaganda for American global hegemony, plain and simple. As Dudziak reconstructs in *Cold War Civil Rights*, the Cultural Affairs, Psychological Warfare and Propaganda Division of the US Department of State took the lead in shaping international perceptions of African Americans in the early Cold War (79–115). The United States Information Agency and the Voice of America kept its posts busy throughout Asia, Europe, and especially sub-Saharan Africa creating and disseminating radio broadcasts, films, newspaper articles, and pamphlets to explain to an attentive world how to understand American race relations through liberal paradigms.

As Dudziak establishes, "The Negro in American Life," a widely distributed USIA pamphlet written in 1950 or 1951, was the best-developed government position on race (49–55). It obscured racial contradictions in the United States through a developmental life narrative that, in a temporizing move, depicted the steady maturation of "the Negro" from childhood to adulthood as an index of the health of American democracy. Representing an entire social group as a single individual ("the Negro"), the pamphlet naturalized racial inequality as the inequality of a child, contending that access to education would eventually enable "the Negro" to mature gradually into a "man" and citizen, able to persuade his white fellow citizens of his equal status and rights through reasoned argumentation.

To reinforce propaganda about the anonymous "Negro in American life," the USIA distributed more particularized life narratives publicizing the success of famous Black Americans in newspapers throughout the nonwestern world. A few of these published in West African newspapers in the 1950s include "Working for World Peace: Dr. Bunche in History," "Harry Belafonte's Crusade for Americanism," and "Negro Hurdler is determined to win Olympic event" (Von Eschen, "Who's the Real Ambassador" 117). For the State Department, the prominence of famous Black individuals in America was to verify that "the Negro" as a whole would one day achieve the elevated status predicted for him in generalized narratives such as "The Negro in American Life." To this end, Ralph Ellison was vigorously promoted as a "Great American Novelist" and Jackie Robinson as America's sportsman—ambassador to the world.[6]

In addition to publicizing the lives and achievements of accomplished Black Americans, State Department speaking tours brought African Americans who embodied middle class professional status to Africa and Asia to verify the Black witness that Cold War propaganda constructed. For example, as Dudziak relates, the USIA was particularly pleased with the speaking tour of Max Yergan, the founder and executive secretary of the Council on African Affairs. On a USIA-sponsored trip to Lagos, Nigeria, in 1952, Yergan witnessed that he enjoyed "ever-expanding rights and privileges which his grandfather, a Negro slave, could only dream of" (quoted in Dudziak 56). To the same degree that the State Department promoted and facilitated the travel of individuals like Yergan, it worked to discredit and to restrain the movements of African Americans opposed to Cold War foreign policy, such as Du Bois, Robeson, and Josephine Baker.[7]

With the narrative of the "American Negro" as "America's witness," racial liberalism achieved political centrality in the US and as an ideology of US expansionism during the early Cold War. For US national culture, the narrative worked to change the dominant reference points of national identity by powerfully inserting a narrative of the "Negro" as fully "American" into an earlier story of US manifest destiny, portraying the "American Negro" as an instrument for bringing US-style freedoms to the world. It revamped nationalist narratives of American history to include Black American progress against racism as a chapter in the story of the progressive development of American democracy. At the same time, the narrative of the "American Negro" as "America's witness" censored an earlier anti-imperialist global political economic critique of race and racism, which as

Von Eschen establishes, was an important component of the Black public sphere in the US in the 1930s and 1940s (*Race* 7–21). Cold War liberals ostracized Du Bois precisely because he continued to advocate for this earlier understanding.

Soliloquy against US-Led Neocolonial Capitalism

As Kate Baldwin persuasively argues, the United States ultimately turned the Soviet Union's criticism of racial violence and Jim Crow to its advantage: it set the conditions for the US to disseminate a narrative of a promised resolution to racial strife, which served to guarantee rhetorically the moral legitimacy of US global leadership and to distract attention away from the ambitions of US-based capital and goods seeking investment and markets in the decolonizing world (Baldwin 177). Precisely because African American life narratives played such a critical role in the American exceptionalist racial drama orchestrated by the United States, successive US administrations made a concerted effort to silence African Americans who allied themselves with the social and economic goals of the Soviet Union or who continued to approach racism as part of a nexus of imperialism and capitalism, such as W. E. B. Du Bois, Paul Robeson, W. Alphaeus Hunton, and others. Du Bois, for example, was tried in 1951 in federal court as an agent of foreign powers for his work with the Stockholm-based Peace Information Center. Although he won an acquittal, the impression remained that he was guilty of treasonous conduct. He was informally criminalized, and his passport revoked, cutting him off from advocates and audiences outside the US.[8]

In response to his silencing and to its failure, to the new global context of expanding American hegemony and the role of African American life stories in its ideological management, Du Bois, we argue, invents an oppositional practice of autobiography *in The Autobiography of W. E. B. Du Bois: A Soliloquy on Viewing My Life from the Last Decade of its First Century*. Rupturing the liberal narrative of the "American Negro" as "America's witness," Du Bois reappropriates the African American life story as a witness against the expansion of US-led neocolonial capitalism. From the period of the publication of *An American Dilemma* (1944) to the time of the writing of the *Autobiography* (1958–59), McCarthyite red baiting decimated the Left and progressives in the United States and disunified further in the face of revelations of Stalinist violence. In contrast, racial liberalism, once part of a left-of-center agenda, became part of mainstream Cold War politics and achieved prominence in American national culture and identity. In light of this development, we can perceive the urgency of the efforts of the *Autobiography* to keep alive a leftist agenda expressly in the name of racial justice, as well as the degree to which it threatened and undid Cold War racial political meanings and thus was consigned to illegibility within them. That the *Autobiography* was first published in the USSR, China, and the German Democratic Republic in 1964–1965, with its first US publication not appearing until 1968, testifies to the text's global ambitions, its strategic use by communist bloc countries, and its invisibility to US conversations (Aptheker 561).

To appreciate the oppositional practice of autobiography we find in *The Autobiography of W. E. B. Du Bois*, it is important to remember the loaded genealogy of African American autobiography, a genre in which the literary and the political have always been inseparable from one another. Emerging as slave narrative, African American autobiography began with the paradoxical project of arguing for Black humanity. This condition placed a founding constraint on the genre: that "the parameters of what could be said [were] always attenuated by the less lenient powers of what could be believed" (Baldwin 160). By the mid-twentieth century, as argued above, African American autobiography had to cope with the determining condition that, in the United States, the meaning of Black humanity had become inseparable discursively from the ideological legitimization of US global leadership. Along with this condition came the injunction that African American autobiography serve as evidence and therefore it could be interpreted along positivist and explanatory lines. This injunction effected the reading not only of autobiography, but also of novels written by African American authors, which were interpreted as "autobiographical" even when it was rationally difficult to do so.[9] To offer "proof" of the progressive development of American democracy, the narrativity of African American life stories had to be suppressed.

In contrast to Cold War liberalism's treatment of African American life stories as evidence and explanation, Du Bois in the *Autobiography of W. E. B. Du Bois: A Soliloquy on Viewing My Life from the Last Decade of Its First Century* underscores the narrativity and the literariness of his own intervention, as the subtitle *A Soliloquy* implies. "Soliloquy," which we can define as nondialogic discourse from the self to the self, seems to signal a deliberate withdrawal on Du Bois's part from the constructed political community of liberal nationalism. A second meaning of "soliloquy" is a literary or dramatic mode of performance, where a character speaks in the presence of others (the audience or other characters), performing deliberately crafted "truth," a species of metanarrative, as if it were intimate self-revelation. Considered in the context of the *Autobiography* as "A Soliloquy," this second definition of "soliloquy" as crafted "truth" seems to indicate a deliberate move to free the genre of African American autobiography from the positivism racial liberalism ascribed to it. By practicing autobiography as "to soliloquize," Du Bois foregrounds narrative technique to nurture a critical imagination about the meaning of Black lives in the United States. The goal, in the first place, is to help readers resist the story of capitalism that Cold War liberal narratives were telling through insinuation and elision as they worked to restrict racial meanings to a story of US freedom. Du Bois inscribes as real an African American life story that memorializes the history of race in the development of modern capitalism to arrange desire for an alternative to US neocolonialism. To do so, he breaks sharply with liberal nationalist protocols for the telling of African American lives.[10]

As the Library of America anthology of Du Bois's writings reports, the *Autobiography* is made up to a large degree of previously published material, with some two hundred pages adopted from *Dusk of Dawn* (1940) and substantial text taken from *In Battle for Peace* (1952), *The Souls of Black Folk* (1903), and work published in the *National Guardian* during the early 1950s (*Writings* 1308). As McCarthyism in the US shrank Du Bois's circle of friends and influence, Herbert Aptheker's undiminished ties to both Du Bois and the Communist Party marked a deeply felt trust between them. In moving to Ghana in October 1961, Du Bois left his papers and correspondence to Aptheker's home. Over the following years, Aptheker and his wife Fay categorized the archive materials, and, with consultation and consent of Shirley Graham Du Bois, he became the charge for finding a suitable institution to house them. Using Du Bois's carbon copy of the autobiography completed in Ghana, Aptheker and Fay typed out the manuscript as well as a selected bibliography, collected photographs, and notes and explanations (Murrell 199–205).[11] The amount of text that Du Bois recirculates from *Dusk of Dawn* is interesting, for it demonstrates the proactiveness of Du Bois's thinking, that is, the degree to which he anticipated the link between liberalism, capitalism, and US global power that became the central themes of race relations in the early Cold War. Byerman has interpreted Du Bois's recirculation of work in the *Autobiography* as an attempt by the author to control his self-representation and to self-anthologize work that received too limited an audience ("Recovering the Self" 66 and *Seizing the Word* 223). Building on Byerman's insight with an eye toward Du Bois's later positions against US neocolonialism, we suggest that Du Bois in the *Autobiography* positions his earlier work as steps on an intellectual journey to develop a critical consciousness about race that drives him to witness for an ideal of communism against actually existing US capitalist democracy. The fact that *Dusk of Dawn* predates Myrdal's study and the Cold War yet comes to many of the same conclusions about the destructive links between race and capitalism strengthens the prosocialist and anti-neocolonial witness of the *Autobiography*.

Shirley Graham Du Bois, a well-regarded Leftist in her own right, was a key interlocutor in Du Bois's later years, despite appearing in the *Autobiography* primarily in the role of spousal support, "my wife, Shirley Graham." For example, she assisted in editing the fiftieth-anniversary edition of *The Souls of Black Folk* (Horne 149) and, when he was too ill to travel, delivered his speech to the "All-Africa Conference" in Accra in December 1958 (Du Bois *Autobiography* 401–4). Graham Du Bois's constant companionship to her husband was bound not just by love but in their shared social, political, and ideological commitments.

The *Autobiography* opens by flouting the Cold War liberal injunction that stories of African American lives articulate themselves with the story of the nation; it begins on the day of Du Bois's long-awaited escape from US territory, August 5, 1958, after having been denied a passport for eight years on the grounds that it was "against the country's best interests" for him to go abroad (11). Part One of the *Autobiography* is a 50-page travelogue of his journey, which Du Bois narrates as moving providentially eastward, from the declining metropolises of Western European to the new world of socialism emerging in the Baltics, the Soviet Union, and what for Du Bois was a colored People's Republic of China.

The opening travelogue serves to extract Du Bois's life story and the motif of the African American life story in general from the context of Cold War imaginings of the international as the space where American freedom fights Soviet communism. Instead, they are placed within a context of the international where anticolonial socialism struggles against neocolonial capitalism. Making the recontextualization obvious, Du Bois declares the need to rethink his life story in light of the world conflict that his journey from the parasitical West to the striving East revealed to him: "I mention the trip in some detail because it . . . had wide influence on my thought. To explain this influence, my Soliloquy becomes an autobiography. . . . Who and what is this I, which in the last year, looked on a torn world and tried to judge it?" (12).

Du Bois further distances his telling of the African American life story from liberal nationalism. He denationalizes and internationalizes African American racial formation by reconstructing it within the racial history of colonial capitalism. As he travels through Western Europe, Du Bois travels through time as well as space, excavating the social and economic histories shaping the present. He finds a red, white, and blue thread, the prehistory of present US neocolonialism, woven into the fabric of European colonialism. Visiting Holland, for example, Du Bois locates his own family history and the genesis of US racial capitalism within the history of British and Dutch slave-trading and Dutch empire in Southeast Asia:

> It was a Dutchman who in the early 18th century kidnapped my great grand-grandfather on the coast of West Africa and sold him into slavery in the valley of the Hudson. This was the century in which the Dutch began to take part in the stealing of labor in Africa. . . . The British in the 18th century succeeded in displacing them as the world's greatest slave traders and established slavery in their American colonies. This commercial rivalry between the Dutch and the British resulted in a system of Dutch colonies which covered Southeast Asia. (17)

Telling the story of his progenitor's entry into the future space of the United States as Dutch slave property, Du Bois articulates his transnational family history to illuminate the role of racialization in the global development of colonialism and capitalism. At the same time, he traces the origin of US racial capitalism back before US statehood, back to the stem where it becomes indistinguishable from European empire.[12]

Centering African American racial formation within the history of racial capitalism, Du Bois claims an identification with a socialism responsive to this context. The *Autobiography* narrates this socialism to be emerging most forcefully in China. It dramatizes a powerful, imaginative identification for African Americans with China, based on nonidentical yet shared experiences of the culture of racial capitalism as dehumanizing. It then depicts this identification to generate the possibility for an affirmative cultural style to support a new kind of transnational belonging. In particular, Du Bois depicts "American Negroes" and "China" to share a contiguous culture animated by a habit of self-sacrifice formed in reaction to separate yet overlapping historical experiences of oppression. Du Bois first relates "American Negroes" to "China" in a passage that asserts China's greater suffering: "I used to weep for American Negroes, as I saw what indignities and repressions and cruelties they had passed; but . . . I know that no depths of Negro slavery in America have plumbed such abysses as the Chinese have seen for 2,000 years and more. They have seen starvation and murder; rape and prostitution; . . . oppression and contempt . . . from Tartars, Mongolians, British, French, Germans, and Americans [and] from the Chinese themselves" (50). Praising China's ability to survive and to be transformed by suffering, Du Bois next personifies "China" as a Black singer of spirituals, crooning the song "O, Mourner, get up off your knees" (52). While the collapsed signification appears at first to be a strange elision of cultural difference, Du Bois here seems to use literary devices to entice the reader to accept an existing cultural continuity between "African Americans" and "China." He asks the reader to imagine the major producer of "culture" (understood broadly as that which gives one a sense of self in the world) not to be religion or language but historical experience, specifically, the historical experience of oppression organized through regimes of racial capitalism (coolie-izaton, segregation, colonialism). This common experience, Du Bois suggests, generates shared alternative cultural norms to the culture of US-European capitalism.

The *Autobiography* has been criticized for its blindness to the abuses and the imperialism of the PRC and the Soviet Union.[13] In consideration of this critique, it is important to recognize that Du Bois was highly motivated to see China and the Soviet Union—and communism in general—in a favorable light. In the first place, we might assert that Du Bois narrates a story of China as a nonwhite socialist Utopia, the better to oppose liberal narratives of the United States as a postracist white Utopia.[14] Importantly, for Du Bois, there was no capitalism that was not always already racial capitalism, and communism served as a kind of placeholder for an alternative ethico-economic relation where racial and economic democracy (a term Du Bois sometimes preferred to socialism) would flourish together. We might describe Du Bois's total project in the *Autobiography* as the construction of an antiracist argument in favor of communism through the telling of an emblematic African American life story (Du Bois's own) that memorializes the negative history of race in the development of capitalism.

In a section entitled 'Interlude" inserted between the opening travelogue and the retelling of his life story, we find the *Autobiography*'s most important declarative statement, in which Du Bois formally declares a belief in communism.

> I have studied socialism and communism long and carefully in lands where they are practiced and in conversation with their adherents, and with wide reading. I now state my conclusion frankly and clearly: I believe in communism. I mean by communism, a planned way of life in the production of wealth and work designed for building a state whose object is the highest welfare of its people and not merely the profit of a part. . . . Once I thought these ends could be attained under capitalism. . . . After earnest observation, I now believe that capital and free enterprise are leading the world to disaster. . . . Democratic government in the United States has almost ceased to function. . . . We are ruled by those who control wealth and who by that power buy or coerce public opinion. Who now am I to have come to these conclusions? And what if any significance are my deductions? What has been my life work and of what meaning to mankind? . . . This is the excuse for this writing which I call a Soliloquy. (57, 58)

In these passages, employing italics to mimic the sense of a spoken pledge, Du Bois turns the Cold War loyalty oath on its head. Rather than witness for the United States, Du Bois witnesses against the existence of democracy in the US—a larger point Andre Johnson's chapter in this volume also explores—avowing that "[democratic] government in the United States has almost ceased to function." In the last lines of the passages above, Du Bois reverses Cold War orchestrations of the "American Negro" as "America's Witness." He frames the telling of his life story as a means to account for how he came to believe in communism (defined in ideal terms as planned production and redistribution within a state) over and above liberal nationalism. In doing so, the *Autobiography* counters the narrative in *An American Dilemma* of the conversion of white Americans into liberal antiracists with a narrative of an African American conversion to communism.[15] In providing a Black witness against US neocolonialism to counter liberal nationalist stories of a Black witness for America, Du Bois's declaration of belief in communism comes across as something other than a dogmatic show of support for the Soviet Union.

In contrast to Cold War liberal discourse, which anchored the witness it extracted from African American life stories in the presumed truth of African American being, Du Bois bases his oppositional witness on what he learned to think: the point of his life story is the formation of a critical consciousness about race in the development of capitalism. Following the "Interlude," telling of the life in the *Autobiography* proceeds chronologically, as is conventional, but its narrative focuses on the author's intellectual development, on what he has to learn to be able to perceive "race" as a consolidation of hermeneutics and social forces inseparable from the genealogy of global capitalism. This break, then, becomes an interpretative optic that gives meaning to Du Bois's life and work and arranges a desire in the author for an ameliorative and revitalizing socialism.

Du Bois begins rethinking his intellectual formation with his youth in Great Barrington, Massachusetts, and then moves on to his student years at Fisk and Harvard universities and the University of Berlin. In particular, the narrative investigates how Du Bois's formal education prevented him from grasping economic organization at all, completely obscuring the primary entanglement of modern capitalist social relations with racialist ideologies. At Fisk, his lessons "on the whole avoided economics" teaching, for example, "the moral aspects of slavery, not the economic" (126). At Harvard, Du Bois finds the environment poisonous to lessons that contradicted the interests of the institution, now a "defender of wealth and capital, already half ashamed of Charles Sumner and Wendell Phillips" (189).

As he retells and rethinks his life story, Du Bois subjects his earlier intellectual formation to a reparative autocritique. Specifically, in his rethinking he supplies the political economic critique of race in the history of modern capitalism that he lacked previously. Often Du Bois's reparative autocritique comes across as an awkward exercise in rough historical materialism. He replays his thinking as a student and then juxtaposes his past perception with his new understanding of concurrent international developments in colonialism and racial capitalism. Below, for example, Du Bois subjects to critique his decision to make Bismarck the topic of his Fisk University commencement oration:

> I took as my subject "Bismarck." This choice in itself showed the abyss between my education and the truth in the world. Bismarck was my hero. He made a nation out of a mass of bickering peoples. . . . This foreshadowed in my mind the kind of thing that American Negroes must do, marching forth with strength under trained leadership. On the other hand, I did not understand at all, nor had my history course led me to understand, anything of the current European intrigue, of the expansion of European power into Africa, of the industrial revolution built on slave trade and now turning into colonial imperialism; of the fierce rivalry among white nations for controlling the profits from colonial raw material and labor; of all this I had no clear conception. (126)[16]

Even as Du Bois remarks on the gap in his knowledge, he begins to fill it in, repairing his education at the same time he recounts its failings. He corrects his earlier miscomprehension of Bismarck as a praiseworthy nationalist leader with a new understanding of Bismarck as a colonial exploiter of Africa.

Du Bois's reparative autocritique provides an opportunity to narrativize a political economic history of race that Cold War anticommunism obfuscated. For example, in the passage below, Du Bois juxtaposes his flawed earlier understanding of the 1887 Queen's Jubilee next to his better, later comprehension of the event:

> The Queen's Jubilee in June 1887, while I was still in Fisk, set the pattern of our thinking. The little old woman at Windsor became a magnificent symbol of Empire. Here was England with her flag draped around the world, ruling more black folk than white and leading the colored peoples of the earth to Christian baptism, and as we assumed, to civilization and eventual self-rule. (142)

> The Queen's Jubilee, I [now] knew, was not merely a sentimental outburst. It was a triumph of English economic aggression around the world and it aroused the cupidity and fear of Germany who proceeded to double her navy, expand into Asia, and consolidate her European position. Germany challenged France and England at Algerciras, a prelude to the World War. Imperialism, despite Cleveland's opposition, spread to America, and the Hawaiian sugar fields were annexed. (207)[17]

In his later understanding, Du Bois learns to look beyond the Queen's Jubilee as a convincing symbolic representation of Progress to see it as a diacritical indicator of economic rivalry among US-European imperialists. Thus, Du Bois's reparative autocritique constructs a Black witness based in an intellectual understanding of the interrelations of capitalism, imperialism, and colonial ideology that, by situating capitalism as interwoven with antidemocratic political forms, clearly conflicts with Myrdal's conception of a Black witness for the legitimacy of US-style capitalism and political democracy.

As the *Autobiography* moves forward, the focus changes from what Du Bois was unable to think to what the study of race enabled him to think. By World War I, systematic inquiry into race relations for Du Bois had come to serve as an intellectual lever for thinking outside the matrix of social relations, values, and norms supporting the "economic development into which [he] was born":

> Had it not been for the race problem early thrust upon and enveloping me, I should have probably been an unquestioning worshipper at the shrine of the established social order and the economic development into which I was born. But just that part of the order which seemed to most of my fellows nearest perfection seemed to me most inequitable and wrong; and starting from this critique I gradually, as the years went by, found other things to question in my environment. (155)[18]

As Du Bois narrates it, the "race problem" becomes a bit of meaning-making for him, a marker of difference and reversal, which he deploys scientifically to reckon against reified common sense. Mapping continuities in condition among "the darker races" of the world and searching for a synthesizing explanation, Du Bois narrates a learning process where he begins to comprehend the instrumentality of racialization for modern capital development. He concludes that robust, international racial equality would mean the end of modern capitalism, reasoning that racism's historically deep saturation with capitalist social relations puts the expansion of capitalism into contradiction with racial justice to the extent that victory over global racial inequality would necessarily have to coincide with the transition from capitalism to socialism. Whereas in *Dusk of Dawn: An Essay Toward an Autobiography of a Race Concept*, Du Bois offered his life story as an example of how the meaning of race is lived in the world, in *The Autobiography of W. E. B. Du Bois*, he offers his life story as an example of how to relearn the meaning of race to demystify the development of modern capitalism and hence to see the continuity between territorial colonialism and the tactics of US neocolonialism.

Du Bois narrates a second witness that follows from his hard-won insight into Black experience with US racial capitalism: a story of African American racial formation as fit to bear the rationality of socialism. By this we mean that Du Bois finds ripe conditions for critical thinking that cathects to habits and values conducive for socialism in the historical dialectic between the self-consciousness of Black people and their contemptible material conditions under regimes of US racial capitalism, an idea of African American experience and epistemology utterly lacking in Myrdal's binary conception of African American formation as either all American or pathological. Du Bois calls this consciousness-in-solution in African American racial formation "an inner Negro cultural ideal" (391). Although from his terminology, it might sound like Du Bois's "ideal" represents an essence intrinsic to African American being, by 1960 his "inner Negro cultural ideal" is overwhelmingly historical materialist like his thinking about race in general at this time.[19] In the *Autobiography*, he tracks the "inner Negro cultural ideal" through its phenomenology, that is, through structures of experience presenting themselves to consciousness in attitudes, habits, and behaviors.

Du Bois describes the "inner Negro cultural ideal" as a consciousness "developed by memory of slavery and experience of caste" (*Autobiography* 391). Present and continuing in African American racial formation, rather than immanent or inherent within it, Du Bois makes it contingent on cultural memory and material conditions (such as the relative absence of class differentiation) and therefore capable of growing stronger or weaker.[20] In fact, Du Bois portrays the ideal to be growing weaker within African American racial formation throughout the 1950s, diluted by Cold War distortions of Black history, weakened cultural memory, and increased socioeconomic mobility for middle class black professionals. As

Du Bois recounts, where he once "had faith" that the "inner Negro cultural ideal . . . would drive the Negro group into a spiritual unity that would preclude the development of inner class struggles," by 1960 he determines the contingency has become "improbable" (*Autobiography* 392). Nonetheless, according to the protocol of the *Autobiography*, we must evaluate Du Bois's narrativization of the "inner Negro cultural ideal" to be an attempt to inscribe it as real along the lines of "to soliloquize" and thereby prop it up in the name of a future revitalization.

The most important facet of "the Negro cultural ideal" that Du Bois tracks is a reactive ethic of self-sacrifice. Formed in reaction to the long historical experience of the culture of US capitalism as a mode of dehumanization and dispossession, the ethic of self-sacrifice is not a racial property but a habit of relation to others that breaks the rules of possessive individualism and other values conducive to the accumulation of private wealth. The forms of appearance of the ethic of self-sacrifice are multifarious and sometimes subtle. He first introduces the ethic of self-sacrifice in the figure of an uncle who works without wages for a decade to support the unexpectedly impoverished white family that "employs" him. Another early figure is Josie, a young African American woman he meets while teaching summer school in rural Tennessee. Noting the sacrifices she makes in pursuit of an education for herself and her siblings, Du Bois remarks on her "unconscious moral heroism that would willingly give all of life to make life broader, deeper, and fuller for her and hers" (*Autobiography* 116). When he goes South for the first time to attend Fisk University, Du Bois finds self-sacrifice to be characteristic of a "half-awakened common consciousness" among Black people there, sprung from shared emotive experiences ("common joy and grief") and especially from shared material conditions ("a common hardship in poverty, poor land, and low wages") (*Autobiography* 212). He later extols Atlanta University for instilling in future race leaders a determination "to spread with their own hands the Gospel of Sacrifice" and traces the impulse animating the Niagara Movement to "the spirit of willingness to sacrifice" that John Brown exemplified (*Autobiography* 111).[21]

For Du Bois, the ethic of self-sacrifice answers the question that all socialist theory must engage: what motivates unselfish behavior? As depicted in the examples above, Du Bois's ethic is open and multiapparitional. It is agential in itself rather than owned and deployed. Some of its forms cluster around the idea of material foregoing that Du Bois opposes to the culture of private wealth accumulation. Others (such as the example of John Brown) lean on the Latin roots of "sacrifice" ("sacer (sacred) + facere (to do)") to prioritize sacred-making behaviors over profit-making ones. All of the examples esteem other-directedness over self-interest. Du Bois asks the reader to imagine the ethic of self-sacrifice to be a present and abiding reflex (although beginning to dissipate) onto which the redistributive logic of socialism might be grafted. The first step is to put the material history that illuminates its formation back into the public record. While

Cold War liberals such as Myrdal employed African American life stories to reconfigure nationalist symbols and to recreate national identity, Du Bois stages an ethic of self-sacrifice as an alternate value around which a constituency for global socialism can coalesce. He depicts it to be present not only in African American formation, but also in the motivations of Chinese communism and the cultural heritage of pan-Africanism. For example, in his speech for the 1958 All-Africa Conference in Accra, reprinted in the penultimate chapter of the *Autobiography*, Du Bois depicts it to be a key component of a culture that will sustain pan-Africanism: "As I have said, this is a call for sacrifice. . . . If Africa unites it will be because each part . . . gives up a part of its heritage for the good of the whole. That is what union means; that is what Pan-Africa means" (404). Du Bois's Black witness thus calls for international alliances and affinities radically at odds with Myrdal's conception of a Black witness to ratify the US as leader of a "free world" coalition against communism.

Set against Cold War distortions of African American persons and history, Du Bois's life story comes across strongly as a countermemorialization of the story of race in the development of capitalism that he makes the point of his intellectual formation. We can venture that this countermemorialization was intended to anchor a process of imagining transnational ties in the name of an alternative geopolitics.[22] In this, we vouchsafe Bill V. Mullen's representation of W. E. B. Du Bois as a "committed global revolutionary thinker and typologist of world revolution," whose life "may be best understood as the evolutionary political embrace of the Un-American years before the political label became the Cold War cloak designating his marginalization and dishonor" (Mullen 7). In the end, Du Bois's "soliloquy" does not so much signal a lonely withdrawal from the constructed political community of the United States as a jeremiad against the historical amnesia on which he saw postwar US neocolonialism situated to thrive, as well as a conjuration of an ethical and radical antiracism, beyond the scope of liberal political calculation.

Disloyalty as a Hermeneutic in the Trump Era

Returning to the *Autobiography* in the era of Trump and the Black Lives Matter movement, we see that many of the conditions that enabled Du Bois's witness for communism to nurture a critical consciousness of racial capitalism have ended, notably the end of communism in the Soviet Union (not that Soviet communism ever realized an alternative to racial capitalism). Yet the work of Black freedom struggles and other movements to conjure new political communities and ethical and radical antiracisms able to take on the injustices of capitalism continues. Even as right wing, libertarian and social conservative agendas demand even less accounting for racial equality (and thus even more leverage for white supremacy and economies of dispossession), Black, Native, queer and Palestinian-led social movements introduce visions of conditions for wellbeing and relationality that exceed conservative or liberal political thought, and in that way, can be affiliated with Du Bois's 'ethic of self-sacrifice.' The first year of Trump's presidency was a year of toppling—or seeking to topple—Confederate monuments. Du Bois's address to the "Almighty Dead" in the *Autobiography* reminds us that it is not enough to erase the symbols and rallying points of white supremacist power. Rather, the witness of past oppression demands the active creation of a future that develops out of a critical consciousness of the past. Once again, discourses of loyalty and criminality seek to suppress critical thinking in the name of nationalism, and the norm is increasingly to inhibit critique of precisely racial capitalist modes of brutal and slow violence, from police killings to environmental racism. So, we return to Du Bois's important, yet flawed witness for communism as an alternative to racial capitalism in the *Autobiography* as an example of the difficulty—and necessity—of keeping hermeneutical activism about racial capitalism alive in the face of US nationalism and the criminalization, delegitimation, and censorship it can bring to bear.

NOTES

Portions of this article appeared as Jodi Melamed, "W. E. B. Du Bois's UnAmerican End," *African American Review* 40/3 (Fall 2006): 533–50. Thanks to the John Hopkins University Press for permission to present portions of the earlier article.

1. Though much of Melamed's reading of the *Autobiography* remains intact, this version seeks to extend a hermeneutical activism about racial capitalism to the Trump era. The trajectory of dominant thinking of race has shifted from a framework of "multiculturalism" that appeared to be sensitive and humane to difference even as it operated within ideologies of American exceptionalism to an "all-American nativism," which uses racially divisive rhetoric and policies to justify banning, deporting, and detaining migrants from Mexico, Central America, and Arab- and Muslim-majority countries. Daniel Denvir argues that Trump "speaks nativism" and thus theorizes the management of racial Others as an effort to make good on the promise that "a country made white 'again' will be great." See Daniel, Denvir, *All-American Nativism: How the Bipartisan War on Immigrants Explains Politics as We Know It* (London: Verso, 2020), 383–404.

2. For more on the history of state-sanctioned or official antiracisms after World War II, see Jodi Melamed, *Represent and Destroy: Rationalizing Violence in the New Racial Capitalism* (Minneapolis: University of Minnesota Press, 2011), 2–50.

3. *An American Dilemma*, a near national bestseller, proclaimed as a masterwork by Harry Truman and W. E. B. Du Bois alike, dominated national discourse on race at all levels in the late 1940s and 1950s, from the academy to government to the kitchen table. While Myrdal was the sole author of the study's two volumes, he relied on research reports compiled for the project by a prestigious, interracial group of social scientists and other scholars (primarily from

the University of Chicago schools of sociology and anthropology), including Ralph Bunche, Charles Johnson, Louis Wirth, Melville Herskovitz, Arnold Rose, Sterling Brown, Alaine Locke, and W. E. B. Du Bois. For a history of the Carnegie Corporation's initiation and participation in the study, see Ellen Lagemann, *The Politics of Knowledge: The Carnegie Corporation, Philanthropy, and Public Policy* (Middletown, CT: Wesleyan University Press, 1989). For a discussion of the importance of *An American Dilemma* as a foundational text of modern social science, see David Southern, *Gunnar Myrdal and Black-White Relations: The Use and Abuse of An American Dilemma, 1944–1969* (Baton Rouge: Louisiana State University Press, 1987); Daryl Michael Scott, *Contempt and Pity: Social Policy and the Image of the Damaged Black Psyche, 1880–1996* (Chapel Hill: University of North Carolina Press, 1997); Steven Steinberg, *Turning Back: The Retreat from Racial Justice in American Thought and Policy* (Boston: Beacon, 1995); Walter A. Jackson, *Gunnar Myrdal and American's Conscience: Social Engineering and Racial Liberalism, 1938–1987* (Chapel Hill: University of North Carolina Press, 1990).

4. We follow Robinson's usage of the term "racial capitalism" to designate the historical agency that ensues from the originary and continuing permeation of capitalist economic and social relations by racialism, a process that shapes the development, organization, and expansion of capitalist societies and social ideologies alike. See Cedric J. Robinson, *Black Marxism: The Making of the Black Radical Tradition*, Foreword by Robin D. G. Kelley, Preface by Cedric J. Robinson (Chapel Hill: University of North Carolina Press, 2000), 2–3.

5. In addition to the exceptional work of Aptheker in disseminating and interpreting Du Bois's late body of work, several Du Bois biographers must also be recognized as attentive to its importance: David Levering Lewis, Gerald Horne, Manning Marable, and Arnold Rampersad. Levering Lewis's encompassing second volume of his Du Bois biography has corrected the common misperceptions of Du Bois at the time of the writing of the *Autobiography*, but also to a degree reinforced them. Although Levering Lewis draws a straight line back from Du Bois's late radicalism to his earlier activism and scholarship, he continues to portray Du Bois in later life as alienated and lacking in critical judgment, *W. E. B. Du Bois: The Fight for Equality and The American Century, 1919–1963* (New York: Holt, 2000). In *Black and Red: W. E. B. Du Bois and the Afro-American Response to the Cold War 1944–1963* (Albany: State University of New York Press, 1986), Horne more forcefully recovers the late Du Bois as an active and engaged radical and intellectual. He also illuminates how common misperceptions of the late Du Bois are byproducts of Cold War historiography as well as government efforts to discredit Du Bois in the 1950s. Unfortunately, Horne's revisionary history has not gotten the attention it deserves. Although more compressed than Horne's study, Marable's *W. E. B. Du Bois: Black Radical Democrat* (Boston: Twayne, 1986) puts the late Du Bois back into the mainstream of African American and progressive politics in the 1950s. Marable also offers his own meritorious theory for the tendency of Cold War critics to distort Du Bois's later social thought: "the refusal to draw any correlation between Marxism and democracy" (216). Rampersad's 1976 biography *The Art and Imagination of W. E. B. Du Bois* (Cambridge: Harvard University Press, 1976) is exceptional for its attention to the role of Marxism in Du Bois's total intellectual genealogy and its insight into the importance of dialectical materialism for the late work (263–64).

6. It is ironic that despite Ellison's condemnation of *An American Dilemma* for its inability to recognize that "Negroes have made a life upon the horns of the white man's dilemma," Ellison's own image, as crafted by successive State Departments, served as a black witness for America within the parameters Myrdal's study laid out. See Ralph Ellison, "An American Dilemma," in *Shadow and Act* (New York: Vintage, 1995 [1953]), 316.

7. On the State Department's persecution of Robeson, see James Ellison, "Paul Robeson and the State Department," *The Crisis* 84 (May 1977): 115–33 and Martin Duberman, *Paul Robeson* (New York: Knopf, 1989). On its campaign against Josephine Baker, see Mary L. Dudziak, *Cold*

War Civil Rights: Race and the Image of American Democracy (Princeton: Princeton University Press, 2000), 67–78, and Josephine Baker and Jo Bouillon, *Josephine*, trans. Mariana Fitzpatnck (New York: Paragon, 1988 [1976]). On the federal persecution of Du Bois, see Horne, *Black and Red*, 201–23 and Lewis, *W. E. B. Du Bois*, 496–571.

8. Horne persuasively argues that these attempts to undermine popular support for Du Bois inside and outside of the United States were never as successful as Cold War historiography maintains. He reconstructs how Du Bois in the 1950s was more closely embraced and embracing of working class African American political movements and left progressive movements than ever before. According to Horne, in the eyes of a majority of nonelite Black Americans and of leftists battling Cold War repression, Du Bois's resistance to McCarthyism and Cold War national sentiment only augmented the high regard in which they held him. After Ghana won independence in 1957, the State Department could no longer afford the negative publicity of refusing "the Father of Pan-Africa" the right of egress and restored Du Bois's passport. See Horne, *Black and Red*, 133–66.

9. Barton, for example, reads Chester Himes's novel *If He Hollers* as an autobiography (not even "autobiographical fiction") in spite of glaring discrepancies between the novel and Himes's life. (The protagonist of the novel is falsely charged with rape and impressed into the military to avoid a prison term.) In another example, Frederic Wertham determined that Richard Wright was Bigger Thomas insofar as the character's "unconscious determinants" were the emotions and events that Wright had experienced as a fifteen-year-old boy employed in a white household in the Jim Crow South. See Molly Rae Rhodes, "Doctoring Culture: Literary Intellectuals, Psychology and Mass Culture in the Twentieth Century United States" (University of California San Diego, PhD dissertation, 1997), 82–106.

10. For an alternative interpretation that reads the *Autobiography* as failing to demonstrate Du Bois's interiority and thus failing as "soliloquy," see William E. Cain, "From Liberalism to Communism: The Political Thought of W. E. B. Du Bois," in *Cultures of U.S. Imperialism*, eds. Amy Kaplan and Donald Pease (Durham: Duke University Press, 1993), 307.

11. The US edition was published by International Publishers in 1968. Upon reading the page proofs in 1967, Shirley Graham Du Bois remarked to Aptheker, "I know that yours was a work of devotion and love, that your reward springs from the memory of love and faith which W. E. B. always had in you. Any other thanks is superfluous," quoted in Gary Murrell, *"The Most Dangerous Communist in the United States": A Biography of Herbert Aptheker* (Amherst: University of Massachusetts Press, 2015), 205.

12. Throughout the travelogue, Du Bois leans on this intertwined economic history to create a counternarrative to post–World War II portrayals of the US as savior of democratic Europe. Instead, he depicts their relationship to be that of old coconspirators revising the terms of their alliance to reflect the US's new dominance. While Cold War McCarthyism sought to reduce all expressions of disidentification with "America" to attacks on democracy writ large, Du Bois makes it clear that his own disidentification cannot be so reduced: it proceeds from remembering race as a technology of western colonialism, which makes visible this new epoch as one of the consolidations of US-led neocolonial capitalism under the rubric of an international alliance of free and democratic nations. See Du Bois, *Autobiography*, 15–43.

13. See, for example, Cain, "From Liberalism to Communism."

14. Thanks to Grace Kyungwon Hong for this observation.

15. Thanks to Steve Karian for this formulation.

16. The passage is to be found verbatim in *Dusk of Dawn*. See W. E. B. Du Bois, *Dusk of Dawn: An Essay Toward an Autobiography of a Race Concept* (New Brunswick, NJ: Transaction, 1997 [1940]), 32.

17. These passages are to be found verbatim in *Dusk of Dawn*. See Du Bois, *Dusk*, 52.

18. This passage is to be found verbatim in *Dusk of Dawn*. See Du Bois, *Dusk*, 22.

19. The phrase "inner Negro cultural ideal" is dated terminology for Du Bois by 1960. It harkens back to his phrasing in the 1898 pamphlet "The Conservation of Races." Here Du Bois described a "Negro ideal" very much in Hegelian terms as a sort of biologically-rooted *Volksgeist* ("Conservation," 40). Warren describes the 1898 "Negro ideal" as "the epitome and expression of the intellect of black-blooded people in America" that would represent the Negro's unique contribution to civilization. We argue that Du Bois uses the term "inner Negro cultural ideal" in 1960 to describe a consciousness that he associates very much with Black experience but that he drops the blood-taint that Warren accentuates. See Kenneth Warren, "Delimiting America: The Legacy of Du Bois," *American Literary History* 1.1 (1989): 172–89.

20. Du Bois pinpoints the golden age of African American fitness for socialism at just after World War I. At the time, he asserts, African American economic cooperation was viable and might have acted as a catalyst for a larger national reorganization: "I did believe that a people where the differentiation in classes because of wealth had only begun, could be so guided by intelligent leaders that they would develop into a consumer-conscious people, producing for use and not primarily for profit and working into the surrounding industrial organization so as to reinforce the economic revolution bound to develop in the United States and all over Europe and Asia sooner or later" (*Autobiography*, 291).

21. We must note that the lack of an active imaginary about gender seems to truncate Du Bois's vision of an ethic of self-sacrifice. James notices this limitation in Du Bois's late political thought in *Transcending the Talented Tenth*. As James remarks, despite Du Bois's ability to unlearn his class privilege and his early rejection of patriarchy, he never discards a masculinist conceptual framework. Ultimately, his privileged, oppositional subject is a male intellectual animated by an ethic of self-sacrifice. See Joy James, *Transcending the Talented Tenth: Black Leaders and American Intellectuals* (New York: Routledge, 1997), 35–61.

22. To this end, Du Bois reprints nearly a dozen speeches delivered to audiences around the world: in Peking on his ninety-first birthday, in Chicago on a tour to raise funds for his upcoming trial; in Moscow at a Soviet peace conference; in Accra, Ghana, for the 1958 All-Africa Conference. Translating the speeches from spoken to written performances, Du Bois implicitly figures a collectivity of "listening" audiences, allowing the reader to imagine a collective audience to be responsive to the form of antiracist, anti-imperialist global politics for which the *Autobiography* ultimately witnesses. See Du Bois, *Autobiography*, 396–408.

CHAPTER 12

Geography of Freedom: Partnership in Preservation and Public History at W. E. B. Du Bois's Boyhood Homesite

—Camesha Scruggs

At 612 S. Egremont Street in Great Barrington, Massachusetts, the site looks unassuming. There sits a large maroon sign and a parking lot, adjacent to a two-story house. At the rear of the lot, there is a sign with a photo of William Edward Burghardt Du Bois that is recognizable. The photo is his countenance, complemented with the distinguishable hair, mustache, and goatee. At the scheduled times and dates, it is at this spot where the guide greets visitors, and the tour begins. The guide and the visitors commence the performance of public history and preservation, simultaneously creating a community bound by their experience.

Throughout this chapter, my practicum experiences as a tour guide at the W. E. B. Du Bois Boyhood Homesite will be in conversation with scholarship regarding Du Bois, memory, and preservation. This chapter examines the various elements and instances of public history that occur on and around this site. I argue that Du Bois spearheaded his own preservation project while providing guidance to the communities that manifested the site into fruition. Through his writings about this place and actions of friends and supporters, the plans for the site are shaped by them. The communities that were and continue to be built are based on their connection to the site while continuing to create a memorial imprint of Du Bois. The memorial imprints from these communities expand the geography of freedom in addition to being active participants in preservation.

This chapter threads together autobiographical reflections as a tour guide at W. E. B. Du Bois's Boyhood Homesite with scholarship, public history, and historical memory. Unlike scholars such as Amy Bass, Dennis Loy Johnson, and David Levinson, who write about Du Bois's life in Great Barrington, my contribution is

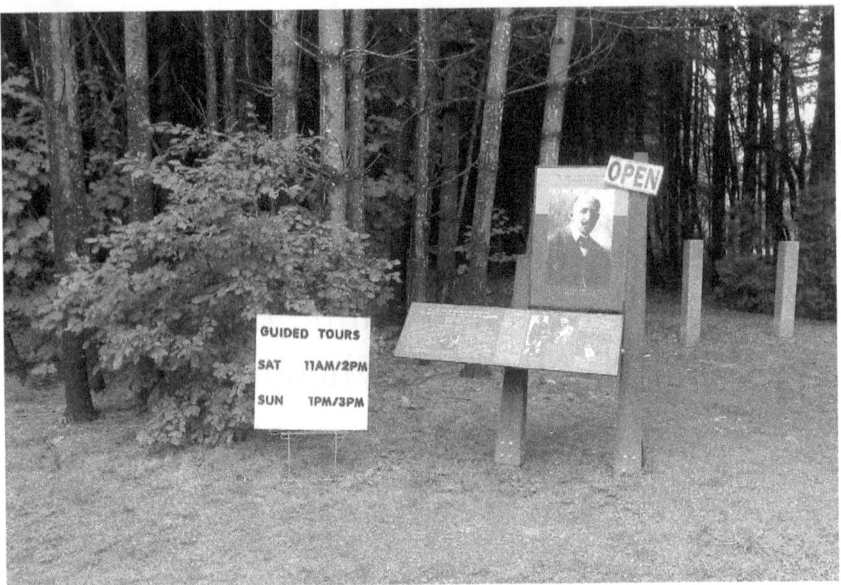

W. E. B. Du Bois Boyhood Homesite, Trail Entrance. Photo by the author.

an intervention and engagement through the practice of public history over an extended period.[1] I've had the privilege of guiding individuals and groups along a wooded trail, leading to his boyhood homesite, while talking about Du Bois, a hometown native and son of Massachusetts. In what follows I'll include descriptions of a typical tour of the homesite alongside a historiographical analysis of place, space, and sites of memory as it pertains to Du Bois.

The year is divided into two major seasons; summer tour season, which occurs between the Independence and Labor Day holidays, and non-summer tour season, which occurs during the academic school year. To orient visitors, I begin with a chance for them to tell me what they know about Du Bois. The information varies from nonexistent to expansive, giving visitors a chance to take in the feel of the space and mentally prepare for the tour. Additionally, I survey the group, inquiring about their reason for visiting. The reasons range from curiosity to pilgrimage. In the hour-long walk, we discuss the major things that he is known for, such as being a founding member of the National Association for the Advancement of Colored People (NAACP) and a Harvard graduate. We discuss his impact on the field of sociology through his work *The Philadelphia Negro*. Some of the visitors know of Du Bois because they have read *The Souls of Black Folk* as a requirement. During the tours, we discuss the impact of Du Bois on the local and larger memory. In the short distance of a one-half mile, we discuss the career trajectory of Du Bois from scholar to activist. Upon arriving at a wooden platform and a partially demolished fireplace foundation, visitors

W. E. B. Du Bois Boyhood Homesite, Physical location and Excavation Site. Photo by the author.

have the chance to stand on the land once owned by him and his ancestors. They have the chance to connect to the ideas of home and its significance to him and those like him. To challenge perceptions and connect visitors to ideas of a home place as a historic site is rewarding as a public history practitioner.

Upon entering the site, one feels as if they are in an unusual place. The trees extend upward with a cathedral-like arch, setting the tone. This visual imagery makes visitors feel as if they are entering an intimate yet sacred space. At the first stop, we discuss Du Bois's birth and death dates. Some are surprised that in his life span of ninety-five years, one can see the transition from the end of the Civil War to the modern civil rights movement in the United States.

The geographical focus on the tour expands and contracts. We begin with the local focus, expand to a global impact, contract to a national focus, contract to a local focus, with the final stop focusing on his global impact. Through this method, visitors have the opportunity to examine and explore his life from a variety of perspectives. Yet, they can see his local impact on a broader world.

At the first stop of the tour, we examine the signage that shows Du Bois sitting at his faculty office desk at Atlanta University, where he was a professor. We discuss Du Bois as a scholar and his academic appointments at Atlanta University, Wilberforce University, and the University of Pennsylvania. An informal survey of the group reveals that the most well-known work is *The Souls of Black Folk*.

I mention that scholars consider Du Bois an integral part of sociology. Through *The Philadelphia Negro*, Du Bois examines social and economic conditions of Blacks in a northern city. The question above the photo asks, "Would America have been America without her Negro people?"[2] Some answer no. However, I pose that if any ethnicity, (dis)ability, gender, or sexual orientation were to replace Negro, could that question still have relevance. At the bottom of this sign is a photograph of the silent march on Fifth Avenue in New York City, which took place on July 28, 1917. In the photo, I point out Du Bois. I ask them to notice the children, raising a pointed question regarding their positioning. We talk about the symbolism of that action, which was to send a message to President Woodrow Wilson to enact legislation so that "children will not have to face the possibility of being lynched."[3] On a particular tour, one of the visitors realized that this photo had been recently memorialized as a Google Doodle of the Day. The doodle commemorated the centennial of that event to a broader audience. The connection to modern-day technology and the historic past is one that I attempt during these tours. While the site is historic, there are points of relevancy to the modern day that can be made to allow visitors to see the connections, making public history palatable.

As we advance along the trail, visitors ask questions predominantly about the Black population and his childhood in Great Barrington. Based on archival sources, Du Bois was an intelligent young man, graduating at the top of his class from Great Barrington High School. Du Bois observed Great Barrington as an attendee at town hall meetings and worked at various jobs in the town. The visitors attempt to determine if Du Bois is an anomaly and the possible correlation to how progressive Great Barrington was at the time. Although the population of Blacks was small, the Burghardt family was known in the community. Du Bois and Blacks in the Berkshire area experienced a freedom similar to other colonial areas that formally ended slavery prior to the nineteenth century.

Next, we arrive at the second stop, where tree trunks and logs provide places to sit; fashioned like a space for a pseudo campfire circle or outdoor classroom. The featured photo shows Du Bois standing upright. Contrary to my childhood memorialization of Du Bois as a tall man due to his significance in Black history, we discuss his actual height of being slightly above five feet tall. A photo of Du Bois at the Paris Exposition of 1900 helps to tell the story of his award-winning exhibition of African Americans there, an authentic narrative of Blacks on a global stage. This leads to a discussion of Du Bois and involvement in global affairs. We discuss his education at Humboldt University in Germany and immersion into the field of sociological and economic thought. Du Bois is an early participant and supporter of the Pan-African Congresses, and the signage displays archival material about it. We discuss his invitation to and eventual interment in Ghana. However, the striking quote above the photo that states, "The problem of the twentieth century is the color line,"[4] is one that sparks discussion amongst the

W. E. B. Du Bois Boyhood Homesite, Interpretive Wayside. Photo by the author.

visitors while posing the question of whether the quote should be updated for the twenty-first century.

We move further on the trail to the third stop, arriving at a vegetation-covered boulder. It is at this spot we discuss the role of community in regard to Du Bois. We discuss the purchase of land, leading to the creation of a memorial site. Additionally, we discuss the communities that supported Du Bois during the accusation of supporting communism. Community is a central theme from this point forward on the tour.

The fourth and fifth stops discuss home as an important place. I ask visitors to consider how they feel about their homes and hometowns. Through popular culture, I make the connection to productions of *The Wizard of Oz* and *The Wiz* with the memorable line of "There's no place like home" by Judy Garland and the selection of "Home" by Diana Ross. The signs present Du Bois surrounded by family. Finally, we approach the actual homesite. Du Bois speaks affectionately about this place and claims it is "The first home I remember."[5] To continue the connection to home, we discuss the process of the archaeological work performed at the site and the significance. In rudimentary terms, I provide the analogy of how an Amazon purchase history can provide a socioeconomic glimpse into a household. These ideas make the site visitor community closer to understanding the significance of home and Great Barrington to Du Bois's life.

Finally, we go in reverse towards the last stop before returning to the entrance and the parking lot. It can be confusing because we encounter the sign immediately after the tour begins. The last sign is a photo of Du Bois and his second wife Shirley Graham. The sign discusses Du Bois and relationships with groups domestically and internationally. There's a picture of Du Bois with artist Pablo Picasso, a local NAACP branch, and writers for an Afro-Asian literary conference. However, I advise visitors to view the sign last because it culminates several of Du Bois's ideas and issues a challenge to seek global democracy, making the concept of freedom have elasticity.

Author and Great Barrington native Amy Bass provides a nuanced perspective of Du Bois in his hometown in her work, *Those About Him Remained Silent: The Battle Over W. E. B. Du Bois*. She discusses the controversies and celebrations surrounding Du Bois's memory in Great Barrington. Bass provides an objective look at the local efforts and the implications. Regarding the site Bass states, "This plot of land is now considered to be an archaeological site by the University of Massachusetts, which took the title for the land from the Du Bois foundation in 1988."[6] It serves as a living lab and classroom for the university.[7] We have had the opportunity to perform archaeological digs on the site to learn more about his maternal ancestors. We use this site to educate the public about one of the most interesting persons in the larger freedom struggle. Visitors are able to stand on land once owned by Du Bois's maternal family for two centuries. It materializes the concept of Black land ownership that was rare for the time. Du Bois's reclamation of this plot of land was significant in several ways. Du Bois was continuing to create a geographic area of freedom with connections to linear and historic pasts. The land is in proximity to Sheffield, the site of Elizabeth Mumbet Freeman's quest for freedom. His ancestors obtained the land after manumission, within the decade of slavery's abolition in Massachusetts in 1783. This corresponds to anthropologist and archaeologist Whitney Battle-Baptiste's claim that "the House of the Black Burghardts becomes the site of family history, a place to decipher the complexity of a figure like W. E. B. Du Bois, and the basis for a larger discussion of Blackness in New England. The House is the physical site of Du Bois's maternal line and provides the means to address interesting issues such as the invisibility of race in New England's historical memory."[8]

Pierre Nora's work, "Between History and Memory: Les Lieux de Memoire," examines the concepts of memory, history, and preservation. Seen as a theoretical framework to preservation, Nora argues that there are distinctions between memories and histories with the claim, "memory is a perpetually actual phenomenon, a bond tying us to the eternal present; history is a representation of the past."[9] Nora warns against preserving just for the sake of doing so. Preservation should be a strategic method to ensure against the erasure of history. An interesting observation are the trinkets left behind at the entrance, boulder, or platform of the homesite. Before each tour weekend, I would walk through to note any changes or needs to the site that may need to be remedied such as fallen branches, etc. There would be notes, coins, stones, and photos left there. The idea of memorializing a place that was important to Du Bois employs the notion that those who preserve, protect, and visit the site are active participants in enlivening a place that is important to his identity. Each visitor leaves the site with a greater understanding of the homesite and the significance of this place in regard to his life. The ideas, memories, and efforts of Du Bois regarding this place are impressed on the visitors to the site. As visitors leave the site, they have an opportunity to sign the visitor log. Collected in small 5×7 inch notebooks, a diverse group of authors leave comments, concerns, critiques, and suggestions. These expressions of gratitude and honor to Du Bois reflects a personal connection to those visitors that leave such items, supporting Nora's concept that "memory takes root in the concrete, in spaces, gestures, images, and objects."[10]

Community, in proximity to the site, can be defined by a few groups. In the first group, Du Bois speaks of family living nearby, creating a community that contributed to his identity. In a second group, Du Bois's work of writing for and on behalf of the Black community in Great Barrington connected them to other Massachusetts Black communities through the *Springfield Republican*, as a corresponding journalist, and as a secretary for the Clinton African Methodist Episcopal Zion Church women's sewing circle. Another group to consider are the individuals who raised funds and gave Du Bois his childhood home as a birthday gift in 1928 and established a community that cared for him and shared his aspiration to save his childhood home. The community created through the Friends of Du Bois organization to establish a memorial park in the mid-twentieth century continued the tradition of saving Du Bois's childhood home. Each of these communities are concentric. Despite the unbound geography, each of these communities partially employ Benedict Anderson's idea of "imagined community." Anderson defined imagined communities as people tied together by ideas and not geography. Specifically, "the members . . . will never know most of their fellow-members, meet them, or even hear of them, yet in the mind of each lives the image of their communion . . . [and] is always conceived as a deep, horizontal comradeship."[11]

Architectural historian Max Page provides an accurate description regarding the purpose for visitation and preservation of historic sites. He claims that "historic buildings and landscapes are the open doors Americans walk through to enter the past; to learn from it . . . we are drawn to historic places. We believe in them. We crave them. They appeal to some of our deepest desires."[12] This desire is conferred when Bass states, "Regarding the Burghardt property, University of Massachusetts anthropologist Robert Paynter suggests that in the nineteenth century, the family farmed the land and also took in some boarders."[13] This complicated the narrative of African Americans' association to land in the late nineteenth and early twentieth centuries. The Burghardts were landowners and landlords, exercising a freedom unknown to most at the time. "The homestead represented the family of Du Bois's mother as well as of the famed civil rights leader, descendants of one whose good turn in the American Revolution gave him his freedom and put his roots in Great Barrington with the earliest of its settlers."[14] According to archaeologist Whitney Battle-Baptiste, "For Du Bois, the house of the Black Burghardts was his homeplace, the place that had a significant impact on his identity and cultural formation."[15] As a team member in the University of Massachusetts field schools of the Du Bois site and director of UMass Amherst's W. E. B. Du Bois Center, she understands the significance of home and the tangibility of freedom. Specifically in this geographical space, Du Bois considers this to be a paradise, far extending beyond perceived or imagined boundaries. Battle-Baptiste confers this by stating, "[the Black Burghardts of Great Barrington] created the playground and the place where young boys and girls of the next Burghardt generation would play and experience a life in a secure, safe and insulated space quite separate from the realities of racial and class distinctions."[16] Bass and other scholars who write about Du Bois's life in Great Barrington preservation and historic sites build a scholarly community and create an intellectual memorial imprint by "showing just how complicated the politics and culture of memory can be, and how public space can serve as the front line for battles regarding how various social groups are represented and defined."[17]

During my tenure as a site guide, there have been challenging moments. Following the 2016 election, there was a personal concern for the site and possible vandalism. Anxiety gripped me as I approached the site and inspected the boulder, signage, and the platform. Although the site has the designation as a National Historic Landmark and is under the conservatorship of the Commonwealth of Massachusetts, there is no visible protection in the form of security or surveillance. However, there was great relief to discover that the site was undisturbed.

At the site, discussions of democracy and controversy over Du Bois's affiliation with the Communist Party tend to be part of the dialogue amongst visitors to the physical site. These events occur within the correspondence through and to the website as well. There have been instances at the site and via messages of individuals questioning the existence of the site. Through the usage of selected sources, individuals attempt to challenge the necessity of a site devoted to an avowed communist. For an educator, a steady calm elucidates these inquisitors with selected sources to counteract their claims.

Obversely, there have been discussions of whether Du Bois would support the Black Lives Matter movement or Colin Kaepernick's form of protest. During one of the tour seasons, a trademarked Black Lives Matter sign suddenly appeared in the parking lot. Visitors would ask if I strategically placed the sign and was it supported by the university. My response was that unknown persons placed it there. However, the spirit in which it was done, Du Bois could have possibly supported it and commented about it in *The Crisis* if he were alive. That act connected a past historical figure to a present historical movement, giving the memory of Du Bois an opportunity to reside outside its chronological boundary.

For the site guide opportunities arise to promote the space in media formats, which can include YouTube videos and television appearances. A particular opportunity arose to create content with a local media company. By shooting at the Du Bois Boyhood Homesite, we created a video narrative of the site and its significance, placing them on a YouTube channel. Another opportunity was creating a question for a local high school television quiz show. Shot on location, a question was presented and broadcast at a later date. These visual formats present the site in a nontraditional manner, a digital deed of memory as it were. These virtual communities contribute to the reach of the Du Bois narrative while creating a memory and digital imprint.

One rarely has the opportunity to meet individuals affiliated with the initial developments of a historic site. For example, I would never have the opportunity to meet Shirley or David Graham Du Bois because they died before my involvement with the site. However, to meet someone that was directly associated with the initial park proposal and land acquisition made the decision to serve as guide priceless. It happened when in between scheduled tours, a vehicle approached the site. The group emerges, yet an elderly gentleman stays behind. They stated that they wanted to just walk the site, without a guided tour. I discover the gentleman in the car is Dr. Edmund Gordon, one of the cofounders of the site. We spoke about the site and how much it has changed since the land purchase. He told me about the land acquisition process, and I thanked him for his work and hoped that the current site was just a small portion of his vision. Gordon wrote previously about his contribution:

> My wife Susan and I purchased his childhood home site, were able to get it designated as a National Historic Site, and gave the property to the University of Massachusetts to be converted into a memorial park honoring our friend. My older son and I became members of the advisory committee to the university's considerable effort to establish its archive of Du Bois's papers and to name its university library the Du Bois Library. Professor David Levering Lewis, Dr. Du Bois' biographer, and I became friends.[18]

At the site, race is a prominent theme. However, gender is one of the subthemes at the site. Throughout his life, Du Bois was surrounded and influenced by women. Although his mother and wives appear on the signage, I try to bring gendered perceptions and approaches into this historic site during the tours and talks. I discuss these women in addition to Elizabeth Mumbet Freeman. We discuss his views regarding women's suffrage as expressed in one of the quotes on the signage, which states, "Every argument for Negro suffrage is an argument for woman suffrage; every argument for woman suffrage is an argument for Negro suffrage; both are great movements in democracy."[19] That can be difficult to integrate when the site can be placed in the Thomas Carlyle "Great Man/Hero Worship" context, which partially agrees that great men shape history through their personal attributes. Of course, Du Bois speaks extensively of his childhood in Great Barrington. However, Whitney Battle Baptiste's *Black Feminist Archaeology* allows us to explore the impact of the women of Du Bois's Great Barrington childhood. Starting with Lucinda Burghardt, the land that is now the site was acquired by her and passed down through various family members, eventually to his grandfather and great uncles. Battle-Baptiste supports this by stating, "There were clear decisions about property and inheritance that were made and maintained by these women."[20]

I advise visitors that in addition to seeing the transition from Civil War to civil rights through his lived experiences, we also see his consideration towards gender as evidenced in scholarly works such as "The Damnation of Women" and *The Souls of Black Folk*. Du Bois's interaction with women can be seen in the instance when, as a child, he describes a calling card being declined, introducing him to the ideas and notions of race; realizing that there is a veil in regard to race relations. Du Bois speaks with respect and admiration for his mother Mary, first wife Nina, and daughter Yolande. He protects these women through a series of actions. With respect to his mother, he works as a young man in Great Barrington in various jobs to provide a small sense of financial security. When Nina gives birth to Burghardt, it takes place in Great Barrington. During the riots in Atlanta in 1906, Du Bois sends his family to Great Barrington as a place of safety. These instances and individuals are vital to our understanding of Du Bois and the impact of women in his life.

Additional opportunities to expand Du Bois's geographical reach occur through guest lecture events. During these events, speakers highlight the local connections. Using Du Bois's writings and archival material, local communities feel closer connections to him. Using the seminal work, presenters explore *The Souls of Black Folk* and its reference to and descriptions of Western Massachusetts. Some lines include, "I was a little thing, away up in the hills of New England, where the dark Housatonic winds between Hoosac and Taghkanic to the sea"[21] and "I fled faster and faster away from the flickering sea into my own Berkshire hills that sit all sadly guarding the gates of Massachusetts."[22] Anecdotes of Du Bois missing an engagement at a local institution provide a glimpse into his humanness and grants relevancy to a historic person. By the mention of local places such as Mount Holyoke College, the audience once again feels closer connections to him and places that are still in existence.

With the lack of wireless service at the homesite, there have to be alternative ways to connect visitors to the site. Photocopied images used along the tour further illustrate some of the points of Du Bois's life in Great Barrington and in the wider world. Additionally, anecdotes about the sources in the archives help visitors connect to Du Bois's humanity. For example, when children are on the tour, I ask them how they connect with their grandparents. Some of the answers include telephone, emails, or FaceTime. I explain to them that Du Bois connected to his grandparents as well. We discuss a letter in the archives Du Bois wrote to his grandmother at around nine years old. This instance brings children into the experience as well as creating a dialogue for realizing that this great man was once a child with similar experiences. Another example is event planning for an adult child. I mention locating the receipt to a printmaker for Yolande's wedding invitations. Also, I bring up the guest list. In this list, certain individuals are not allowed, despite submitting a reservation card in advance. The harsh pencil marks on some names can be interpreted as a protective parent or a frugal father concerned about the rising costs of this celebration. Of course, I suggest visitors go to the Du Bois Special Collections website and use search terms in Credo such as grandmother and wedding to find digital copies of these specific items discussed on the tour.

Connecting through modern concepts and ideas help visitors understand preservation. At the boulder, we discuss the efforts of Edmund Gordon and Walter Wilson. Gordon, an educator and friend of Du Bois, partnered with Wilson, a real-estate developer. These gentlemen created a Friends of Du Bois organization. This organization created an archaic GoFundMe, raising money to purchase acres of land near the homesite. When I introduce this concept to visitors, they connect to the idea of community fundraising for a mutual cause. Also, the local community that participated in the cleanup efforts at the site did not have the luxury of creating a Facebook group or an online petition via change.org. Yet these communities were able to purchase land, create a space and assist with the efforts to make the site a National Historic Landmark in 1979.[23] Once again, these concentric communities are expanding the geography of freedom and memorial imprints.

As I reflect on my experience, I engage with these interacting communities and see myself as a partner with Du Bois on this preservation project. Du Bois possibly would not consider himself to be a preservationist by modern standards, yet he truly was. His participatory acts of preservation ranged from writing about his boyhood home to taking the effort to rebuild on the site of the home. One of his primary reasons for building the fireplace was so "the tongs can rest on the fire of worship in the house of the black Burghardts."[24] What better motivation for preservation than to pay homage to the past while creating a future?

The Special Collections and University Archives at the University of Massachusetts, which house over a hundred thousand items, served as the knowledge repository during the tours. This repository was beneficial when individuals sent emails before and after visits in addition to the general public phone inquiries wanting to know about Du Bois. Herbert Aptheker, historian and former custodian of Du Bois's papers, agrees and claims, "The University of Massachusetts will be a mecca for scholars in Du Bois lore for a long time."[25]

In addition to using the Du Bois archives at the university, there is the privilege of consulting with anthropologists Robert Paynter and Whitney Battle-Baptiste, historians David Glassberg and Bernard Drew, and former site guide Felicia Jamison. This particular group of scholar-practitioners have participated in the design charette and archaeological digs, drafted extensive reports, published scholarship, and led tours at the Du Bois Boyhood Homesite.[26] Their conversations and insight provide contours to understanding the physical and intellectual space. Their work guides the script for tours and assists with the inquiry requests that are submitted. Their contributions, advice, and guidance has proven to be immeasurable to this experience. The fiscal support from the Housatonic Heritage Association ensures that marketing and publication support is provided. A historic site is more than just a physical structure or cherished and significant piece of land. These interacting communities work together towards a common goal of preserving and presenting a historic site.

At the end of the tour season, I take one last walk through the site by myself; giving me the chance to reflect on the visitors and their experiences. Although every image and header quote on the signs are committed to my memory, there seems to be a different interpretation during these reflections. As I reach the last signpost, depicting a photo of Du Bois and his wife Shirley, I begin to walk backwards from the sign. My reasoning for doing so is metaphorical; so that I may not turn my back on Du Bois's legacy. As I get closer towards the entrance of the site, I turn and walk forward; as if I am walking out into the world, inspired by Du Bois to make a change for the greater good. As a public historian, my desire and mission are to make history accessible to others, so that they may learn about the past in order to impact the future. If I can make that happen with a walk in the woods and discussing Du Bois, then I have done my work.

On October 18, 2019, the 50th Anniversary Commemoration of the site dedication took place with various groups in attendance, similar to the original event. Scholars, musicians, celebrities, Great Barrington citizens, and supporters of Du Bois crowded beneath the tent at the entrance of the site. Speakers discussed the importance of Du Bois's legacy and the significance of this place. Modern video cameras and cell phones captured the program like the archival footage in the

Conducting a Tour at the W. E. B. Du Bois Boyhood Homesite. Photo by the author.

W. E. B. Du Bois Papers. Unlike the original site dedication, there was no surveillance or riot gear. Just a network of van shuttles to transport attendees from the nearby airfield transformed into a parking lot for the morning's events. However, the imagined community gathered once again to celebrate the life of Du Bois with events in Great Barrington throughout the day. Before the program, a large group took an abbreviated tour at the site. When we reached the boulder, I asked the group to imagine the scene half a century ago and discuss what has changed since. At that moment, they became active participants in preservation, by partnering with the past and memorializing the legacy of Du Bois for future generations. Traversing a geography of freedom in Great Barrington offers one way to think about the deeds of memory preserved in Du Bois's own personal, local history.

NOTES

1. For works with a primary focus of Du Bois's life in Great Barrington and the attitudes towards celebrating his life in the late twentieth century, see Amy Bass, *Those About Him Remained Silent: The Battle Over W. E. B. Du Bois* (Minneapolis: University of Minnesota Press, 2009); Dennis Loy Johnson, "In the Hush of Great Barrington: One Writer's Search for W. E. B.

Du Bois," *Georgia Review* 49, no. 3 (1995): 581–606; David Levinson, *The African American Community in Rural New England: W. E. B. Du Bois and the Clinton A.M.E. Zion Church* (Great Barrington: Berkshire, 2018).

2. W. E. B. Du Bois, *The Souls of Black Folk* (Chicago: AC McClurg, 1903), 263.

3. https://www.google.com/doodles/100th-anniversary-of-the-silent-parade.

4. Du Bois, *Souls*, xv.

5. W. E. B. Du Bois, "The House of the Black Burghardts," *The Crisis*, April 1928, 133–34.

6. Bass, *Those About Him Remained Silent*, 9–10.

7. Robert Paynter, "The Neglect of Du Bois in His Hometown of Great Barrington, Massachusetts and the Subsequent Efforts to Overcome That Neglect" (paper presented at the annual meeting for the Association of the Study of African American Life and History, Cincinnati, Ohio, 2009).

8. Whitney Battle-Baptiste, *Black Feminist Archaeology* (London: Routledge, 2011), 156–57; Whitney Battle-Baptiste and Phillip Luke Sinitiere, "Excavating History and a Homeplace: An Interview on W. E. B. Du Bois's Impact, Influence, and Legacy," *Socialism and Democracy* 32, No. 3 (2018): 251–58.

9. Pierre Nora, "Between Memory and History: Les Lieux de Memoire," *Representations* 26, Special Issue: Memory and Counter-Memory (Spring 1989): 7–24.

10. Nora, "Between Memory and History," 9.

11. Benedict Anderson, *Imagined Communities* (London: Verso, 2006), 6–7.

12. Max Page, *Why Preservation Matters* (New Haven: Yale University Press, 2016), 13.

13. Bass, *Those About Him Remained Silent*, 10.

14. Bass, *Those About Him Remained Silent*, 116–17.

15. Battle-Baptiste, *Black Feminist Archaeology*, 139.

16. Battle-Baptiste, *Black Feminist Archaeology*, 142.

17. Bass, *Those About Him Remained Silent*, xxi.

18. Edmund Gordon and L'Tanya Watkins, "Race Man and Philosopher of Education: A Reflection on W. E. B. Du Bois," *American Educational Research Journal* 54, No. 15 (April 2007): 48–52

19. Du Bois, "Woman Suffrage," *The Crisis*, April 1915, 285.

20. Battle-Baptiste, *Black Feminist Archaeology*, 159.

21. Du Bois, *Souls*, 3.

22. Du Bois, *Souls*, 208.

23. Department of the Interior, National Park Service, National Register of Historic Places Inventory-Nomination Form, W. E. B. Du Bois Boyhood Homesite, https://npgallery.nps.gov/AssetDetail/NRIS/76000947.

24. Du Bois, "The House of the Black Burghardts."

25. Bass, *Those About Him Remained Silent*, 112.

26. Specific works include Robert Paynter and David Glassberg's "Conflict and Consensus in Great Barrington: Remembering W. E. B. Du Bois," *Museum International* 62, No. 1–2 (August 2010): 57–60; Bernard Drew, *Dr. Du Bois Rebuilds His Dream House* (Great Barrington: Attic Revivals Press, 2006.). A 2009 final planning report, "W. E. B. Du Bois Boyhood Homesite and Great Barrington: A Plan for Heritage Conservation and Interpretation" by Michael Singer Studio is available at http://www.duboisnhs.org/vision.html.

Afterword

—Eric Porter

I am inspired by the insights and new approaches brought to the late career of W. E. B. Du Bois by the contributors to this excellent volume. I say this as someone who tried his own hand at engaging Du Bois's twilight years a while back with a book focusing on his post-1940 (although generally not post-1955) intellectual work and biography. What eventually became *The Problem of the Future World: W. E. B. Bois and the Race Concept at Midcentury*, drew significantly from the extant scholarship on Du Bois's final decades but was still predicated on the assessment that we still had a lot of work to do on the period.[1]

Thankfully, the scholarship on the late Du Bois has grown significantly over the past decade. Bill Mullen's *Un-American: W. E. B. Du Bois and the Century of World Revolution*, Nahum Chandler's *Toward an African Future: Of the Limit of World*, and Phillip Luke Sinitiere's companion to the present volume, *Citizen of the World: The Legacy and Late Career of W. E. B. Du Bois*, are among the noteworthy book-length additions to this conversation.[2] With each contribution our understanding of the late Du Bois becomes richer. Scholars bring new approaches to bear on his work and address a growing set of challenges stemming from those engagements. *Forging Freedom* adds mightily to this project.

Du Bois, of course, has long had a phenomenally wide reach as inspiration and touchstone. Choosing to write about Du Bois today, regardless of the period of his career under consideration, is an interesting, often challenging, endeavor because so many other people have already done so. In other words, not only does one get to think with Du Bois but also with the extraordinary people working in African American history, Black studies, African studies, feminist studies, critical theory, sociology, philosophy, and other fields who have engaged his ideas—even when ostensibly writing about something else. Individually and collectively, we channel Du Bois and then Du Bois channels us, as we are drawn to him and seek to understand him. We engage him because of his great insights about what he called "the problem of the color line" and, later, what he termed "the problem of the future world" as well as about related issues like economic injustice, war, imperialism, education, and the carceral system. We also write about him because of his resonance as an icon who has embodied African American history, Black identity, radicalism, and so on. Moreover, he has been a model for a methodological orientation that encourages us, even when situated in particular disciplines, to read widely, to deploy narrative strategies rooted in multiple fields, and do whatever else is necessary to address the problem at hand.

So, all the more a problem it was that up until recent years, people were not generally engaging the later work with the same frequency and rigor with which they addressed the early part of the career. For it was in these later years, generally speaking, that aspects of his understanding of the coproduction of racism and capitalism, of imperialism as a racial project, and of the limits of democracy, globally, were becoming more nuanced. And, more generally, he was coming to terms with the ways that race, once it became destabilized as a concept and lost some of its scientific credibility, became in some ways a more powerful and more insidious force within the realm of geopolitics and knowledge production. Du Bois was, in other words, concerned about the persistence of race and racism not just in spite of but as a consequence of collective beliefs that their exclusions were being overcome.

It was the radical dimensions of Du Bois's vision, warts and all, products of his deeper dive into Marxism and engagement with anticolonial thought during this period, that continued to sustain (despite the personal and professional setbacks) his lifelong commitment to understanding the complicated Gordian knot of race and racism, to find a language that could make sense of race's shifting ontology and paradoxical nature (its simultaneous reality and unreality), and to imagine a different future. And it was precisely this radical vision that made his insights relevant then and continue to make them relevant today.

Forging Freedom contributes powerfully to this excavation of Du Bois's insights, as its contributors examine how his thought around various issues shifted over the decades. In some cases, we learn how familiar Du Boisian critiques, typically explored through readings of early- or mid-career texts may be understood differently by focusing on later works. Lisa McLeod, for example, shows that we get an enhanced account of Du Bois's interrogation of whiteness and, more specifically, of an intransigent white racism that hides behind presumptions of white innocence, if we move from *Black Reconstruction*, the familiar source of such critique, and bring *Dusk of Dawn* and the *Black Flame* novels into the analysis. Charisse Burden-Stelly, meanwhile, tells a different story about Du Bois's often-complicated relationships with Black women activists by focusing on the "radical period" and shared Cold War critiques rather than on his earlier civil rights organizing and the politics of his 1920 essay "The Damnation of Women."

In other cases, *Forging Freedom* helps to broaden our understanding and sharpen our analyses of the range of intellectual influences that shaped his later work. We learn, for example, in Murali Balaji's chapter, that it wasn't simply the political and solidaristic potentiality of Indian thought and activism in general that inspired him but the Hindu concept of *dharma* in particular that shaped his synthesis of socialist and anticolonialist ideals. And, like many of the best edited collections, we learn something from the implicit or explicit disagreements among its contributors. Christopher Cameron's chapter emphasizing the humanistic elements of Du Bois's Marxism, his growing disenchantment with Christianity, clashes somewhat with Phillip Luke Sinitiere's rooting of Du Bois's radical thought in "the moral and ethical idioms of the Christian tradition." But we can take away, in the end, that there are both religious and agnostic dimensions of Du Bois's radicalism.

Forging Freedom is also a useful barometer of the range of present- and future-oriented concerns that scholars, activists, and other thinkers bring to Du Bois. As indicated above, Du Bois had tremendous prescience. He anticipated in earlier texts what would happen late in his life, and in his later years he offered many insights into phenomena that would continue or emerge after he was gone. This process of using Du Bois's later works and deeds to diagnose the present and future began almost immediately after his death. As Robert Greene II's chapter shows us, Martin Luther King Jr., in a speech near the end of his life, invoked Du Bois's radical vision, as well as his victimization by the "obsessive anti-communism" of the 1950s, as a means of offering a critique of the Cold War–driven war in Vietnam.

Forging Freedom's contributors express an important range of present-day scholarly and political concerns even as they rigorously historicize Du Bois's work. The various authors mine his thought and biography for a critical perspective relevant to our times. In addition to concerns alluded to above, we have Andre Johnson's account of how Du Bois's pessimistically prophetic refusal to vote in the 1956 election potentially offers important critical perspective on the present-day ethical dilemma of whether to exercise one's vote or not in an unjust electoral system; Carlton Dwayne Floyd and Thomas Ehrlich Reifer's examination of the continuing relevance of the analysis in *Black Reconstruction* for twenty-first-century Black freedom struggles and human emancipation more generally; Werner Lange's assessment of how Du Bois's peace activism from the early Cold War can provide inspiration in the present for those still working to eradicate nuclear weapons; Reiland Rabaka's analysis of how Du Bois's anticolonial and antiracist democratic socialism maintains the ability to animate a progressive politics in our political present; and Camesha Scruggs's account of how Du Bois helped shaped the public memory about him, as evident in its reproduction at the Great Barrington site of his childhood home, and how multiple levels of engagement with Du Bois's legacy at that site offer guidance for the further development of the field of public history.

Of course, as the contributors make clear, whether explicitly or implicitly, drawing lessons from Du Bois for the present can be a perilous journey. His analytical shortcomings (his elitism, the limited depth of his gender analysis, and so on) have, as others have argued, helped set the limits of certain analytical trajectories in Black and critical race studies. One also has to be mindful of anachronism when bringing the concerns of the present to the study of past figures like Du Bois. In my own work, I tried to take to heart Stuart Hall's instructions to late-twentieth-century scholars wanting to employ Antonio Gramsci's "conjunctural" ideas for contemporary social analysis. "To make more general use of them," Hall argues, "they have to be delicately dis-interred from their concrete and specific historical embeddedness and transplanted to new soil with considerable care and patience."[3] We can locate the imperative for such moves also in Du Bois's own intellectual project, which often sought to transform theory (empiricism, pragmatism, Marxism) to fit his contemporary social world. The challenge is to understand the limitations of presentism and historicism alike, as Adolph Reed has suggested, refusing the illusion that the past can be represented simply and accurately without any recourse to present concerns while avoiding the tendency as well toward decontextualized historical readings that opportunistically serve the present.[4]

But we must also accept the fact that even when we're careful, our own interpretations will be temporally and contextually bound. As Jodi Melamed and Tyler Monson note, Melamed's chapter on Du Bois's posthumous *Autobiography* was originally written in 2006—at a moment of heightened neoliberal multiculturalism and a market-friendly postracialism—and its fundamental orientation was to engage Du Bois's work as a means of understanding these formations as racial capitalism. Revisiting the piece in a Trumpian moment, however, the authors argue it was Du Bois's account of what his critics assumed were his criminality and disloyalty during his later years that seems most pertinent to the present conjuncture. For his work helps us to gain insight into how the suppression and censorship of antiracist critical thinkers sustain racial capitalism.

Similarly, I have often, in the aftermath of November 2016—increasingly and painfully aware of the growing visibility of old-school, recrudescent racism that enabled and followed the events of that month—questioned *The Problem of the Future World*'s focus on the racial regime of postracialism, beginning with my situating of Du Bois's theoretical work vis-à-vis race during the 1940s as a political-intellectual response to this "first post-racial moment." I find myself thinking that if I were wrapping that project up in 2023 rather than shortly after the election of Barack Obama to the presidency, I may well have paid more attention to Du Bois's work on fascism's colonial underpinnings and his concerns that elements of it would survive into a putatively democratic future. As I perhaps discussed too briefly, the parallels between the racial projects of Germany and the United States during the early 1940s were not lost on Du Bois: "With all our tumult and shouting and pious rage against Hitler," he suggested, "we are perfectly aware that his race philosophy and methods are but extreme development and application of our own save that he is drawing his race lines in somewhat different places." "Democracy cannot have a rebirth in the world," he continued, "unless it firmly establishes itself in America. . . . otherwise they are setting before the world a vision of continual struggle, of continual recurrence of war after war, the end of which no living man can see."[5]

Moreover, the last few national election cycles have witnessed the rapid escalation of the Republican Party's racist projects of gerrymandering, voter suppression, and disenfranchisement. And, we have seen many times in recent years how the composition of the US Senate (i.e., two senators per state regardless of population) serves to overrepresent elite white citizens' interests in the US Congress while enabling a politics of fictive white solidarity that diminishes the collective interests of working people across the board. With that in mind, I might also have been compelled to say more about Du Bois's critique of electoral politics in *Color and Democracy*. For there he was concerned with how disenfranchisement combined with the overrepresentation of white voters in western and southern states with relatively small populations enabled, through the election of officials with investments in the racial status quo, a general rightward thrust in the political sphere. Ultimately, he argued, these phenomena "[force] the United States to abdicate its natural leadership of democracy in the world and to acquiesce in a domination of organized wealth which exceeds anything elsewhere in the world."[6]

Ultimately, Du Bois's later work remains valuable for generating useful critical perspectives on the multiple futures he cautioned us against as well as on those futures he did not quite imagine. And even our interpretations of Du Bois that become somewhat obsolete—although perhaps, in some cases, only temporarily so—are also, in the end, generative. To return to this collection's epigraph, Du Bois is among the dead who continue to speak to us through their deeds, and we have done our best to dream with them. *Forging Freedom* will become part of the collective memory of Du Bois's twilight years. His deeds, his dreams, but also our temporally bound, politically shaped engagements with them, will ever more compose the shifting archive orbiting this great thinker. *Forging Freedom* is fundamentally important for what it brings to Du Bois studies now, for the insights that it shares, and it will remain important for future engagements even when the needs of the present are different, when we think different questions should be asked and alternative interpretations posed. Certainly, one lesson in Du Bois's late work, as these essays make clear, is his perseverance, his willingness to continually reanimate his critique for a changing world. And as the critical conversation about him grows, we have more to work with in the hopes of achieving one of the better future worlds that he imagined.

NOTES

1. Eric Porter, *The Problem of the Future World: W. E. B. Bois and the Race Concept at Midcentury* (Durham: Duke University Press, 2010).

2. Bill V. Mullen, *Un-American: W. E. B. and the Century of World Revolution* (Philadelphia: Temple University Press, 2015); Nahum Chandler, *Toward an African Future: Of the Limit of World* (London: Living Commons Collective, 2013); Phillip Luke Sinitiere, ed., *Citizen of the World: The Late Career and Legacy of W. E. B. Du Bois* (Evanston, IL: Northwestern University Press, 2019).

3. Stuart Hall, "Gramsci's Relevance for the Study of Race and Ethnicity," in *Stuart Hall: Critical Dialogues in Cultural Studies*, eds. by David Morley and Kuan-Hsing Chen (London: Routledge, 1996), 411–40.

4. Adolph L. Reed Jr., *W. E. B. Du Bois and American Political Thought: Fabianism and the Color Line* (New York: Oxford University Press, 1997).

5. W. E. B. Du Bois, "The Future of Africa in America" (April 1942), in W. E. B. Du Bois, *Against Racism: Unpublished Essays, Papers, Addresses, 1887–1961*, ed. Herbert Aptheker (Amherst: University of Massachusetts Press, 1985), 183–84.

6. W. E. B. Du Bois, *Color and Democracy: Colonies and Peace*, reprint, with a new introduction by Herbert Aptheker (Millwood, NY: Kraus-Thomson Organization Limited, 1975), 85–91.

ABOUT THE CONTRIBUTORS

Murali Balaji is a lecturer at the Annenberg School for Communication at the University of Pennsylvania, where he also oversees diversity and professional development. He is a journalist, author, and academic with over twenty years of experience in diversity leadership. He is the founder of Maruthi Education Consulting and has consulted for numerous nonprofits, government agencies, corporations, and political campaigns on diversity, equity, and inclusion issues. Balaji has also served as the education director for the Hindu American Foundation, where he was recognized as a national leader in cultural competency and religious literacy. He cofounded the Voice of Philadelphia, a nonprofit geared to help high school dropouts (or pushouts) develop media literacy and citizen journalism skills. He has also been a professor at Temple University and Lincoln University, where he chaired the mass communication department and engaged in multi-method research. His areas of research include political economy, race and media, and the connections between masculinity and nationalism. He worked as a journalist for nearly a decade, covering politics, sports, and demographic changes. He won an Independent Press Association of New York award for covering racial justice issues and was honored by the St. Paul City Council for his work on covering policy issues.

Charisse Burden-Stelly is associate professor of African American studies at Wayne State University. She is the coauthor, with Gerald Horne, of *W. E. B. Du Bois: A Life in American History* (ABC-CLIO, 2019) and coeditor of *Organize, Fight, Win: Black Communist Women's Political Writings* (Verso, 2022) with Jodi Dean and *Reproducing Domination: On the Caribbean Postcolonial State* (University Press of Mississippi, 2022) with Percy Hintzen and Aaron Kamugisha. Her book *Black Scare/Red Scare* will be published with the University of Chicago Press in fall 2023. Additionally, Burden-Stelly is the guest editor of the "Claudia Jones: Foremother of World Revolution" special issue of the *Journal of Intersectionality*. Her writings appear in peer-reviewed journals including *Small Axe, Souls, Du Bois Review, Socialism & Democracy, International Journal of Africana Studies*, and the *CLR James Journal*. Her public scholarship can be found in venues such as *Monthly Review*, *Boston Review*, *Black Perspectives*, and *Black Agenda Report*.

Christopher Cameron is professor of history at the University of North Carolina at Charlotte. He received his BA in history from Keene State College and his MA and PhD in American history from the University of North Carolina at Chapel Hill. His research and teaching interests include early American history, the history of slavery and abolition, and African American religious and intellectual history. Cameron is the author of *To Plead Our Own Cause: African Americans in Massachusetts and the Making of the Antislavery Movement* and *Black Freethinkers: A History of African American Secularism*. He is also the coeditor of *New Perspectives on the Black Intellectual Tradition* and *Race, Religion, and Black Lives Matter: Essays on a Moment and a Movement*. His research has been supported by the Gilder Lehrman Institute of American History, the Massachusetts Historical Society, the American Philosophical Society, and the American Council of Learned Societies.

Carlton Dwayne Floyd is associate professor of English, affiliated faculty in women's and gender studies at the University of San Diego (USD). He was formerly the associate provost of inclusion and diversity and the cofounding director of the Center for Inclusion and Diversity at USD. His interests include African American and interracial literatures and cultures, cultural studies, metaphor, myth, and migration. His publications include works on August Wilson, Equity for African Americans in Education, and the implications of metaphors in current social and political situations, and he is a coauthor, with Tom Reifer, of *The American Dream & Dreams Deferred: A Dialectical Fairy Tale* (Lexington Books, 2023).

Robert Greene II is assistant professor of history at Claflin University. He is coeditor, with Tyler D. Parry, of *Invisible No More: The African American Experience at the University of South Carolina*. Dr. Greene II is also senior editor of the award-winning *Black Perspectives* blog of the African American Intellectual History Society and publications chair for the Society of US Intellectual Historians. He has also written for various publications, including *The Nation*, *Dissent*, *Jacobin*, and *Oxford American*. Currently, Dr. Greene II is working on his book, *The Newest South: African Americans and the Democratic Party, 1964–1994*, which details how the Southern leaders of the Democratic Party in the post-Civil Rights era crafted strategies to attract, and hold onto, the Black vote across the nation.

Andre E. Johnson, PhD, is associate professor of rhetoric and media studies in the Department of Communication and Film and holds a University Research Professorship at the University of Memphis. Grounded in an interdisciplinary understanding of scholarship, Johnson studies the intersection of rhetoric, race, and religion. He teaches classes in African American public address, rhetorical criticism, religious communication, prophetic rhetoric, homiletics, and the rhetoric of social movements. He is author of the award-winning *No Future in this Country: The Prophetic Pessimism of Bishop Henry McNeal Turner* (2020) and editor of *The Speeches of Bishop Henry McNeal Turner: The Press, the Platform, and the Pulpit* (2023) with the University Press of Mississippi. He is also coauthor, with Amanda Nell Edgar, of the forthcoming *The Summer of 2020: George Floyd and the Resurgence of the Black Lives Matter* (2024), also with the University Press of Mississippi.

Werner Lange was born in the rubble that was Germany after World War II and began his life in America as a "displaced person." A grant from the National Defense Education Act enabled him to attend Ohio State University, where he earned two degrees, a BA in sociology and an MA in anthropology. After his service in the US Peace Corps in Thailand, he continued his graduate studies at the Johann Wolfgang Goethe University in Frankfurt, and became engrossed in the Critical School of Sociology, a liberating paradigm that shaped much of his lifelong scholarship. Through the auspices of the Frobenius Institute he participated in ethnological fieldwork in southwestern Ethiopia. Several publications resulted, including "The History of the Southern Gonga of Ethiopia." In 1975, he earned a PhD from Goethe University. He also taught a course on US progressive social movements at Karl Marx University in Leipzig. As a NEH Fellow at Brown University, he participated in the dedication of the W. E. B. Du Bois Papers in 1980 at UMass. Lange was one of the earliest scholars to extensively review those invaluable documents on microfiche in Amherst. This research produced publications such as "W. E. B. Du Bois and First Scientific Study of Afro-America"; "Du Bois: Man of Peace"; and "A Voice in the Wilderness: W. E. B. Du Bois on Peace." Lange has remained active in the peace movement for over fifty years, and currently serves as director of the Ohio Peace Council. He is an ordained minister and received a DMin in 1994. His most recent publication is *Onward Christian Soldiers: The MAGA March toward a Fascist America.*

Lisa J. McLeod is a philosopher and political theorist who works on Du Bois and also in critical race theory, feminist studies, and carceral studies. She did her undergraduate degree in philosophy at the University of California at Santa Cruz, then received her JD in 1990 from UCLA School of Law. After four years doing capital appeals and habeas investigations with the State Public Defender's Office in Los Angeles and San Francisco, she returned to academia, receiving a PhD in philosophy from Stanford in 2000. At Guilford College, in Greensboro, North Carolina, she teaches in the philosophy department, as well as the programs in women's, gender, and sexuality studies, african american studies, environmental studies, and health studies. She is on leave in the academic years 2021–23, working in Boston on issues of white supremacy, democracy, and freedom in the work of W. E. B. Du Bois.

Jodi Melamed is associate professor of English and Africana studies at Marquette University. She is the author of *Represent and Destroy: Rationalizing Violence in the New Racial Capitalism* (University of Minnesota Press, 2011) and has published many articles and chapters in a wide array of journals and editions. She is a coeditor (with Jodi Byrd, Alyosha Goldstein, and Chandan Reddy) of a special volume of *Social Text*, "Economies of Dispossession: Indigeneity, Race, Capitalism" (Spring 2018). Melamed is the recipient of numerous awards, fellowships, and grants, including a Fulbright, a Woodrow Wilson Postdoctoral Fellowship, and grants from the American Studies Association, the Social Science Research Council, the Mellon Foundation, and the Wisconsin Humanities Council. She is currently at work on a new book project titled *Operationalizing Racial Capitalism.*

Tyler Monson is a research lecturer in women's, gender, and sexuality studies at Dartmouth College, and formerly a postdoctoral fellow and assistant director of the Dartmouth Consortium of Studies in Race, Migration, and Sexuality. He has research and teaching interests in post-1945 American literature, queer of color criticism, militarism, and data and surveillance studies. His current book project, *Unmasking Militarized Masculinity: Sissies and the Security State,* argues an ideology of militarized masculinity to be a key criterion of inclusion to the US nation-state for some racial and sexual minorities, and instigates a mode of critique from the epistemological position of a sissy figure.

Eric Porter is professor of history, history of consciousness, and critical race and ethnic studies at UC Santa Cruz, where he is also affiliated with the music and Latin American and Latina/o studies departments. His research and teaching interests include Black cultural and intellectual history, US cultural history, jazz and improvisation studies, urban studies, and comparative ethnic studies. Among his books is *The Problem of the Future World: W. E. B. Du Bois and the Race Concept at Midcentury* (Duke University Press, 2010). He is currently completing a book on the history of San Francisco International Airport with attention to how that history offers insights into a broader set of phenomena that have defined the Bay Area as a metropolitan region.

Reiland Rabaka is professor of African, African American, and Caribbean studies in the department of ethnic studies and the founder and director of the Center for African and African American Studies at the University of Colorado Boulder. He is also a research fellow in the College of Human Sciences at the University of South Africa (UNISA). Rabaka has published seventeen books and more than eighty-five scholarly articles, book chapters, and essays, including *Africana Critical Theory*; *Against Epistemic Apartheid: W. E. B. Du Bois and the Disciplinary Decadence of Sociology*; *Forms of Fanonism: Frantz Fanon's Critical Theory and the Dialectics of Decolonization*; *Concepts of Cabralism: Amilcar Cabral and Africana Critical Theory*; *The Negritude Movement*; *The Routledge Handbook of Pan-Africanism*, and *Du Bois: A Critical Introduction*. He is also a poet and musician.

Thomas Ehrlich Reifer is professor and former chair of sociology; affiliated faculty in ethnic studies and women's and gender studies at the University of San Diego; and associate fellow at the Transnational Institute, a worldwide fellowship of committed scholar-activists. He was formerly a research associate at Focus on the Global South (Asia) and the Fernand Braudel Center for the Study of Economies, Historical Systems and Civilizations (SUNY Binghamton). Dr. Reifer has published widely on global social change, is a Freedom Writers Teacher, and helped in *Dear Freedom Writer: Stories of Hardship and Hope from the Next Generation*, by the Freedom Writers with Erin Gruwell (New York: Random House, 2022). He is coauthor, with Carlton Floyd, of *The American Dream and Dreams Deferred: A Dialectical Fairy Tale* (Lexington Books, 2023).

Camesha Scruggs completed her doctorate in history in 2022 at the University of Massachusetts Amherst and received a certificate in public history. A native Texan, she received a BA and MA in history from Texas Southern University. Her research interests are in twentieth-century US, African American, and gender and empire histories. She serves on the executive boards of the Association for the Study of African American Life and History and the National Collaborative for Women's History Sites, organizations committed to educating others on marginalized histories. She performs volunteer work for various community preservation initiatives, bringing stories to broader audiences. She has worked with the Du Bois Boyhood Homesite since 2016 as a docent and consultant on various projects.

Phillip Luke Sinitiere is professor of history at the College of Biblical Studies, a predominately African American school located in Houston's Mahatma Gandhi District. He is also the scholar in residence at UMass Amherst's W. E. B. Du Bois Center. A scholar of American religious history and African American studies, his recent books are *Protest and Propaganda: W. E. B. Du Bois,* The Crisis, *and American History* (University of Missouri Press, 2014), *Salvation with a Smile: Joel Osteen, Lakewood Church, and American Christianity* (NYU Press, 2015), *Citizen of the*

World: The Late Career and Legacy of W. E. B. Du Bois (Northwestern University Press, 2019), and *Race, Religion, and Black Lives Matter: Essays on a Moment and a Movement* (Vanderbilt University Press, 2021). Sinitiere has received research funding from the Lily Endowment, the Houston Public Library, Rice University's Center for Engaged Research and Collaborative Learning (CERCL), the Society for Values in Higher Education, the American Sociological Association, and the Andrew W. Mellon Foundation.

INDEX

CPSIA information can be obtained
at www.ICGtesting.com
Printed in the USA
BVHW040922210523
664546BV00005B/10